Three Rivers
of the Amazon

Three Rivers
of the
Amazon

Tim Biggs

Three Rivers of the Amazon
Published in 2007 by Tim Biggs
Suite No. 244
Private Bag X6
Cascades, 3202
Pietermaritzburg, KwaZulu-Natal
South Africa
E-mail: timbiggs@futurenet.co.za
Website: www.timbiggs.co.za

ISBN: 978-0-620-39816-9

Layout and design: Marise Bauer, M Design
Editors: Steve Vorster, Bill Bizley & Sally Hines
All artwork and illustrations: Tim Biggs

Photographs courtesy of:
Fanie van der Merwe: pages 107, 118;   François Odendaal: pages 53, 55, 61, 06,155;   Graeme Anderson: pages 270, 273;
John Ivins: page xii;   John Lee: page 6;   Kyle O'Donoghue: pages 241, 244, 249, 286, 292;   Matt Carlisle: pages 13, 14;
Piotr Chmielinski: pages 160, 169, 170;   Richard Smithers: page 138;   Ross O'Donoghue: pages 254, 255, 257, 260, 278, 291;
Shaun Biggs: pages 262, 265, 280;   Zbigniew Zbecek: pages 36, 153, 163, 173, 181, 182, 185, 188, 191, 196, 214.

The majority of the remaining photographs were taken by Tim Biggs.

Contents

Foreword

Rivers around the world have been called many things. The 'Everest', the 'mightiest', the 'most dramatic' and so on…all opinions, but there's only one river on earth that can be called the biggest. The Amazon River dumps more water into the ocean than any other river…period, and there's only one man who's kayaked all three of its main source tributaries from high in the Andes Mountains to their confluences in the Amazon jungle, and then onwards towards the Atlantic Ocean.

Tim Biggs, living quietly in South Africa, is one of the unsung legends of paddle sports. I first met him when I was ten years old (in the mid eighties). He had just returned from his 1985 Amazon Source to Sea Expedition, and featured in Joe Kane's book, *Running the Amazon*. My friends and I used to sit in awe, whispering about his accomplishments as he paddled.

Now we get his story firsthand. It paints a compelling picture of the type of man that sets out on such an exploit, and includes the colourful life that he's lived as a farmer in rural South Africa, specializing in grueling downriver marathons. We visit his philosophies and values; we join him on his first Amazon adventure – the zero budget expedition down the Urubamba River, where he lived for months amongst the South American Indians. We're ultimately carried through to 2004 where Tim, now in his fifties, teamed up three young South African paddlers (and an eager filmmaker) to accomplish his bold, lifelong goal of running the third and final fork of this massive river.

Apart from being one of the nicest guys on earth, one of the things I've always enjoyed about Tim is the way he tells his stories. They are told with excitement and passion but with humility towards himself, whilst cleverly adding twists and turns to the tale at just the perfect moment. Shortly before writing this book he asked how it should be written: I said that if he wrote in the same way that he tells his stories, he'd write the best kayaking adventure book ever. I believe that he's done just that. *Three Rivers* does precisely what it's supposed to do. It draws you in and lets you feel exactly what it's like to be on an expedition, in a faraway place. At the same time it makes a necessary and important contribution to the history of paddle sports and adventure in general.

I'm excited that Tim has put his stories on paper for us, and future generations, to enjoy. Trust me when I say that reading this beautifully illustrated book is nothing short of inspiring. Kayakers and non-paddlers alike will be delighted!

STEVE FISHER – professional kayaker
Steve Fisher travels the world, kayaking the most extreme white water on the planet. He is acknowledged as the world's top big water kayaker.

Preface

A Dream Come True

I want to tell you my story. It's a story about my life, but it's mainly about a dream I had many years ago when I was in my early twenties. It was one of those things that began small, and then through the years and life's twists and turns, grew, and then, unexpectedly, blossomed.

My dream was to explore the tributaries of the Amazon in far-off South America. It was first born when a friend, François Odendaal, approached me to suggest we look at exploring the world's greatest river, the Amazon. 'Yes, Frans – I'm on, there's nothing I'd like to do more,' I spontaneously replied to his invitation.

The timing was perfect. I needed a challenge in my life, and besides, I was feeling strangely empty after spending years on the canoe racing circuits of South Africa.

That was the moment a mysterious door opened to me. Through it led a narrow path winding down into a range of towering, arid mountains. The path overlooked a river cascading and clawing its way through steep valleys and sheer-walled canyons. The river seemed to be alive. The river was the Urubamba, the major tributary to the Amazon. After spending four months travelling through this majestic rock-strewn waterway, yet another door opened which led down into the unknown and daunting chasms of the Apurimac River, the longest tributary and supposedly true source of the Amazon.

A third tributary to the Amazon still lay waiting to be navigated – the Marañón. Early Portuguese explorers believed that this was the source of the Amazon, as it was the largest of the three rivers. Twenty-four years after beginning my quest, this final door opened before me, revealing the thundering waters of the Marañón, and bringing the chance to kayak the third river.

In this book I have also included the stories of my early experiences of an expedition down the Limpopo River, of a wild sailing voyage, and of an epic wilderness expedition down the Colville River in Alaska. It was during my running of the Amazon Rivers that I discovered a new river – a river that challenged my every attitude, my belief system and even my view of God. These adventures were all integral aspects of my quest to kayak the rivers of the Amazon.

Acknowledgements

To Margie my dear wife, you gave me the freedom to partake in the Apurimac and Marañón Expeditions (and many others). Without your support and love, my dream to explore the Amazon's rivers would never have happened. To my beloved children, Sam, Keetah, Ben and Jonathan: you have all been an inspiration to me and have added immeasureably to my life in every way.

To my late Mom and Dad who always loved and supported me in all I did, and who would have loved to have seen this book published.

To Scott Rolason, my inspiring American missionary friend, who 'kicked my backside' and got me going with my book, and for his advice and input.

To my editors, Steve Vorster, who has become a great friend of mine, and to Bill Bizley. A huge thank you, guys. To Sally Hines and Steve Vorster for proofreading. These three people each deserve a medal for the way they wrestled through my rough drafts and poor grammar.

To Marise Bauer for the magnificent job she has done with the layout, and for her endless patience.

To Sean Wisedale, for inspiring, encouraging and mentoring me along the road to self-publishing. I hope we can kayak a river together one day.

To Rory Pennefather, my friend and racing partner for reading through my text and for his advice.

To all the teammates whom I have been so privileged to kayak with these past 25 years, and who have all influenced my life. Without them not a single trip would have happened. Here a special mention of François Odendaal for sharing his vision to explore the Amazonas with me, and for all we've been through together. Thank you, Frans.

To our many sponsors who over the years have made our expeditions possible by donating and assisting with craft and equipment. Special thanks to Perception Kayaks for their kayaks which were used on the Urubamba and Apurimac Expeditions; to Fluid Kayaks and GWV Industries for the kayaks we used on the Marañón Expedition. Also, thank you to Stohlquist Gear, Polartec Clothing Sportron and Varig Airlines.

To the hundreds of friends we made in Peru, and who so warmly helped and supported us with all aspects of our journeying during the past 25 years; part of my heart remains with you in Peru. You are wonderful people!

And by no means last, my Savior and friend, Jesus Christ, for being my shepherd and closest friend along my journey through life. Lord, I give you all the praise and glory.

Celebrating my 53rd birthday over 'Thrombi Falls'.

Early Days

UMKOMAAS EXPERIENCE

We all spotted it at the same moment, as it came spiralling into view.

'Look, it's a tree, an enormous tree.'

Squinting upstream we watched spellbound as the convulsing water carried the slowly-rotating tree towards us. Sinking and reappearing, it swept past us and accelerated as it found the deeper, faster current. We saw it crashing through the roller-coaster waves at the approach to the Stae Braes rapid. It careered towards the cliff, and then disappeared as it was buried by a pillow of water that rebounded off the rock face. Seconds passed before one of the tree's broken limbs finally punctured the surface and re-emerged, some hundred metres downstream.

A silence fell. I could feel my dad's common sense kicking in.

'I don't know if you should try this one, Tim.'

Running my first rapid on the Umkomaas River. Seconds after this I capsized
~ boat broke in two ~ never to be seen again.

'Ja. It's bigger than I thought,' I replied, trying to conceal my jitters.

What we had just witnessed had prophetically transported me through time. It was as though I had watched myself in place of that battered old tree. Dad, Mum and I stood in silence on the hot, round rocks that were the banks of the Umkomaas River. The roar of the river in flood was bass to the background of hundreds of high-pitched cicadas. Indecision, adrenalin, spirit – these were all ingredients of my racing thoughts.

This was no small moment in my life. I was 17 years old and about to attempt my first paddle on a river. Beside me lay my newly-acquired craft, a sleek flimsy, 17-foot-long fibreglass 'Pointer' canoe. I was dead silent, a mental battle was raging inside me.

'You're mad to try it – you'll wrap your boat.'

But then another voice countered with: 'Come on. You can do it.'

It was almost as though a force within that churning, crazy water tugged at me. At that moment, as we stood there, something took over.

'Okay, Dad, I'm going to give it a try.'

Neither Dad nor Mum replied, their silent disagreement almost loud with resistance to my decision. Dad quietly stooped and picked up the tail-end of the canoe. I picked up the front.

'Where do you want to put in?' he asked.

'There,' I said, 'just upstream of that boulder.'

We wedged the boat on the rocks, half in and half out of the choppy water. I struggled to stretch the nylon spraydeck over the cockpit. My mouth was as dry as a sun-baked rag. I tried to block from my mind what the next few minutes might bring.

I pushed off from the bank. 'Good luck, Tim,' shouted my mother. 'See you at Josephine's' (the bridge 8 km downstream where they would be waiting for me).

The first few metres were relatively calm, then the current gripped, lifting the boat, and sweeping me away downstream. The canoe's nose dived and wal-

My first taste of a canoe race on the Umgeni River.

lowed in the roller-coaster waves. Surges of powerful water immediately took control of my course. I was in the hands of the river.

For a brief moment I wanted to scream with exhilaration and excitement. Something was happening to me that I had never felt before. It was terrifying. It was thrilling. I found myself accelerating toward the cliff at tremendous speed. Nothing responded to my frantic efforts to turn my canoe. Seconds later a wall of water rose up and engulfed me. Darkness crashed over me, and the roar of the river was silenced. I capsized. I ripped frantically at the spray cover that was trapping me in the cockpit. With lungs bursting for air, I kicked and fought my way free and struck for the surface. At last I emerged, choking, coughing, and swimming with all my might. I caught a glimpse of the blue nose of my canoe rising vertically, barely 20 m from me. It pointed skyward and then disappeared in the brown water. The next rapid was approaching with speed. I was exhausted, too tired to swim and with only energy enough to gasp for air. A kilometre downstream from the rapid, I found I could at last drag myself from the river, looking like a drowned rat. Sprawled on the rocks, I could hear my dad's distant voice drifting toward me.

'Tim, are you all right?'

'Yes, Dad, I'm okay, I guess . . . that was terrible! I had no chance.'

'Well, good show for trying.'

We stood again, searching for any sign of either paddle or canoe. Even my spraydeck and shoes had been ripped off me.

'That boat was in two pieces. I doubt we'll find anything now. Let's go,' said my dad, trying not to be discouraging.

Slowly we turned from the river and began a disappointed walk back to our old Peugeot pickup which was parked on the riverbank. I had been initiated! Harshly initiated.

Something happened to me that day – a day that I have never forgotten. For the previous year or two at school and on the farm I had sensed a kind of void in my life. I could not pinpoint it, but I knew it was there. What happened that day, despite the disappointing outcome, seemed like a glimmer of light, an answer to some far-off call deep in my being. I wanted to do more of this, much more. The seed was sown.

Kayaking ~ hard to beat!

Life on the Farm

Our farm, Murchison, was situated some 12 km outside the farming village of Ixopo. It was a beautiful place with rolling hills and wooded valleys. Half the farm was cultivated, the other half was wild thornveld, where my dad grazed his cattle through the dry winters. There were five children in our family, all high-spirited and keen for anything.

We all loved our dad intensely. Dad was strong, self-disciplined and a man of few words, passionate about farming, and who spent as much time as possible outdoors. Farming the African soil had taught Dad the true meaning of patience, determination and perserverance. Whether the frost lay thick on the ground, or the sun beat down, Dad would be dressed in khaki shorts and shirt. When a humorous twinkle appeared in his eye, we were warned that a practical joke was on the way.

My mother, despite being only 5 foot 3 inches tall, was a tower of mental, spiritual and physical strength. For 20 years she devotedly drove the 25 km, gravelled route to school and back. These trips were eventful to say the least. We had a name for every tree, bend, hill or dog along the route and we would chant the names as we passed by: 'Henny Penny suicide crossing', 'sprinkly stream', 'black dog tree'. Many tales could be told of my mother's less-than-average driving skills on these trips. During the summer rains, mum often displayed raw courage, while having to negotiate flooded streams in our old Willy's Jeep. On many an occasion, and much to our delight, the Jeep would execute a perfect, yet out of control, 360-degree spin while speeding along the slippery road.

I loathed school. I simply could not understand why the idyllic farm lifestyle had to be interrupted by such an uninspiring pastime as school. One of my favourite talents was climbing trees and raiding birds' nests, an activity that saved me from many a long day at school. As Mum bundled us into the Jeep for

Going to school was a real shock to the system.

4

school each morning, I would often make a break and race up the highest tree in our sprawling garden, peering down through the branches at my exasperated mother.

During those years my younger brother Dan and I developed a love for cross-country running. Instead of spending long afternoons waiting for our elder brothers and sisters to finish their sport activities, we would head out over the hills for home, running along winding cattle paths, exploring the shortest route home. For both of us the sensation of racing over broken terrain, stooping under low branches, leaping from rock to rock over streams, became a passion and a lifestyle.

A typical scene - mum and Dad on the front verandah.

Caroline, David, Barbara, Dan & me.

A year's military training, followed by university, opened a new era in my life. After the military, university opened up many vistas, drawing me in every direction. Lecture theatres, new friends, initiation, rowdy parties – but, above all, an environment tailor-made for excelling at sport. I embraced my 'new love', canoeing, with all my heart. A single training session per day soon became two, then three, combining gym training, running and paddling. A new dream began to emerge and grow, a dream that consumed me. I wanted to race for South Africa! To reach this goal, however, I needed 120% effort. My paddling

mentors and my heroes with whom I had trained, had now become the competition I had to beat! Being the smallest of the group, I realised that I had only one option: I had to train harder and longer to finish first. My sights were set.

One day, while I was preparing for one of the daily training sessions, a strange meeting took place. A fellow student with a slight limp and loping walk approached me and introduced himself.

'Hello, I'm François Odendaal,' came an almost Germanic Afrikaans accent. 'I saw your canoes, and I thought I must meet you. I also have a Klepper white water canoe, and I would really like to use it while I'm here. Could I perhaps join you for a paddle sometime?'

'Of course, join us now!' I replied, still shaking hands with my new acquaintance. 'We're just off to the river now. Let's go.'

As I got to know François I realised that he was different to anyone I'd ever met before. He exuded enthusiasm and drive. Spending time with him inspired me, and our friendship began to grow. François was, unlike myself, a first-class academic and a passionate zoologist. He had the reputation for being one of the country's top students. It wasn't long before he invited me to join him on a trip he was planning on the Limpopo River. I gladly accepted.

Little did I suspect how this man was going to influence my life over the next 10 years.

THE LIMPOPO

Hippos and Crocodiles

It was in the summer of 1976, my third year at university, that we embarked on the trip down the great Limpopo River. We chose to put in near the source of the Limpopo near Thabazimbi on the Crocodile River. Our destination was the Indian Ocean. The Limpopo winds its way lazily through South Africa, Botswana, Zimbabwe and finally Mozambique, where it enters the Indian Ocean at Delagoa Bay.

I had motivated François to allow my fellow students and racing friends, Matt Carlisle, Jerome Truran and Neville Slade, to join the team. François agreed. Together we had already done a couple of short trips on the Umkomaas, Tugela and Umzimkulu Rivers of Natal, but nothing on the scale that the Limpopo promised. The idea simply hooked me, as it was to be my first genuine long expedition.

Our young team, consisting of inexperienced but high-spirited 20- and 21-year-olds, headed out into the African wilderness to share a month that guaranteed incredible experiences. From the outset our days were action-packed and exciting; we operated as hunter-gatherers, shooting ducks and geese, fishing and restocking on essentials such as beans and rice from isolated farms along the river.

Much of our time was spent trying to out-manoeuvre the huge pods of hippos which romped and grunted in the deep pools. Upon arriving at such a pool, the dominant bull would mock-charge us, defending his territory, making it clear there was no way past. This would send us scattering in all directions, only to regroup cautiously to discuss our next move while they also regrouped, plotting who-knows-what! The hippos were vocal and upfront in their approach, and for a good 10 minutes would send off challenging rallies of snorting and water-spouts, clearly warning us not to enter their territory. Intimidated and nervous, we would wait for their rage to calm before sprinting for our lives around the likeable but deadly beasts, never sure when to expect a hit from below!

On many nights grunting hippos kept us company. They would graze around the camp while we would lie dead still, hoping that they would not take fright, stampede through the camp, and flatten us. Luckily they never did. Where the river became braided and channelled, hippos would often find themselves separated from their pod. If we unexpectedly came upon these lost ones, a crashing of under-growth would follow as the startled animals stampeded in

7

Limpopo team: Matt, Jerome, François, Tim and Nev.

all directions. On one such occasion, an enormous cow flung herself into the river, missing my kayak by no more than a metre; I don't know who was more terrified.

Numerous crocodiles along the way guaranteed that our adrenalin levels remained fully charged. At Mabalel's pool, a famous crocodile-infested pool, described by the Afrikaans poet, Eugene Marais, we had a breathtakingly close encounter with these reptiles. An enormous olive-green canopy of mahogany and wild fig foliage overhung the green, greasy waters of the deep pool. We carefully entered it, suspecting that danger was near. François spotted it first.

'Watch out! Crocodile!' he yelled.

We rocketed into panic mode, searching frantically for our adversary, unsure where to escape to. Then I saw it: an enormous 20-foot-long crocodile had slipped into the muddy brown waters and was now charging in our direction. To my horror I realised that the giant reptile's path was directed straight for me! Its two red eyes locked in on me like a heat-seeking missile. I leapt into action, sprinting off at right angles to my attacker's course. A quick glance behind me confirmed my greatest fear: in a few seconds the croc would be on me. I had no chance. A half submerged log some 3 m to my left caught my eye. I desperately veered towards it and had narrowly cleared it when an explosive splash behind me rocked my boat. Not daring to look behind, I sprinted wildly on towards safety. The crocodile had swerved at the log, lost its momentum and disappeared under the murky waters.

My worried and wide-eyed friends finally caught up to me.

'Phew, Tim, that was close! We thought it had you,' François called.

'Ja, me too. That was definitely too close for comfort,' I replied, still shaking from fright.

We paddled out of Mabalel's pool in silence. That poet clearly understood the place, and now we did too. It was a pool that would remain engraved in our memories for a long time.

After a full day's paddling, nothing beat the long and relaxing evenings spent sprawled out on the white, sandy riverbanks. With stomachs full and hearts contented, we would enjoy the stunning and cool starlit nights; gaze into the orange, hardwood coals of the campfire, and relate and exaggerate the incidents of the day.

Days merged into weeks as we journeyed through one of Africa's most beautiful rivers. We fell in love with the forested river, and with this new and care-free way of life.

Politics on the Water

For François this trip had a completely different meaning. Two years earlier he and a group of friends from Pretoria had set out to paddle the same stretch. None of the team were experienced paddlers, and in a tragic sequence of events, François's dream to follow the Limpopo to the sea turned into a nightmare. The river had flooded that summer, a chocolate snake of coiling bends and turns, winding its way through the African bushveld plains. After the first week, only François and his friend Johan Smit continued downstream as the rest of the team had pulled out. The two paddlers arrived at a man-made weir across the river. After they had scouted this dangerous obstacle, they agreed to run it. François would go first while

Operation Donkey - we found this donkey trapped on a mud cliff - too scared to jump into the crocodile infested waters.

Matt bags a Spurwing goose for supper - what a treat!

9

Terrafou Farm - François leaves the team.

Johan took photographs from the weir wall; once François had made it, Johan would follow him.

François lined up his kayak and sprinted towards the chocolate brown lip of the fall, pulling with all his might; the fibreglass kayak dived, rose slowly and the nose lifted vertically from the churned back-wash, stalled and looped over backwards into the deadly and inescapable keeper wave of the weir (the last photograph that Johan took recorded this). François was sucked out of his cockpit with frightening force and recycled time and time again by the unrelenting backwash of the weir. Fear and emotions slowly slipped away from him as he began drifting into unconsciousness.

François came around, finding himself wrapped around the half submerged branch of a tree. Finally a local passer-by spotted the corpse-like shape in the tree and called for help. He was hauled out with ropes and carried to the nearest farmer. Johan had photographed François from the bank and when he rea-

lised his friend's life was in danger, had plunged into the deadly turbulence to help him. Unfortunately, the Limpopo was not as forgiving as it had been to François, and Johan's drowned body was discovered four days later. The camera was found on the weir wall, the last photo being that of François dropping over the weir.

I never had the privilege of meeting Johan Smit, but he must surely rate among the unsung heroes of African river stories.

It was now two years later, and François was reliving the tragedy; was he hoping that doing the same route would magically remove the deep fear of water and death that had plagued him since that fatal journey of 1974? Was that the reason he was so sombre compared to his four light-hearted companions?

We were indeed an interesting, unlikely team. Not only did Afrikaner nationalism and apartheid cause deep divisions between the Afrikaner and the black population, but it also alienated the English-speaking people from a great number of Afrikaans-speaking citizens. This hailed back more than a hundred years to the time of the Anglo-Boer wars, and unforgiving stories and memories lived on between the two cultures.

During the second week on the Limpopo, an unfortunate argument broke out. Our daily routine had been to break camp at first light, paddle until the midday heat became unbearable, and then enjoy a three-hour siesta under the shade of the riverside forest. It was during one of these siesta breaks, when our tongues lacked the control of our hazy minds, that an unfortunate political argument broke out between François and the rest of the group; the siesta ended unhappily with some hurtful wounds and the group became polarised.

Several days later we arrived at Terrafou, François's family farm, where he announced that he would be leaving us to finish the trip on our own. Surprised, and sad that our relationships had turned sour, we bade François farewell as he left for Pretoria.

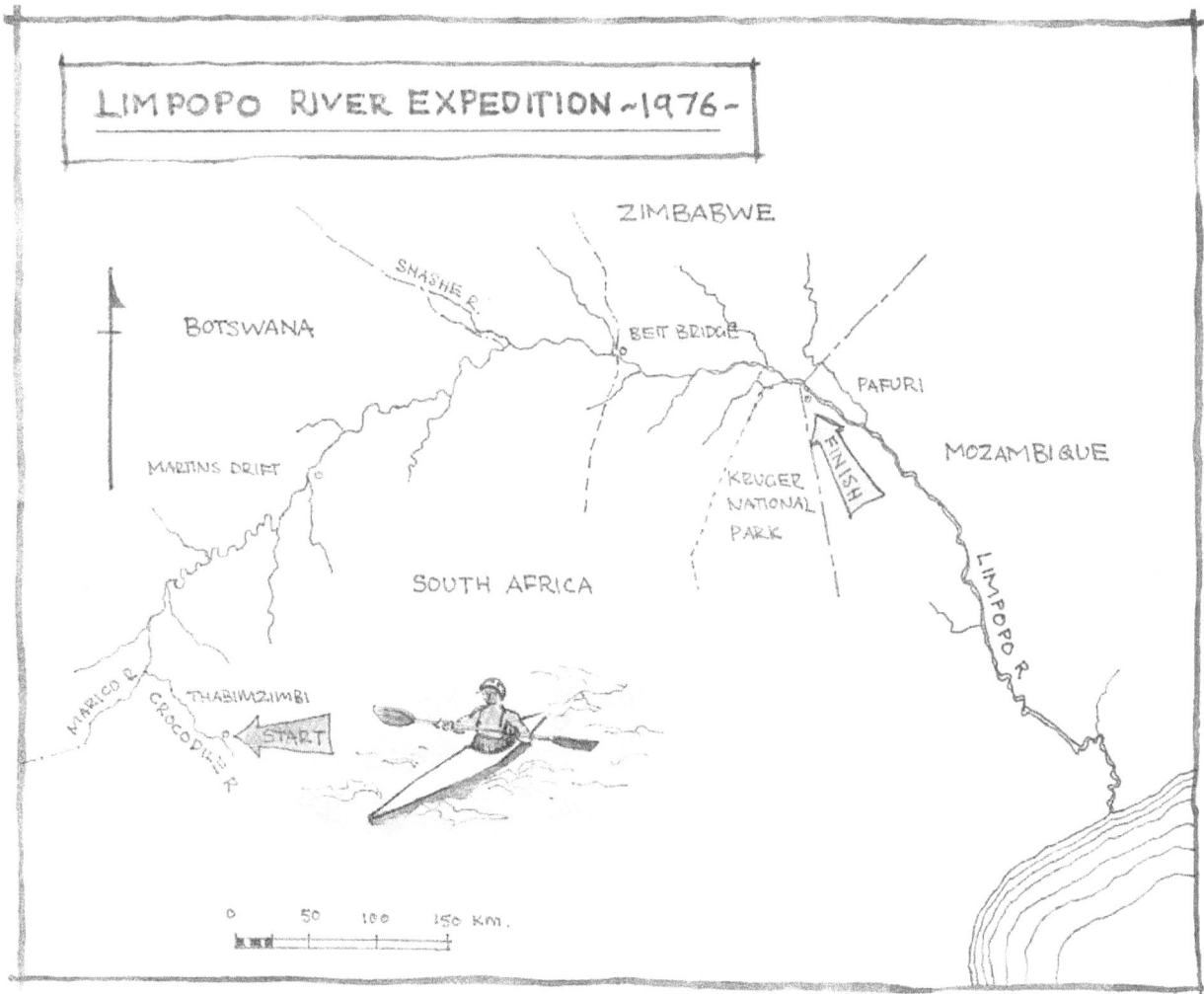

LIMPOPO RIVER EXPEDITION ~1976~

Snooze – You Lose

Farmers along the river had informed us that a guerrilla war in Mozambique was raging, and our dream to reach the ocean would not be possible. We would end our trip at Pafuri on the Mozambiquan border. On our second night without François, we camped on an enormous creamy-white beach several hours below the confluence of the Shashe and Limpopo Rivers. At 6:30 p.m., tired after a long day's paddling in the blistering December sun, we dragged our heavily laden kayaks up the 300 m of clean sand expanse. 'Surely that's enough,' Matt panted, 'I can't see the river rising this high overnight.'

In unison we agreed, leaving the boats scattered over the beach, removing only what we needed for our camping. The mosquitoes were already out in their droves and we threw together dry firewood and soon sat huddled in the relief of the protecting acrid smoke. Sleep came almost instantly after supper and we slept deeply to the sound of grunting hippos.

At the first light of dawn, lilac and mauves haloed the river forest. We woke to witness the most incredible sight. Huge islands of frothed, brown foam were floating lazily around our sleeping bags, submerging our beautiful white beach. The brown waters of the Shashe River had flooded her banks. To our dismay and alarm we were horrified to find Matt's and my canoe were gone, along with much of our gear which had been left in plastic waterproof buckets. I leapt into Jerome's kayak and paddled downstream, where to my relief I found Matt's boat, tail sticking vertically out of the water.

Hastily packing our remaining gear, Matt, Jerome and Neville raced downstream, hoping to recover our lost gear, but alas, my sturdy craft was amiss, swept away by the floodwaters of the Limpopo.

Beit Bridge lay only 65 km downstream and so we held a hasty conference to discuss our strategy. Matt, Jerome and Neville would paddle downstream, while I would run and make my way through the bush to rendezvous at Beit Bridge. All day I ran, often startling herds of buffalo, wildlife and large game as I wove through the Limpopo bush. At one point, I hitchhiked a lift on the back of a rickety old tractor and trailer, sharing the ride with four Venda men who were gathering firewood. The old wizened driver looked me up and down suspiciously, and then snapped in Afrikaans, 'Okay, get on, but I'm not going very far.' Border terrorism and violence were rife along the river and I respected his suspicion.

Eight hours later, exhausted and dehydrated, I was stopped in my tracks by the familiar rattle of an R1 rifle being cocked, followed by a familiar Afrikaans command, 'Who goes there?' Two powerfully built young South African Defence Force troops circled me with cocked rifles.

'Hold fire – I'm a canoeist, I've lost my canoe and I'm looking for my friends. I have just run from the Shashe River,' I stammered, probably looking like a mad man. The Beit Bridge patrol had been alerted by the earlier arrival of my three friends, and they had been expecting me. We spent a memorable night braaing boerewors with the troops, drinking beers and exchanging tales of the bush.

We had a dilemma: three boats and four paddlers. It was Nev who came forward. 'Guys, I'd like to miss this next stretch, my feet are killing me, and I can't get rid of this darn diarrhoea – how about I meet you at Pafuri on the border?' We agreed, and I took over Nev's kayak.

It was now Matt, Jerome and I who pushed on downstream through the Malala and Que Que Falls section of the river, and finally into the Kruger National Park. All the while our ordeals with grumpy hippos and aggressive crocks intensified.

This trip was starting to take its toll on us physically, with the humid January heat often reaching 48 degrees Celsius, and the relentless reflection of the sun inflicting servere sunburn. Festering and infected sores from cuts and scratches covered our bodies. We had run out of sun cream and were burnt to a dark tan; my lips were swollen and blistered. All of us had contracted severe athlete's foot and Matt could barely walk. Coping with ongoing diarrhoea had become a way of life; we were truly weary and deeply tired.

A shout came as Matt, Jerome and I finally rounded a densely forested bend.

'There it is, there it is! There's the flag!' Matt yelled.

A small red flag, suspended by a long, bowed bamboo pole, protruded through a gap in the canopy of emerald-green foliage. The South African military at Beit Bridge had offered to radio the Pafuri border post, requesting they hang a flag over the river in case we overshot the mark and entered Mozambique guerrilla territory. We dragged our kayaks up onto the grassy banks of the Pafuri border post and cau-

Jerome in the rapids approaching the Malala Falls.

13

tiously walked into the shaded tropical forest. Not a soul was in sight; we walked on and came to a camouflaged army tent.

'Anyone home?' we called. A movement deep in the bush caught our eye, a trooper carrying his rifle moved towards us, unsure of our status. We quickly explained our mission and were led along a winding footpath to the camp's HQ (a small prefabricated building), bristling with radio masts and aerials. Mike English, the sergeant in charge of the camp, stepped towards us.

'I was expecting you, you made it sooner than I thought you would, but hey, you boys are in a bad way. I'm sure you can do with a good meal and some doctoring up,' he observed as he looked us up and down, seemingly amused at our bedraggled, malnourished state.

Our first expedition had ended. The Limpopo experience had created deep bonds amongst us. We had seen the best and worst of each other – and our passion for wild rivers had been stoked by this wonderful adventure.

Afterword: A year later Graeme Pope-Ellis happened to be visiting a friend who farmed on the Limpopo upstream from Beit Bridge on the farm Nottingham. Keith Knott showed him an old fibreglass kayak which he had found protruding from the dry riverbed. Graeme had immediately recognised it as my boat and returned it to me in Pietermaritzburg. What a coincidence.

This was my kayak which was lost & found a year later~ buried in the mud.

A SEA VOYAGE

Exciting and challenging years sped by; races and marathons came and went. It was a rewarding season of my life: I graduated from university, was honoured with national colours for long-distance canoeing, and – to the relief of my family – I started a career as an engineering geologist. My modest list of personal achievements had not removed that empty, lost feeling that had haunted me ever since my school days. Try as I might to follow my dreams and to win races, a void remained that I could not fill. A bad dose of infectious hepatitis caused me to sit out a season of racing. In depressed self-pity and introspection, I often wondered why it was that I was plagued by this nagging emptiness while leading a dynamic and exciting life, and while surrounded by friends.

It was during this time of reflection and recovery that the phone rang and François's familiar voice came across the line.

'Hey, Tim. What about those plans of ours to go exploring? I'm off to Australia for a year, but meanwhile we must plan to do something good on rivers. What about South America?'

'I'm dead keen, but why wait so long!' I blurted out, without thinking. Maybe this would be the cure for my unsettled soul.

We met within a week at François's home in Pretoria, and we drew up a rough plan to explore the tributaries of the Amazon. We had seen little of each other over the past three years, and I had often wondered how we would get on after our tough experience on the Limpopo River. François soon dispelled my fears. He seemed to have excelled in his career, and indeed held no small reputation in the competitive world of scientific research. It was not difficult to regain the old rapport that we had shared back at university.

François had been pondering the idea of exploring the major tributaries of the Amazon River for some time. We poured over maps and atlases and

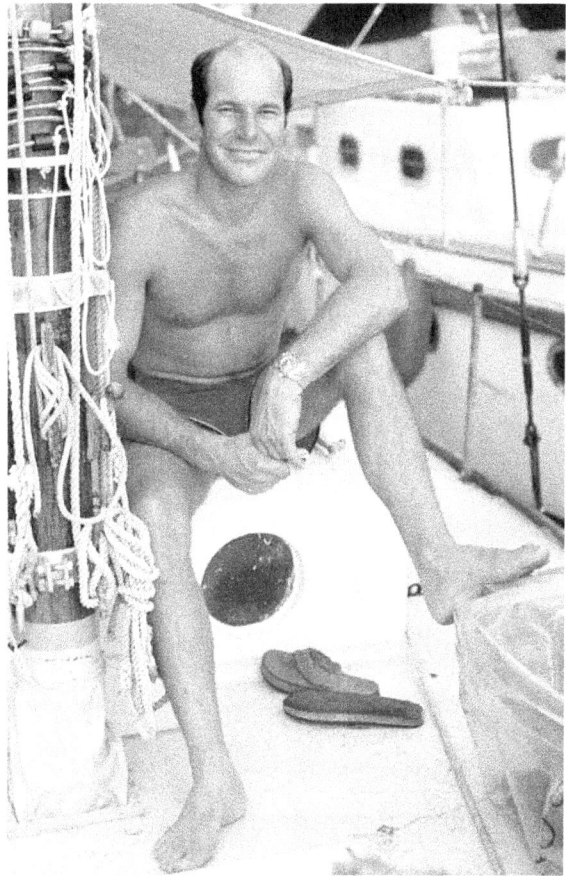

My wild skipper – John Beadon.

found ourselves returning with fascination to the tributary of the Amazon known as the Urubamba River. We could see that it rose high in the peaks of the Andes and then cut its way down to the jungle through 800 km of canyons. Spontaneously we agreed that this was 'our' river, 'our' challenge. Our meeting ended with a promise: we would meet again, in Peru, in the autumn of 1981, where we would tackle the mighty Urubamba.

Shortly after that Pretoria meeting, I got a surprise call from my sister Barbara who put me in contact with one John Beadon, a British skipper who was urgently looking for crew to help him sail his yacht from Richards Bay to Israel. Two weeks later I boarded a small,

Jaho - a yacht with character (and many vices).

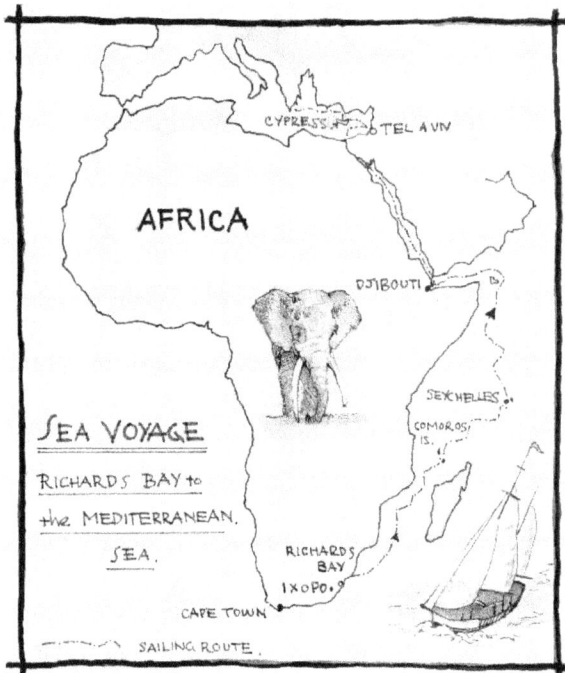

SEA VOYAGE

RICHARDS BAY to the MEDITERRANEAN SEA.

stubby 32-foot yacht, *Jaho*, and within hours my world had become a storm-ridden sea with white horses. For days on end we were relentlessly battered by a storm so severe that the crucial automatic steering gear and much of our rigging were smashed; an absolute greenhorn at sea, I was thrown in at the deep end, and handed the tiller in these wild seas.

'Try and hold her on course and run with the waves,' shouted John. 'I need to check the rigging.'

Jaho's stern rose, a giant swell lifted her high, and she accelerated down a long wave, her hull vibrating to a high-pitched scream, and the tiller wrenching at my straining arms. The yacht seemed determined to veer diagonally across the face of the wave as I wrestled with the rudder.

'No, no! Don't let her get sideways, we'll go over, dammit!' screamed John, diving for the tiller and straightening us out just in time.

Again I was handed the tiller and again I hung on to it for dear life, fighting to hold our course. For three days we careered through mountainous seas and breaking waves, fighting off a howling southwester. We were permanently drenched, we had little or no sleep, and my servere seasickness and dry retching grew increasingly painful. It was only on day eight, off Europa Island, that the weather eased and John could at last fix the steering mechanism.

'Sundowner time, Tim,' came his call from below.

John appeared through the hatch with a bottle of Johnnie Walker whisky and a dish of savoury snacks. We sat back soaking in the crimson sunset and enjoying our first moment of relaxation since our departure.

Four weeks later, we sailed triumphantly into the small port of Mahé in the Seychelles Islands. Any expectations of on-shore pleasures rapidly evaporated as we found the island gripped by political turbulence and guarded by Tanzanian soldiers. John sold *Jaho* to a local Buddhist resident, and was commissioned by a French Naval officer, Philippe, to sail his 40-foot steel-hulled ketch to Djibouti, as all French 'ex-pats' had been given two days to leave the island. Philippe would fly to Djibouti where he would meet us, and we would then fly on to Tel Aviv.

I again signed up as crew, and was now marginally more experienced than at our first departure. Our two-man team set off for Djibouti en route to Israel, where John had been offered the unusual job as a dolphin trainer for the Israeli military. It was on our voyage across this lonely stretch of ocean that, at the Horn of Africa, we found ourselves wallowing haplessly on a glassy, oily sea, becalmed and without any diesel fuel. In temperatures of 45 degrees Celsius we spent our days hiding from the relentless sun, following the small patch of shade cast by the sails on deck, and trying to dodge the stream of cargo ships that were headed for the Suez Canal. Our voyage was eventful: on one occasion we were shadowed for three days and nights by an Arab dhow; threatened by an Ethiopian gunship; and nudged by an over-friendly sperm whale.

As we approached the sheer cliffs of the Djibouti coastline, a thick fog enveloped us for days, denying us any opportunity to locate our position with our sextant – we were lost. Then miraculously before our eyes, the fog momentarily cleared and the grey cliffs of the coastline reared up ahead of us. A slit in the rock mystically revealed itself as the swirling fog lifted.

'Yes, yes!' shouted a stressed John. 'It's the entrance, all right! There it is, we've found it.'

We rounded the 300-m high bluff and exploded into whoops of jubilation. Djibouti at last! But our pleasure was short-lived. A yacht came sailing straight towards us.

'Hey, that's *Esprit de Vent*,' John shouted. The owners, Richard and Jean Newby Frazer, had moored alongside us in the Seychelles, and had departed for the Red Sea two weeks before us.

'Look, Richard's trying to tell us something,' I called to John across the deck.

Richard was leaning over the bowsprit, and as we approached we could hear him shouting, 'Tim!

Dolphins – they escorted us for days on end.

Get your gear, jump aboard with us. They'll kill you if you go in there. They hate South Africans. Hurry, they're watching us. Come now!'

My skipper had no doubt about the urgency in Richard's voice.

'Get your passport and go, Tim, I'll catch up with you in Israel,' he reassured me. I raced to my bunk, scooped my few belongings into a backpack, and leapt across to the *Esprit de Vent*, shouting a farewell to John. A grey gunship was already speeding towards us, bellowing unfriendly commands in Arabic through a loudhailer. We needed no further encouragement. Richard opened up the six-cylinder Perkins motor and, with a roar, we sped from those sinister cliffs and the even less friendly 'welcoming committee'.

Eight months had passed. We had sailed safely to Tel Aviv, and then on through the Mediterranean along the Turkish coast and Greek Islands. I had collected two letters from François in Tel Aviv, and passion for our adventure on the Urubamba was fanned to life again. The river with its ancient Inca history and intrigue, its windswept peaks and towering rock walls was calling me.

It was time to move on.

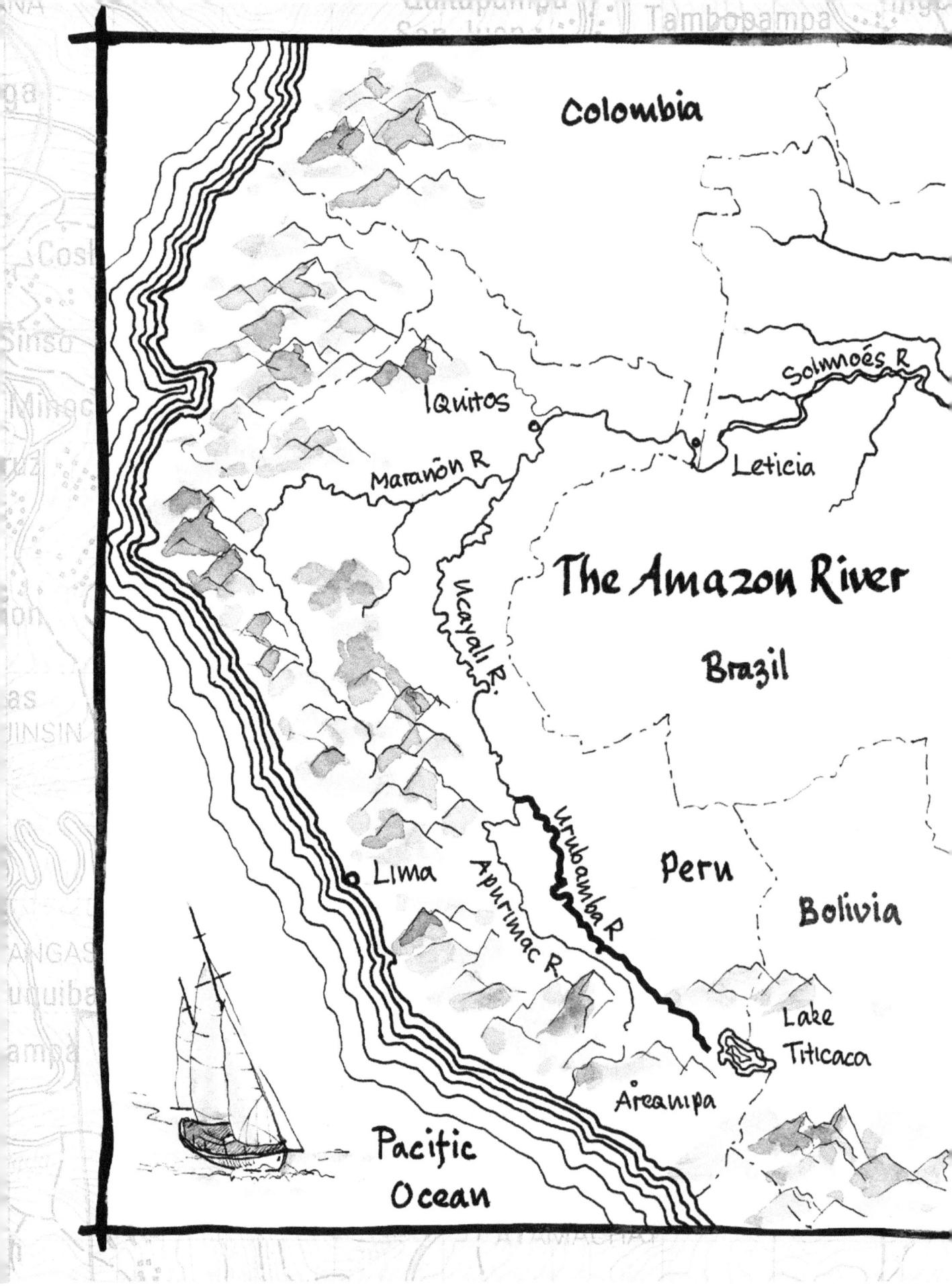

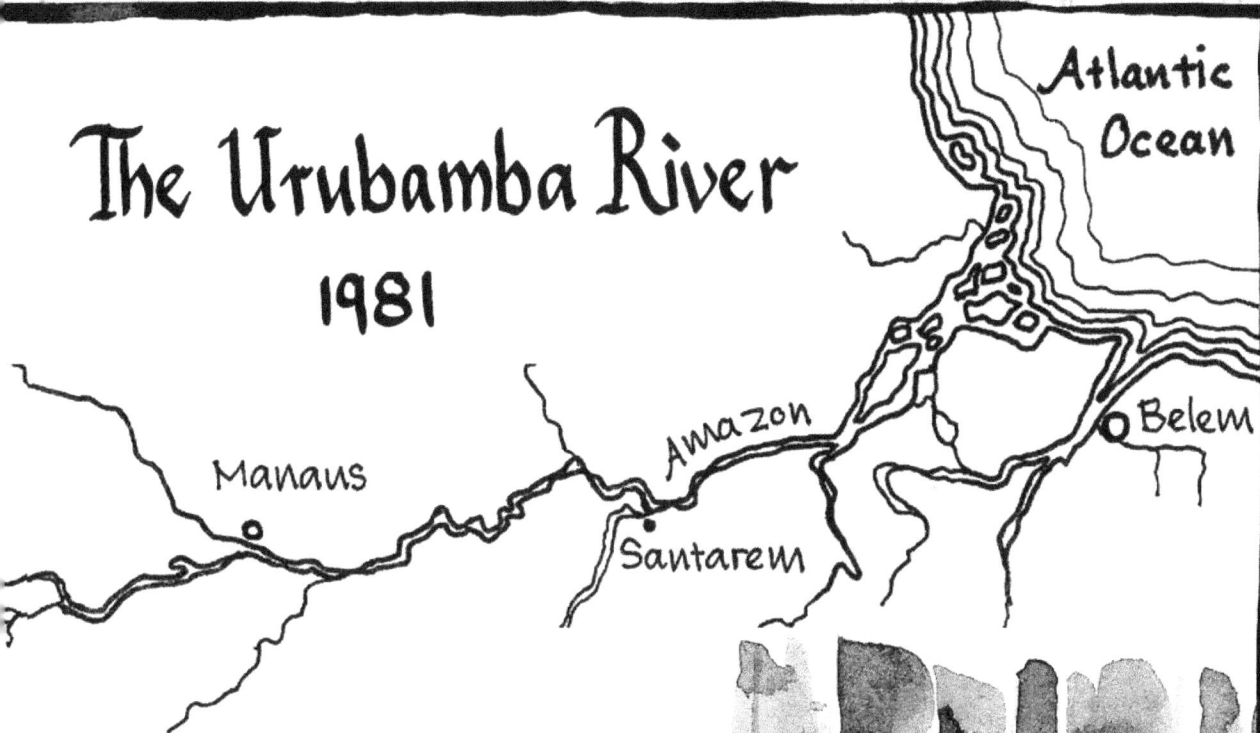

The Urubamba River
1981

Atlantic
Ocean

Amazon

Manaus

Santarem

Belem

N

PART 1

```
0        200      400      600
```
Kilometers

Chapter 1

URUBAMBA PREPARATION

First Impressions

In America, everything is very big, especially its generosity. Soon after I arrived in New York in September 1980, I was swept along, 'American' style. I hitched the New York–Denver route to join a kayak trip down the Ladoore Canyon. Gary Lacy, a member of the US white water team, whom I had raced against in Ireland, had arranged for me to join them. I had my first taste of American kindness as my friends not only arranged my schedule from town to town, but also lent me a kayak plus a full set of gear. I had hardly had time to adjust to life in the States before the invitation of a lifetime arrived – a place on a 19-day expedition down the Grand Canyon. As I had only planned to get to Peru three months later, I was ready to relish any adventure that came my way.

Our Grand Canyon Team - ready to roll.

My first meeting with the 15-man team was an embarrassment. At a filling station at Steamboat Springs, Colorado, I stepped out of Gary's pickup and took my first step towards the assembled group. The bootlace of one of my boots snagged the hooks on the other, and I was brought down onto the concrete like a ton of bricks! I won't forget the startled faces of the group as I scrambled to unravel myself.

'Hi, guys, I'm Tim,' I introduced myself as I struggled to my feet, trying to conceal my embarrassment.

Their expressions were filled with mirth, and we all laughed loudly at my dramatic entry. That broke the ice and I immediately felt welcomed and adopted by the team. One of the top kayakers of this group was someone who was going to play a large part in my North and South American adventures. He was Chan Zwanzig, a Chinese American and quite easily one of the most unusual and eccentric people I'd ever come across. Chan was of medium height and build, had a protruding 'goatee' beard, long straight dark

The magnificent Grand Canyon.

hair, thick tinted glasses, and an intense manner of addressing anyone. He was a true product of the 'hippie' era – a college graduate who had taken up work as an equipment operator simply to have money and time for his first love – kayaking.

Beneath the layered walls of the canyon, our team plunged through the enormous breaking waves and the powerful rapids. Within a week, the treacherous, turbulent Colorado had quite humbled me, apart from leaving me with both my shoulders badly wrenched. The crashing white water completely deflated my self-confidence. At the end of each day I would crawl to a quiet corner of a sandy beach to brood on my woeful realisation: I was pitifully ill-prepared for the South American rivers that we were headed for.

Chan came to the rescue. Amused by the way I had hurled myself headlong into the rapids – to take beating after beating – he began coaching me.

'Dumb South African,' he would chide. 'Don't go in there like that, you'll be torn apart! First figure out what the water's doing. Plan your strokes – how you'll brace when you paddle into a breaking wave, or when best to make a sweep stroke or bow rudder stroke.'

Gradually, with Chan's hasty coaching and my own keenness to learn, I began to understand the dynamics of big white water hydraulics. I mastered the easier moves, and my self-confidence grew with each triumph in this preparation run for the Urubamba.

After the Grand Canyon, Chan, Chuck McNulty, Jim Stohlquist and I crammed into Jim's old Dodge and headed out in search of some good kayaking in the freezing rivers of British Columbia. Between bouts of paddling, I scraped together dollars working on building sites, kneading dough in pizza restaurants, driving trucks, and even manicuring marijuana buds, until I had enough to equip myself with quality gear for kayaking in South America. I liked these Americans; they were warm, generous, fun loving and hard-working. But even as I learned new kayaking skills the thought weighed upon me that my South African

teammates – Matt, Clive and François – would simply not get this first-hand exposure to American rivers that I was getting. They were good paddlers on southern African rivers of much smaller volume. How would they cope with the gradients and volumes of the Andean rivers? I was thinking especially of François who had now spent two years in an Australian desert and had had no opportunity to paddle at all! He was an outstanding planner and visionary, but his river skills were undeveloped for the trip we had in mind. There was no doubt that we needed stronger paddlers on our team, and preparation time was beginning to run out.

Chan and the Other Troops

During these North American expeditions, Chan became increasingly interested in our plan to run the Urubamba. I could feel his immense desire to be part of our team, and that presented me with a dilemma. As much as I recognised our need for a strong kayaker of his calibre, Chan was not the easiest person to get along with. To be totally frank, he was too outspoken, had an unpredictable temperament, and a good portion of self-centredness. He was certainly not suitable for a long and testing expedition such as the one that lay ahead of us. On the other hand, Chan was dedicated and had all the knowledge and expertise we would need. Would I jeopardise the success of the whole venture by including Chan in our team? Then there were my friends, of course. How would they take to Chan?

I mailed an express letter to François (who was the overall leader of the expedition), explaining my predicament. From the deserts of Australia his reply came in under two weeks.

'Tim,' he wrote, 'it's your choice. If you think he's okay, we can take him, although to me he sounds a bit wild.'

Being the 'on the water leader' of the expedition, it was up to me whether to include Chan or not, and

François Odendaal

Matt Carlisle

Clive Curson

Chan Zwanziq

Tim Biggs

François was mature enough to approve of and trust my judgement. There were only two weeks before I would fly to Peru and after some serious deliberation, I decided to take the risk and include my eccentric American friend as the fifth member of our team.

Matt Carlisle, one of my best and most enduring friends, had been my first choice for this expedition. A talented paddler and a muscular athlete, he had the rare quality of a relaxed and warm temperament, underpinned by strong and uncompromising principles. Matt had accompanied us on the Limpopo River and as the most tried and tested of our team, I thought him the best paddler of us all. At this time, he was reading for a teacher's postgraduate degree at Bath University in the United Kingdom and he had won several prestigious gold medals in international long-distance kayaking events.

Clive Curson was a quiet, intense marathon-racing friend of many years. He and I had trained together, raced together, and then represented South Africa together in a marathon tour in Europe. As a young and brilliant chemical engineer, Clive thrived on planning and logistics. Here was someone who could focus on a mission and accomplish it with clinical precision. Clive and François were responsible for the logistics of the trip, including finding sponsorship and sourcing equipment. Like me, Clive was something of a loner, often appearing to be in a world of his own. Although mentally he was as hard as steel, he also sported an unpredictable wild streak. During our marathon-training days we had shared a love/hate relationship, but it had resulted in a rock-solid friendship.

The long awaited moment came, and I found myself on the last leg of my journey to the Urubamba: a journey that had lasted over a year. Concerned messages from loved ones and friends back home were trickling in: 'On which continent are you now, Tim?' and 'What are you doing, Tim?' and 'When will you be coming home?'

Our new expedition had at last come together and my gut feeling was that this would be the adventure of a lifetime.

Lima, Peru

The first challenge in South America greeted me at 1:00 a.m. on Valentine's Day 1981, when I landed at Lima Airport. It seemed that I would not be immune to that universal airport virus – missing luggage! My backpack with all my worldly possessions, together with $1 800 hard-earned cash that I had carelessly hidden in its side-pocket, was missing. This was one Valentine's Day where sweet little surprises would only be a dream!

With much gusto, together with the use of a Spanish phrase book and animated sign language, I raced around the terminal buildings vociferously

EQUADOR

COLOMBIA

PERU

IQUITOS

AMAZON RIVER

Ponao de
Retema

BAGUA

MARANON R

QUIVILLA

PUCALLPA

UCAYALI R

BRAZIL

QUEROPALCA

ATALAYA

URUBAMBA R

APURIMAC R

LIMA

PACIFIC OCEAN

N

MACCHU PICCHU

CUZCO

BOLIVIA

CHILE

25

demanding attention from the blasé officials. A small group of spectators gathered to witness the show as performed by a lone and excited gringo (as English-speaking people were derisively called by Latin Americans). After an exhausting and unproductive hour, I finally conceded defeat. My backpack had not arrived in Lima, leaving me without luggage or money. I was soon wallowing in a mixture of self-pity and despair when, as so often happens at low points, help came from an unexpected source. On this occasion, it came from Ruth, whom I had befriended on the flight from California. She spotted my distress and came to the rescue. Small she might be, but this dynamic, dark-haired Peruvian girl soon had the officials scuttling in all directions, obeying her sharp commands. But alas, it was 2:00 a.m. and I was still without a backpack. With traditional Peruvian hospitality, Ruth invited me to her parents' home in downtown Lima. I embraced the offer, grateful that someone in that vast, foreign city cared for me. Ruth had returned to Peru after six months' study in the United States, and her welcome-home party was a thunderous affair. Her entire family, together with extended family, neighbours and friends, all lined up to welcome her and her indebted guest from Africa.

Within minutes, bottles of pisco were cracked open and the potent drink began to flow freely. A typical celebration began, each glass tumbler charged to the brim and a toast made to the person closest to you. After downing the pisco you refilled with a loud 'salude amigo' and passed your glass on to the intoxicated friend nearest you. The stomach-warming liquid would disappear; the tumbler be refilled and passed around the cheering circle once more. After the fourth round, my head was swimming and I retreated from the jolly circle and collapsed onto a comfortable sofa. So began my South American initiation, the merriment raging on until the early hours of the morning.

Two weeks later and after dozens of trips and time-wasting phone calls to Lima Airport, and when I had almost despaired of my cherished backpack, it miraculously showed up. A bureaucrat notified me that it was at the Lost Property counter. The money was there too, hooray!

The next group of friends I made was at the South American Explorers (SAE) Club, based in a dreary building in Lima. Tom Jackson, a slightly built, wiry Californian with river-rafting experience, ran the club. He had first-hand experience of rafting on the Urubamba River with fellow American Lazlo Berty, and he would often thrill me with dramatic descriptions of some of the classic sections on the river. His stories included that of a 100-m wide whirlpool that sucked down an entire craft, of endless class 5 and 6 rapids, and of chilling near-death incidents. I sat listening to Tom's stories feeling like a young sailor hearing of the monstrous Moby Dick for the first time.

What were we letting ourselves into? Were we trying to bite off more than we could chew?

The SAE Club became my Lima base, and the help and information I gained from this kind, well-informed group proved invaluable as I prepared to head into the unknown regions of the Andes. It was nearing the end of March and there were only four weeks to go before my teammates would arrive. I decided to carry out a preliminary reconnaissance of the Urubamba, and set out for Cuzco in a packed, overloaded Ormeno bus. After a 63-hour ride, including five punctures, two front spring repairs and various life-and-death escapes, the bus finally rattled into Cuzco town. I was exhausted.

Cuzco, Southern Peru

Radiant light, reflecting off Cuzco's gold-plated walls and temples (dedicated to the Sun god), together with all the magnificence of Incan architecture, have struck approaching travellers for centuries as they have looked down on the former capital of the Inca Empire. At least that is how the story goes, but it was not the case on the freezing morning when I stared numbly through the vibrating window of the bus at the sprawling masses of reddish-brown Spanish-tiled roofs. Although impressive, Cuzco seemed to exude a latent spirit of sadness – was it a restless under-current left from the ransacking and looting by the Conquistadors centuries before? I did not know, but the hand-hewn cobbled roads and the giant building blocks aroused in me a perception of a city of legends that I had not experienced before.

Chando Malonari, a sturdy, genial Peruvian tour operator, welcomed me and keenly shared all he knew of the Urubamba. He showed me photographs of the American kayaker, Lazlo Berty, venturing into the yet uncharted Torontei gorge, his kayak a minute

More cataracts on the Urubamba.

speck against the enormous grey rocks and the continuous fury of the water. Looking at those terrifying photos, I knew I just had to see that river for myself.

First Glimpses of a Monster

At first light the following day I boarded the train for Machu Picchu, 80 km northwest of Cuzco. The railway line apparently followed the east bank of the Urubamba for the complete length of the notorious Torontei gorge. In my backpack, I had enough food for a three-day hike along the Inca Trail, which passes over the mountains and ends at the Machu Picchu Inca ruins. As the passenger train descended into the valley of the Incas, my heart leapt at what unfolded before me – torrents of water cascading down each small quebrada (gully), joining waters, storming through narrow confined walls, doubling in size and then doubling yet again as the river careered down the steep Andean slopes. I had never seen anything like it. According to the rainfall statistics, that season was the wettest in 50 years. It did not surprise me – all that water had to come from somewhere! Eventually the creaking, squealing train entered the Sacred Valley of the Incas and my own excitement reached a new high.

A kaleidoscope of images of the chocolate-brown river – flashing past the windows – left me breathless. Hundreds of swollen rivulets pushed such volumes of water into the boulder-choked riverbed that the river became a raging monster, fighting to force its waters through the constricting banks. As the train clattered and swayed along the track I stood at the window, mesmerised, a knot in my stomach reminding me that this was what we were destined to paddle!

'No, it's impossible. We can't possibly run it, it's unthinkable!'

Gloom and doubt began to set in. My dream of navigating the river became blurred. Why even bother to start the expedition if we could not tackle this main section?

27

The Urubamba in full fury.

Sing for your Supper

A clear, strangely comforting young voice pulled me back to reality. A small Peruvian cholo boy stood commandingly in the aisle, reciting poetry at the top of his voice and capturing the attention of the entire coach. Fascinated I watched the obviously poor kid perform to earn gratuities from the travellers. He ended his recital with a beautiful Quechuan shepherd's song for which his intrigued audience applauded loudly. They, too, sensed the lad's courage and positive spirit.

How could I not get the message?

It was as if someone was rebuking me: 'Come on, Tim, pull out of it. Don't "psyche yourself out" so easily. Look at that young boy – he has nothing, no family, no support, but look at his courage! He's out there; doing what it takes . . . you go and do the same.'

I sat gazing at the passing river – our river!

'Yes,' I said, responding to myself. 'I must do what it takes. We've got to do it.'

To my surprise, the boy seated himself next to me.

'What's your name?' I asked in broken Spanish.

'Amberto, señor.'

'How old are you?'

'Twelve years, señor. I have no parents, I must do this to help feed my younger brothers and sisters.'

'I'm Teem, hola,' I said to him, trying to sound as Spanish as a matador. We shook hands and chatted. I liked this brave, young boy and sensed an understanding and a bond between us. We both had goals to reach – a dream to live and we both meant to make it. Watching the river, I realised that Amberto, in a peculiar way, had helped me to win a major mental battle.

All of a sudden, he pointed at me, then at the river. I nodded and mimed a paddling action with my arms. He understood and looked me over with a quizzical expression.

'Muy peligroso señor, muy peligroso!' (very dangerous, sir . . .).

I agreed, 'Si, muy peligroso.'

We stared at the flooding river, each in silent thought.

Losing the Inca Trail

The shrill whistle of the train shrieked, signalling its arrival at 'km 88', the start to the Inca Trail. I had decided to include the famous trail in my reconnaissance. I crossed the roaring river on a swaying footbridge and soon caught up with a group of Israeli hikers. We walked together for several hours until I decided to push ahead at my own pace, climbing two high ridges before I set up camp under a small cluster of trees. A steady drizzle set in and I spent the night alone, gazing meditatively into the glowing coals of my campfire. I needed this time alone to sit and grasp the reality of what lay ahead. I felt more positive than I had in a while, thanks to the brave boy on the train and because of the river shouting its challenge. I was not going to surrender, surely not before I had even tried!

The following day I caught up with a slow-moving group of European hikers. Their guide, Guiyermo,

was sure I could make Machu Picchu by nightfall if I pushed hard. Reluctant to spend another wet and lonely night in the elements I raced on, pushing myself hard. Rain set in during the afternoon and I realised that my trail was petering out. I retraced my steps for a few hundred metres to where the trail had forked. My map had become wet, soggy, and useless. Clouds of grey mist were billowing in and I knew that there was no hope of reaching Machu Picchu that evening. I would walk for another hour and then camp for the night, facing the elements. The path faded and then picked up again. Believing it was still the Inca Trail, I walked on along a hillside that gradually became choked with cane and reeds.

'Another 100 m, and if I can't get past this darn stuff, I'll turn back.'

However, the cane thickened and towered above my head.

'I am crazy to be walking in this jungle of —'

Before I could finish my sentence, the ground under my feet gave way. To my horror, I began sliding and falling down a steep slope. Desperately I grabbed for handholds, found a small shrub, held onto it for a few seconds before it too gave way. My momentum picked up. I was bouncing at uncontrollable speed down a steep slope on my back. Then I struck a protruding ledge with a loud thud. It launched me into the air, and into silent semi-darkness. I was freefalling to a certain death.

'Oh God, help me!' I cried out.

Falling

Soundless seconds passed – then the explosive shock of impact – then an eerie darkness enveloped me. This was surely the end! Thousands of miles from home I had fallen to my death on some mountain, chasing an impossible dream. The darkness did not lift; it grew heavier, spreading over me like death's cold blanket.

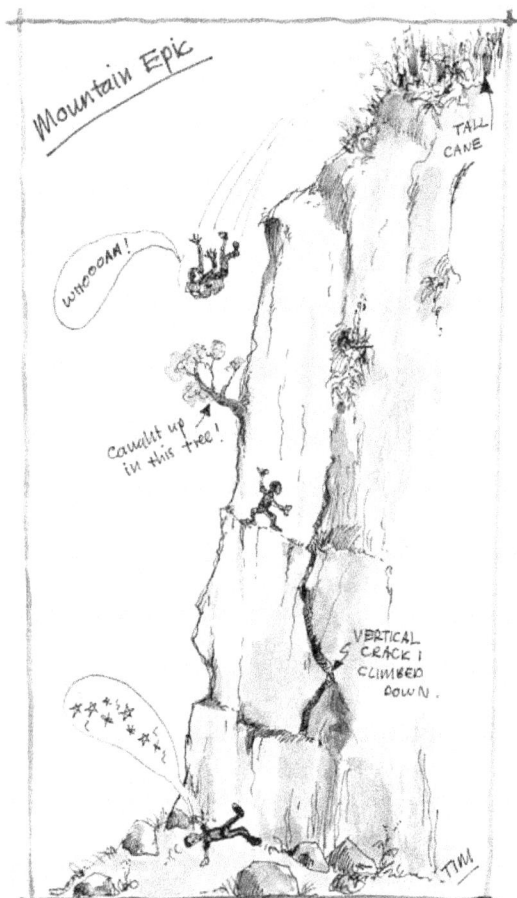

Mountain Epic

WHOOOAH!

Caught up in this tree!

TALL CANE

VERTICAL CRACK I CLIMBED DOWN.

TIM

Another close shave.

'Where am I? Am I alive?' I muttered some time later. It was now completely dark. Gingerly I reached out with my hand and touched something – it was the rough, woody texture of bark. Slowly I realised what had happened; the magnitude of it astounded me.

'It's a tree, I've been stopped by a tree!' I mumbled in astonishment. Through an intense dizziness, I recalled my fall: the sensation of falling free, the terrible collision, and the darkness.

'Did I break my back?' I wondered. I carefully shifted my position. It was painful, but I could move, and relief swept over me. I slowly tested each limb, my neck, and my back. I was all right, but I did not know where I was.

Darkness, drizzle and the faint outline of a cliff face behind me were all I could register. Groping about, I realised I was wedged in the fork of a spindly tree. Reaching for the sling and caribena that were strapped to my backpack, I painfully clipped myself to a branch and slumped back against the tree, exhausted but re-assured.

Making it through the Night

Hanging there between heaven and earth, I assessed the situation: I had survived a massive fall without fracturing a single bone; I miraculously landed in a tree where my backpack had obviously broken my fall. I did not know how far I fell, or how far below the ground was. The morning would bring those answers.

I had no company, except for glumness and shock. What if I could not get off the cliff face; who would hear my frantic calls? I would hang in the tree until I starved to death, or died of hypothermia. At once, long, uncontrollable shivers gripped me as shock set in; the freezing Andean wind sucked the warmth from my body, as though it was clearing out the warmth from my very soul. I cursed myself loudly for my stupidity and for continuing along that path knowing it was the wrong trail. 'Was I absolutely crazy?' I asked, knowing the answer.

The night dragged on and on and I did not know if I would see another morning again. Somehow, after a long, blind struggle, I had managed to ease out my backpack and clipped it to the tree. In its side pocket, I scavenged around and found some biscuits, cheese and my old harmonica. I pressed the instrument to my cold lips and the quivering notes of Kris Kristofferson's *Bobby McGee* soon drowned in the velvety, pitch-blackness of the unnerving night. But this boy was not busted flat in Baton Rouge; this boy was 'flat' in some tree, with nowhere to go! All the while, my mind rambled through many things: my life, my parents, and my friends back home. What would my folks think if they saw me perched in this tree like a bedraggled and injured egret chick?

I had never been one to pray, but that night I frequently called out to God to spare me. I was scared.

Sleep came at last and carried me off into a restless doze. Some time later I awoke with a fright, clutching at the branches, thinking I was falling again. It was with elation that I realised I was still alive – and not falling to my death. As long as I was alive I did not care that it was somewhere in a tree who knew how high above the ground. Dawn had arrived and shifting masses of white mist rose upwards towards me. Suddenly there was a break in the white blanket and I gasped in utter horror at what unfolded before my stunned eyes...

. . . terra firma was 100 sheer metres below me!

A Second Chance

A sheer cliff face dropped away below me onto enormous angular boulders forming the scree slope some 100 m below me. Above me, overhanging granite slabs forbiddingly blocked any hope of an upward ascent. Then the enormity of the whole situation struck me: I was clinging to the only tree on the entire cliff face!

I should have been dead.

Realising this, I began to chuckle at the absurd predicament I found myself in. That chuckle triggered off spasms of hysterical laughter. I roared and howled manically until I almost toppled out of my perch. Weak from laughter, I quickly sobered up as the cold wind swallowed up my empty, wacky mirth. It was time to get down to business and find a way to get out.

Not being an experienced mountaineer, I scanned the rock face below me for signs of a route down. During my years in Cape Town, I had rock-climbing friends who often dragged me up many of their climbs

and taught me the basics of rock climbing. Sitting pretty in my perch, I knew I had only two options: wait for someone to take me down or climb down myself. The choice was obvious.

'Come now, Biggs, stop your whining and go for it. If you make it, you make it; if you don't, you don't. What the hell, rather die trying than die of thirst up here.'

I spotted a crack in the rock that led downwards, intercepting a narrow ledge that I figured I could traverse along. Along the edge, a series of rock slabs appeared to offer handholds to a point approximately 40 m below me. From there, my envisioned route disappeared around a bulge on the cliff face; I would just have to gamble that it wouldn't turn out to be a dead end. That was the last thing I needed.

'Okay, let's do it,' I shouted to myself. Carefully emptying out my backpack, except for the last of my rations and my harmonica, I watched as each item thumped onto the rocks far below. With adrenalin pumping, I slowly edged out of the fork in the tree and wedged my fingers into a vertical crack. The granite rock was solid and tight. My feet found the small footholds, which allowed me to lower myself down the rock face onto the ledge. Traversing out along the ledge I inched my way forward, barely finding fingerholds on the rock. Then the unthinkable happened: there were no more foot- or handholds. Desperately I searched for something to grip onto, my forearms beginning to cramp. I couldn't go backwards or forwards – I was stuck. In a last chance bid, I stretched my arm further along the rock for a fingerhold.

Yes, there was something . . . a minute crack!

I jammed the tips of my bleeding fingers into the minuscule crack and lunged forward. It was my only chance; would my fingers support me? For a fleeting second, it felt as if I was losing my grip, and then my left foot found a slight edge. The seconds seemed like an eternity as I teetered, clinging to the rock with the last of my strength. I had to make it, I could not fall, I just had to make it. I moved again, my foothold held;

I was onto a ledge again! Shaking, I hugged the rock, its grainy texture cold against my clammy cheek, my mouth dry and gasping for breath.

'I must keep moving,' I motivated myself and had to reach the bulge before I could think of a rest. The climbing eased as I worked my way down through the massive slabs and the small ledge at the base of the bulge. I peered around the corner in suspense.

'Phew,' I sighed in relief. There seemed to have been some kind of route edging across the face diagonally. Huddling up against the wall behind me, I rested, chewing on dry bread and raisins, longing for a sip of water. Again I had to venture out along a totally exposed route, depending on minute fingerholds to support my weight.

My final challenge was a 3-m drop onto a narrow ledge at the end of the diagonal route. Now only 15 m away from the scree slope, the end was in sight! I lowered myself, hung from my arms, and searched for a foothold. Without warning, the rock I was clutching came loose in my hand. I dropped like a stone, striking the lip of the ledge and landing with a crunch. Clawing at the rock with raw fingers, I fought to stay on the narrow ledge, but to little avail: I felt my fingers slip and then I was falling again, crashing against the rock wall followed by the terrible impact and immediate blackness.

My head throbbed with pain. I groaned and squinted into the bright light, touching my forehead; it was wet with blood. I lifted my head off the ground and sat up dazed, then slumped back onto the soft, green grass. I was on terra firma, and I was alive.

'Yes, I made it, I'm alive!' My gamble had worked. I lay back again, thanking whoever, whatever for helping me through the ordeal. 'Thank you, thank you,' I mumbled, 'I thought I was a goner.'

With a parched tongue and an incredible thirst, I proceeded towards the lush, green forest below, but not before looking back up at the small, lone tree protruding from the cliff some 100 m higher. I just shook my head.

I turned around and staggered shakily down the boulder-strewn slope, towards the forest below, where I knew I would eventually find the Urubamba.

Troops Arrive

D-day had arrived; the team was finally on its way. François was the first to come. I was supposed to meet him at Lima Airport but sadly I disgraced myself by arriving in Lima a day late after having been tempted into joining a group of attractive German tourists to a seaside resort. François was not impressed, but forgave me after a couple of beers, and soon we started discussing our plans late into the night. I had carried out my reconnaissance thoroughly and had scrolls of maps with invaluable information. It had been almost two years since we had met in Pretoria to discuss our Urubamba dream and we had much catching up to do. We discussed our different roles in finer detail, wishing to avoid confrontation and confusion once the expedition had begun. François would be overall leader of the expedition, with Clive Curson his deputy. I would be the 'on the water leader' and in charge of the practical side of operations.

Our seven sponsored 'Perception' kayaks from the USA then arrived on the Danish liner *Charlottenberg*. It was good news, but then the Peruvian Customs Department unexpectedly launched a bitter broadside, demanding US$20 000 for the release of our kayaks – an amount we just did not have. I spent two weeks in fruitless negotiations, but the officials would not budge, leaving us devastated. (A similar story of a German climbing team sent home before they even got to the Andes did little to lift our morale.) The entire expedition seemed to be in jeopardy. We refused to give up, having put so much effort into planning it. The entire team (with the exception of Chan, who was in America), along with mountains of provisions and equipment, had arrived in Lima. Apart from having no kayaks, we were ready to roll.

URUBAMBA PREPARATION

We assembled in a small hotel room, sitting on boxes of provisions and equipment, getting to know one another and discussing the trip. It was the first time we had been together as a team and spirits were high despite the kayak fiasco. François Odendaal was there, Clive Curson, Matt Carlisle, Fanie van der Merwe (the cameraman who would only stay with us for the first month) and me. There were two additional teammembers, our team doctor, Doc Curson (Clive's dad), and Donata Gallucio, our team physiotherapist.

I was taken aback when I learned that the attractive Italian Australian was actually François's girlfriend, and had been invited aboard as the team physiotherapist. I was even more surprised to find that Donata had no previous expeditioning experience and had never been on a river. I respectfully accepted our leader's decision. However, I could bet money on it that her presence would at least add spice to the trip.

With Fanie only staying a month due to other commitments, François and Clive seemed determined that we should plan the entire expedition to suit Fanie's tight filming programme. The upper sections would therefore be run in 'relay style' in order to cover the huge distances, while the key section of the Torontei gorge was also too high-risk to run at present semi-flooding water levels. To top it all our kayaks were still lying impounded in customs. In good faith we hoped that all would eventually work out, and our kayaks would be released. The team would split in two. One group, consisting of François, Fanie and Donata would push up into the mountains in search of the source at Lake Sibinacocha (6 000 m high). The rest would continue the battle against customs for the release of our kayaks, and begin searching for alternative kayaks in Peru.

With the future of our long-planned expedition now swinging precariously in the scales, we were unsure whether our setting off on a kayak expedition without a single kayak was outrageously foolish or courageously optimistic. Trying hard to conceal our dejection and low morales, we bade each other good luck, and the mountain team departed from Lima and set off for the source of the Urubamba.

Chapter 2

THE URUBAMBA
(April – July 1981)

First Blood

If real life had soundtracks, then that great American crooner Dean Martin's *Memories are made of this* would have played loudly when Matt, Clive and I slipped into the swirling waters of the Urubamba on 10 April 1981. This was the day when my attempt to navigate the three major tributaries of the Amazon River started. Although it only materialised over two decades later, this was the day that stirred my emotions like no other.

It was the realisation of a lifelong dream. As my kayak carved through the water, I could not believe it was finally happening. It felt as though an age had passed since François and I first dreamed of passing through that mysterious doorway to launch our kayaks on the rivers of the Andes. Now it was here, happening, and making memories.

Our starting point was Combapata, where the small Rio Salca flows into the Rio Vilcanota at some 4570 m (15 000 ft) above sea level. Our topographic maps indicated that the Rio Salca was the longest tributary of the Urubamba and that its source was Lake Sibinacocha. It was to this lake that François, Fanie and Donata had already departed in their attempt to lay eyes on the very first drops of the river.

Chan and I had waited on in Lima, continuing our search for replacement kayaks. We eventually found two second-hand Perception Quests, and two rickety fibreglass kayaks from the American ambassador, Alf Cooley, and his friend Tom Jackson. The ongoing struggle with the Peruvian customs had taken its toll on my sense of humour, and when Chan volunteered

The Rio Salca. Just upstream from here it plunged underground.

to stay on in a final attempt to secure our confiscated kayaks, I was extremely grateful. Chan would meet up with us once negotiations with the Peruvians either failed or succeeded.

With this minor setback behind us, we turned to the task at hand. The river was high after the unseasonable rainfall. Fortunately the stretch we started on was swift but straightforward, allowing us time to settle into our kayaks and tune ourselves to the rhythm of the river before entering the small Checacupe gorge, some 30 km downstream. For a while we acted like boys, shouting at each other in excitement, frolicking in the small surfing waves as we cruised along at 20 km/h (12 m/h), with the banks of the river rising steeply to form a small, narrow gorge.

'I need to work on my seat and hip pads,' I yelled across to Matt and Clive. 'I'm too loose in this old boat; I won't be able to roll.' I had taken Tom Jackson's old fibreglass kayak, a long, awkward boat that had no fixed footrest.

'Let's do it once we're through this section,' Clive yelled back. 'It doesn't look too difficult.'

With that prophetic forecast, the situation rapidly deteriorated. Looking downstream, I could see the gradient increasing as the river charged over 'pourovers' and between massive boulders. I turned my kayak upstream to ferry-glide towards the bank, but the slow-turning vessel was caught sideways by the current and sucked backwards over a powerful pourover and into a boiling, recycling hole. Frantically bracing myself against the surging water, I felt a stabbing pain shoot through my right shoulder, signalling what I had dreaded most: the recurrence of my old shoulder injury.

In an instant I was over, tugging at my spraydeck, and in a second was out of my boat, swimming in the wild water. An eerie, silence swept over me as the current pulled me down. Just as suddenly it released its grip and I surfaced, choking and gasping for air. In some pain, I began the long swim for the shore. Eventually reaching the bank, I dragged myself out

We spent the night with this family. The mother (above), was grumpy the next morning.

of the water, cursing myself for my stupidity. As I recovered on the shore, there was no sign of Matt and Clive. My two friends were probably a mile or so further down the river by now, oblivious to the fact that the Urubamba had almost swallowed me on the first day of our journey! I stood up and began working my way along the base of the steep banks, searching for my kayak, my paddle, and my friends.

Around a corner, parked in an eddy, was Matt in his kayak. He was holding on to my kayak, but there was no sign of Clive. I hurried towards him, relieved to see him and my kayak after my maiden swim on the Urubamba.

'Where's Clive?' I asked.

'I last saw him heading downstream, chasing your paddle,' said Matt. 'He should be back any minute. I hope nothing has happened to him, maybe we should wait for him here.' He cast a concerned glance downstream. Ten minutes later, Clive had still not appeared.

I scaled the steep bank and began jogging through the undergrowth in search of my friend, leaving Matt with the kayaks. In the distance, I spotted Clive des-

pondently picking his way through the boulders towards me.

'Clive! Are you okay, buddy?' I called out.

'Tim, I've never had a swim like that. I almost drowned,' a pale-looking Clive said as he sat down on a boulder and described what had happened to him. While chasing after my paddle, he too had dropped over a ledge and into a hole. He had missed his roll, was separated from his kayak, and had to swim

After spending the night at this homestead, I sat on a rock and sketched - my fingers were frozen!

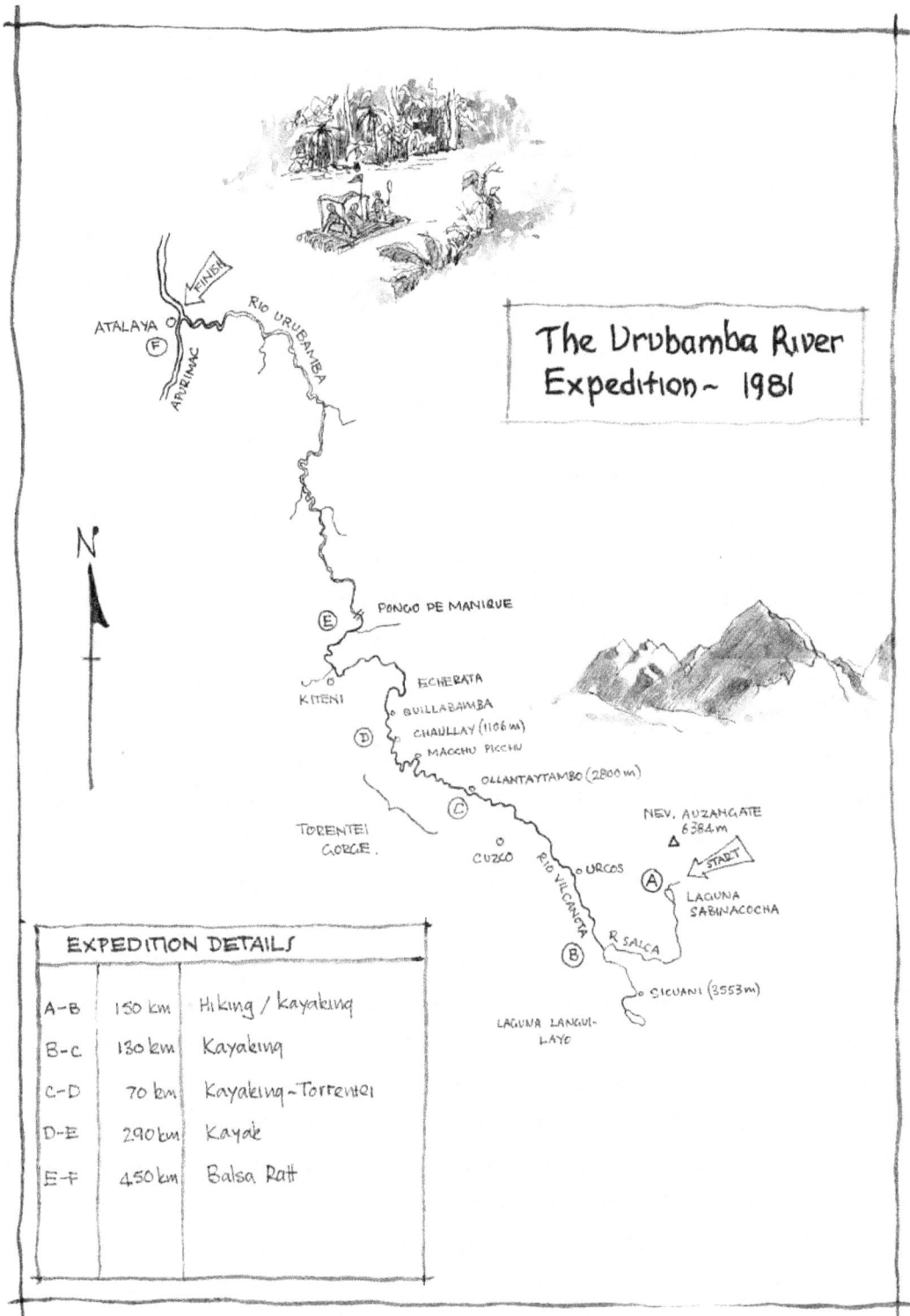

The Urubamba River
Expedition ~ 1981

ATALAYA
FINISH
F
APURIMAC
RIO URUBAMBA

N

E PONGO DE MANIQUE

ECHERATA
KITENI
QUILLABAMBA
D CHAULLAY (1106 m)
MACCHU PICCHU
OLLANTAYTAMBO (2800 m)

C

TORENTEI
GORGE.
CUZCO
RIO VILCANOTA
URCOS

NEV. AUZANGATE
6384 m
△
START
A
LAGUNA
SABINACOCHA

B
R SALCA

SICUANI (3553 m)

LAGUNA LANGUI-
LAYO

EXPEDITION DETAILS

A–B	150 km	Hiking / kayaking
B–C	130 km	Kayaking
C–D	70 km	Kayaking ~ Torrentei
D–E	290 km	Kayak
E–F	450 km	Balsa Raft

38

1981 UPPER AMAZON KAYAK EXPEDITION

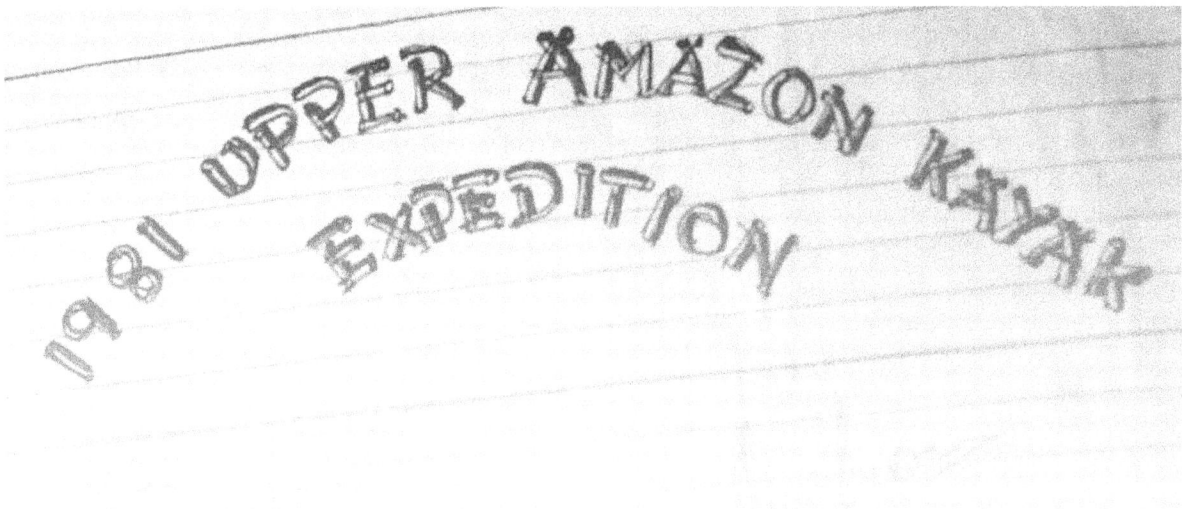

through a kilometre of rapids. Just when Clive was about to surrender to the Urubamba's power, it mercifully spat him out into an eddy where his half-submerged kayak was randomly circling. Looking at my friend, I was glad that we had both survived.

Matt caught up to us and the three of us sat on our kayaks, our morale at a new low. We were very aware that we had failed our first test on the Urubamba dismally.

'Sorry, guys,' I said, finally breaking the awkward silence. 'It was all my fault. I should never have swum. I don't know what got into me.' Although I realised that it could have happened to anyone, I felt responsible for the disastrous start to the day. 'Next time I'll fit my boat out before the rapids,' I scolded myself.

'Well, it's a good wake-up call for all of us,' said Matt. 'We will be fine from now on if we just sharpen up.'

'Yes, I don't want to swim like that again,' Clive muttered while removing a splinter from his finger with a penknife.

Matt was right; we had to be sharper. The Urubamba was not to be taken lightly. It demanded respect and vigilance. As it was, it had drawn first blood; it hit hard, and held nothing back.

The game was on. Boy, was it on!

A Leader in Trouble

Once bitten and twice shy, the three of us continued cautiously through the gorge. Some four hours later, we spotted our seconds, Doc and Jose, and immediately saw that something was wrong. Their body language screamed out 'bad news'. My first thought was that something had happened to the other group.

Doc, with a concerned and furrowed expression, strode towards us.

'There's a problem with François's team,' Doc confirmed my suspicion. 'We've just heard over the radio that three foreigners are sick and dying in the mountains near Pitumarca. It could only be our guys,' Doc concluded.

Highly concerned, we loaded our kayaks on to the Land Cruiser and hurried towards Santa Barbara. Passing the police station at a small Andean village, we stumbled upon Don Juan, a weather-beaten Quechua mountain man, who had first relayed the message of woe. He had been informed by our sister group's guide, Domingo, that François was seriously ill with a potentially fatal case of *soroche* (altitude sickness). According to Don Juan the group's greatest concern was that in order to descend to an altitude where François might recover, they first had to climb several hundred metres to cross a low pass. Apparently, no one in the group wanted to risk this move as it could finish off François. The team faced a dilemma.

Alarmed by the bleak description of the situation, Doc and Matt immediately headed back to Sicuani village in search of a rescue helicopter, while Clive and I continued up the mountain towards our friends. Hiking hard up the slope, we came across a second messenger; Julio gave us a cigarette box on which Fanie had scribbled the following: 'We are going to try to get François down, will head for Sucu Pallca. Need medical and food provisions urgently. François very ill, be quick.'

We loaded Julio with our provisions and hurried him back up the mountain while we rushed back to Santa Barbara where we left a note for Doc and Matt to cancel the helicopter bid. Packing enough provisions into our backpacks for a long hike, we set out for Sucu Pallca to meet François's party. The thin, crisp air bit into our lungs as the altitude reduced our pace to a slow walk. Exhausted, we stumbled over the rocks until we came to the three-hut village of Sucu Pallca. It was already 9:00 p.m., and struggling through the driving rain and the sub-zero temperature, we knocked on the door of the largest hut. A small, hunched Quechua woman ushered us inside after we begged for accommodation. Our gracious hostess then show-ed us to a candlelit croft where we made full use of the dusty floor space.

Sharing the single-room homestead with the family of seven (and ten guinea pigs!) was a humbling experience. Moments before I fell asleep, I heard the restless scuffle of guinea pigs and the suppressed giggles of the children. It was most definitely a first for this Quechua family to have bedraggled visitors like us spending the night!

Clive and I rose early the next morning, and after thanking our hosts, we marched through the thick frost, pushing on to Chancopampa, the next village along the mountain trail. We hiked in silence through the mountain wilderness, the only sounds being that of our own breathing and the crunching of the frost underfoot. Dawn's first rays of light silhouetted the craggy, snow-covered skyline ahead of us, raising our hopes for a clear day.

Clive broke the silence. 'Isn't that them coming down that far ridge? Look over there, Tim!' he called.

A small procession of two mules, a horse and a few slow-moving figures were making their way across a ridge in the distance.

'Yes – those aren't Quechuas, they're gringos,' I called, squinting against the glare of the snow. 'Yes, yes – it's them all right. Let's run to meet them!'

The ultimate in riverside real estate.

Andes
rescue
bid drama
Daily News Reporter

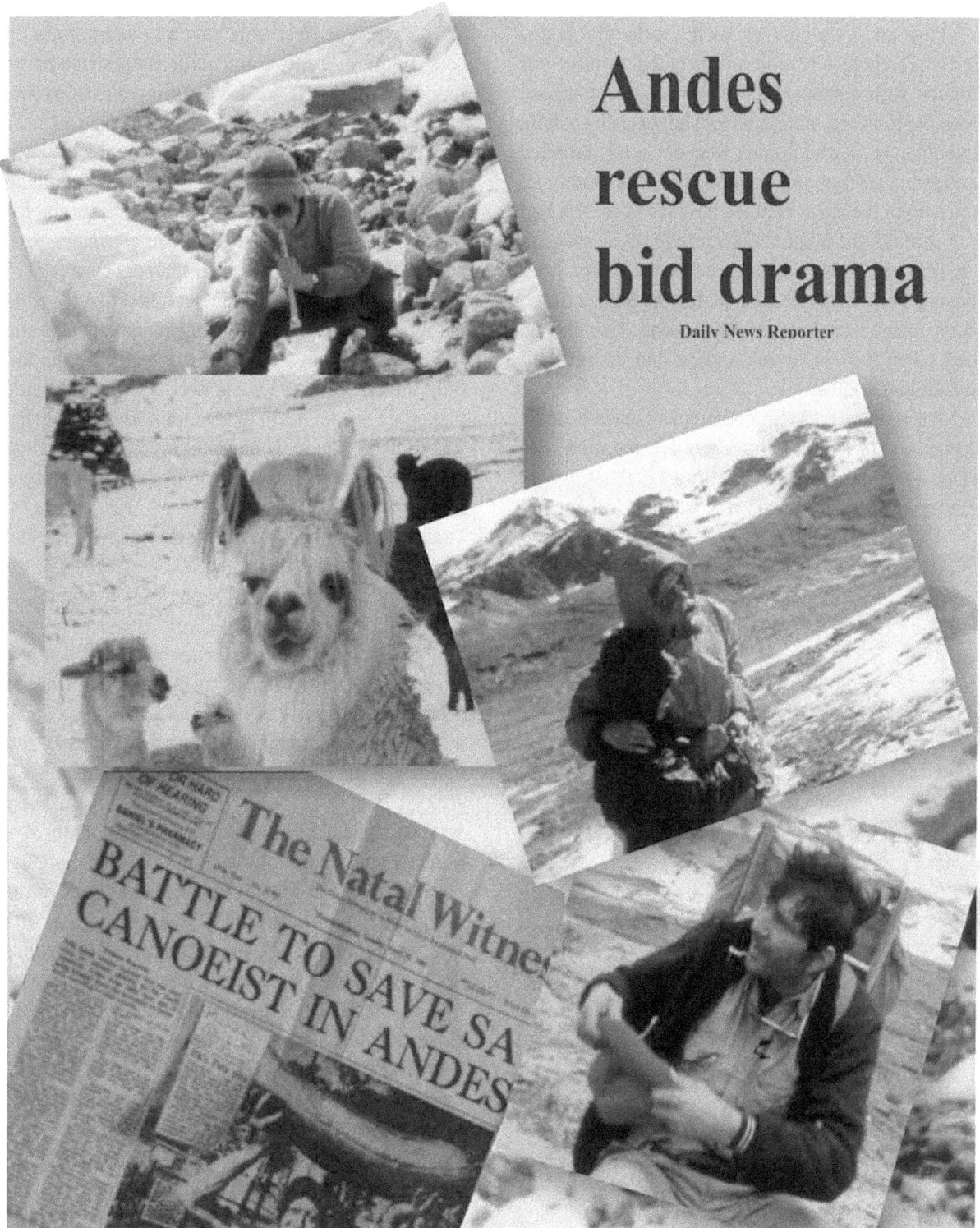

The Natal Witness

BATTLE TO SAVE SA
CANOEIST IN ANDES

Clive and I sprinted across the rocky and boggy terrain, forging a stream and running to meet our friends with whoops and yells. François, slouched over the back of a mule, was looking pale and ashen, but alive. Fanie and Donata were obviously fatigued and strained. They looked happy to see us. Domingo, the hero of the party, beamed from his horse. He had run through the night to deliver the SOS message to the police at Sicuani, a distance of some 70 km. After having a bite to eat, he immediately set off at a run to climb to the team at Lago Sibinacocha. The mission had taken him 36 hours, and he had arrived half frozen and limping.

The reunion was reminiscent of a fairytale movie scene, where long-lost travellers are reunited. The saga was finally over, and with great relief, we all made our way back down to the waiting Urubamba.

Domingo the 'Good Shepherd'.
He carried the sos message down to
the team ~ had a bite to eat ~
then ran back through the night ~
36 hrs on the trail.

Back on the river trail, safe and snug around a cosy campfire, François and his group described their mountain ordeal. He had felt the symptoms of *soroche* when they reached the high mountain plateau near Lake Sibinacocha. As excessive carbon dioxide built up in his muscles, severe cramps racked his failing body. He finally collapsed in a panic, his lungs starved of oxygen. Then, in a state of semi-consciousness, scenes of his life unfolded before him: old memories of his near-drowning on the Limpopo River many years earlier, his parents, and faces of old relationships and friends. Eventually the will to survive left him, and only the presence and support of Donata and Fanie prevented certain death in the mountains. During the following 24 hours his lungs began making gurgling sounds, confirming that pulmonary oedema – present in the advanced stage of *soroche* – was setting in. Fanie and Donata feared the worst, and with the bad weather and snowfalls, it had become impossible for a helicopter to fly in, even if one was available. All they could do was wait.

During one of the short breaks in the bad weather, Fanie and Donata slipped away from François to search for the source of the river. Following a small stream that ran into the lake, they struck it lucky and discovered the magical birthplace of the streamlet. It trickled from a rock and gradually became a lively watercourse. Being deeply concerned about François's plight, Donata picked up a fragment of the angular black rock as a memento. While hiking back to the camp, they discussed a plan for François's rescue. With him lapsing in and out of consciousness, the team's decision was unanimous to attempt the risky descent.

This decision called for an ascent over a steep ridge, before making the descent. As the team of four climbed the 500-m high ridge, François showed dangerous signs of cramping, and suffered uncontrolled spasms. There was no going back now – the only way forward was up and over the obstructing ridge. At what seemed a snail's pace, animals and humans trudged up the steep incline. Would François survive

The Andes - where many rivers are born.

the higher altitude? What if he went into a coma? Then, suddenly, without realising it as all attention was on François, they had reached the summit and were already moving down the other side!

The psychological relief from the burden of tension and fear was welcomed. Instead of a dying leader, the group now had a François who was beginning to show signs of improvement, and as the oxygen-rich mountain air reached his lungs and vitalised his body, he visibly regained strength. Steadily the team descended the steep mountain path, a new optimism in the air.

The Arrival of Chan

With François recovering and the source of the river found, we climbed back in our kayaking 'battledress' and launched our boats. This next section would take us to Pisac. With only three kayaks in reasonable shape among the five of us, we had to take turns paddling the long fibreglass doubles kayak (brought along for the flatter sections). François, still physically and mentally battered after his ordeal, helped Fanie with the filming, and rested, while enjoying the attention from his physiotherapist, Donata. The two of them planned our sequences and came up with some amazing footage. We had to shoot some of the scenes repeatedly until the two filmmakers were happy.

Chan had arrived at last from Lima with disappointing news about our kayaks. Our expedition was dealt a hard blow, with the unyielding Peruvian bureaucracy still refusing to release our kayaks.

That night we camped at the end of the small Checacupe gorge where Matt had found some huge logs. Together we built a monstrous bonfire, celebrating our first night together as a full team. There was much laughter and bantering and as the beer flowed, our river stories took on dramatic and exaggerated proportions. A cold drizzle finally drove us into our tents in the early hours of the morning.

Camera, Lights…

Every kayaker understands the effect of having a camera rolling while he makes his run. It is like injecting him or her with an extra dose of courage and bravado. As we approached the beautiful town of Ollantaytambo, it was time for the cameras to roll. The camera crew was on a tight schedule and hungry for some exciting action footage. Chan pulled his kayak to the side and signalled to the camera vehicle that we had found a suitable filming spot – a 1.5 km section of class 3 rapids, ending in a massive series of crashing 'stopper waves' spanning the width of the river.

As Matt, Clive and François had opted for setting up safety below the Huarang rapid, it was up to Chan and me to run the section. While Fanie and some of the others set the cameras in position, Chan and I nervously speculated about the possible routes.

'I'll take the line through that 1-m gap, break through that hole, then into the eddy on the left-hand side,' Chan speculated with his usual confidence. 'What line will you take, Tim?'

It was a nerve-racking decision. A dud run would be on film for all the world to see and laugh at. Chan's line was more technical, although miss it and you would be slaughtered. The other option was to charge the recycling hole and crash through it by sheer force. 'What the hell,' I thought to myself, 'it won't kill me, so why not go for it!'

Being the more experienced kayaker, Chan went first. With his usual polished skill, he ran the small tongue that cut through the edge of the first roaring hole, broke through the crest of the second, and spun his kayak neatly around to reverse into a small eddy. All this with the ease and calm of a ballet dancer. It was a single take and any moviemaker's dream.

Then it was my turn, and I just had to go for the the big drop. I lined up, fully aware that a good hiding at the hands of the Urubamba might well be on the cards. With a dry mouth and a racing heart, I worked my way through the approaches and struck

Nothing can humble you like a fierce river. Huarang Rapids.

out with all my might over the lip of the 2.5-m trench. As I plunged into the trough, I was dismayed at the size of hydraulics about to engulf me. Tons of brown water crashed over my head. Its force and violence stunned me as my boat repeatedly and uncontrollably cartwheeled, the violence of the water hurling me back into the hole. I was unable to escape the river's strong grip. Eventually the thrashing water calmed and I knew I had been flushed out. I struck with my paddle to roll, failed, struck again and failed, then desperately clawed myself up, guarding my still tender shoulder all the while. My waterlogged kayak sluggishly righted itself, I broke the surface, gasping for air, relieved. During the run, my spraydeck had 'popped' and I now sat somewhat subdued in a half-submerged boat. Chan and Matt were quickly at my side; the amusement on their faces clear as they scrutinised me. I knew they were waiting to say something. The Urubamba had just thrashed Tim Biggs (again) and this was a fine opportunity for a wisecrack. Chan paddled up.

'Well done, Tim – you hung in there through a good class-5 hiding,' he said encouragingly. 'Your kayaking is improving at last! Maybe you'll be up to the Machu Picchu stretch after all.'

Yes, I thought, I must be.

Changing Plans

We had now reached the beginning of the Torontei gorge – the gateway to the famous Machu Picchu ruins. Chilca siding, at 76 km along the Cuzco railway line, marked the point where the Urubamba changed gear, so to speak, and accelerated into its fiercest section, the notorious Torontei gorge. From a mere 5 m/km, the gradient increases to 23 m/km for the duration of a relentless 65 km (45 miles). With the high water levels from the late rains, the combination of steep gradient and high volume lifts the bar several notches, making this section borderline suicidal for kayakers of our calibre and experience. The doubt in our minds

Machu Picchu.

45

Fanie filming at Machu Picchu

happy with the state of affairs and grumpily helped to load the kayaks on the train for Machu Picchu. There was no sense in rebelling against the decision; it would have been in bad taste and might polarise the team. Anyway, once in Machu Picchu, Fanie spent a day filming us where we paddled around the base of the towering granite peaks. A day later, near the village of Escherate, he filmed us running a magnificent class 4 rapid. Once Fanie left, François would be responsible for documenting the journey on film.

The time came for Fanie to say goodbye and head back to South Africa. He had certainly won our respect and friendship, and as one who had led an expedition himself, his presence, maturity and experience helped hold our diverse group together. Fanie had been the one who could defuse a heated argument, injecting humour into it, and turning it around so that we all parted as friends. After the trial on the mountain François had grown especially close to Fanie, knowing his friend's mountaineering experience might have averted a tragedy.

'Cheers!' we yelled as Fanie drove off with Jose. 'Thanks for everything!'

'Thank you, guys. See you back home.' Fanie's lean and sun-tanned face grinned back at us from the departing Land Cruiser.

With Fanie gone, we returned to our schedule and started navigating the river at the village of Chaullay.

François Disappears

We had leap-frogged the 70-km Torontei gorge from Chilca to Chaullay – where we had found the first section of river that looked reasonably navigable. The Torontei gorge was too dangerous to attempt while the water level was that high. Chan and I volunteered to run it later (some time after we had reached the confluence of the Urubamba and the Apurimac).

In the back of our minds we knew that the imposing jungle was only days away. That thought brought a welcome anticipation, as from there all

about this section persisted. Could we hope to run it? Wouldn't it be safer to simply walk round the gorge? Only time would tell what the group would decide.

We had been together as a group for almost two weeks, and had begun to gel as a team. In the meantime Fanie's time with us was running out, and with only four filming days left, we would have to skip sections of the river in order to complete the film project. A clear 'tail wagging the dog' situation had developed where the making of the film was taking precedence over the running of the river. I was not

The mystical mountains of Machu Picchu.

road access ended, and we would be self-supporting and on our own. We excitedly offloaded the kayaks and prepared to set off for Kiteni and the Pongo de Mainique, now only 120 km downstream.

It was here at Chaullay that François began his maiden paddle on the Urubamba. Our leader was understandably nervous. He had not paddled for the two years leading up to the expedition, and the *soroche* attack had certainly been a physical, as well as an emotional, setback. After scouting the first rapid, he decided to put in further downstream in calmer waters. There he would wait for the rest of us.

The moment we entered the river, we realised that we had once again grossly underestimated its strength. The river might have looked manageable when looking down on it from a height, but at water level, what had appeared to be an insignificant wave, was now a wave crashing over our heads. The river had also increased in volume from 60 m³/s (2 000 cf/s) to a staggering 500 m³/s (18 000 cf/s).

From the road, we had scouted what had looked like a reasonable class 4 rapid. Now, as I led the descent, we swept into dangerous pour-overs and thrashing waves. Within seconds, I found myself flying over

Journal sketches of Quillabamba.

Rapids, and notes of river.

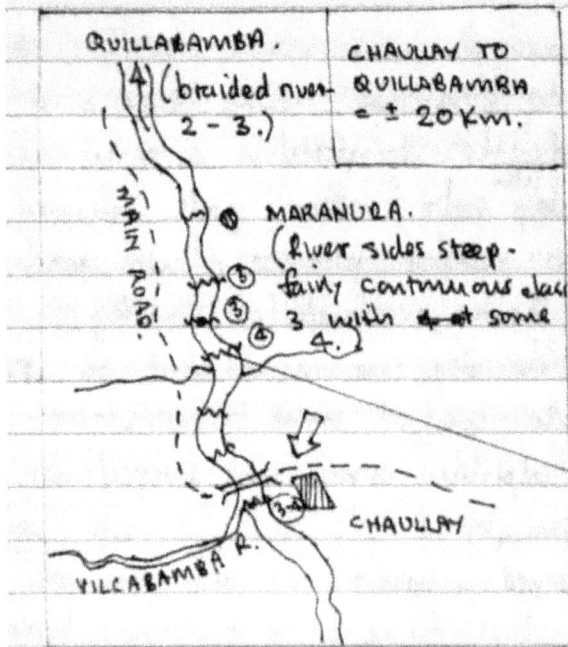

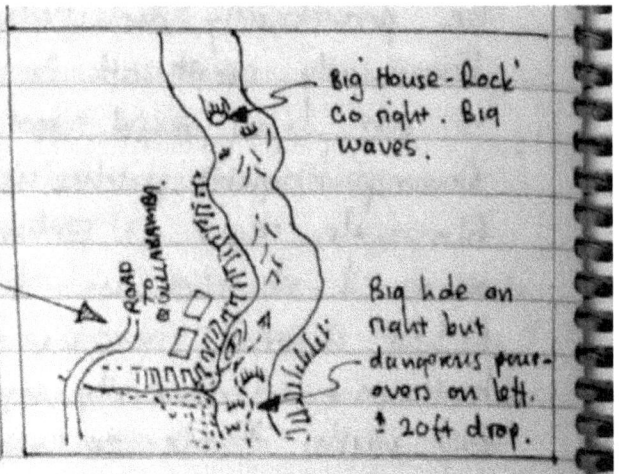

a pour-over and into the waiting turbulence below. The water whipped me over and while upside down I managed a quick roll and surfaced. Wide-eyed I fought my way down the remainder of the rapid, more out of control than in. Matt and Clive joined me at the bottom, also wide-eyed at what we had just run. Before we could discuss our next move, the river swept us along to the next rapid where we manoeuvred our way through potentially disastrous recycling holes. Thankfully eddying out at the end of the kilometre-long section of rapid, we realised that we had not seen François, who we were supposed to have waited for at the end of the first rapid.

I grew cold and hoped that nothing had happened to him, especially not on his first voyage on the river that he had been dreaming about for so long. That would have been some cruel irony indeed.

We waited for 10 minutes and when he did not show, we speculated that François had taken fright at the sheer size of the rapids and probably put in lower down the river. We set off, navigated the next two rapids, but still found no sign of our leader or his kayak. We were now 3 km from our starting point and the option of running back along the riverbank would have taken too long; besides, François was clearly not on that stretch.

'Let's push on,' I suggested uneasily. 'François has obviously pulled out. This water is too fierce for him to start on.' I was silently feeling guilty for allowing a breach of a fundamental river principle – never allow a team to split up.

'Yeah,' said Clive. 'He would have been waiting on the bank if he was paddling. Remember that he set off 20 minutes before we started. If we had somehow missed him, he will walk back to the Land Cruiser when he realises we have gone on.'

Clive's words made some sense and we continued down the river more relaxed. At Quillabamba, 15 km downstream, an agitated, cursing Doc waved us in.

'Why the hell did you leave François? What did you think you were doing letting him paddle on his own?' Doc exploded.

In total silence, his angry words soaked in; François must be paddling on his own some way behind us. I could only helplessly point out that François had set off by himself. That, of course, was a weak excuse and certainly not one that would bring François to safety. With an hour of daylight left, Matt and I decided to head upstream in search of our leader. We loaded our kayaks onto the Land Cruiser and a fuming Doc drove us back to our starting point.

Not wanting to waste time, Matt and I paddled hard through the rapids, scanning the riverbank for any signs of François. Despite our efforts, darkness caught up with us and dropped over the river like a velvet curtain. We were now breaking another river principle by paddling in the dark. We tried to stay as near to each other as possible, shouting warnings to each other as we moved downstream, twice narrowly missing malicious pour-overs. We continued, calling out François's name, but there was no sign of him. Finally, the twinkle of a single light signalled the bridge at Quillabamba. Relieved to have survived the ordeal, we dragged the kayaks through the dark and wet undergrowth towards the bridge where Doc was waiting for us – angry and molested by the vicious swarms of mosquitoes.

A technical run.

Big water.

What kind of news did he have for us? Good? Bad?

'He came in,' reported Doc brusquely. 'He is okay, but it could have been nasty. He has cut his hand pretty badly and almost lost his boat.'

'Phew – well, at least he's in,' I sighed. 'I was pretty close to losing my own boat paddling in the dark,' I added feebly. 'Sorry, we won't do it again – we were wrong in paddling on, we should have waited longer.' My abject apology did little to calm our seething second.

Meanwhile François had recovered and was sitting with a beer in hand, reliving the adventure of his solo run to Quillabamba. It turned out that he had been working on his seat on the riverbank, when we had paddled past him, somehow missing each other. When we failed to arrive below the rapid as we had arranged, François waited 25 minutes and set off on his own, having forgotten to fit buoyancy bags to his kayak. He had bravely battled his way through the powerful rapids – portaging some, running some – and experiencing close encounters in others, cutting his hand in the process. We listened in silence, wondering how we had managed to chalk up so many mistakes in such a short section.

'Sorry, Frans, we shouldn't have gone on without you. It was a bad mistake, we should have known better,' I said apologetically.

After I had quietly scolded François for kayaking without buoyancy in his kayak, the incident died a silent death.

Meeting the Locals

Somewhat like an overloaded mule, the expedition battled on downstream through the swiftly flowing river. We had now reached the hilly forested region, which boarded the adjacent jungle. Although the river's gradient had lessened to 10 m/km, massive rapids, interspersed with flat water sections waited for us. We came to a grinding halt when the dirt track alongside the river ended abruptly. Ahead of us, as far as the eye could see, sprawled millions of square kilometres of virgin jungle, penetrated only by the snake-like Urubamba.

At the point where the track ended lay Kiteni, a busy trading village where two worlds meet. Here, traders from the vast jungle to the east carry in coffee, cocoa, cocaine and other valuable bounty harvested from the huge jungle storehouse. From the mountains to the west and south, other traders come to load brightly decorated eight-ton trucks with goods. The marketplace is the interface between the two cultures; the melting pot where they barter their wares, noisily settling deals over bottles of the local San Juan jungle beer.

It was here that Doc and Jose would head back home, leaving us to press on with a smaller, more manageable team. Our arrival in Kiteni aroused a great deal of interest, especially when word spread that we would be navigating the dreaded Pongo de Mainique – the notorious river gorge that separated the jungle from the mountain regions. This lay some 50 km downstream.

'Señores, I have lived here all my life. Many, many, people have never returned from the Pongo – many drown in the whirlpools, others killed by the Machiguenga Indians, you must not go.'

These were the words of Daniel, the local restauranteur, who soon realised that he was wasting his breath trying to deter us. We did not, however, ignore his advice completely, as it was consistent

We crossed the river to celebrate at the local watering hole. Unfortunately, on the way back at midnight, we became stranded halfway across, and spent a cold night sobering up.

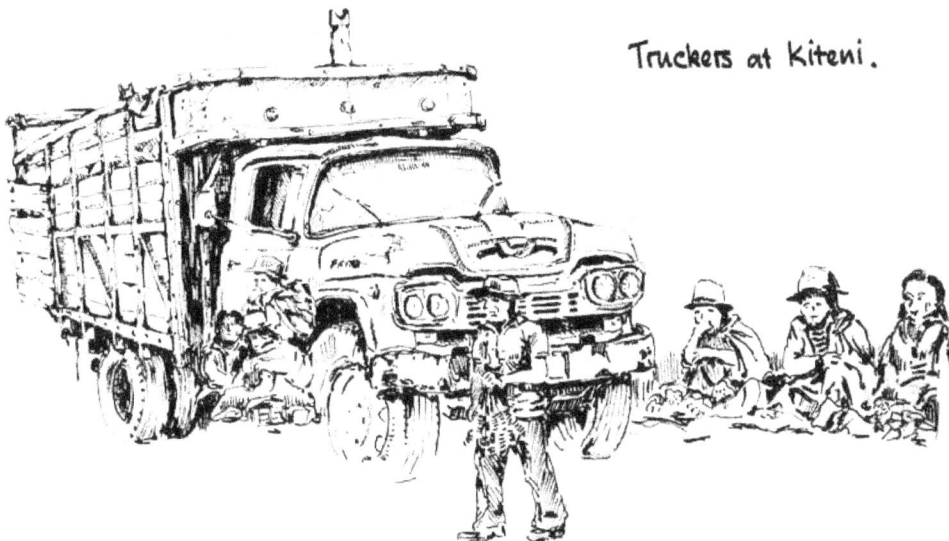

Truckers at Kiteni.

51

with the tales of woe shared by Tom Jackson and the US Consul, who had both shared tragic stories of drowning in the Pongo, and of groups of anthropologists who had been killed by Indian tribes. Being an opportunistic businessman, Daniel then appointed himself as our manager, recruitment officer and adviser. He also turned out to be quite an authority on the 'evils' of the dark jungle and supplied us with an endless list of dos and don'ts. Since we were doing the rest of the journey without seconds, we had decided to construct a raft to carry our luggage (and Donata). For this we needed balsa trees. Without hesitation – and without invitation – Daniel engaged the services of two locals, Rudolpho and Crispen, to get us to the village of Saniriato where there was a small forest of balsawood trees. Crispen would transport François and Co. there on his 10-m long motorised lancha. Once there, Crispen and friends would help us build the raft, at a price, of course. Saniriato was only a few kilometres away from the dreaded Pongo de Mainique and seemed an obvious place from where to launch our attempt.

After a full day's paddling – Chan and I in single kayaks, Matt and Clive in the double kayak – we reached Saniriato (where Crispen's home was). The village consisted of five mud huts, all clad with banana frond roofs. Here we learned that Crispen had bargaining skills second-to-none, and after hours of arguing and crafty negotiation, we agreed to pay him a deposit of $250 (108 000 soles) to get work on the raft underway. We arranged to pay the balance once we were safely through the Pongo. Crispen was happy with the terms and ferried us across the river to a balsawood forest on the southern slopes of the Urubamba.

We enthusiastically felled the pulpy balsa logs and dragged them down to the pebbly *playa* where a debarking operation was in full swing, with Clive, Matt and Crispen debarking and lashing the logs together with lengths of peeled bark. Pinning the logs together with ironwood stakes, we finally completed the raft with cross spars lashed to the main beams with bark and vines. And voilá: soon we were looking at a brand-new, creamy white, slippery vessel, 6 m long and 1.6 m wide. Our able guides looked satisfyingly at their handiwork, and unexpectedly announced that the raft was now ready for its launch, and that we should depart for the Pongo early the next morning.

That was not the agreement as we remembered it. Voicing our objection sparked off a hostile reaction from Crispen. We argued in vain that we had agreed to build a much wider raft over a period of

Matt and I wiping out in the Escherate Rapids.

three days, which would allow the balsa logs to dry. Crispen was resolute and refused to change his mind, denying most of the conditions that we had agreed to, adding that only small rafts had any chance of surviving the Pongo in any case. Unsure why he had turned against us, we reluctantly yielded to his demands, and began preparing ourselves for tomorrow's first taste of travelling by balsa raft. Gringo/Peruvian relationships dropped to an all time low.

Out of Control

At 8:00 a.m. the next morning we launched our brand-new balsa raft, but with shock and disappointment it dawned on us that we would never fit onto the flimsy platform, let alone our mountain of provisions. To rub a fair dose of salt into our wounds, the thing barely floated! It wallowed, three quarters submerged in the brown water. My sense of humour had left me some time in the night and pessimism now clung to me like a wet blanket. We nevertheless decided to soldier on. At that time, and at that place, we did not have an alternative.

Using our kayaks, Chan and I were to guide the raft through the rapids and bends while Clive and Matt would paddle the K2 (the doubles kayak). François and Donata would ride ahead in Crispen's Johnson-powered canoe. Twenty minutes before the main party departed, we pushed the raft into the current. As I paddled after it, I noticed that Chan had decided to unpack and repack his entire kayak, tinkering with his boat, showing no sense of urgency at all!

'Come on, Chan,' I yelled, 'the raft has floated off.'

'I'll catch you later,' came his casual could-not-care-less reply.

'No, Chan, I can't escort the raft on my own. Let's go.'

Soon we were in a shouting match that resulted in Chan staying put, while I had to race after the raft, fuming at Chan's indifferent attitude.

Berty the Balsa under construction.

We were now in our fourth week, and Chan's attitude and unreasonable behaviour were steadily deteriorating. As I had invited Chan on the trip, I felt personally responsible for managing my friend's erratic showdowns, and I was even starting to wonder whether I had made the right decision in inviting Chan on the expedition. Donata had also expressed frustration at Chan's chauvinistic and unreasonable attitudes, which in turn had dragged François into the fray. How would we survive another three weeks together on this confined and cramped platform?

As though possessed by some jungle demon, the raft had an uncanny way of heading straight for the only obstacle in the river. (Of course the raft was not possessed, but out there in the middle of the jungle, strange thoughts easily find a way into your head.) The raft also appeared determined to wipe itself out at every sharp bend. All the while the river speed was increasing and the rapids were growing in size, meaning that the Pongo was near. I noticed the sky had transformed into a greyish-green with enormous storm activity building up over the dark green canopy of the jungle. Crispen's canoe, with François, Donata and all our stuff, had caught up with me and assisted in guiding the raft. Chan, however, was still conspicuous by his absence and I cursed him under my breath. The day's journey had also taken its toll amongst Crispen and his crew, whose tension levels were electrically high. The slightest mention of the Pongo would trigger off an angry reaction in Crispen and Co; if the Pongo had that effect on the locals, maybe it was as bad as they made it out to be. Cracks in the relationship between François and Donata were also appearing, and looking at them on the raft together, the answer was obvious: conflict. Up to now Donata had only been part of the hiking and support teams. This was Donata's first venture out onto the river, into a totally new and forebidding environment about which she was totally unfamiliar. Donata was in a difficult situation. She was François's girlfriend, and had been invited to join the trip as such, but with the unclear role of acting largely as the team physiotherapist and general support member. Now being included in the raft team, she found herself handicapped without the technical skills required for the ordeal ahead, and she was exposed to the full brunt of personal tensions among the river running team.

To improve the raft's steering and ability to avoid colliding with the riverbank around every sharp bend, I secured the long rope from Crispen's canoe to a cross spar on the raft. Meanwhile, the sides of the river grew steeper and the waves became more powerful. As we rounded a bend, Matt and Clive, who had paddled on ahead to scout, urgently waved us down from the left bank. Immediately downstream lay a 100-m (328-ft) rapid with breaking waves, and below that an even bigger rapid that led directly into the high rock-faced entrance of the gorge. It was crunch time!

'Go for the side!' I yelled to Crispen.

To my annoyance, he did not respond. The craft and Crispen's canoe were now heading swiftly for the rapids.

'Frans, tell him to head for the bank!' I hollered again.

Still, no one responded. Couldn't they see they were heading for disaster? While thinking about everyone's ill-timed passivity, a shout of alarm from Matt caused us all to look his way. An enormous green snake had arrowed out of the jungle, slithered over the canoe between him and Clive, and then disappeared into the river. We looked on in amazement. It was a typical jungle moment.

Eventually Crispen began steering his boat towards the bank, but – too late! A faster current had caught the raft and it sped past Crispen's canoe, turning the canoe back to front. In a wild response, Crispen opened the throttle to the maximum and a bizarre tug of war between the motorised canoe and the 'possessed' raft (I was really starting to think it had a bloody mind of its own!) ensued. Both vessels surged sideways into the waves, completely out of control. I raced after them, watching helplessly as the fiasco intensified. The canoe had now overtaken the raft and the rope between them had snagged across the canoe's gunwale, tilting it dangerously to one side. One of Crispen's crew dived for a machete and hacked at the rope wildly, the two ends twanging as they parted.

The raft was now free, but it careered straight under the hull of the canoe, where it jammed firmly, hoisting the stern of the canoe into the air, its motor screaming and the crew and passengers simultaneously yelling orders at each other. Disaster was imminent. Both vessels had now entered the next rapid where huge waves crashed over them. It was now surely a matter of time before Crispen's canoe would succumb to the power of the water and capsize, sending all and sundry into the ferocious Pongo. Canoe and craft, locked together like bizarre Siamese twins, now ploughed through one monstrous wave after another. After another massive wave, the two vessels unexpectedly swerved towards the bank. Crispen's canoe lunged forward and the raft followed it into the welcome safety of an eddy. Barely 200 m (656 ft) downstream, the gaping throat of the Pongo de Mainique waited, ready to swallow whatever came its way. Man, that was close!

Everyone was dumbstruck by what had happened, and the shouting and screaming temporarily ceased as they realised how close they had come to a real disaster. As if divinely arranged (by either the jungle gods or another) to coincide with our arrival at the Pongo, the sky now opened its reservoirs, pelting us with sheets of rain. Rolls of thunder resounded above the roar of the river while the lashing rain came down on us. We all leapt ashore in a hurry and secured the raft and the canoe to a huge tree trunk. After a strenuous struggle, and much heaving and levering, we managed to separate the canoe and the raft, before towing them upstream against the current to a safer mooring position, as we feared that the rain might cause the river to rise, sending both vessels into the Pongo.

Comrade Chan only then arrived on the scene and paddled into the eddy to join the stranded expedition. His face was wild with frustrated anger.

Chaos at the Pongo after the raft collided with the boat.

'What the hell do you think you're doing!' he screamed, gesticulating rowdily at Crispen and his crew. 'Don't you know how to steer your own bloody boat?'

His outburst was uncalled for and was the last straw for our hired boatmen, and ourselves. They could take the pressure no longer and a wild, almost comical drama unfolded in which everyone screamed at everyone else. It served no purpose except to serve as a 'pressure release' for the preceding tense river adventure. When dusk arrived a while later, the pointless arguments and din thankfully ended. I approached Chan about his day's performance.

'Chan, we needed your help today with the raft, where were you? I couldn't cope on my own steering that darn thing! It smashed into the bank on almost every bend,' I complained grumpily.

'Sorry, Tim, I guess I needed some peace and quiet, time on my own you know – away from everyone for a while.' I left it at that.

We had better things to do like finding a suitable place to sleep, and so in the darkness and rain, we scaled the slippery bank in search of a campsite for the night.

The Pongo De Mainique and Other Surprises

The next day we woke feeling jittery, and as glum as it may sound, that did not surprise anyone. We had a restless night behind us and the misadventures of the previous day were still fresh in our memories and aching bones. Crispen was in a foul mood again and it quickly spread to his crew. Crispen, like all of us, was nervous about the Pongo. After all the horrifying stories and fables we had heard about it, we were on the verge of experiencing the Pongo for ourselves. As though the morning was not downbeat enough, Matt and Clive approached François and dropped a bombshell.

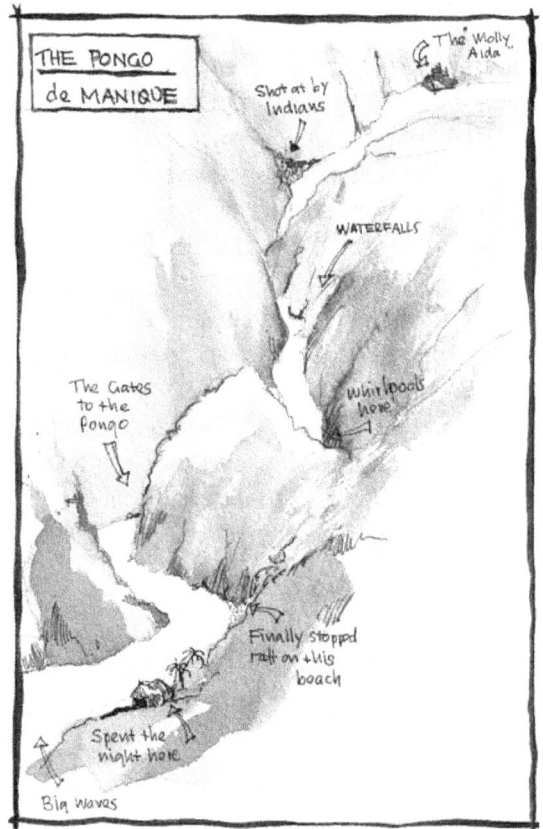

THE PONGO de MANIQUE

The Molly Aida
Shot at by Indians
WATERFALLS
The Gates to the Pongo
Whirlpools here
Finally stopped raft on this beach
Spent the night here
Big waves

They were pulling out of the expedition – immediately. The team was shocked and bewildered and the twosome's announcement took some time to sink in. Hadn't we planned to complete the Urubamba expedition together? As friends? As teammates?

Clive was unflinching in his stand. 'We need to get back to South Africa,' he explained. 'If we continue on the river now, we might miss our flight. Besides, Matt's feet are in really bad shape.'

No amount of persuasion could swing their decision. I felt disappointed and somewhat let down, almost betrayed, and I suspected that other issues than the ones they had put forward, were involved. Was the tension of the past few weeks too much for them? I did not really think so, as Matt and Clive were both tough guys mentally. No, I had known both of them for years and experienced their unflinching determination in tough situations. Was the expedition too physically demanding for them? I doubted that too, although Matt's feet were indeed in a mess – covered with a mass of infected sores and fungal infection. Still, I believed there were other reasons for their decision, possibly the thought of spending weeks on end cooped up on the raft, possibly unhappiness with François's leadership. Matt and Clive had been stalwarts during the past month, and I would miss their company and friendship. Anyway, as a gesture of goodwill they agreed to see us through the Pongo before they departed.

The Urubamba had risen several inches overnight and lateral waves surged angrily onto the rocks. We pushed the raft into the current and watched as it floated, rising and falling on the giant swells that now swept it towards the black rock walls of the Pongo de Mainique. François, Donata, Matt and Clive would make the trip through the Pongo on Crispen's boat, while Chan and I would follow in our kayaks. We launched, and were immediately lifted by the powerful surges and swept towards the Pongo's entrance. What lay beyond those towering walls? With adrenalin pumping through my system, I glanced over my shoulder to glimpse Crispen's canoe as it pushed off from the bank. There was no turning back now. We were all in this together, fully committed, our differences temporarily set aside.

Crashing through the roller-coaster waves we passed through the sheer-sided walls, craning our necks to see what followed – what a relief, our first glimpses showed no man-eating rapids or killer whirlpools, only a series of surging waves and boiling turbulence. Chan and I raised our paddles, a signal that all was 'okay', before we floated into a magical setting – a light drizzle had set in, and the mist rising off the water shrouded the dark, austere cliffs, and the overhanging tiers of dense jungle vegetation. The river had now narrowed to a mere 25 m. A spectacular waterfall cascaded over the right sidewall, plunging 60 m, pumping out plumes of white spray

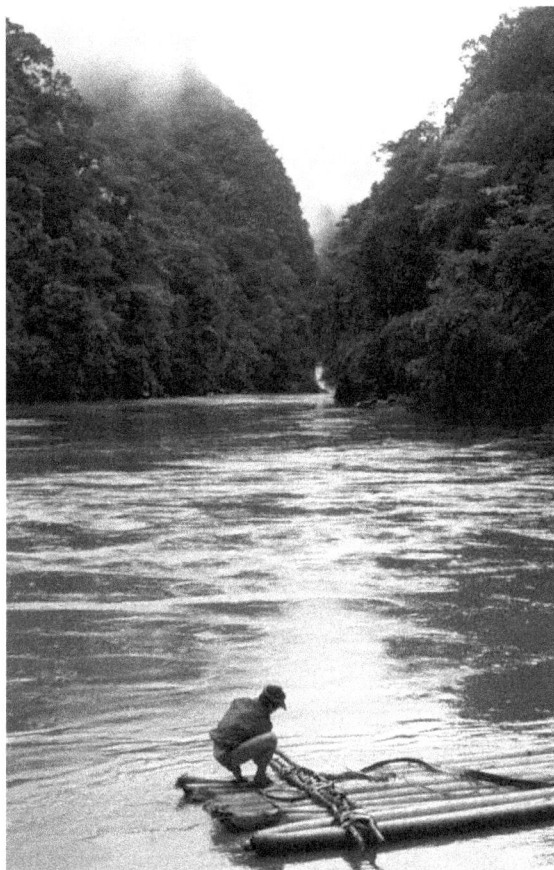

Repairing our raft after the Pongo.

from the heaving river. A 6-m wide whirlpool cycled menacingly.

'Look up there at the high-water mark!' shouted Chan. 'It must be a good 5 m above river level.'

'Now I can understand how so many people have drowned in here at flood levels in these whirlpools; it would be deadly,' I replied.

Five kilometres later, we were through the Pongo de Mainique, and the immense tension literally washed off our shoulders. Where were the deadly whirlpools and steep drops we had expected? We shouted with delight at having negotiated the notorious gorge. Crispen had skilfully skirted the big waves, and, apart from almost sinking from shipping water, he had chosen good lines through the gorge. Our raft was still spinning its way down through the successions of whirlpools and side eddies, and we jubilantly pulled up onto a white sandy beach to await its arrival.

Our unpredictable friend Crispen immediately broke the magic of the moment by reminding us of our financial obligations. Since the venture was a success, greed had overcome him, and he shrewdly demanded double the agreed-upon price. By this stage we were well attuned to his tactics and decided to play him at his own game by staging a sit-down strike on his own canoe, refusing to budge an inch. Tension had now reached fever pitch, the four boatmen were agitated, and a good old-fashioned punch-up looked imminent. Then a strange thing happened: we could no longer hide our mirth and burst out laughing. Crispen and his stern-faced cronies stood motionless, probably thinking that the gringos had finally caught some jungle fever. Then, ever so slowly, Crispen started to smile. Moments later a broad grin spread accross his face.

The stalemate was broken. For a few moments, Crispen's boatmen appeared rather uncomfortable before they, too, broke into smiles. Seconds later all the gringos roared hysterically with laughter. It was a strange sight indeed. Within a few crazy moments, the animosity and conflict of the preceding days disappeared and Crispen gladly agreed to ferry Matt and Clive back to Saniriato, and to drop Chan and I upstream so that we could escort our raft. François carefully counted out the balance of $100 owed to Crispen and his crew, before we bade farewell to Matt, Clive, Crispen and the merry boatmen, who roared off upstream against the swirling current.

Arrows and Merry-Go-Rounds

We must have been a sight – four pale-skinned, weather-beaten gringos on a small beach in the Amazon jungle! We had two kayaks and a raft (in great need of repairs). We gazed downstream to where the Urubamba disappeared into the jungle-clad hills, trying to imagine what lay ahead. The odds were slowly turning against us now, our expedition thinning out at every corner and with totally unknown territory ahead. Turning around was not an option.

The raft had taken a battering on its passage through the Pongo, with several punishing collisions as it was pulled into eddies and whirlpools, and bashed against the sidewalls. We began to search for some suitable balsa trees in the canopied jungle and it did not take long before we spotted some fine specimens in a narrow ravine leading off the small beach. Having acquired the basics of raft construction from our boatmen friends, we quickly felled four well-grown, straight balsa trees and dragged them to the beach. To pin the logs together, we used the same black chonta (ironwood) for pegs that the locals had shown us, hammering them into the sturdy beams with the river rocks.

Working on the raft, we realised that its flexibility (that we had earlier scorned) was actually its strength, as it would allow the structure to absorb the terrific beatings that it would have to endure. After a rainy night, we completed our handiwork by lashing and pinning three extra logs to the raft. For stowage space, we strapped a 1-m² tea box onto the platform, which would serve as seating space and a lookout stand for scouting ahead when approaching a rapid.

Bar a sun canopy, our new, improved raft was ready for its maiden voyage. François ceremoniously broke our only bottle of cheap Peruvian champagne over the bow and christened her *Berty the Balsa* (a name that seemed to suit our everything but streamlined, wallowing craft). Returning to the steep ravine,

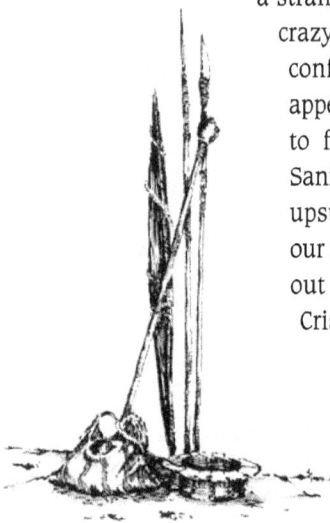

François and I found several straight saplings for the sun canopy, felled them and were about to return to the beach when the crashing sound of a falling tree, followed by a yell from François, stopped me in my tracks. I was about to call out to him when the distinct fluttering sound of a fast-moving projectile swished past my head.

An arrow!

I froze. There was movement in the bushes, barely 15 m away from me. In Kiteni, we had heard some horrible stories about poisoned arrows, never dreaming it could happen to one of us! My invisible assailant shot another arrow, missing me by inches. Never mind the sun canopy, I thought, and with a yell I dropped the saplings just as François came hurtling past me, screaming, 'Go, Tim, run – I've been shot at!'

I needed no encouragement and hurled myself down the steep ravine, sliding and tumbling through the thick vegetation. I reached the beach first and shouted to Chan and Donata, 'Let's go, guys, we've been shot at, let's go, let's go!'

'Who? Where?' responded Chan, looking calm.

François's arrival and frantic yelling finally convinced Chan that this was no practical joke. Pandemonium broke out on the beach.

'Push the raft out! Move it!' I bellowed.

Frantically we hurled our belongings onto the raft and pushed off into the river. Chan leapt into the kayak, while François, Donata and I clambered aboard the raft.

'Man, that was close. Two arrows nearly hit me,' François gasped.

'Did you see anyone?' I asked.

'No, but there was movement in the bush not far from me.'

'Watch out, guys, watch out – the cliff!' came Chan's warning shouts.

To our dismay, we were heading straight towards the cliffs on the bend where mounds of water careered into the rock wall, creating a high foam pillow.

'Paddle to the right! Paddle!' I screamed.

My good friend Frans Odendaal aboard "Berty the Balsa" TRIOMF

Our efforts to steer right were too late, we couldn't hope to make it. *Berty* was going to crash on her first voyage (just like that other big ship). I strained on my paddle and braced my feet between the slippery newly-fitted logs. The next moment, my left foot slipped and disappeared through a gap between the logs, trapping my ankle in a vice-like grip. With a yell of pain, I yanked my foot free from the logs only to go flying backwards; my paddle flew from my hand striking Donata squarely on the forehead! She survived the blow, but seconds later *Berty* collided squarely with the rock face. She lurched at the impact, projecting all three of us forward as we clutched at anything we could hold on to. *Berty* hovered for seconds, creaking and shuddering as the torrent hurled it mercilessly against the rock. Water surged over the deck. 'Here we go,' I thought, 'we're going to capsize this darn thing.' Then the Urubamba simply released us and washed us to quieter water.

Looks peaceful ~ but don't believe it.
Two weeks together on the raft
s we were ready to kill eachother.

As if in a game, the raft unexpectedly spun around and entered the same reverse orbit of the eddy, sending us back towards the cliff face. Chan followed helplessly in his kayak, yelling out instructions and commands. The Urubamba had us in her grip! We slowly floated in a wide circle, gathering momentum, until the force of the water propelled us broadside towards the cliff. With a loud cracking sound we again collided head-on with the black rock face. Then, for a third time, the same sick cycle began: floating slowly in the reverse orbit, picking up speed, waiting for the blow. Chan was now screaming commands and curses at us for failing to follow his instructions. Determined to avoid another collision, I moved to *Berty*'s bow, and pushing with all my might, braced my paddle against the cliff. Without warning, my feet slipped on the slimy logs and down I went, landing on my back with a loud thump! There I lay, gazing up helplessly at the 60-m high cliffs towering over me, waiting for our ill-omened raft to crash against the rock once more. Third time lucky, the saying goes, and so it was. The river miraculously released us – no cheeky recall this time – and we glided swiftly downstream. As though sensing that it had won this round, *Berty* lazily performed 360-degree spins as it flirted with the swirls of the river.

'Man, this is going to be one hell of a trip! This damn raft has a will of its own,' I bemoaned loudly. 'You can't budge it, it just does whatever it wants.'

'Look out!' Chan shouted from his kayak. 'There's another bend coming up.'

'Oh no,' I groaned, 'I can't believe this is really happening to us.'

François and I manned our stations, straining at our paddles, determined to prevent another merry-go-round episode. This time, thank goodness, we narrowly cleared the cliff and moved downstream quite happily.

How had the myth arisen that this stage of the expedition would be a pleasure cruise?

Ship Ahoy!

What materialised before us around the very next bend in the river was more like a scene from a far-fetched fiction novel, than from our small adventure down the Urubamba. It was just 'totally' unbelievable.

'Look, look, a ship!' Donata had shouted with elation a few seconds earlier.

'What?' François had barked, spinning his head around, his paddle frozen in his hands.

Come on, Donata, I had thought.

I looked anyway, squinting into the glare of the late afternoon sun. Sure enough, there was something on the far side of the river, close to the right bank.

'What on earth! What the —' I stammered. 'I can't believe it. We are thousands of kilometres from any seaport. What's an ocean steamer doing here?'

We managed to manoeuvre *Berty* into an eddy, our eyes never leaving the spectacle that sported the name of *Molly Aida* (painted in bold red letters on the black, rusted background of the ship's bow). Someone on board spotted us and waved in a friendly manner. Soon others collected, staring and excitedly pointing down at us. Minutes later a small dingy approached us and a swarthy, semi-naked Machiguenga Indian man beckoned us to come aboard. We did not hesitate and tied *Berty* off against a tree, loading some of our luggage onto the dingy. As we sped across the river it dawned on us that we had no idea what the steamer and its crew were doing out here in the middle of nowhere. They might have been guerrillas or drug dealers for all we knew. The temptation, however, of spending some time aboard a decent vessel far outweighed our apprehension.

'No ~ I can't believe it ~ it's a ship!'

61

'Do you have any cigarettes or beer?' one of the men on the dinghy asked.

'Sorry, my friend, we were about to ask you the same,' replied François, and started laughing. Soon everyone chuckled at the common nicotine and alcohol predicament.

'Would you people like to spend the night?' another friendly crewmember asked.

'Sure, we'd love to,' we responded in unison.

Once on board we found that the crew of the *Molly Aida* was as kosher as could be, and as unlucky as one could get. It turned out the steamer had travelled 2 500 km upstream from the inland port of Iquitos in northeastern Peru to the unexplored regions of the Urubamba in order to assist in the making of *Fitzcarraldo*, a movie on the legendary explorer of the same name. However, the river had the last laugh, and during the filming the river level had dropped, leaving poor old *Molly* beached on a submerged gravel bar. Now a skeleton crew of nine kept a lazy vigil over the steamer, waiting for the summer rains and high water to lift her off the sandbar.

The crew were low on rations, and we gladly shared our scanty provisions with them. Even so, we spent an enjoyable evening on board sharing anecdotes, stories and experiences. Donata with her Italian flare soon became the centre of attraction, enjoying the attention from the all-male crew. By this time, I had had the opportunity to get to know Donata and to build a friendship; I could only respect and like her for her courage and resilience in coping with this jungle ordeal. Chan, meanwhile, had challenged the skipper, a dark American Indian of about 40, to a game of chess. The skipper later shared with us the fascinating history of Fitzcarraldo, a pioneering entrepreneur during the time of the rubber boom. He and his brother had been murdered by the Machiguenga Indians while scouting the Rio Mishagua. As the

Meeting fellow rivermen - we struck an immediate rapport.

night wore on and the whisky flowed, so the tales of jungle intrigues and adventures became increasingly dramatic. The most exciting (and disappointing!) bit of information was that the stars of the movie, Klaus Kinski and the beautiful Claudia Cardinale, had left the steamer only two days before our arrival! Wouldn't it have been something sharing this unique experience in the romantic and pristine jungle, with the beautiful Miss Cardinale? Sadly, it was not to be.

Early the next morning we sadly waved farewell to the *Molly Aida* and her brave crew, having established a warm bond of friendship. Now we were once again guests of our grand hostess, the mighty, and sometimes pitiless, Urubamba.

The Whirlpool Blues

An orange had never tasted as good as the one I enjoyed when our raft found a few kilometres of relatively peaceful and calm water. It was our second day since the Pongo. I sat back against the wooden tea box in Huckleberry Finn mode, relaxed and contented with life, peeling and eating oranges while enjoying the serenades of the rich bird life and the chatter of monkeys. Blankets of mist shrouded the low hills, and giant trees craned spectacular canopies over the lower tiers of dense jungle forest, draping their necklace-type vines over the swirling river. The magical moment had François and Donata in the palm of its captivating hand, too. Chan had paddled ahead in his kayak to scout for rapids.

'This is the life!' marvelled François. 'Just listen to those bird calls.'

Calls of the indigenous birds floated across the water, their sounds like no other I had ever heard – the 'squeak' of rusty gates, shrill traffic 'whistles', resounding foghorns, animal howls, clicks, beeps, bellows and roars.

'Here's breakfast, Donata,' I called. 'Have some orange. It had a worm, but I've cut it out.'

'Tim, do you think this is a second-class restaurant? How dare you! We have got to maintain standards, you know,' Donata joked back in her distinctive Australian-Italian accent.

I was beginning to take to this lively physiotherapist. I had previously viewed her selection to the team negatively, as it appeared that the main reason for her being there was for François to have a girlfriend on the river.

In a way, I pitied Donata. She was in a difficult position since she had none of the essential skills required for a river trip like this. However, she had steadily won our respect with her tremendous courage and grit; I never once so much as heard her utter a complaint. A disturbing post-Pongo revelation we had discovered about Donata, however, was that she could not swim a stroke! Talk of a twisted irony.

'Ah-ha, here is our first rapid of the day,' reported François, climbing onto the square tea box while peering ahead. With white pith helmet and a scraggly beard, he was anyone's image of a typical eccentric, colonial explorer. What he saw were the vigorously dancing plumes of white water that drew a thin line across the disappearing river ahead of us. That could mean trouble.

'Chan! Where the hell is Chan?' shouted an exasperated François. 'He's meant to be scouting for us, showing us a line! He's never here when we need him.'

The raft accelerated.

'The river runs sharp left. I'll stick to the inside of the main current,' François reported and then added, 'We're goners if we hit anything at this speed.'

Waves crashed across the creaking, flexing balsa logs as we ploughed clumsily into the approaches to the rapid. The river had literally eaten through a hillside that lay between truncated red cliffs, 60 m high.

'Oh, no! Watch out, whirlpool on the right!' I yelled.

On the right-hand side of the bend was a whirlpool the size of half a football field. Clinging to the raft as we swept down the rapid at 25 km/h, water crashing over us, we straddled the frothing interface between the main and the reversed current of the whirlpool. The result was dramatic: *Berty*'s entire starboard side disappeared under the thrashing water as the two converging currents locked in fierce combat.

'Hold on, hold on!' François and I screamed together.

We were now completely at the river's mercy. For a second time our raft swung around in slow motion, entering and re-entering the reverse current until it swept us off in the opposite, upstream direction. Meanwhile, micro whirlpools sucked and tugged at the raft's flexible platform, spinning us around uncontrollably. We were in deep trouble! On our second lap around the edges of the whirlpool, we managed to claw our way out of its clutches and ended up in an eddy on the steep side of a mud bank. We sat there for a while, knowing it was impossible to climb the cliffs to safety. There was only one route out . . . to break through the circular current.

About to attempt another run, Chan finally arrived in his kayak, paddling hard on the outer orbit of the immense hydraulic cycle. Carefully he worked his way to the raft, yelling a mixture of garbled instructions and abuse for allowing the whirlpool to capture the raft. This was the last straw for François.

'Shut up, Chan!' François retorted. 'When are you going to be where you should be for a change?

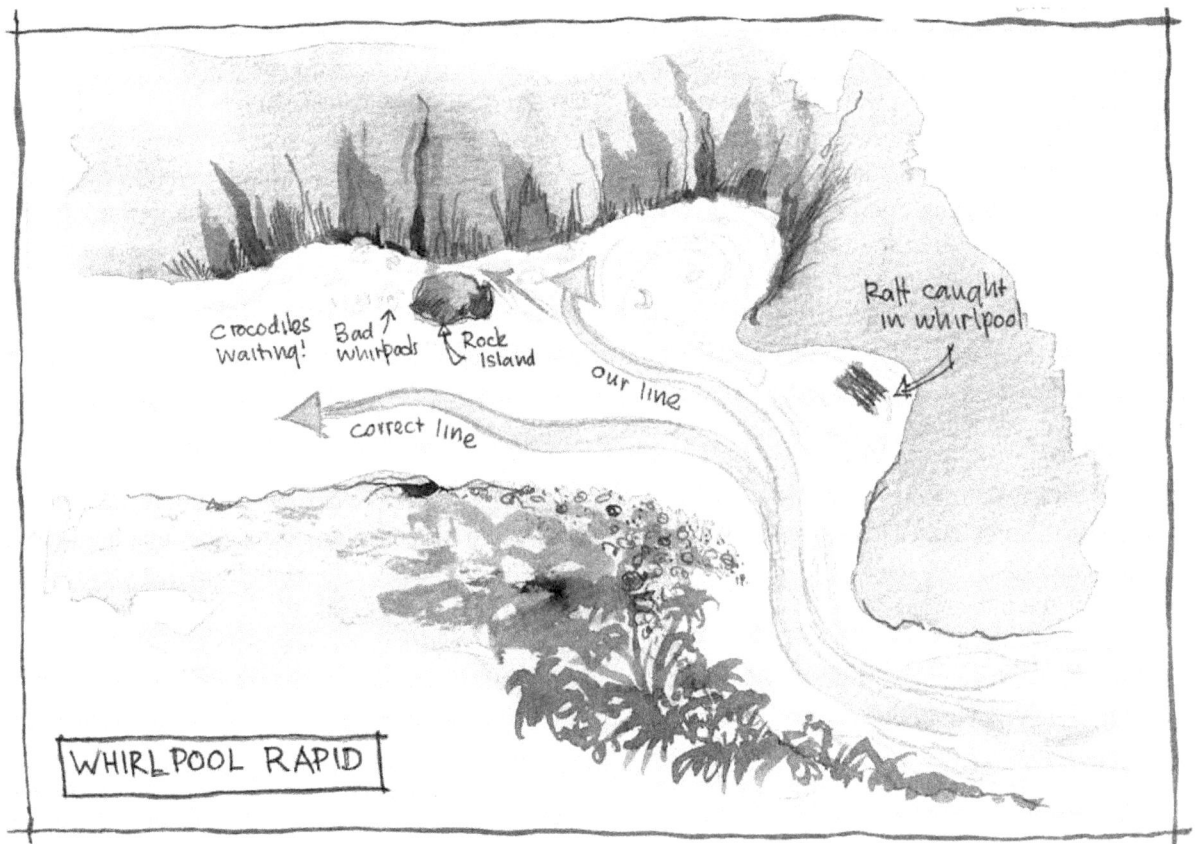

Crocodiles waiting! Bad whirlpools Rock Island our line Correct line Raft caught in whirlpool

WHIRLPOOL RAPID

Pitching up when it's too late to help, and then yelling at everyone will get us nowhere!'

Feeling that we had an outside chance of making it through, I called out to Chan, 'Load your kayak on the raft and help us paddle. We can only get out of this with some serious paddling!'

'Hang on, Tim,' François interjected. 'It's no good going at it again. We have already been around the whirlpool twice. We must make another plan. This raft will break up if it gets another work-over.'

'No, Frans,' I said insistently. 'Our only hope is to break through the surge on the right, and then head for the small opening between the rock island and the cliff. We've got to keep trying.'

Through all of this, Donata had remained seated on the tea box, offering encouragement to François and me. With Chan aboard now, we manned our paddles and again entered the wild whirlpool.

'Listen up, when we get to the far end, paddle like mad!' I yelled.

Seconds later we were there, at the edge of the thing, ready to burst through, or die trying. 'It's now or never. Paddle!' I hollered. We paddled for all we were worth, but to no avail – we could not escape the whirlpool's swirling vortex.

When Chan saw that we had once again missed our line, he began yelling hysterically at François and me. 'No, don't paddle like that, paddle like this! You're going the wrong way. Don't go there, go here! Can't you see you are being stupid? Why can't Donata paddle? She just sits there doing nothing. Tell her —'

François could take no more. 'Leave Donata out of it! You bloody well paddle yourself; don't waste your time looking at us. You are the problem, not us. Donata can't paddle here; she'll drown if she ends up in the water. You know she can't swim.'

Doing our fourth power-sapping lap around the whirlpool, we again missed the breakthrough point, and it began to look as though François was right: we were trapped indeed. We could not pick up and carry the raft around the steep cliffs, and we had no way of rejoining the main current. We could not even abandon the raft and construct another one downstream because we were no longer in balsa tree country. We seemed to be squarely 'stuffed', as another jungle saying goes!

'Come, guys, just one more try,' I begged. 'It's our only chance.'

François shrugged his shoulders and reluctantly agreed. Morale on the raft was now almost non-existent, and our paddling was weakening by the minute. For the fifth time, the raft repeated its long circle around the whirlpool, and as we approached the 'only-hope' gap, we gained momentum and strained with all our might to shift the wallowing raft to the left. Suddenly an unexpected micro whirlpool sucked down Chan's side of the raft, spinning us wildly. Overall it was getting too much to handle.

Enduring this latest crisis, and as if possessing human qualities (it did have a mind of its own, of that I was sure), *Berty* let out alarming creaks of distress, her timber beams flexing dangerously. Then just as things looked at their bleakest, the back of the raft whipped around, almost catapulting us overboard. The timing was impeccable! The raft surprisingly veered towards the exit gap and at precisely the right moment it surged through the mound of turbulence that had been our Nemesis so many times.

'We're through! We've done it! Keep her straight now.' The joy in my voice was over the top, but we weren't in the clear just yet.

The narrow gap between the island and the cliff was fast approaching. Would the raft fit through it? If we spun now, we would undoubtedly crash broadside into the rocks, and that would be the end of the whole caboodle. Our dependable *Berty*, however, swept through the gap with the grace of a slalom kayak, plunging through the tongue of water that took us to safety. At the sides of the chute two menacing, deep whirlpools circulated, ready to devour all who ventured into their orbit. They would not get us this time.

Several caymans (alligators) lay as though asleep metres from the whirlpools. Looking back upstream, we saw the red cliff and the narrow chute safely behind us. We could relax again.

'This rafting business is getting scarier by the day,' François remarked.

Soup of the Day at Fever Camp

The deeper we penetrated the mighty jungle, the more the rafting lifestyle became second nature to us. We had more or less adapted to *Berty*'s antics, had figured out the best corner on the raft to relax or find much needed solitude, and, of course, the skilled affair of boiling a brew of tea while rafting.

A couple of days into this part of the journey we realised that we were lost, and our actual position on the small scale map was a mystery. The tributaries were our only relevant pointers, and these did not always correlate with the map. Well, we figured that as long as we were still on the Urubamba we couldn't go too far wrong, except that it messed with our finer logistics. Good, sandy campsites had become more difficult to find and we would often drift for hours before finding a suitable spot to camp. To avoid this aimless drifting, Chan would scout ahead in the kayak to allow us time to manoeuvre the sluggish raft across the river, which was now some hundreds of metres wide. Almost without fail this exercise developed into arguments, with Chan being either uncooperative or not warning us in time of a good site, and after a long, hot day's rafting, that would be the last straw. On one such occasion, we had spotted two dugouts pulled up on a sandbank some distance ahead. François yelled at Chan to make contact and find out where we were and if there were any villages nearby. Paddling ahead of us, clearly within hearing distance, Chan showed no response, leaving it to the heavy raft to reach the bank. We paddled furiously to

the sandbank, reaching it just in time before the strong current could wash us downstream.

Apart from the two dugouts, there was no sign of any habitation. Chan agreed to watch over the raft and the equipment, while the rest of us set off to explore the area. We had learnt that it was best to announce one's arrival by calling out, 'Bueños dias, bueños dias.' We did, but there was no response. Donata spotted an overgrown path leading up a high bank and we scaled it until it became a level terrace. Although the vegetation was dense, I spotted the top of a thatched roof peeping through the trees. We cautiously edged forward, the entire time calling out our greeting with dwindling enthusiasm. We had sensed that things were not normal – surely, the inhabitants must have heard us already. Then we suddenly stumbled upon seven or eight huts on stilts, and what I saw will stay with me forever.

Brown, emaciated, limp bodies lay strewn across the raised bamboo floors of the timber huts. The sweet, dank smell of death and sickness hung heavily over the scene. We could not help staring at the bone-thin, hollow-eyed faces that were gazing at us, a desperateness in their fading eyes.

'My God, they are dying,' whispered an emotional Donata. 'This is too terrible.'

The aura surrounding the colony was so oppressive we began to retreat, we just had to get away from it. Unexpectedly, a voice spoke from behind us. We spun around, startled, and found a sombre, expressionless Machiguenga Indian man facing us.

'My people are all dying. They are sick, they have the fever,' he announced without introducing himself, his expression unchanging.

'Is the whole village dying?' François asked.

'No, the others are across that small river over there,' he said. 'You may go there, you will be safe. Ask for Hefe, he can also speak some Spanish.'

We were thankful to leave the horrible scene behind us, knowing that we were not able to assist

Huts in the Yellow fever 'death colony.'

even if we had wanted to. We followed the path that the old man had pointed out and crossed the stream. In a clearing, we found a small encampment of grass and pole huts, with raised floors and banana-clad roofs. A group of Machiguenga Indians, all dressed in their traditional hessian garments, immediately approached us. A man dressed in semi-western attire stepped forward. It was Hefe, and he invited us to his hut. Not wanting to offend our host, the three of us single-filed up a bamboo ladder and into a scantily furnished room. Here he beckoned us to sit on roughly sawn logs that were neatly placed around a single-board table.

In broken Spanish, he explained that he was the teacher and the chief of this village and that an epidemic of the deadly yellow fever (caused by female mosquitoes) had broken out recently, smiting two thirds of the community. The extent of the tragedy stunned us, and we silently pondered on it. Hefe's wife, an attractive woman, then broke the depressing atmosphere by serving us yuca, and in large wooden bowls the thick, white drink masato chicha. Not having had a decently prepared meal for a while, we were grateful. While eating and drinking away as

good guests should, Hefe explained how they prepared the fermented yuca (made from an indigenous liliaceous plant). Women would seat themselves around a central clay bowl, and chew the root before blending it with saliva and the mucus of the nasal passages. I noticed Donata turning a shade greener after our host's vivid description, and I had to fight back a compulsion to vomit out what I had just eaten. Honourably we struggled on with our meal, determined not to offend our hosts, especially out here in a South American jungle. Hefe then told us that they pour the brew (after the addition of the finger-licking ingredients!) in a deep wooden trough where it stays until it becomes intoxicating. For some inexplicable reason the fermented yuca has an incredible effect on the locals, apparently turning them into stupefied, fighting savages. The fermented masato chicha has a cool, clotted feel to it, and has a sour, sweet quality that really works the palate!

We gingerly continued to ladle the yuca and masato chicha into our mouths, struggling to keep our imaginations from running wild. Then another appetite killer struck: something was lurking in the

A Quechua pick.

depths of my bowl – what was it? I scooped it up and was almost bowled over when I saw a tiny hand – resembling that of a young child's – emerge with its slightly curled fingers pointing upwards! François and Donata spotted my dilemma and giggled impolitely as I struggled to pick the flesh from the monkey's slender bones. The meat was not bad at all.

Hefe offered us a place to sleep for the night, but when he told us that the village of Camisea was only two hours downstream, we decided to push on. We thanked our host for the meal and made our way back to Chan and the raft, still chuckling about my monkey hand soup!

'What took you so long?' Chan called out, irritated. 'The mosquitoes have been eating me alive! Why didn't you tell me you would be half the damn afternoon?'

We were all in excellent spirits, and I was determined not to let Chan spoil our cheerful mood. I had loved the interaction with the villagers, despite the tragic yellow fever.

The village where we dined with the chief. Special of the day ~ monkey hand soup and fermented chicha.

'Sorry, Chan. The chief invited us to a five-course meal of jungle delicacies and to watch his pretty dancing girls,' I teased with a laugh. 'We just couldn't refuse, you are lucky we even came back at all.'

'The sky is turning pink, guys – last time it was pink it poured with rain that night – remember. It's late and I am sure it's going to rain. We must go.'

'Pink skies in the morning, shepherd's warning. Pink skies at night, shepherd's delight. That's what my Dad always told me,' I chirped back.

We punted the raft into the current. Above us, the late afternoon sky had magically transformed into an artist's palate of mauves, pinks and gilded clouds. Once afloat, the current swirled about us, creating whirls and micro boils of muddy sediment that patterned the surface. A crescendo of bird and animal calls silenced our idle chatter. We listened, enchanted, completely absorbed by the strange but beautiful repertoire of jungle song.

Night Riders

With darkness closing in on us, and with the Urubamba widening to an impressive 200 m, we were running into serious trouble as Camisea was still nowhere to be seen. We had been on the river for almost four hours now and according to Hefe's directions should have reached it long ago.

'It'll be dark in a few minutes. Where is this Camisea?' grumbled François. 'What do we do now – keep on going or try to find a campsite?'

'I haven't seen a single beach for the last hour. I suppose we just keep going,' Donata suggested.

Darkness had captured us with its velvet veil. We had no option but to keep moving downstream. The moon had not yet risen, and the stars offered no navigational assistance. Giant trees lined both riverbanks, their branches and contorted roots hanging low over the river.

'If we get washed into that lot, we're goners,' François remarked. 'Chan must scout carefully now. Where is he? Hell, that guy drives me mad! He should be scouting ahead. Chan, where are you?'

Chan did not respond.

With our vision disabled by the darkness, our sense of hearing increased to a new pitch of awareness, monitoring the intensity of the waves slapping the log beams, and the rush of water on the riverbanks.

Suddenly my heart froze. 'What's that?' I called out. 'Is that a rapid ahead?' We all recognised the low-pitched roar of water crashing over rocks.

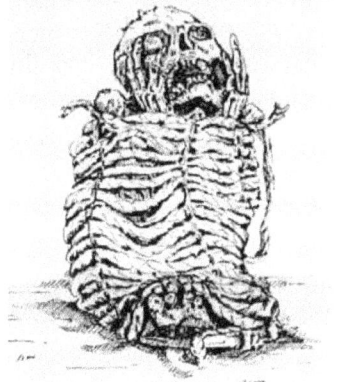

A beautiful dwelling.

'Chan, Chan – where are you?' we yelled into the dark. It would have been comforting to hear him respond, even if it was in his usual blasé way. Only silence and the steady roar of the approaching rapids answered us.

It was impossible to see which way the river turned. If we ended up crashing into the overhanging branches along the bank, we would be in real trouble. That could sink the expedition within seconds – literally. My instincts told me that the river turned right at this point, and Donata agreed with me. Anxiously I suggested that we paddle towards the right of the mainstream, beach ourselves on a gravel bar and stop this crazy runaway wooden horse of ours. Waves were beginning to wash over the raft, and the faintest semblance of white water was visible ahead; the raft timbers creaked and flexed as we accelerated into the current. Three successive waves poured over us, soaking us completely, while we tensely waited for that lethal collision with a rock or a low branch.

'Try to stay in the main current,' I shouted above the roar. Our raft was now careering through waves, the spray drenching us.

Then a familiar voice bellowed out from the pitch darkness. 'Come to the right! There's an eddy here. Paddle hard! To your right!' Chan shouted.

'Paddle, paddle!' François yelled with renewed vigour.

We attacked the water like madmen, determined not to miss Chan's eddy that lay invisible in the night.

'Here it is!' shouted Chan. 'You're almost past it. Paddle, man, paddle! To the right!'

Slowly *Berty* swung into slow-moving water as we broke out of the current and into the eddy. We could not see Chan, but kept moving in the direction of his voice. Things were looking a whole lot better, dark or not!

'There's a gravel bar on the right bank,' Chan shouted. 'I think we can camp here.'

To our relief the raft ran aground on the bar. François and I both jumped off into thigh-deep water, and with the bank still 20 m away, pulled and shoved the raft towards it, securing a rope to a large log as an anchor. François then probed the darkness with our only working (dim) flashlight, revealing a small patch of dry, sandy mud for a campsite.

'I'm happy to sleep in a tree,' I chuckled, 'rather than on this runaway raft.'

'Uh-oh,' François said alarmingly. 'We've got company. This beach doesn't belong to us – there are crocodile tracks everywhere!'

The thought of the giant reptiles circling around us while we waded through the waste-deep water in the pitch dark energised us.

'There they are, look at their eyes, look – all around us!'

As François shone the dull beam across the water, five or six pairs of ruby-red eyes studded the darkness.

'I'll be joining you in the tent tonight, ladies and gents,' I announced, happy to be on terra firma.

'So will I. We're in for a cosy night,' added Chan with a chuckle.

We only had a two-man tent between us – (the bigger tent had accidentally returned with Matt and Clive). François and Donata had understandably com-

Another day at the office.

71

Donata preparing onions for lunch - François looking hungry.

mandeered the small tent, and Chan and I only sneaked inside when a major cloudburst spoiled our sleep. Most nights we would huddle close to the campfire with shirts over our heads to keep off mosquitoes and vampire bats.

That night, however, all four of us shared the tent and slept like babies.

True Colours

As our journey's hourglass slowly began running out, we had eventually mastered the navigating of our old raft. After missing the village of Camisea, we finally reached the village of Shepahua where François, Chan and I disgraced ourselves by overindulging at the local watering hole. Donata, concerned about our well-being, was not at all happy with the state of affairs and scolded us severely.

During the last couple of days there had been a noticeable yet subtle change in our attitudes towards

each other – a weird acceptance of each others' and our own weaknesses. The Urubamba in her quiet and patient way had humbled us. We were beginning to bond. The conversation that night, like most conversations around a late night campfire, had steadily slowed down, with long silences between the chatter. Chan, who had been sitting quietly gazing into the dying coals, broke the silence.

'Hey, François, I've been thinking about our expedition. We really have only two problems.'

'And what's that, Chan?' asked François, on the defensive.

'You and me!'

'Oh no,' I thought, 'here we go.'

A moment of surprised silence followed. In the flickering light, I spotted a slight smile creep across Chan's face, and then François smiled. I began laughing and soon Chan joined in, then François, and then Donata. The four gringos shrieked and roared with fits of uncontrollable laughter, rolling on our sides in the sand. The pent-up tension between us was disappearing, layer after layer.

How utterly ludicrous we had been with our bickering and scrapping! There we were floating down the planet's greatest river, and yet we had fallen prey to petty arguing like children in an overcrowded classroom. What was the matter with us?

When our laughter at last subsided, François got up from the sand, his eyes watery from all the laughing. 'Chan, you're right, I know. But with all our nonsense and rough edges, we remain compañeros, journeying down the same river together.'

Seldom had truer words been spoken on the banks of a river.

Berty Breaks Up

Our final destination – the confluence of the Apurimac and Urubamba – was now only 70 km downstream. We had spent an interesting night at the Sepa Penal Colony – a police control post where all river travellers had to register. A tense-looking soldier had ordered us ashore to report to his commandant. And after an hour-long interrogation, we were found not guilty on any charges of trafficking drugs, spying or disorderly conduct. The stern interrogations were surprisingly followed by an invitation to spend the night at the colony. We gladly accepted and spent an unforgettable night drinking beers and listening to the officers relating tall stories of jungle life. The penal colony held 400 prisoners, mainly hardened criminals with 50-year sentences. Our host, the lieutenant, tapping his Colt 45, boasted that not a single prisoner had managed to escape during the past decade.

Extending his hospitality even further, the lieutenant had offered us a military flight in a Dakota to Atalaya. Without hesitation, Chan and Donata accepted the offer. Once in Atalaya, they would arrange our flight back to Lima.

Two weeks after running the Pongo de Mainique, it would be up to François and I to complete the final leg of the jungle voyage. As we pushed off from the bank at the colony, I noticed an old convict, stooped and with flowing white hair, watch us intently. How obvious it was that he also longed to be free! A dangerous-looking soldier must have read my thoughts. With a waving motion of his rifle he signalled us to move along. I couldn't resist passing him a mock salute as the river swept us downstream.

The water level had risen by almost a foot overnight and there was new energy in its swirling current. After the hustle and bustle of the penal colony, it felt good to be on our own. We sat back on the raft and soaked up the magnificence of the scenery. A low river fog was gradually lifting, indicating a clear day ahead and wild geese honked choruses to each other as they flew low above the water.

'Let's try to get a brew of tea going,' I suggested. 'We're in a long straight section. You steer, I'll get the Primus going.'

The familiar hiss of the paraffin stove completed the leisurely atmosphere as we sat back, waiting for a hot brew of tea, sweetened with condensed milk.

'Look, Frans,' I called out. 'Tree ahead, over there in the middle of the river.'

'Shouldn't be a problem, it's still a long way off. Let's just watch it a bit.'

We remained seated, eying the fast-approaching obstacle which was now no more than a hundred metres from us.

'Which way?' François queried. 'Right or left?'

'Left, I reckon.'

We raised ourselves from our comfortable seats, lazily putting in some corrective strokes. The raft did not move from its course. I stiffened up. We were hurtling along at 15 km/h and we were now heading straight for the enormous tree trunk that was protruding from the river. This was a potential ship wrecker!

'The left, paddle to the left,' I called out anxiously. 'Paddle, Frans, paddle! We're heading straight for it.'

Berty the Balsa – the raft with a mind of its own – did not veer one inch and was still heading directly for the massive, inclined tree trunk.

'Let's try right,' François shouted. 'We're not going to make it left.'

'No, no – left man, keep left, we can't change now!'

It dawned on us, in that slow-motion movie way, that it did not matter whether we tried left or right, we were going to hit the only obstacle on the entire river. I could not believe it.

A second later our world exploded with a ripping, tearing shudder of breaking timbers. The leading edge of the raft veered upwards onto the inclined ramp. The collision rocketed me into the air. Below me I glimpsed a spectacular sight. *Berty the Balsa* was in pieces! Balsa logs, kayaks, clothes, the tea box, paddles, and sleeping bags – all were flying and floating in different directions. Then I was fighting my way to the surface of the swirling water. With a mind that still could not believe what had happened, and eyes blurred by the muddy water, I spotted half of *Berty* floating past. I swam furiously towards it, pulled myself onto the fragmented timbers, and looked back at the scene of the accident. The other half of *Berty* protruded from the river, still pinned against the tree, tilting crazily skyward.

What happened next was a blur. François was some distance downstream swimming among the flotsam that now littered the river. I dived for our one kayak as it floated past, climbed in, found a paddle and raced from one piece of flotsam to another, retrieving possessions. In the meantime, François had managed to pull himself aboard the breakaway section of the raft. I finally caught up with him and manhandled the kayak and myself onto the new 'larger' half of *Berty*.

We were stunned. How on earth was it possible that one single obstacle in this huge river could wreak such havoc? We paddled across to a small beach to regroup and assess our losses, then lay back on the clean white beach and roared with laughter.

'I'd do anything to have that smash on film,' I laughed.

Our second kayak was lost, along with much of our gear. My favourite blue cotton shirt, which I'd worn through a whole year of travelling, was now part of the Urubamba. Miraculously our filming equipment and camera had survived the big dip and appeared to be in working order. Ten minutes later a peci-peci chugged upstream, towing our lost kayak and paddles! The Machiguenga riverman saw us and grinned, miming our accident and subsequent swim. We nodded and laughed with him.

There was no way that we could reach the confluence at Atalaya by nightfall. This trip was not going to end that easily. We gathered a few remaining belongings and lashed them to the larger half of the broken raft. Tonight would be a cold night! We had lost our sleeping bags and all our clothing – I had only the pair of shorts that I was wearing. Ready to face the river again, we once again cast off into the current.

It was dusk when we spotted two naked Machiguenga men standing motionless by their dugouts, observing us as we floated past.

74

'How far to the Rio Apurimac?' François shouted in Spanish.

The men did not stir an inch; it was as though we did not exist. Several kilometres later, a small peci-peci chugged upstream. We waved the boatman down and asked the same question.

'Three kilometres!' he assured us. 'Half an hour only.'

Encouraged, our hopes rose. Maybe we would be celebrating in Atalaya tonight after all. Only a few hundred metres further, we floated past a hut with a banana-thatched roof. A woman was gathering fruit from under a small tree, while a man perched high up in its branches.

'How far to the Rio Apurimac?' we called.

'Twenty kilometres,' came the shrill, confusing reply. A second later there was a sharp crack, and the man in the tree dropped to the ground like a stone! We looked on in amazement, unable to help, hoping we were not the cause of his misfortune.

'Es Peru!' we joked at the bizarre incident.

'Let's not have another midnight cruise,' François proposed. 'The night is here, bro'. Time to camp.'

'Yeah, time to camp.'

Suddenly the raft rocked viciously as it struck shallow rocks. We lurched forward, and François, caught off guard, toppled headlong overboard, cursing loudly as he fell.

'Why don't you just swim to Atalaya, Frans?' I joked as I hauled him back onto the raft.

For the next 15 minutes, we grunted and groaned as we strained to lift the raft off the submerged rocks. Tens of thousands of mosquitoes descended on us and finally drove us off our craft. We moored *Berty* with a throw-line, and waded ashore with our few soaked belongings. Soon we sat around a smoking campfire, François in his wet clothes and me shirtless, hiding ourselves in the coils of smoke – our only deterrent to the mosquito invasion.

'Frans, remember back in Pretoria when we first dreamt of this trip?' I asked reminiscently.

'Ja, I remember, all right. Seems like another lifetime. But here we are – we may even make it to the end.'

An acrid billow of smoke moved lazily over me, stinging my eyes. I grumbled at it and moved my log seat out of its smoky path.

'What do you think about the Machu Picchu section, Tim? Do you still think you and Chan will take it on?'

'Yes – yes, we have to, but that's going to be a story all on its own. Who knows whether we'll survive it or not!'

'Yes, the Torontei gorge is a nasty piece of work. I am not sorry that I won't be doing it, but I'm already weeks late for my work,' François muttered.

We both sat silently, each engrossed in our thoughts and memories of the time spent on the Urubamba. I reached forward and nudged the glowing coals with a stick. A small, orange flame leapt playfully up out of the coals.

Eventually I broke the silence. 'Hey, Frans, thanks for bringing the whole trip together. It's been a huge thing, and here we are. It's been a dream come true for me and I've loved everything about it.'

'So did I,' he responded. 'Thanks for your support, Tim. Many times I also wondered if we'd ever make it to Atalaya.'

The breeze shifted direction, blowing warm smoke in my face again. It was time to sleep. A half moon rose above the jungle skyline and the clear call of a nightjar drifted across the water. This was surely our last night on the river.

There

We were up before first light, stiff with cold. The river had dropped slightly during the night, and had left the raft perched on the rocks. We wrestled it off the rocks using lengths of driftwood to lever it inch by inch until we reached waist-deep water, then clambered aboard and floated through the heavy mist that hung over the water. Giant mahoganies and intertwined vines hung over the narrow channels. As we silently slipped past islands and concealed channels, for the first time I felt we were actually part of this incredibly beautiful wilderness environment. It was as though we had finally gained acceptance from her waters. At last, daylight's warming beams of light began to penetrate through the upper tiers of jungle canopy, spreading slowly across the glassy river surface. I fired up the battered old Primus and boiled river water in last night's baked bean tin. Huddled on the tea box, we sat silently, enchanted by the waking jungle. A green-and-orange speckled snake glided effortlessly through the water ahead of us while a noisy band of monkeys chattered excitedly in the dense canopy above. Everywhere different species of birds were singing, each distinctly different.

Suddenly the left bank seemed to have receded several hundred metres. There was so much water! We stared and looked again.

'It's the Apurimac,' we whispered in unison. 'We are here.'

The Apurimac's waters were not as discoloured as the Urubamba's, and were a third less in volume. Here two of the Amazon's greatest tributaries join to become the Ucayali, which in turn flows through 1 800 km of pristine jungle before merging with the third tributary, the Marañón.

Filled with emotion, we paddled across to the right bank and unpacked our gear. Our *Berty* looked a sorry sight with its missing beams and without gringos and their shabby belongings. The familiar beat of a peci-peci approached and soon a low-slung dugout chugged into view, hugging the right bank. I waved the boatman down.

'Can you give us a ride to Atalaya?' François asked.

Flying out of Atalaya in a Cessna. I sat with a sheep accross my lap.

Jungle wilderness from horizon to horizon. (Urubamba in far background.)

The wiry old man inspected us and our luggage shrewdly, then, without saying a word, held out eight fingers.

'Eighty soles?' François asked.

The man nodded his head. We loaded our box in the dugout, tied the kayaks behind it, and pushed *Berty the Balsa* (the one with a mind of its own) off into the current for her final voyage.

'Where have you come from?' the semi-naked man asked in broken Spanish.

'Upstream,' I replied, pointing back to the Urubamba, 'from the mountains.'

He stared at me for several moments, nodded understandingly, and then turned his gaze towards Atalaya.

We edged our way on upstream.

Chapter 3

TORONTEI GORGE

Preparing for the Gorge

It was 3:00 p.m., 11 July 1981, when the door to my hostel room burst open and a beaming Chan, radiating enthusiasm, strode inside. He was convinced that the river level was low enough to paddle Torontei gorge.

'I looked at it yesterday, and I'm sure we can do it,' he said, still bubbling over.

Apparently, the water was down by about a metre, and a good deal less vicious than it had been a month before. I was thrilled with the news and had had more than I could stand of this eternal waiting. It was now almost three months since we reached Atalaya.

'Yes,' I said, 'I am ready when you are. We can take tomorrow's train to Machu Picchu. We could even be on the water by midday.'

The time had arrived for the biggest challenge of our lives. I felt the mix of rushing emotion, pumping adrenalin, and the struggle to concentrate. Tomorrow we would come face to face with the Urubamba's fiercest section: the Torontei gorge. There was nothing quite like it, dropping almost 2 000 m over the 70-km river.

François, Matt, Clive and Donata had all left Peru in May, leaving Chan and I to complete the unnavigated gorge. In the small room of the Hostal Miraflores, we spent a heady evening, packing our gear, double-checking our kayaks, and bidding farewell to our Cuzco friends. One of these friends was Raphael Hansa, or, because of his slightly 'euro' look, 'Gringo' for short – a laid-back, friendly Peruvian. Built like a rugby front-ranker, he combined the roles of surfer and Andean tour guide. He had spent years working with Andean Adventure Tours as a guide and porter. When he heard of our plans to run the Torontei unsupported and alone, his brow furrowed with concern and disapproval. He stepped forward and made an unexpected proposition.

'Guys, I'll help you! I'll carry your gear. You just cannot run that crazy river without help; you won't make it. I will walk along the riverside, following the railway. I can fit everything in my poncho. Look, I am a strong guy, I'll look after you!'

Gringo's proposal was amazingly generous, but by this time, our coffers were rock bottom. We hardly had enough money to buy provisions for the trip, let alone get ourselves back to Cuzco. We certainly could not pay for a support team. We explained to Gringo that we would love to have him along, but that we had no money. We could perhaps put something toward his living expenses, but that was it. Our budget was at rock bottom.

'No problem,' said Gringo. 'Money no big problem for me. I'd like to help you. We go!'

Chan and I discussed Gringo's offer and accepted it without second thoughts. The advantages of having him would be enormous. His presence alone would bring moral support and much needed humour, and secondly it meant that our boats would be much lighter – a great help in such difficult water. Privately, I also knew that Gringo's presence would relax and dilute the tension that always simmered under the surface between Chan and I.

We accepted gratefully; the deal was on. Our plans, after almost two long months of waiting, were at last coming together. At 5:30 a.m. the next morning, on a cold stone-paved Cuzco station, a pinkish-mauve sky was breaking through the Andean peaks. In the thronging crowd of travellers there was no mistaking our odd-looking, little group – a Chinese American, a South African and a Peruvian, heaving gigantic bundles of gear and provisions, and struggling to fit two kayaks onto the crowded train.

'Urubamba, here we come!' we shouted. We were now familiar with the spectacular train ride down 76 km of line to the point where we would set off down the river. The railway follows the 75-km gorge all the way, offering great scenery to the tourist, and making the logistics of a kayak expedition much simpler for us. At Chilca siding, at kilometre post 76, the train grounded to a shuddering halt. Chilca was nothing more than a rickety, rusted, corrugated iron building. Its residents were a small and humble Quechua family who eked out a living selling roasted corn and fried chicken to passengers in transit. We had only two or three minutes to hurl off our gear and leap to the ground before the train rumbled away with a piercing whistle, disappearing slowly as it wound its way between the sheer cliff sides.

A New Team

So, this was it, we had arrived. The river was no more than 200 m down from the train line. I pushed my way through thick vegetation, hunting for a marker-tree I had used these last two months to monitor the water level. The notches I had cut into the bark with my penknife were still clearly visible. I had cut the first in early April when I first set eyes on the Urubamba. They were now 2 m above surface. A notch I had made a month ago was now 1 m above. The river was certainly much tamer, without those crashing, exploding waves that still rang in my memory. Not only was it less violent but it had also changed colour from chocolate brown to a slightly muddy green.

I stared at it, aware of the nerve-racking build-up that had prepared me for this moment. Was I up to it? It was certainly more difficult and more dangerous than anything I had previously attempted, and if one valued one's life one wouldn't take a swim in this water! An inner voice warned me that I was engaging with something rather too big for me. It was like a novice boxer thrown into the ring with a heavyweight champion. For a moment the thought flashed through my mind – there's still time to quit, now's the moment to bolt for it.

I looked up at the towering, forested walls and tried to redirect my racing thoughts. It was difficult to think straight without emotion swaying me. This was my last chance to pull out. What would my father have said? Dad would have looked at me calmly and said, 'I think you've bitten off more than you can chew with this river, but on the other hand you've got this far, maybe you should give it a go.'

I could clearly hear my mother's voice: 'No, Tim, I don't think you should do it. Come back when you've had more experience. The river will always be there. Just look at it, it is far more dangerous than the Umkomaas or Umzimkulu Rivers back home.'

Another restraint was my poor relationship with Chan. Here we were, about to trust our lives to each other, and yet the last months had exposed an increasing irritation between us, even exasperation. The months of waiting had led us to a sort of saturation point – it was an open question whether we had the intimate, mutual trust that could take us through the gorge. In kayaking, the inter-dependence just never lets up: you depend on each other all the way.

TORONTEI GORGE

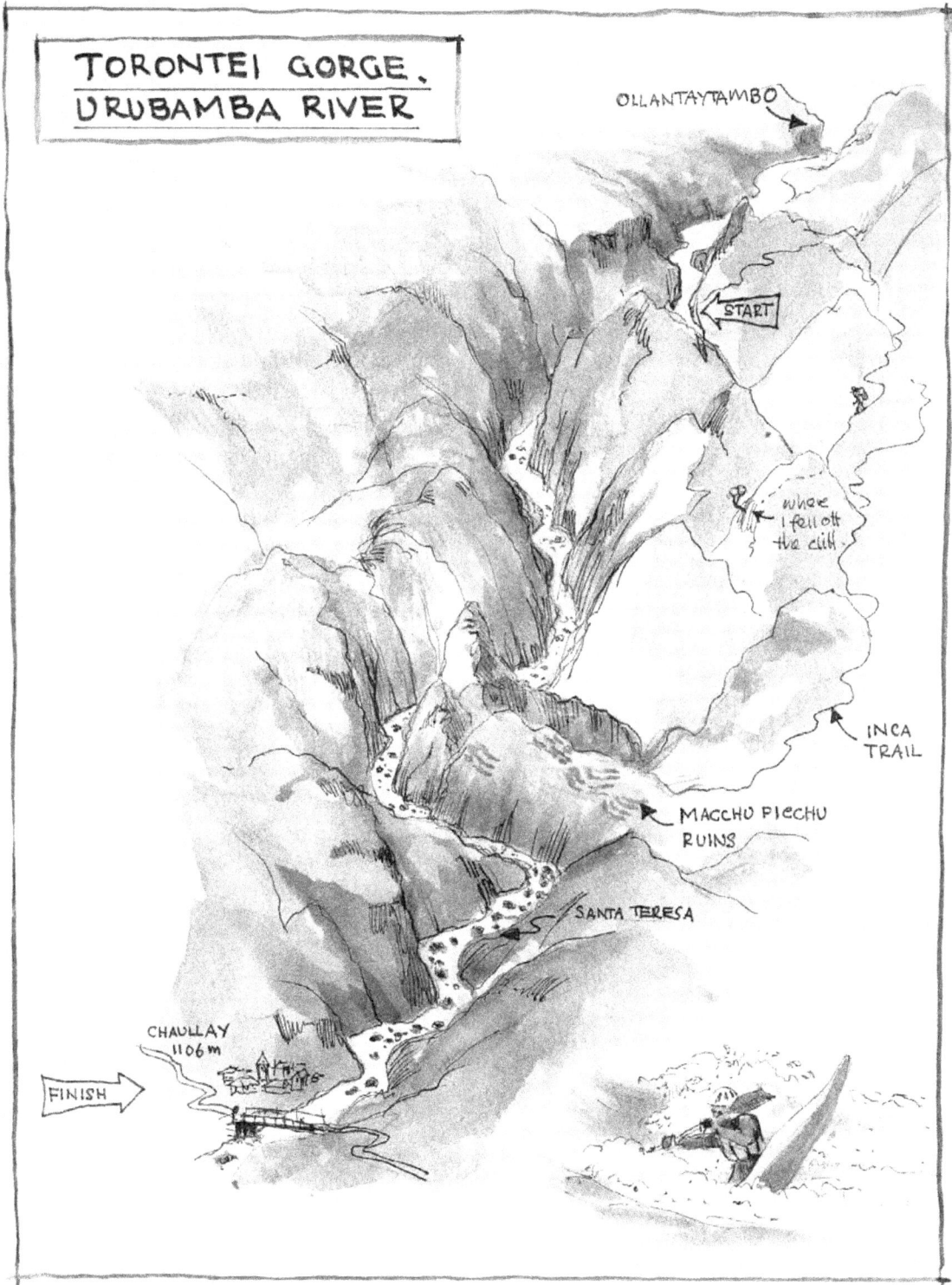

TORONTEI GORGE,
URUBAMBA RIVER

OLLANTAYTAMBO

START

where
I fell off
the cliff

INCA
TRAIL

MACCHU PIECHU
RUINS

SANTA TERESA

CHAULLAY
1106m

FINISH

Chan packing his boat.

Chan and I stood there motionless, both fighting with our thoughts and emotions.

'We can make it, Chan. It's now or never, we can make it,' I said.

'Yeah, I think we can.'

Gringo sat quietly with the equipment, watching us.

'You guys be okay. River is good now, I'm sure you be okay,' he said reassuringly. With no more ado, he bundled our gear and provisions into a massive el paco poncho, pulled it tight from the corners, and, with a roar like a bull, heaved it on his back.

Chan and I looked at him, knowing our time of truth was near.

'Okay, guys,' Gringo said, 'I see you downstream in 4 or 5 km. Take it easy; the water is still strong. Be careful.'

I stared at the surging masses of water, searching for a line we could run. Trying to block out the roar from the river and focus, I followed my imaginary line down to the next eddy, 100 m downstream. 'Yes,' I said to myself, 'there is a line. Small, but definitely there.'

Chan and I turned to each other and laughed. This was it. Our porter had left us no choice but to get into the water and start paddling. The game was on.

'You had better have a fire and a hot meal waiting, you old bastard!' we yelled after him. There was no

Our friend Gringo - he could carry the load of 3 men.

reply, his powerful frame disappeared behind the rocks, as he walked back to the railway line. In an intense silence, Chan and I pulled on anoraks, fitted spraydecks, life jackets and helmets. We checked and tensioned each buckle and strap, a routine as natural to us as eating and drinking.

Going In

We sit perched in our kayaks, ready to slide into the water. Chan pushes off. His boat slides crocodile-like down the bank. In a flash he is swept out of sight. Now it is my turn. I am alone with the river. Fear cramps my gut; the roar of the racing water floods my brain. I hesitate, and then – against all my instincts – I push off the bank and follow Chan downstream.

Instantly the current catches my bow and my kayak is whipped downstream. I have seriously underestimated the water's force. With two strong sweep strokes, I break into an eddy. From behind a low, smooth rock, I peer backwards over my shoulder in search of Chan. I catch sight of him 20 m downstream, tucked in an eddy and watching me intently. We both peer downstream over our shoulders, catching shafts of spray from the rapid we are about to run. How different the river looks at surface level! We nod to each other, and Chan, breaking out of the eddy, leads our charge.

The river sweeps through an S-bend between two giant boulders, then drops over a 2-m-high chute, with an eddy below it. Chan is swept out of sight. I glimpse the orange kayak before he disappears. I wait and wait. At last, the orange nose flashes vertically up into the air – and then disappears again. Chan has been 'endoed' (cartwheeled). It's obviously bigger than we thought. Is he okay? I had better go and see. I peel out of my eddy and swing into the hard-hitting turbulence of the current. Waves break over me. For a moment I see only a haze of spray before I can clear the water from my eyes. I brace hard against the diagonals that rebound off the right bank. I must cut the corner sharply to make the tight

Chan hanging in for dear life.

S-bend. Waiting until the kayak is perched on top of the wave crest, I manage two sweep strokes before I narrowly round the corner. The chute is now directly ahead of me. My kayak accelerates with the sliding mass of water that funnels into the chute. As I perch on the lip of the fall, I glimpse Chan's raised paddle signalling that the run is clear. At least he is okay. The next moment I am diving down the chute, and there is a muffled stillness. Tons of water pound my kayak's back deck, and I am catapulted vertically in a 'tail-walking' endo. I hit the water upside down, 'Eskimo roll', and haul frantically to reach the eddy where Chan waits for me. I narrowly miss being being swept into the next rapid. As we pause, we pass concerned glances at each other: this is going to be a tough run.

The next rapid needs scouting from the bank. Chan scrambles up the rocky bank and yells, 'Okay, Tim, it's not too bad. The river smacks into that boulder on the left. You must turn hard right before you get to it, cut the corner, then paddle hard towards the right bank. The far right drop is okay, so be sure not to miss it.'

Running a rapid on your partner's instructions, without seeing it for yourself is always scary. The person on the bank can see the entire rapid, whereas the kayaker on the water cannot see more than a few metres ahead of him, as the river drops over the horizon line. I was about to push off from the bank, and run the rapid blind, depending on Chan's animated hand signals, when my alarm signals flashed: get out and look at it yourself, Tim!

Chan noticed my hesitation.

'What's the problem? Don't you trust me?' he shouted, annoyed that I doubted his judgement.

'Yes, of course I do, but I just want to see the thing for myself.'

'Okay, then, I'll go first. Stay in your boat.'

'No, I still want to look at it myself.'

I scrambled up a pockmarked boulder and surveyed the scene. 'Thank goodness I've seen it from here,' I thought to myself, it was far more hectic than I'd imagined.

'Hell, Chan,' I shouted, 'this is tricky stuff; class 5, not 4. If you miss that right drop and go over the middle chute you land dead centre of that huge hole.'

'Yeah, but that's exactly why you must turn hard to the right,' Chan responded.

It was pointless arguing. 'Let's keep going,' I called.

Chan was already in his boat, understandably annoyed that I had challenged his judgement. I signalled to him that I would be on the bank with a throw-line if he needed help. His orange boat swept into the maelstrom. I gasped at what I saw: he had missed his line, his kayak disappearing under the wall of water. Above the roar of the rapid, I heard the clunk of his paddle as he threw himself against the rock, trying to save his upstream rail from being pulled under. For seconds he hovered there, side-surfing the cushion. Suddenly the boat was released, and his boat slipped backwards down a smaller chute to the left of the rock. Disaster seemed imminent. Chan whipped around with a lightning reverse stroke, corrected himself and broke through the current. Another graceful stroke and he was right on line, powering over the drop before disappearing under water. I marvelled at his quick reactions. For two to three seconds there was no sign of him. Then, when the upside-down hull appeared, Chan's roll was instant and he was up in a second, but obviously still in trouble. He had overshot the eddy behind the rock and was swept into the next rapid. A quick glance over his shoulder showed him that he was not going to make it to the bank. I started running down the bank, leaping over slippery rocks, trying to get to the next rapid. We had not yet scouted this one. At first glance, it looked harmless, with just a big wave or two. Then I saw two menacing holes, lurking beneath the spray . . .

Chan, with his usual calmness, spun his boat around and steadied it even as he swept toward the

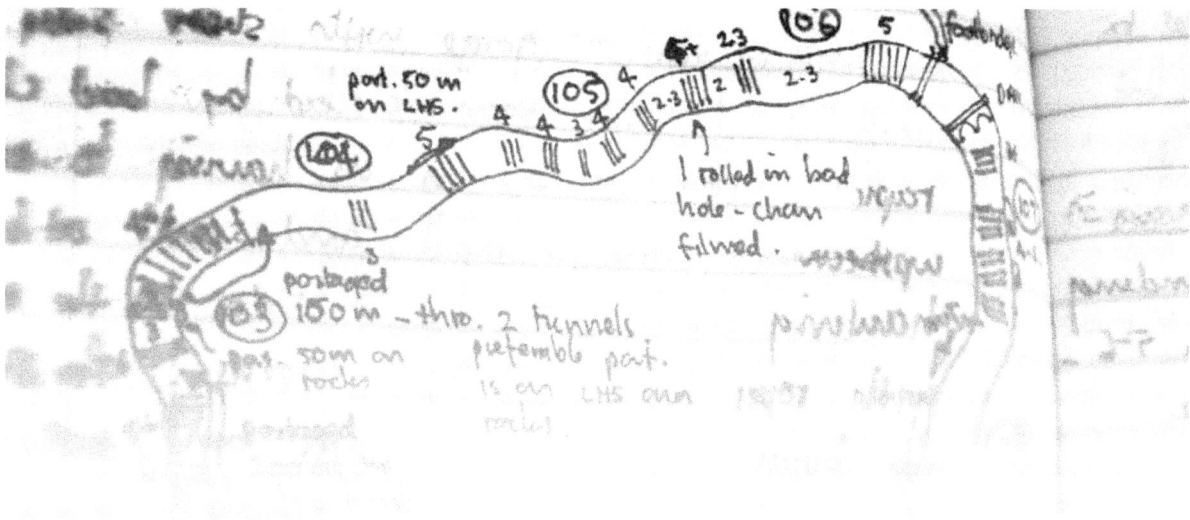

Water-stained diary notes.

rapid. He glanced up at me on the bank, looking for direction. Wildly I pointed my paddle to the right, directing him away from the dangerous holes. He understood the signal and skirted the side of the first, clipping the second before slipping into the safety of an eddy. A minute or two later I caught up with him, breathing hard.

'Well done, man! You hung in there magnificently!'

'Yeah, that bottom drop was way more powerful than I realised.

'Look, Tim, this water is pushy. Maybe we should wait until the level drops off a bit. Fact is that I am at my limit in this water. It's just too fast.'

It was now my turn. If Chan had miscalculated with some of his moves, what would I do? Uneasily I walked back upstream, climbed into the cockpit of my kayak, and slid off the bank. I broke into the current, determined not to be broached sideways against the boulders as Chan had been. I paddled furiously, with the result that I cut the corner too sharply and spun out in the messy eddy. Not a good start! I lost momentum and found myself bounced

mercilessly by two conflicting currents. Disaster seemed near. Then in an instant the current gripped my kayak, swept me clear of the boulder, and into the three standing waves, The kayak's nose was shoved into the air and its stern buried in a wave, stalling my entry. I found myself heading sideways without speed for the massive hole. There was no avoiding it; I would have to run it as best I could. I spun my boat around and managed two frantic forward sweeps

A HOLE
Cocacambila Rapid.

before I plunged over the fall, ready for a thrashing. As I dropped, I spotted a small tongue of water funnelling through the hole. My boat responded to a quick stroke, I took a deep breath, water crashed over my head, pummelling my kayak. I was over, upside down. Seconds later I was up again, disorientated, looking around.

Chan was yelling from the bank, 'Paddle, paddle for the eddy!' It was too late. I had swept past the eddy and was well on my way into the next rapid, working it out as I went, somehow making it through. Chan was on the bank with a throw-line.

'Well done, Tim. We made it by the skin of our teeth. You did a good roll. Let's keep going.'

The adrenalin was now in full flow, and with a loud 'yeeeha', we pushed on downstream taking it in turn to lead.

Still in battle mode, we fought our way through another kilometre of water until we spotted Gringo standing at the side, waving wildly to attract our attention. We were exhausted and yet exhilarated by our five hours' of intense kayaking. Gringo came to the bank and helped us drag out the boats. From his wide eyes it was obvious that he had witnessed some of our closer shaves. There was a touch of consternation in his voice.

'You sure you guys okay on this water? Maybe not a bad idea to wait until river drops more?' Gringo asked.

'Come Gringo, too much talking!' we replied. 'Just get that tea going.'

'Okay,' replied our faithful porter. 'Okay, I make, I make.'

Ten minutes later we sat round an expertly made campfire, sipping hot tea with condensed milk. Exhaustion overtook me; I felt emotionally drained. I lay back against the smooth granite rocks and snuggled into the soft sand. Huge trees towered over us and granite cliffs reached into swirling mist clouds. 'This is the life,' I said to myself. Who would have believed that only a night ago we were partying in

Cuzco? I dozed, aware of the cooking sounds of Gringo preparing supper.

'Hey, Gringo,' I said, 'we never expected you to do all the cooking. We should be serving you. You carry our bags, we look after you.'

He laughed. 'I wouldn't trust you to cook for me anyway. I cook today.'

A near-full moon was rising precariously from behind the jagged peaks, soaking the mountains with golden light.

'One more cup of tea, and I'm off to bed. Thanks again for helping us, Gringo. It's great having you along,' I heard Chan mutter.

The fire flickered and crackled as we drifted contentedly from consciousness to sleep.

Fighting the River

It was day three of our expedition, 16 July 1981, and Chan and I set off early. The day started badly with an early morning squabble over the valuable rolls of film that were waterlogged during the previous day's paddling. We grumpily proceeded to pack our boats, disappointed that our film was ruined.

The river had dropped about two inches, and I was grateful for the short break of calmer water, before we entered the long and continuous rapids.

We were now familiar with each other's signals and commands. I could tell by Chan's body language and expression how dangerous any rapid was that he was piloting. Subconsciously he would perform a mini-drama as he acted out an imaginary run, making hand and body movements to match the rapid. If it was a very difficult run, he would stop and look intently ahead, and then quietly shake his head. This was the sign that I had to get out and inspect the section for myself!

The notorious Km 87 arrived, a steep series of unrunnable class 5 and 6 rapids. We decided to run the approaches before portaging. First up was a class 4 drop, which I led without a hitch. Chan was following close behind, but, as I turned to watch his run, his kayak dived deeply, and emerged upside down. I waited for him to whip up as he normally would, but to my surprise he missed his roll and flopped upside down again. Things were getting tense. The class 6 section was now only 25 m further, signalled by a great cloud of mist and spray that pumped up from the collision of water masses. Chan attempted another roll and missed. Horrified at what was unravelling before me, I began sprinting towards him. Something was wrong. I knew Chan's style; never before had I seen him miss more than two rolls. The upturned kayak had caught the faster current, and was acceler-

ating towards the falls. Chan's paddle weakly broke the surface in an unsuccessful bid to right himself. Then, to my horror and disbelief, the great mass of sliding water swept him mercilessly over the falls and into the spray pumping up from below. I could not believe what I witnessed. Would I ever see him alive again?

My mouth was dry with fear and apprehension for my friend. I did not know what to do; following after him would be suicidal. I paddled furiously towards the left bank, only just avoiding being swept over the fall by the current. Gasping, I reached the bank, leapt out, grabbed my boat and bounded along

Big holes ~ big eyes!

from boulder to boulder. On the polished surface my foot slipped and I went sprawling, my boat crashing down on top of me. Furious with myself, I leapt up and continued racing along the bank. Looking across the rapid I could see Chan's kayak cartwheeling in a massive hole beneath the second drop, disappearing, bobbing up again, re-submerging – with no sign of Chan. My eyes scanned the riverbank frantically for any sign of him.

Nothing!

A cliff, dropping sheer into the river, now blocked my path. With throw-line in hand I dived into the water, swept past the cliff, then clawed my way back to the bank. At that moment Chan's kayak appeared. It came floating past me heading straight downstream, and disappeared over another wild drop, still no sign of my friend. Was this it, then? Was this the moment we had always dreaded and never spoke about: had Chan drowned? It was impossible to prevent that awful possibility from occupying my frightened mind. I scanned the whole river scene for a sign of Chan. I would not accept that this was the end. It could not be.

Scrutinising the area, I at last spotted something blue. It was Chan's blue life jacket! And there lay Chan himself spread eagle, half in the water, half out. I raced up to him as fast as I could and lifted his head.

'Are you okay, Chan? Are you okay, buddy?'

He groaned, and then retched up a stream of water. He was alive! I propped him up against a warm rock. Slowly his eyes focused and his mind regained itself. At last he found words.

Chan through a drop.

The rapids just went on & on.

'Tim,' he said weakly, 'I thought I was drowning. That hole just would not let me go. I had given up completely.' A few moments' pause, and Chan asked 'Where's my boat? Have you seen my boat?'

I had last seen it in the second hole, before it disappeared. I told him to stay where he was, and that I would run downstream and look for it. As I ran, the thoughts 'Chan's alive, he's alive!' raced through my head. On I went along the river until I caught sight of his kayak, its orange nose rising from the swirling water. Running and chasing along the boulder-strewn bank, I finally caught up to it, diving into the river as it floated past. I grabbed hold of the handle on its nose and swam the mangled kayak to the bank. Then it struck me that the paddle was missing.

There was nothing to do but to run on further downstream, hoping that the paddle would still be in the vicinity and not already way down the river. At last, to my amazement, the paddle appeared, circling round and round, together with tons of driftwood in a 20-m-wide eddy. Plunging in and shoving through the driftwood, I retrieved it. It was a long but somehow satisfying walk back to Chan. By the time I reached him, he was standing up, looking shaken and pale.

'Chan, I thought you were history,' I chided, more from relief than anything else. 'You're giving me grey hairs. Look, you didn't even lose your glasses!'

Chan laughed feebly. His thick, tinted glasses strapped to his head and covered by his helmet, were a permanent fixture.

'Lose these, and I'm as blind as a bat. You'd have to lead me by the hand all the way back to Cuzco,' he said, already sounding and looking more like the pre-traumatised Chan.

It was now well into the afternoon, and time for lunch. I hauled out lunch for the day – a tin of tuna, biscuits, some cheese, and one block of cooking chocolate.

After lunch we both lay on the rocks, soaking up the sun.

'I'm broken,' Chan groaned. 'I've had enough of this bloody river, enough.'

I could not blame him, after what he'd been through.

'I reckon we camp right here. Don't worry, man! Tomorrow you'll be as fit as a fiddle.'

As things were, with Chan's condition and his buckled and mangled boat – in need of a major overhaul – we could not think of going any further that day. If the sun was hot the next day, the battered kayak might straighten itself out.

Meanwhile we had to consider that Gringo was on the other side of the river. He had overtaken us, seen us, and had walked back upstream. I paddled across and explained to him how Chan's boat was not merely out of action but in need of some serious panel beating. I took our camping gear from Gringo and paddled it back to Chan, so that this night we would sleep on opposite banks. Back at the campsite, I scratched together some firewood and got some tea underway. We were exhausted. Chan lay on his back, bemoaning the plight of his boat and his shattered confidence. This was the first trip where I had seen Chan swim, a sight that I had not expected. The Urubamba was putting us through our paces, testing us to the limit and beyond. Luckily, the clouds and drizzle cleared that night, unfolding a magnificent starry sky. From my campsite position, lying flat on my back, I took comfort in the Southern Cross, arching across the sky and framed by the sides of the canyon.

By 8:00 a.m. the next morning a deep blue sky reigned over the scene, and two hours later Chan's deformed kayak was magically beginning to soften and regain its shape. We carefully weighted the ends and began wedging out the creases and dents in the buckled plastic. Even the support pillars almost fitted again. By noon the hot, softened plastic resembled the definite form of a kayak.

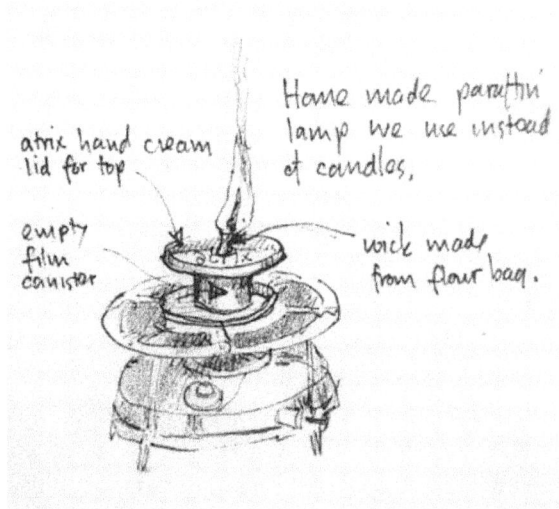

atrix hand cream lid for top.

empty film canister

Home made paraffin lamp we use instead of candles.

wick made from flour bag.

'Hey, Chan,' I said, 'look, your boat's got more "rocker" now (banana-shaped – ends bent up). Maybe you'll be able to make the turns easier. Perhaps I'll do the same to mine!'

After many months of living together, I was discovering something amusing about my old friend Chan. He was more pleasant to be with after he had taken a hammering. Meanwhile we needed no encouragement to spend the rest of the day at rest.

'I'm utterly finished, and I don't want to see any more damn rapids,' Chan grumbled.

I agreed. We camped and rested in the cool shade, overlooking the series of spectacular drops. As evening approached, a crescendo of birdcalls rose from the forest, accompanied by the high-pitched chorus of mosquitoes.

Nearing the End

I woke early on the fourth day, my morale still oppressed by the previous events. The river does not care whether you are scared or not, injured or not, brave or petrified, good or bad. The river is its own boss, flowing by its own rules. You don't mess with a river like this, I mused to myself while I lay in my sleeping bag.

Freezing with cold, I gingerly tested my right shoulder, which I had wrenched in the demanding water, moving it carefully, not sure what to expect. To my relief, my shoulder did not feel too bad. I was heartened, and could lie there in the early light analysing our trip.

There was a personal element in this reflection. Despite us having gone to the outer limits of survival together, my shore-side relationship with Chan was not healthy. I was sure that it was not only my taut nerves that were causing the difficulty; Gringo, too, was tangibly taking strain with Chan. At one point, he had even threatened to pull out, leaving us to our edginess and mutual bickering. That would have been disastrous: we could not afford to lose Gringo! The

This one's a portage for sure.

human aspect of our impasse weighed more on me than the physical, despite the fact that the biggest rapids were still to come.

However, I also had struggles within myself, the same ones that came to me from time to time. I was depressed to discover a sort of hollowness, an inexplicable loneliness in myself, even now as I was fulfilling the dream of a lifetime. I had to remind myself sharply that I had never expected the Urubamba to be a picnic. No, I told myself, I had to see the thing through, and while at it, make an extra effort to be decent to Chan at breakfast.

I crawled out of my sleeping bag and washed my face in the cold river, trying not to notice that merciless current that roared past only a few metres away from me. I found some consolation in carefully building the morning fire, and watching it burst into healthy, orange flames. The flames gathered heat; I placed our old blackened pot of water on the fire, and then took steaming mugs of tea to Gringo and Chan, saying cheerfully, 'Hi, guys! Tea's up. How did you sleep, Chan?'

A cold drizzle soon dampened my cheer. If ever I needed good, hot sunshine for running the rapids it was that day, but it seemed unlikely. We wished Gringo well: 'See you 6 or 7 km downstream, Gringo. There are some big rapids today.'

Chan and I slipped into the water without a word to each other. He, too, was quite tangibly downcast and lacked his usual early morning confidence. His unique, relaxed style was still there, however, and with minimal effort he entered the mainstream. I watched him disappear into a cloud of spray and turbulence. I closely followed behind: we had scouted this section thoroughly, and were confident about our approach. The shock of the first cold waves crashing into my chest and face jerked me into reality. Glimpsing ahead I saw Chan disappear over a drop. I followed carefully, determined to nurse my shoulder.

The next rapid started with a series of class 5 bends and turns. We worked our way cautiously downstream, one rapid at a time, one kilometre at a time, hardly speaking to each other, and making only the most necessary hand and paddle signals. The alternating leadership took all our concentration, each peering over his shoulder for the next pool eddy, running it, then signalling our partner to pull in alongside. Sometimes there would not be enough room for two boats, and the first would have to break out into the current as the second entered the eddy.

We were now paddling well as a team – watching each other, reading each other's movements, and all the time assessing the size and difficulty of the next drop or chute that loomed before us. The continual 'yes' or 'no' decision-making took its toll, and made the tea break at 10:30 a.m. most welcome. My only mishap that morning happened as I was climbing into my kayak, when, with one foot in and one foot out, an unexpected surge swamped me completely, knocking me flat into the icy water. Frantically I

The best moment of the day ~ lunch on the rocks.

grabbed my boat before the stream took it, and with my other hand, latched onto a tuft of grass, and dragged myself to shore.

'Bad luck,' Chan laughed as I floundered in the water, cursing.

On the seventh day we rounded a bend and there before us was the most breathtaking sight of the whole trip: the thousand-metre-high cliffs of Machu Picchu reaching up almost vertically out of the river, and disappearing into a low layer of cloud that mantled the peaks. A mixture of exhaustion and emotional relief choked our minds. We had both begun to wonder if we would ever make Machu Picchu. Now the sight of the place filled us with new hope.

We were in no great shape physically; we had both lost our river shoes, our feet were a mass of cuts and bruises, I had hurt my shoulder, and Chan his wrist. Our personal relationship had deteriorated from our continual scuffles and scrapping, and we badly needed a break from each other. For all its glamour, however, the small village beneath the majestic ruins was no more than a small and smelly row of riverside houses, discharging tons of litter and garbage into the Urubamba. It is here that flocks of tourists visit the famous ruins that lie high above the village. Machu Picchu's economy depends on sales of food and souvenirs from its makeshift stalls. Well, we were not exactly tourists, and indeed the locals treated our arrival as no small event. An excited crowd thronged around us, not one of whom had ever seen a kayak on these waters. Some excited children carried our kayaks up the steep bank, and when Gringo appeared at last, he had to rescue us from the inquisitive on-lookers. With a due sense of the occasion, he shook our hands. 'Well done, guys,' he said, 'you see, you can do it.'

Indeed. We had made it to Machu Picchu.

The expression on Gringo's face showed relief and happiness – qualities that had been missing these last few days. We knew that this was as far as Gringo would come; our invaluable guide had informed us

that Machu Picchu would be the end of his journey with us. His news had been a great disappointment, and had a negative effect on our morale.

As we were sitting at our camp, Chan announced: 'I think I'm gonna stop here, Tim, the trip has kind of lost its feel for me.' I didn't rush to respond, but pondered over the matter. It hardly came as a surprise, considering the strained mood and the difficulties of the last few days. We had both taken many knocks, and experienced some close shaves during the past eight days. The thought of pitting ourselves once more against the relentless river held no attraction for either of us, neither physically nor mentally.

I wasn't sure whether Chan's announcement was genuine. If it was real, I'd find myself in a fix. To try to run the remaining section alone was not something I wanted to attempt, but dangling like a carrot in front of me was the cold fact that the end was in sight! There were only 35 km of the original 1 800 km of river left, and that fired me up. No, there was no way we could drop out at this point, we had to finish what we had set out to accomplish. Perhaps a day's rest, and some gentle persuasion, would bring Chan to change his mind. We had come too far to simply end here.

I finally responded. 'Hey, Chan, it's your call. Personally though, I think we've had too much of this river. Let's have a break for a day or two and see how we feel.'

Meanwhile, back to the present, we had a decision to make: our finances were now virtually non-existent, do we spend the little we had on some celebratory beers or rent a cosy room for the night? Needless to say we unanimously chose the beers – a less than wise choice as we recognised the next morning, having spent a sleepless night on the riverside, being too uncoordinated to pitch our tent!

We certainly paid for our sins that night, a thunderstorm had developed in the night, and completely drenched us. Waking up late the following morning, we discovered to our dismay that our friendly neighbours had relieved us of a good deal of our meagre material wealth during the night. Our treasured Patagonian fleece jackets, my diary and my flashlights – all had left the party! As might be imagined, our morning's conversation did not reflect high moral standards, and a good deal of loud cursing rebounded from the canyon walls! The expedition was in disarray. Today was a day off. We bade farewell to our loyal friend Gringo, and spent our last few dollars buying him a train ticket back to Cuzco. We waved goodbye as the train moved slowly out of Machu Picchu station, leaving us to face the full brunt of each other's foul moods.

If life can be compared to a river journey ~ this would be the heavy action, aggressive section.

Chan was adamant that he was not going to continue downstream to Chaullay, and it seemed that I would have no option but to head on downstream, unsupported and solo. In a mutual mood of despair and fuzzy heads, we tried to rest, avoiding each other as much as possible, each dealing with his own thoughts and wondering what to do with the tattered Urubamba expedition.

In a bid to free myself from this oppressive frame of mind, I set off on a hike to the ruins. As I climbed, the panorama became more spectacular, and I could look down onto the gorge far below me. Downstream of Machu Picchu the river entered an awesome jungle gorge. Sheer, granite cliffs covered with moss and forest vines, rose 1 000 m from either side of the river. Far below, the Urubamba wound snake-like around the rock bastions of Machu Picchu, before plunging with a double portion of power into an 8-km-long canyon with continuous cataracts and drops. I stared in dismay at the huge rapids far below. Even from this height they looked enormous and dangerous. This was bigger and more demanding than anything we had yet run. Maybe Chan was right. Maybe this wasn't for me. I would not survive it. Dejected, I climbed wearily down the mountainside to our camp, when a familiar voice called out from behind me.

'Hola, Tim – Tim, what are you doing out here?' I spun around to see Talo, my friend from Cuzco, with two attractive young European tourists walking behind me.

'Talo, I can't believe it! What are you doing here, how do you always seem to have beautiful girls with you?'

He laughed aloud and explained that he was acting as a guide to the two German tourists. 'And they call this work! Ah, Tim, life can be so good,' Talo said, laughing again.

Talo duly introduced Jutta and Elke to me. I couldn't help noticing their disapproving glances as they scrutinised me; then it dawned on me: I looked like and, probably smelt like, an outright tramp! I was covered in sores and scratches, had blistered lips and was wearing a filthy T-shirt and an over-sized pair of tattered river shorts. I played host never-theless and invited the party to our riverside camp. How I enjoyed watching the change in Chan's face as I sauntered into the campsite with my Peruvian friend and two attractive girls! Chan, who had been lying sprawled on the grass half asleep, leaped up as though he was under attack. I moved our crude seats (some round river rocks) close to the smoky fire and beckoned our guests to take a seat; a round of tin mugs of tea and soggy biscuits soon followed.

Talo sat and listened intently to our stories and tales of the past seven days. Even as we spoke, I could see his mind working, and then suddenly, without warning, out it came.

'What about it, girls! Didn't you come to the Andes for some real adventure? Come on; let's follow Tim and Chan down the river! It'll only take four or five days, but this will be the first time the river has ever been kayaked – we'll be part of history! Come ladies, it'll be an adventure – we'll be famous!' Talo lobbied passionately.

Talo obviously had a solid relationship with the German girls as they unanimously accepted his pro-posal with excitement and enthusiasm. To my amuse-ment, Chan's mood suddenly swung to one of greater interest. I seized the moment.

'Come on, Chan! With Talo and the girls coming along, the rest of the trip will be a party. Imagine it, lying in our camp under the shade, being served drinks and snacks by two beautiful girls after a hard day's paddle! Come now, Chan, that's world class! We can't go home without finishing this last small section, not after all we've been through,' I said, hoping that Chan's single-mindedness would buckle.

There was a long silence as Chan pondered over his decision. 'Okay, Tim, I guess you're right. I will join you, but I still need at least one more day to relax and rest. I'm still pretty drained.'

Chan

Endo

Close your eyes and go for it.

Talo and the girls cheered and clapped hands.

'That's great, Chan, fantastic! Thank you,' I responded. 'We have been through so much together. Let's finish it off with a bang, once and for all,' I said, so relieved.

I had dreaded the thought of running those rapids alone, but now with Chan back on the team, hope was flooding back.

'Okay, guys, we see you here the day after tomorrow,' said Talo, standing up to go. We watched as the team of three walked off towards the village.

That evening I decided to clear the air.

'Chan, I know we've scrapped and argued all the way, but I want you to know it's been good paddling with you. You have often helped me out of trouble, and you've taught me a hell of a lot about kayaking. I'm grateful, man. I'm sorry about all the times I've got mad at you.'

Chan was taken aback. I could see emotions flying around in his head.

'Okay, Tim, it's fine. Thank you, too,' Chan answered, 'I need to find some sleep after last night – goodnight, sleep well.'

I crawled into my sleeping bag with the sense of a burden lifted, and slept peacefully. We would make it yet!

Victory!

The following day I hiked down to scout the river, enjoying being on my own. It was a time to meditate, think things through, and work up courage for the next day's kayaking. I returned before dark and chatted with Chan about what I had found out. There was no point in even attempting to run the first section of cataracts, they were way beyond our skill levels.

'It's continuous class 5 and 6. You won't believe how bad it is. We are going to have to portage,' I reported.

Chan's jaw dropped. 'More portages,' he moaned.

'Hey, Chan, remember we've got to leave some river for the next generation to run,' I tried to joke. We broke camp at first light, and, moving in silence, slipped off into the swiftly-flowing water. After a kilometre of paddling, we came to our first portage. Thereafter there was another flat section before the river dropped into the maelstrom of steep and continuous cataracts. There was nothing to do but haul our boats up to the railway line and drag them downstream in the direction of Santa Teresa. As we were both now committed to finishing the course, a good deal of the tension between Chan and I had dissipated. We chatted good-humouredly about the sorts of kayaks – and indeed the sorts of kayakers – who would one day kayak this seemingly impossible section.

At last we reached Santa Teresa, where, after our strenuous portages, we treated ourselves to roasted maize, fried fish and banana. Talo had found a porter to carry our gear, and joined by the attractive European contingent, we sprawled on a grassy slope overlooking the river. Downstream we could see the greenish-blue Salcantay River flowing into the muddy Urubamba, increasing its volume by some 30%.

Our next 4 km in class 4 and 5 waters occupied us fully for the rest of the day. The river had grown in volume and was now less technical than before, but

The surf's up!

96

wider, with more powerful hydraulic action and bigger waves. The kayaking was exhilarating as we plunged through the crashing white water, ensuring that we skirted the colossal holes. We were fast coming to the end of our long-planned adventure. The next day we paddled hard for six hours, making only two portages. We could smell victory in the air! This, together with the two-day rest we had given ourselves, worked wonders for our morale. We were now paddling almost by instinct, floating through rapid after rapid, often running them blind, simply reading the river as we went, thrilled by its speed and power. We passed under a bridge spilling over with brightly dressed townfolk, loudly cheering as we swept beneath them. Chaullay was now only one day's paddling away. Our hearts were full, the end was in sight: nothing was going to stop us now.

The concluding hours of our journey were thrilling as the river swept us along. We ran one last spectacular rapid, surging through the long train of enormous standing waves; and there it was, a rickety steel bridge bearing a rusted and flood-battered sign – Chaullay! We paddled hard to gain the bank before being washed past the finishing point. Breaking into an eddy

Good adrenalin below Santa Teresa.

under the bridge, we dropped our paddles and shook hands. This was it: Chaullay – last rapid, last bridge, and last stop of our huge journey through the Andes. Four months had passed since the first part of the trip, when we had launched into the river on the high plains of the Andes. These four months now seemed like the kaleidoscopic view of a lifetime, filled with thrills, spills, highs and lows, exhilaration, fear, danger, all merging with each other. Images came to mind of floating downstream on a balsawood raft, of fending off angry villagers, of building glowing campfires, and, of course, the endless swirling rapids.

Our dreamlike summary was speedily interrupted by shouts and wild activity from the villagers who poured down the steep bank to meet us – surrounding us, touching us, looking inside our kayaks, poking at our life jackets and gear. The mood was infectious and we could not resist joining in with the crowd's laughter and festivities. Eventually the town's mayor proudly descended to the river down some slippery, muddy steps. In broken Spanish, we explained to him who we were and the nature of our mission.

'Of course, we remember you, you and your friends were here three months ago. Come with me, amigos. Tonight you are our guests, tonight you stay with us

We've made it! The whole village poured out to welcome us.

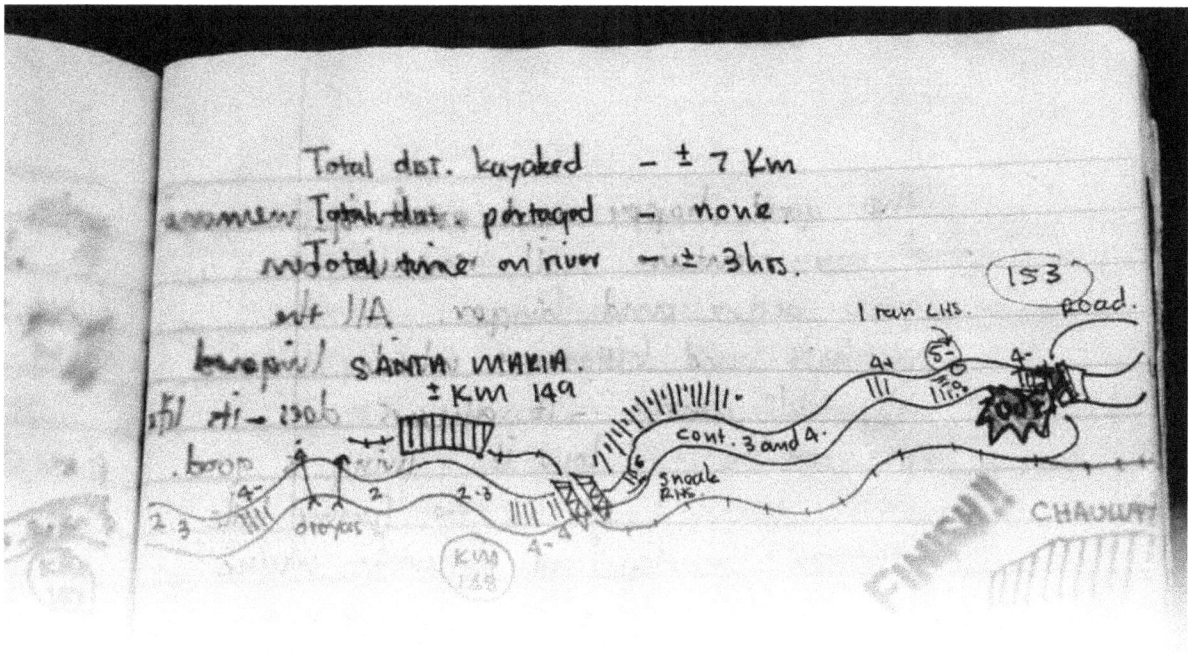

and we celebrate. We have never seen such a thing as this,' the hefe (mayor) announced.

Without more ado our boats and gear were lifted head-high by the colourful and vibrant crowd and we were marched to the village square. The climax to all the hilarity came when a group of young men hoisted Chan and I up onto their shoulders. The atmosphere was fantastic and emotional, the villagers had made us feel like champions. It was as if the river was presenting us with a special gift, saying 'Well done, friends'; it made a perfect ending to our Torontei adventure. Sleep came with difficulty that night as we struggled to adjust to sleeping on a soft mattress. The images of endless waves and racing currents swirled through my mind.

Chan and I shared our last meal together back in Cuzco, sitting staring at each other across a wobbly, small restaurant table. We didn't say much, we didn't

need to. We simply sat quietly savouring the sweetness and the delicious taste of a hard-worked for victory. The key to the mysterious door had been turned, the door had opened, and the Urubamba had allowed us passage through its towering canyons.

We had certainly been an unusual mix – an eccentric South African and an excitable Chinese American. One could hardly expect to find such diverse temperaments, and yet the Torontei experience had made a unity of this odd mix. We laughed about our many arguments along the way, one or two of which had nearly finished off the expedition.

'We've had our ups and downs all right, hey Chan?' I laughed. 'But if you ever come to South Africa, you'll be treated as a guest of honour.'

We laughed again, shook hands for the last time, and parted ways.

Chapter 4

COLVILLE RIVER, ALASKA
(August – September 1983)

California Dreaming

The ringing of the phone eventually broke through my sleep. With heavy eyes, I groped for the bedside lamp's switch.

'There must be a crisis somewhere. I hope no one has . . . well, you know . . . why else would anyone call at this hour of the morning?'

I jumped out of bed, anticipating bad news.

'Hello, Tim, it's François. I'm phoning from California – how are you?'

Immediately I relaxed. I had not seen François for quite a while, and it was good to hear from my old friend and river buddy.

'I'm fine, Frans,' I said, yawning. 'Do you know what the time is here in South Africa?'

'Ah, sorry, but last time it was you who woke me up! How about a testing 1 000-km trip in Alaska this August? The Colville River. I've made some good contacts and they can help us with the logistics. Are you keen?'

It was May now and although I had other trips planned for July and August, it would certainly be a lie to say I wasn't keen. A trip down a river with François always guaranteed something special, if not hair-raising.

'Sure, Frans – that sounds great. Actually, it works out well. I am hoping to join some Polish guys for a trip down the Colca River in July and August. Maybe I could go straight from Peru to Alaska. Yes, why not? Count me in – I'd love to come.'

After we had rung off there was no way I could get back to sleep. My mind was racing.

Folded my old kayak in half and rammed it into the plane.

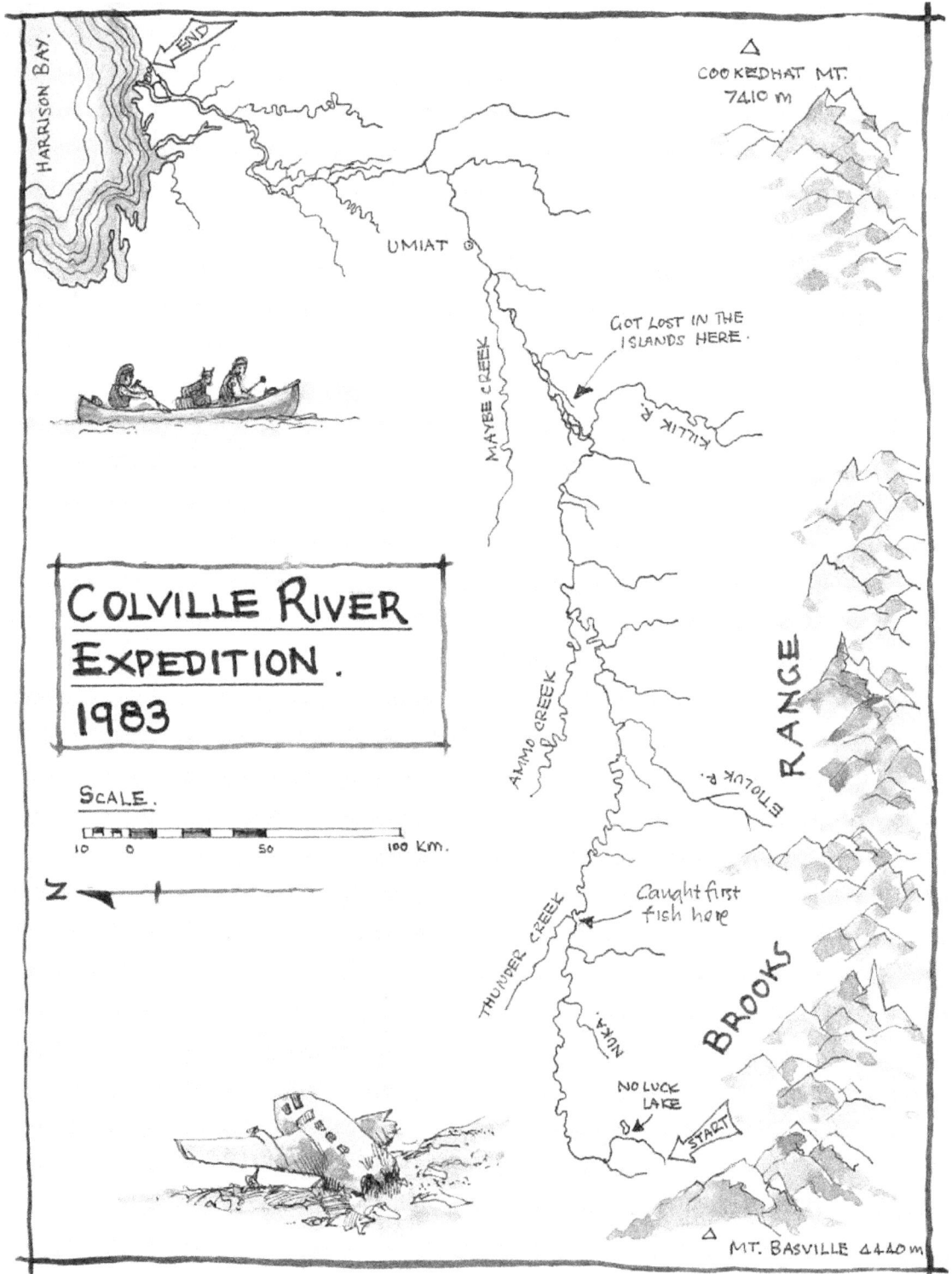

HARRISON BAY.

END

△
COOKEDHAT MT.
7410 m

UMIAT ⊙

GOT LOST IN THE
ISLANDS HERE.

MAYBE CREEK

KILLIK R.

COLVILLE RIVER
EXPEDITION.
1983

RANGE

AMMO CREEK

SCALE.

10   0   50   100 KM.

ETIVLUK R.

N

Caught first
fish here

THUNDER CREEK

BROOKS

NUKA

NO LUCK
LAKE

START

△ MT. BASVILLE 4440 m

The Brooks Range.

Alaska

On 8 August 1983, three months after François's call, our plane bounced twice as it touched down on the uneven runway at Kotzebue, a snowbound Eskimo town just south of the Brooks Mountains in northern Alaska.

We had in the hold one 17-foot-long Coleman Canadian canoe, my blue Hydra kayak that I had used on the Colca, and a heap of gear and provisions. Our team consisted of François, our cameraman Fanie van der Merwe, François's Australian 'cattle dog' Derry, and me.

Our mission was to paddle the full length of the Colville River, which rises from a small ice flow on the northern slopes of the Brooks Range, and then flows northward, bisecting the Arctic tundra on its way to Harrison Bay on the Arctic Ocean, a distance of approximately 850 km. The Colville snakes its way through one of the world's most isolated wilderness areas, and promised extreme weather conditions. François was inspired with the idea of running a river expedition through the unique tundra region. After three months of running the Andean desert rivers in Peru, the change of scenery appealed to me. The two places were quite the antithesis of each other.

As the plane taxied down the runway, with driving sleet beating against its windows, it dawned on me that I might have agreed a little too hastily to join the venture. I was supposed to be an experienced river runner, and it was quite inexcusable that I had not researched the Colville beforehand. At least I had one frightening fact to mull over: the Colville had practically no gradient at all – and that meant no rapids – for almost a thousand kilometres. Horrors! Why, then, had we chosen the slowest craft, an open Canadian canoe, and a white water kayak to navigate the river? In any case, it was too late to turn around and exchange craft; only time would tell how badly we had misjudged the situation.

With good humour, the Eskimos looked us up and down, recognising that we were certainly not the typical 'arctic type'. We soon found our way to the office of a tough-looking Alaskan bush pilot, Ross Hodgers, who was an old hand at flying the Arctic regions and the Brooks Range.

We had so much gear we had to fly two trips with the float plane.

'The only place I can land you,' said Ross, 'is on a small lake, some kilometres from the Colville. Unless of course you want to parachute in,' he added jokingly.

The first flight ferried our canoes and provisions that we had duly strapped to the floats of the four-seater Cessna. Four hours later it was our turn to board the crammed plane. We soared into the overcast Alaskan skies and marvelled at the enormous herds of caribou and moose grazing along the green hillsides, nothing more than specks next to the mountain foothills. Ross pointed to one herd of hundreds of caribou; he dropped the nose of the plane, skimmed over it, then climbed hard to cross the next range of hills. Range after range of ice-capped peaks passed below us, but ahead we could see only the endless expanse of the flat arctic tundra. The Brooks Range spans thousands of kilometres, west to east, dividing the tundra zone from mountainous southern Alaska. Our mood steadily became more serious as we gazed down over the mountain wilderness.

Light was fading fast, and Ross pointed to bad weather that was building up from the south. He

would have to race home to avoid a big storm that was brewing, throwing up enormous banks of translucent cloud. We glanced at each other.

'Here goes to another sort of experience . . . Alaska!' I thought aloud.

No Luck Lake

In the distance a small, silvery, mirror-like lake appeared.

'There it is, mates, No Luck Lake,' said Ross. 'I'm taking you down and then I'm heading straight off. Get ready to offload.'

'What's that on the lake, Ross?' François asked, pointing at a silver object that was perched awkwardly at one end.

'Passenger plane. Crashed here twenty odd years ago – all killed. Hence the name No Luck Lake. No worries, boys,' Ross added with a grin, 'we'll be okay.'

The three of us tried not to look alarmed, but even Derry, sitting on François's lap, put his ears back as though to express displeasure at our pilot's grim humour. The Cessna circled the lake once before coming down, its floats thudding hard as they struck the water and sent up a spray from the icy waves.

Bad omen! ~ a crashed plane on the banks of No Luck Lake.

As Ross roared off - we knew we were a month from nowhere.

When the engines cut out, only the lapping of waves against the floats was there to welcome us.

'Untie your boats and take down your gear,' Ross called out. 'There's the load I left here earlier,' he added, pointing at the bank. 'Guys, I'm out of here, this storm is almost on us.'

We had not realised how intent Ross was on heading back. Derry was jumpy and disorientated and François held him tight on his seat. We unlashed the Canadian canoe and dumped our 100 kg of gear into it. François and Fanie occupied the canoe while I jumped into the kayak. We then paddled our cache of provisions and equipment to the mossy, frosted bank of No Luck Lake, where we called out quick farewells to our pilot.

Ross slipped back into his seat and started the engine. 'If we don't hear from you in six weeks, we'll come and look for you!' he shouted as the Cessna roared into life. Seconds later the plane raced upwind across the lake and was soon nothing but a lonely speck against a stormy sky.

There we were: four forlorn figures on the banks of a creepily-named lake, subdued and silent as the reality of being alone in the wilderness began to dawn on us.

'Hey, Ross, come back. I forgot my toothbrush on board!' I yelled jokingly at the disappearing plane, hoping to break the uneasiness in the group. There were no roads, no airplanes, and the only way to get out of this tundra bog was down the river, 850 km to the closest igloo at the Arctic Ocean. It was 8:00 p.m. and, being the land of the midnight sun, there the sun sat, mauve and red, low on the western horizon. Golden, quilted clouds added a final touch to the spectacular scene.

Fanie broke the silence. 'Come guys, let's go. Here comes a squall.' We looked behind us to see the storm driving in with great banks of bluish-green cloud.

With cold fumbling fingers, we began to unpack our tents, but the kicking wind, gusting at 25 knots, soon changed our minds for us. Hastily we fled to the protective shell of a crashed aeroplane nearby. The fuselage had broken off in the crash-landing, leaving the rear of the plane open, making a near-perfect haven for us to unpack and sort our gear and provisions. Minutes later the storm struck. We heard the roar of the rain first, and then saw the solid water curtain approaching across the lake. Rain lashed and rocked the plane as we huddled in the rearmost corner, but after 20 minutes the storm was over, leaving behind a wild, blue-grey sky.

To avoid the extremes in the weather, François had been advised to plan the trip to fit into a narrow window period between August and September. We would hopefully arrive after the torturous invasion of summer mosquitoes, and be out before winter covered the region with snow and ice. The plan was to take two-and-a-half to three weeks, covering a comfortable 40 km (25 miles) a day. The Colville was a big river, well fed by numerous tributaries such as the Thunder, Ammo and Storm Creeks that flowed from glaciers off the Brooks Range. On studying the maps, the realisation of what we were about to paddle struck home: the total gradient to the Arctic Ocean was only several hundred metres – the equivalent of what was often a single day's descent in the Andes.

This trip was going to be challenging and long!

Our Dingo, our Fitness, our Source

Sleep evaded us that first night. A shrill wind drummed rhythmically against the plane's buckled sides, and at 3:00 a.m., the first thin rays of light filtered into the open-ended shelter. I could hear that my companions were not sleeping. The cold had driven Derry deep into François's sleeping bag, and occasional scuffles and yelps made me wonder whether I should leap to the dog's rescue, or was it only Derry suffering from suffocation? The truth was that I was worried about Derry. It was not the first time that François had surprised me with his choice of a team member. Okay, it was a novel idea to bring a dog along, but in the intense cold, he was already showing signs of distress. Well, we would just have to see.

'Frans,' I whispered, 'are you awake?'

'Sure, I've hardly slept all night. It's been so cold, I'm frozen.'

'We may as well start moving. Let's have a hot breakfast and get going,' I suggested.

We loaded our gear on the boats and paddled across the lake, leaving behind our haven. Now began our overland haul to the Colville River itself. Harnessed like oxen to a sled, we began dragging the flat-bellied Canadian canoe with our equipment in it across a terrain of bog, moss and tufted grass. One foot would be on dry ground, the other in soft, boggy peat. For three days we hauled, grunting, groaning and cursing as we staggered through 4 km of tundra wilderness, looking for all the world like drunken men burdened with heavy loads on their backs. At last our complete cache of provisions lay stacked in a neat pile on the low banks of the Colville. At that point the river was a mere stream, too small to launch our boats. We covered our boxes and bags with a groundsheet and headed upstream by foot, in search of the source of this winding mountain stream.

We hauled our gear through the tundra for 3 days.

Twenty below at the source of the Colville.

Derry had returned to his normal self and raced on ahead of us, scouting in broad circles, chasing after the diving terns and charging after deer and moose. The dog was a matter of controversy among us, but he certainly made our trip unique. François's main reason for bringing Derry along was as a 'celebrity film star' for the proposed documentary, as well as to keep away bears with his fierce, high-pitched bark. Overall, the dog was not the easiest character to get along with. When I was first introduced to Derry in California, François had warned me not to look at the dog. Seconds later the small dog lunged viciously for my face, sending me reeling backwards.

'Sorry, Tim, I should have warned you sooner that the dog was a dingo. I found him while I was studying in Australia. He arrived at our camp from the outback, starving and half dead. I took him in

and we've been together ever since. The only problem is . . . he hates people,' François had apologised.

'Yeah, he sure does,' I mused.

The wind turned southerly, gusting at 20 knots, and blowing icy sleet from the Brooks Range. Dusk arrived late, allowing us extra hours of hiking, and at 8:00 p.m. we finally found the source – a small trickle of a stream flowing from the mouth of an ice flow. It was no more than a foot wide and a few inches deep. All four of us, canine included, huddled up on the frozen moss alongside the glacier. My felt-lined gumboots had done me proud. They were not adequate for Arctic conditions, but they had at least kept out the water as we tramped through the tundra. By contrast, François and Fanie were not so lucky. The mud and water they had taken in was now a frozen paste in their hiking boots.

I pulled out my small thermometer. 'It's minus 20 degrees, guys,' I called, looking at the Celsius measure.

'And dropping,' Fanie added dryly. 'Let's eat and move off before we bloody well freeze out here.'

Clumsily we tore open a packet of biscuits and painfully struggled with frozen fingers to open two tins of tuna with a Swiss army knife.

'Derry's not looking well, I'm really worried about him,' François mumbled, protecting the short-haired dog from the biting wind.

'Yes, he's distressed all right. Can't we dress him up?' I suggested.

'Of course, why didn't I think of it?' François answered. 'Come, Derry, come here, my friend – try this.'

He took a thermal long-sleeve vest and pulled it over the dog's shaking body. We all laughed at the sight.

'Some duct tape, that's what we need,' I chuckled. I had a small roll in my jacket pocket, and taped the vest around his legs and abdomen. 'Those bears will flee when they see you now, old chap.'

Fanie produced his ever-ready hip flask of Cape brandy and we each downed a tot, savouring the warmth as it burned its way into our stomachs. We raised a toast.

'Here's to the source of the bloody Colville,' we cheered.

'If you'd told me it was going to be half as cold, I wouldn't have come near the place,' I confessed aloud.

Finishing our meal in the semi-dark, we filmed the strange gathering of three men and a dog shivering uncontrollably whilst gazing on the small trickle of water running out of the ice. Then, stiff with cold, we packed our bags and began the eight-hour hike downstream back to our canoes. I was certainly im-

Two men and a dog (François, Derry and Fanie).

pressed and surprised at both François's and Fanie's endurance and pace. Fanie had been a competent mountaineer, but as a film producer in Pretoria, his lifestyle had contained a good deal of beer drinking and cigarette smoking. At 6 foot 2 inches, he was still strong and athletic, and displayed a good sense of judgement once out on the trail. François was now a top-flight academic, writing his PhD in behavioural biology at Harvard University. He, too, was the victim of the unhealthy lifestyle of the competitive academic world. Exercising and training very little, it was only on expeditions such as these that he would be forced to draw from his naturally strong constitution. Personally, I had driven myself hard on the three-month Andes trip, and it was only now, here in the wilderness, that I realised how my body was crying out for a rest. I had rushed straight from the Colca expeditions to be here in Alaska four days later, going flat out!

We marched through the freezing night, afraid to stop longer than five minutes lest we stiffen up and not move again. At 3:00 a.m., after three short hours of darkness, the first rays of crimson light dawned in the east, and by 9:00 a.m. we were back at base camp. We pulled off our boots to dry our blistered feet, pitched our tents, and dived into our sleeping bags, utterly exhausted.

Of Novelties and Beginnings

I was up first, peering out of the tent into a clear sky. The wind that had buffeted us had died down and there was not a cloud visible on the skyline. A pungent aroma of tundra scrub filled my nostrils, and I knew we were in a place such as I had never experienced. The remoteness was overpowering. Things were so different here that we might have been on another planet. These were important moments for me, drinking in the immensity of the place. Something deep in my soul communicated with a vast wilderness that was so much bigger than I could

Our canoe carried almost 100 kg of gear & provisions.

fathom, and which quietly answered to the empty, restless feeling in me. This emptiness had been haunting me for so long that it stuck to me like a second skin. It seemed to follow me no matter where I went – to the Andes in South America, or to the big cold nothingness of Alaska!

I primed the small benzene burner and soon had it puffing away to make oatmeal porridge. Breakfast had seldom tasted better – we were famished and still weary from our marathon walk to the source of the river. The sky had changed to a watery blue with a small bank of cloud over the Brooks Range. Happy to launch our canoes at last, we packed our provisions into waterproof bags and began loading the boats. The Canadian canoe, with three weeks' stores

Smoked pancakes for breakfast.

on board, two large men and a dog, floated with its gunwales only inches above the water.

'Hey, guys, no rocking the boat – you'll sink if you do.'

My warning was more than just jest. What would they do if we came to any rapids? Well, perhaps we could dump some gear if we needed to. We launched the boats in the narrow stream, paddled 20 m, and then – crunch! – the heavy canoe promptly grounded to a halt on a gravel bar. We exchanged alarmed glances with each other, as we certainly had not expected this problem. Pushing and shoving with paddles, François and Fanie managed to float the canoe again. All the while, my kayak slipped quietly and unhindered through the shallow channels. François regularly jumped out to pull the canoe through the shallow sections, and then leapt back into the canoe only to find that Derry too had jumped into the river. This solicited infuriated yells from François! As they approached me, it was not always possible to sup-press my laughter at witnessing the crazy dog/master antics. It was not always clear which one was the master!

'Here's a good campsite. Let's pull in, we've had a hard day,' I called out at the end of the day.

François and Fanie were obviously disappointed at the dismal 7 km we had covered on the first day – a far cry from the proposed 40. The difficulty of handling an unfamiliar craft had brought some tension to their relationship. Silently I thanked my good fortune that I was on my own, master of my own canoe, from where I could quietly smile at the squabbles that emanated from the double canoe. Nevertheless, our general mood was positive, and we were all under the spell of the sheer novelty of our environment. No one told us that all novelties wear off sometime, some sooner than others.

Short tundra shrub grew sparsely in the depressions. We gathered some of its fibrous, stringy stems to start a fire, but an acrid, eye-burning smoke was

110

all we could coax from the flames. Taking turns to get the damp wood to burn was more than a challenge as the fire would simply smoulder and then die. This setback raised our stress levels considerably as we had counted on using tundra scrub for most of our cooking. The supply of benzene would certainly not last the whole trip. The landscape between the mountains and the river was gently undulating, but utterly featureless, with not a tree, a rock, or a hillock. A dismal and bleak place indeed.

'How on earth did I get myself talked into this trip?' I rebuked myself. 'I could be paddling in the warm sunshine back home. Well, I'm here now I guess, so I had better make the most of it.' The novelty had already worn off on our first day on the river.

Fanie and I shared a tent, François and his canine the other. That night the wind shrieked around our tent, the cold gnawing through our sleeping bags and into our bones. François coughed a rasping cough late into the night, sending wild thoughts racing through my head. What if François got sick with bronchitis or pneumonia? We would have to dig in and wait for him to recover. Was this wind winter's icy breath setting in, or was this just an unusual cold spell? Questions without answers scrolled through my mind.

I woke to the rustling sounds of François coaxing the fire to life. Dark clouds hung over the olive-green tundra. We cooked breakfast and by 8:30 a.m. had our tents packed and the boats loaded. A herd of moose grazed nearby, showing no fear at all. Two does frolicked up toward us, head-butting the air and kicking their heels.

'Meat won't be scarce on this trip,' Fanie laughed. 'We don't even need a shotgun – I could have caught one with my bare hands.'

'Yes, venison steaks would hit the spot,' said François, 'if we could only make a fire hot enough to roast them!'

Our safety kit included a fishing rod and lures – there simply had to be good fish in the Colville. Little did we know that our fishing rod would save our lives in the following weeks.

We floated off on our second day, but, within 50 m, the canoe again grounded to a halt. François let out a string of curses and jumped out, closely followed by Derry. This made his master roaring mad. 'Get back into the damn boat, you stupid dog!' Derry understood and before François could close in, he nimbly bounced back, soaked to the skin and with his ears pinned back.

It was a frustrating, hard day. However, we passed the Thunder Creek confluence, and the added volume of water enabled us to paddle comfortably without continuous beaching. Huge herds of caribou and moose began to appear, some at least 700-strong, grazing peacefully and quite unperturbed by our presence. Flocks of duck and geese rose into the air with surprised honks as we roused them. François dropped a duck with a shotgun and it flapped around wounded until Fanie managed to catch it and finish it off. Supper would be good tonight. The tundra scrub was also increasing in size and was now at shoulder height. We finally managed to get a fire going but it gave such low heat that it seemed more trouble than it was worth. Because of the shallow waters, progress was still very slow, even after Thunder Creek had joined the Colville. We were now averaging a mere 17 km a day.

The grinding labour gave us huge appetites, and we found ourselves consuming rather more than we could afford. Monitoring the food levels was my job, and my stress levels soared when I realised that if we did not cut back to half rations immediately, we would – in this freezing wasteland – run out of food within a week. My friends did not take kindly to my report that a cutback was necessary. The truth was we were devouring twice as much as we had ever done on the Colca, and were especially using up the oily, fatty foods.

'What about the reindeer moss idea?' Fanie suggested. 'Apparently it has saved the lives of many a hunter caught by an early winter.'

'Ja, the story goes that you eat too much of it and then you start hallucinating,' François joked.

'Okay,' I joined in, 'we'll mix it with our soup tonight and see what happens. This place needs some livening up!' The evening's pea green 'reindeer moss' soup did nothing for our stomachs, besides win some spicy criticism on how terrible it tasted.

'Okay, I guess I'll need to be a lot hungrier than I am now to eat this stuff,' François admitted.

Migration of the Wild

After 10 days on the Colville, we had covered only 250 km. Despite all the measures we had taken, our food supply was low. The trip was not working out as planned, and our attempts at morale building were not succeeding. On the contrary . . .

On the eleventh day the fine weather we had experienced took a turn for the worse. A hard headwind set in, driving a cutting rain, with the result that by 10:00 a.m., we were utterly soaked and too cold to continue. We hauled our boats out of the river and struggled to pitch our tents in the wind. We spent the day lying low, working at the impossible – trying to dry our wet clothes. The rain and wind persisted through the night, and we were forced to spend yet another day bunkered down. We lay in our tents, fantasising about delicious delicacies and wild desserts, with nothing to eat besides rice and reindeer moss, and with tea that had no sugar or milk. We had all shared our best jokes and stories, and the level of conversation began to drop dangerously low.

The rain stopped in the late afternoon and we peered gratefully out of our tents – at least the next day we could paddle again.

We rose early, hurried on by a combination of cold weather and wet clothes. Then the most amazing scene greeted us: thousands of marching caribou and elk stretching right across the horizon, their heads down as they made their way southward.

'They're migrating south. Winter must be here,' Fanie concluded glumly. 'They do this just before

And then the cold set in.

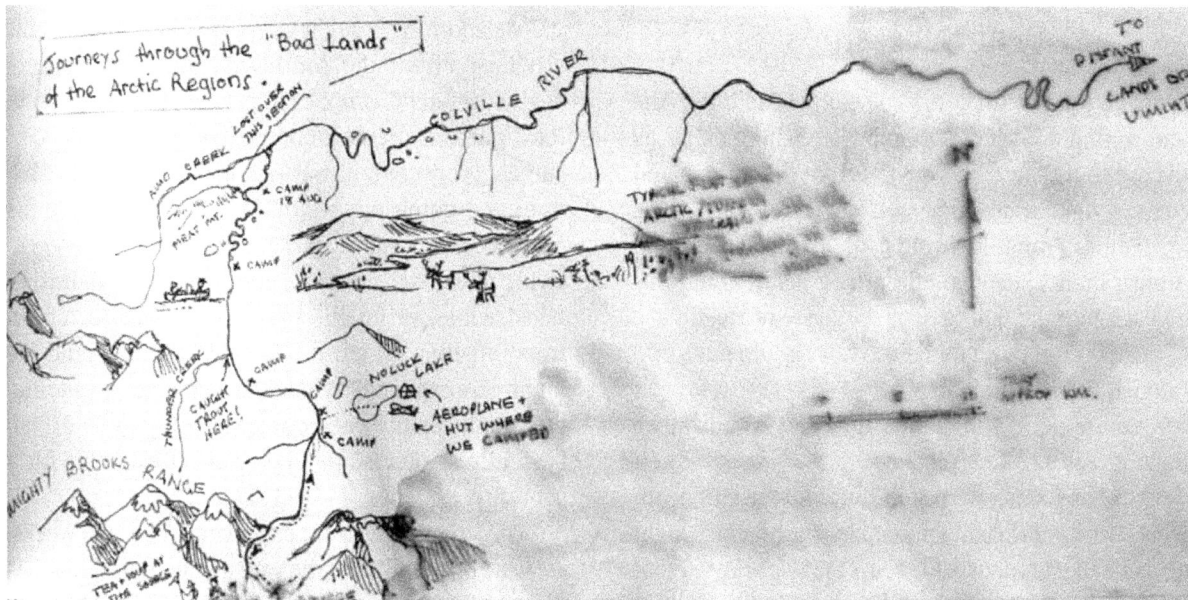

winter sets in. We're in for some interesting weather, chaps.'

François and I said nothing. We were all aware of the looming crisis. The Alaskan winter was upon us: we were not prepared for it, and our source of food was marching away from us.

'Dismal progress, food running out, animals migrating and winter almost here. Things are sure starting to hot up,' François remarked, the irony of his remark not passing unnoticed.

The great migration went on and on. Then flock after flock of duck and geese followed the caribou. We watched in awe; the rush of wings was audible, kilometres away. It was a 'fast food' exodus second to none.

'Come,' said François, 'let's get going. Remember, we still have a fishing rod. Tim, you can be our fisherman. I'll do the shooting and Fanie the filming.'

'Hey, Frans,' I chuckled, 'I'm the worst person in Alaska to be asked to do that. I'm the most useless fisherman, but I'll try.'

'Give it a go,' said Fanie encouragingly.

So we continued, our potential protein supplies disappearing into the distance.

Finding our position on the one-in-thousand maps was becoming increasingly difficult for there were no definite landmarks – another demoralising blow. Also sapping at our morale was our low daily mileage. At last we spotted two peaks in the far-off range which, together with a large bend in the river, seemed to correspond with a position on the map. But our relief soon turned sour on us.

'Guys, if we are only here it means we haven't made anything like the mileage we had thought,' François pointed out. We measured the river on the map with a piece of cotton and correlated it with our actual position, and found we had done 50 km less than we had estimated. The blow was painful; this was equivalent to losing almost three days' progress.

'Maybe we're going to spend the winter in Alaska after all,' Fanie joked grimly.

'That's fine, as long as we find more brandy!' François added.

Slowly, things were starting to fall apart.

Bear Necessities

Early on the twelfth day, I poked my head out of the tent to find a layer of soft snow stretching as far as the eye could see. It was obvious that the caribou and company had timed their trek well.

'Fanie, Frans, look outside!' I called excitedly. Almost immediately, a light drizzle set in and drove us back into the tent to debate our predicament.

'This could go on for days. We've got to push on,' I urged. 'Rain or no rain.'

'You're right, Tim,' Fanie agreed. 'We must keep making miles.'

After breakfast, we headed out into the stiff head-wind. Derry was looking miserable. The previous night he had barked furiously for hours and we guessed that there had been bears around the camp. We paddled hard, determined to make progress.

After lunch, two enormous brown bears watched us from the riverbank as we floated along. Having spotted us, they both began loping through the scrub along the bank, easily matching our pace. At first, we were surprised at their interest, but then we realised that they, too, must be hungry, and that we must appear as a pretty good meal. In those sections where we would have struggled to walk, the powerful animals loped effortlessly. Hours went by and still they tracked us. After eight hours of paddling in light snow, we were soaked through with wet and cold, and ready to camp. We pitched the tents opposite the bears on the other side of the river, knowing that our furry friends would be excellent swimmers, and that the 30 m between us would be like crossing a duck pond for them.

François slept with the shotgun at the ready and I guarded the tent door with a pair of paddles! Derry spent most of the night barking wildly from inside François's tent. After an hour or two I did not know which was worse: having the dog's shrill bark all night, or encountering two Alaskan bears?

We waited, but they never came.

The morning brought worse weather, with squalls driving in from the southwest, and sleet beating against the tent. One of the pegs had come loose in the night and a segment of the flysheet was ripped to shreds. We were still wet and cold from the day before, and going out would be crazy. We spent the next three days inside our tents while the storm raged, trying to dry our clothes. Depression and frustration raged while we fought against our wills to refrain from finishing off our feeble food supply. Would the nightmare ever end? When it appeared to be clearing, we would rapidly pack our goods only to be driven back into shelter 30 minutes later. It was time for a serious conference.

The situation was not improving. After two weeks, we were only a third of the way to the Arctic Ocean. At our present rate of consumption, we had food for only one more week. There were 600 km to go and the weather was visibly deteriorating. We had badly miscalculated our timing. Was there any other way out besides paddling down the river? Studying the map for any possible solution, we came across a single black dot marked Bradie. Surely, this must be a village. It even had an aeroplane symbol, and it was roughly halfway to the sea. I noticed Fanie pricking up his ears.

'Guys, my time's running out,' said Fanie. 'I have deadlines to meet back home, and I can see that we are not going to make it in three weeks. I would like to try to find a pilot who can take me out of this God-forsaken place, and hopefully fly me back to Kotzebue. Let's go to Bradie, what do you say?'

'What if there's nothing there, Fanie?' I answered, not really wanting to lose Fanie so early in the expedition. He was a balancing force in our team that I wouldn't like to lose, always easy-going, calm, with a sense of humour, and with excellent common sense. On the other hand, his departure would mean having more food for François and me. Then again, the thought of just François, Derry and me travelling alone through all those miles made it a tough proposition.

'Well, let's at least go and have a look,' said Fanie. 'We can't lose anything, in fact, we may even find a few more bottles of brandy there. See, it's where this small tributary joins the Colville; if we follow the tributary upstream we should find it.'

'Okay, Fanie, it'll be a pity to lose you, but I can see you're missing those bright lights of Pretoria,' I joked. 'If you have to leave, I bags your boots and jacket, oh yes, and your pocket knife.'

'Ja, and make sure you don't finish the last of the brandy before you go,' François dropped in.

'François, I can see this trip ending up like the Urubamba: just you and me left at the end. Hey, these guys who just can't *vasbyt* to the end,' I teased. 'I suppose I will have to abandon my faithful ole kayak, donate it to the Eskimos, and paddle the old barge with Fransie and Derry.'

Bradie

Three days later we arrived at a tributary which we thought led to Bradie; with no landmarks to check our position against we couldn't be sure. The thought of hiking up the wrong tributary and back was not an appealing one, yet it was a reality. I could see by the strain on Fanie's face that he was more than eager to return home. François stayed with the boats and Fanie and I started out for Bradie, our hopes high that we would find people, more food, and the sort of nutrition that our bodies were craving. We only had 15 km to walk, but, once again, the deceptive terrain fooled us and we only arrived there six hours later, exhausted and chilled to the bone.

'There it is!' I shouted as I spotted a round roof appearing above a rise. We accelerated, hopes high that we would find an aeroplane hangar and a small village, hamburgers, hot chips, greasy food . . . but the reality was devastating. The hut was the only thing in a 'village' that did not exist. We sat down on the doorstep of the iron-sheeted building. The locked door was battered, as though someone had pelted it with a sledgehammer.

'It's the bears,' Fanie said dryly. 'Look, they've even tried to bite their way through!' We managed to gain entrance without breaking the lock. As the door swung open, we saw two bunks and a table, on

Looks like easy hiking - but don't believe it.

115

which there were a few half-finished bottles of jam, some peanut butter and a few slices of bread, brittle as toast. Fanie nibbled on a slice. 'It's fine, like toast, still fresh!'

On a wrapped pack of butter, we found a date – 1979. The food had been here four years and it was still fresh. Ravenously we devoured it, after which Fanie reclined with a few cigars that he had discovered. I took a photo of him sitting in the doorway, smoking a cigar and reading a Playboy magazine that he pulled out of a box.

Well, no aeroplanes, but at least a good laugh, half a meal, and some cigars.

We learned later that the hut was once a survey point. Disappointed, we set off through the tundra bog to arrive back at our camp in the dark, footsore but at least able to share our discovery – and a cigar – with François.

'Sorry, Fanie,' François laughed. 'You aren't going to get rid of us that easily. I'm afraid we're here to stay.'

Fanie's brandy was down to one quarter of a bottle but we treated ourselves to one capful each, toasted one anothers' health and the 600 km that were still to come.

'Don't worry, guys,' I announced. 'Tomorrow I'm going trout fishing. I'm going to catch fish for Africa – big fish. We'll have fish braai (barbeque) every night; there'll be so many fish around that we'll be throwing them back – wait and see!' My boasting was half the result of the tot of brandy, half to cheer up the group.

The following day, although the rain and sleet had stopped, a freezing headwind drove against us, cutting through our damp clothing. For eight hours we pushed ahead, determined to prove that we could make a respectable distance and that we could break the negative mindset that was eating at our spirits. With a line and rod tied to my boat, I trawled a line hour after hour without a single bite.

I was busy winding in with the reel and packing the rod away, when the unthinkable happened. I carelessly let go of the rod and saw it slip into the icy river. The current was fast flowing and only one-and-a-half metres deep. It was then that the impact of what I had just done struck me; I had thrown away our main

Bradie – sketched after Fanie + I
walked 5 hrs to look for food
TIM B.

lifeline for catching food. Desperately I swung my kayak around and paddled hard to find the spot where I thought the rod might be. The water was relatively clear, and I could faintly make out the bottom of the stream. Each time I lowered my paddle into the river to drag it along the surface, the kayak would frustratingly drift a few metres downstream. Again and again I tried. About to give up and ready to tell my friends the disastrous news, I pulled into the bank almost 20 m from where I had lost the rod. I peered into the stream and my eye caught something move.

There was the rod, slowly moving along the bed. I lowered my paddle as deep as I could, lifted it, and it obediently rose and returned to the hands of its master. Overwhelming relief swept through me.

There was still time to land a fish or two before the others arrived, so I pushed ahead to find a spot and to set up camp. A small crystal-clear stream trickled into the river. 'This is the spot,' I said and leapt out and began casting my line, and on the fifth cast the line jerked hard. I slowly reeled in, careful not to make a mistake. There it was, dangling on the end of my line, a one-and-a-half-foot grayling. I couldn't believe my eyes – I had actually caught a fish! I whooped, my confidence soared, and my depression turned to pure joy.

That night we crouched in the eye-burning smoke, attempting to make a fire with wet twigs and kindling. 'I guess this is my punishment for being such a good fisherman,' I grumbled. 'I'm ready to eat the bloomin' thing raw.'

Lost

'Hey, guys,' I reported, 'we're going to have to cut back again on our food rationing, we're completely out of —'

'Well, do something about it – get your bloody fishing going,' interjected Fanie in pure frustration. 'Where are those fish barbecues? Come on, Biggs, make it happen, man!'

Fishing had now become a top priority. I was fishing for survival and for the first time in my life, I began to love it. By this stage, the Etiuluk and Killik tributaries had joined the Colville and had doubled its volume. The river was flowing well and for the first time we were managing between 60 and 70 km a day.

It was now 27 August, but as with most expeditions, we were beginning to lose all sense of time. Life was a cycle of waking to another freezing day, eating, packing the boats, paddling until we could paddle no more, mooring as late as 8:00 p.m., struggling to get a meal cooked, and then crawling exhausted and dirty into wet sleeping bags. Our clothes were greasy, stiff and reeking with weeks of unwashed sweat and dirt. 'I'd hate to think how we are smelling,' Fanie remarked. 'Maybe that's why we don't see bears around us anymore. You see, François, we didn't need to bring Derry to chase away bears after all; we do it ourselves.'

It was during one of these periods of our 'time warp', while I was paddling along one of the thousand, seemingly endless long and boring flat stretches of river, that I called out to my friends, 'I'll paddle on to do some fishing, and find a campsite before dark, see you later.'

'Good luck. We're starving. Catch a big one.'

After paddling hard for an hour, I rounded a corner and came to an unexpected split in the river. The current had accelerated and a large island lay between two channels. The right channel was the obvious choice because of its size, but before I knew it, I was caught off guard and swept down the smaller left channel.

'I'll make it back to the right side as soon as I've passed this island,' I said to myself, but alas, the island went on and on and on. Suddenly it struck me that François and Fanie would probably take the larger right channel. Should I go back and wait for them, or continue? Paddling back was out of the question as the current was far too strong, and to climb out and fight my way through the head-high vegetation would take too long and may cause me to miss them. I decided to keep on paddling, certain that the island would end eventually. I paddled on cautiously until to my horror, the river became braided, breaking into a maze of smaller islands and channels that appeared to stretch out for kilometres. A heavy drizzle had set in and I could barely distinguish these islands through the drizzle and the approaching dusk. I broke into a cold sweat. I knew I was in for an epic!

If François and Fanie went right at the fork while I was floundering around in the wrong channel, they could sail on downstream assuming I had gone on, and we would miss each other. On the other hand, if they arrived at the fork and decided to wait for me while I paddled on, we would still be separated. Without any options, I decided to race upstream and try to meet them before they passed by. I scrambled out on the left bank and began running upstream. Almost immediately, I sank thigh-deep in soft, peaty mud. When I pulled my leg out, my gumboot stayed behind, sucked off by the mud. Plunging my arms into the mud I wrestled it out. Every minute counted. I charged on, ploughing through the head-high scrub, until I plunged headlong into a reed-covered, stagnant pool. Spluttering, I lifted myself out of the muddy slime. 'No, this isn't going to work; I will never make it in time,' I told myself. I had no option but to reverse my plans and head back downstream in my kayak again, hopefully to meet up with them in the main channel. Back in my kayak I sprinted downstream, taking small side channels to my right. Eventually I burst into the main channel. It was almost dark and now raining steadily. I had to make another key decision: wait for them there or continue downstream. With some doubt, I decided that I would wait for exactly 30 minutes. If they hadn't pitched, I would push on downstream. My imagination soon got to work, and I thought of having to spend the night alone on the icy Colville – no food, no tent, and with just the wet clothes I had on. Sure, I had the stove, but not the benzene. No, I simply had to find

François and Fanie. Ten minutes passed – nothing, then 15 minutes – and then 30 minutes, still no sign of them. I began to prepare to move on as they had obviously passed already. We were now well and truly separated.

I decided to wait five more minutes and then paddle to where the islands ended. There I would wait for them, even if it meant a cold night out on the tundra. After five minutes, I turned into the current to paddle downstream. Just then, I heard voices from the dark and my eyes caught some movement . . . François and Fanie drifted into sight. With immense relief I shouted.

'François, Fanie, I'm here!'

They pulled in and we regrouped.

'Hey, Tim, where the hell have you been? We waited for you up at the split for ages; we would have lost each other in the islands. Why didn't you wait for us, man, you didn't think?'

'Guys, I'm sorry. It was stupid of me. The current took me left before I twigged what was going on,' I apologised profusely. The Colville had taught us yet another valuable river lesson – never split up when islands divide the river, and have a plan of action handy in case you do. That night I was in the dog box again. My wrongdoing? No fish for supper!

The sense of humour that had kept us going now reached an all-time low. One had to be blind or deaf not to pick up how we started to irritate each other. François's and Fanie's dialogue had deteriorated into crude Afrikaans joking, followed by extravagant roars of laughter. A definite rift had developed – François and Fanie being old-time Afrikaner friends and me being the Englishman and odd man out. I was determined not to let it get me down. We had to make it to the river's end, and then I wouldn't have to see either of them – or my less than favourite dog – ever again. I did not usually feel or reason like this, but this vast Alaskan wasteland sure had a way of playing with your mind.

Derry Versus Tim

Derry seemed to be the only one who was eating well. The 25 kg bags of balanced dog food that we had brought along were lasting well, and he looked in peak condition. We, on the other hand, looked pale and gaunt.

'Derry, come here boy, how was your supper?' I joked. 'Was it okay, old chap? Let me have a taste of your dessert . . . mmm . . . tastes so good, Derry.' The dog and I had not hit it off from the start. He was a one-man dog, and he did not appreciate my attention at all. Tonight was no exception. All I got for my troubles were pinned-back ears and a low growl.

'Okay, okay, don't take it to heart. But I still want to try your delicacies sometime.'

They certainly smelled and looked better than rice without salt, or the tasteless, green reindeer moss. Not thinking much of what I was doing, I crawled to the back of François's tent and took a handful of the reddish, doughnut-shaped dog biscuits. They were slightly salty and had a good savoury meat flavour. I nibbled one, and then another. With each bite, they tasted better and better.

'Guys, try these, they're great – have some for dessert.' Guffaws came from François and Fanie.

'Tim, we'll have to lock you up when we get back; you're going bananas – too much time in the wilderness.'

'Yeah, I guess I'm losing it. I'm afraid it's been setting in for the past few years. Let me know when I start barking and growling,' I said, as I continued chewing at the biscuits. From that night on my relationship with Derry deteriorated even further. Each time I took a handful, he growled at me menacingly with ears well pinned back.

It was while packing up camp the following morning that I began to pull out a coil of rope. It jammed and I gave it a sharp tug. There was an explosion of action. Derry had been relaxing behind the tent with the rope passing under his torso and between his

Derry - my arch enemy.

hind legs. Rising a full half metre into the air and with a furious yelp, he sprang at me, his incisors sinking into my right hand. I yelled and kicked out with my gumboot, connecting Derry squarely between the legs. There was a shocked grunt as the dog dropped to the ground like a bag of cement. Luckily, François came to the rescue before an out-and-out brawl started. I had the canoe paddles ready for a second round, aiming for his skull.

'Tim, Tim, leave him, man, you'll kill him!' François shouted.

'Won't be sorry if I did,' I warned, nursing my bloodied hand. 'You'd better look after your dog from now on or we'll be having real hot dogs for supper one of these nights.'

François was not amused by my threats. 'Hey, you lay off my damn dog, it's not his fault,' he snapped.

All the while Fanie sat back in the canoe, struggling to stifle a grin.

'Come on, guys,' he called out, 'we've had a hard night, let's not start the day like this. Tim, leave Derry alone, don't be a bully.'

A bad start indeed. If there is one thing that I've always found hard to cope with, it's being bitten by a dog. My temper flares up like a blast in a boiler tube. I felt I deserved the right to sulk for a few hours, paddling on ahead of my friends and my 'favourite' dingo.

The Ice Age

The following day we woke up to falling snow again, the undulating landscape an unending sheet of white, broken only by the shadow of a depression or a slight rise.

Our upturned boats were capped with snow. When I inspected my kayak, I noticed a thick layer of ice protruding from the bank. I placed my foot on it, and a large slab broke off with a sharp crack. The river was beginning to ice up! Calling to my friends, we contemplated this latest challenge. The Collville had dealt us another blow. With snow, one still had mobility, but with the river icing up we would be trapped.

Fanie could not let the opportunity pass for another dry observation. 'Well, at least we won't have mosquitoes to trouble us any more.'

We stood gazing across at the whitened landscape, wondering what to do next. Our clothes and sleeping bags were wet, cold was gnawing at our bones, our feet were continually frozen in wet gumboots, and to cap it all we were starving. Oh yes, and then there was the dog.

The harsh Alaskan wilderness was continuing to work on our minds. Fanie had brought along a book, *Tales from Alaska*, by Robert W. Service. Each night we would read a few of his salty poems, and each night they became more real to us. Stories of how a certain Sam McGee prayed to be burned in an incinerator when he died so that the cold would at last be driven from his bones were a little too real.

There are strange things done in the midnight sun
By the men that moil for gold.
The Arctic trails have their secret tales
That would make your blood run cold;
The northern lights have seen queer sights,
But the queerest they ever did see
Was that night on the marge of lake Lebarge
I cremated Sam McGee.

First the caribou & elk migrated south ~ & then it started snowing.

... and now the river's icing up.

Umiat

I had often pondered how the early explorers who had journeyed to the poles, Scott and Amundsen, survived in those ultra-extreme conditions. The comparison immediately made me feel better. Our trip was a picnic in the park compared with theirs; well, at least we could now relate somewhat to the cold wet and low morale that they must have suffered.

A major landmark was now approaching, Umiat, the sole settlement on the river, positioned, it seemed, about 200 km from the Arctic Sea. If we could only reach it before the river froze completely we might yet survive. Silently we hoped that it would not be another Bradie. On our map, Umiat was indicated by two dots as opposed to Bradie's one. Surely this would be an inhabited outpost! After a short tent meeting, we decided to 'give it horns' and push on to Umiat.

The days that followed were intensely miserable as we fought against strong headwinds and paddled around the long meandering bends of the river. Our journey had now turned into a race against time, a true race for survival. A depressing silence descended as we broke camp next morning in the semi dark. We then paddled two-and-a-half hours before climbing stiffly on to the frozen bank to stamp our feet and devour our rations of two biscuits each. The next stage, another two-and-a-half hours, would find the three of us and the dog sitting huddled together for lunch, struggling with frozen fingers to cut open the tin of tuna. Our benzene was about to run out and tea was off the menu. Fifteen minutes on the water's edge was all we allowed ourselves before we paddled off again for the next four-hour stage.

On 30 August, we spotted a silver galvanised roof peeping over an ice-covered bank. Umiat! We had been on the river for 22 days, and joy and relief consumed us as if we were starving, shipwrecked sailors. We left our craft at the river's edge and clambered hastily up the muddy bank. Two figures emerged from a building, and froze as we appeared over the bank. One then slipped into a hut and came out with a shotgun. We raised our hands and waved. 'Good day, can you help us? We need help and food. Is this Umiat?'

OJ Smith

The big man with the shotgun, who had a fur cap pulled over his ears, approached us cautiously and looked us up and down. We hadn't bathed for a month and we must have reeked; our hair was long and our beards bedraggled.

'Is this Umiat?' François asked again.

'Yes, it is,' came an American accent from the big Eskimo. 'Where on earth have you come from? It looks like you need some help.'

'Yes, we are South Africans canoeing down the Colville,' said François, introducing himself. 'We started in the Brooks Range, but we got caught by the weather, we're out of food. Can you help us?'

The second man began to smile slowly and looked friendlier.

'Food, eat!' he said in broken English, pointing to his mouth and rubbing his stomach.

'Yes, yes, food, eat,' we replied together.

The second man looked at us and I could see the empathy in his eyes. He clearly related to our condition and understood what hunger was.

'I'm O.J.,' the big Alaskan introduced himself. 'Follow me, let's see what we can do.'

A fixed-wing Cessna stood outside a hangar alongside five or six well-constructed metal buildings and fuel tanks. I could sense Fanie rejoicing. We were back in civilisation; we'd found a plane.

It was midday and the seven men posted at the base had finished their afternoon meal. A short chef

Fanie's face lit up when he spotted the Cessna (Umiat).

122

Just couldn't resist the ice cream.

brought us three large plates of food. Our mouths drooled when we saw the venison steaks, vegetables and fried chips. We tried not to disgrace ourselves by shovelling the food down with our hands. Derry could not suppress a long wolf-like howl. The chef watched wide-eyed, disappeared, brought us another helping, and then another. By now five large men had gathered round to watch us with a combination of amusement and alarm at the volumes of food we shovelled down.

'Where's your "dawg" from?' one of them drawled. 'Looks like a cross between a coyote and a mongoose.' We all laughed except François.

'Well, he kept the bears from us,' Fanie threw in, 'and kept ole Tim in hand.' The men raised their eyebrows.

'Ja,' added François. 'He's actually half-wild, half-domestic. The Australians use them for cattle herding.'

Our hunger was uncontrollable, our bodies screaming for oily, fatty foods. My shrunken stomach eventually started to ache unbearably. I had eaten too much too fast. I could see Fanie and François had suffered the same fate. We knew how to resolve it: lie back, move as little as possible, and close your eyes.

'I hope these guys realise that relaxing is the South African way of showing how great the meal was,' I said, stretching my arms and yawning, struggling to keep my eyes open. My whole body was calling for rest and warmth.

We chatted to the two men who could speak English. It seemed that we were at a hunting camp used by wealthy businessmen, who would fly in for hunting holidays. They used two planes, one of which was a floatplane. They told us story after story of narrow escapes and near crash-landings on treacherous, pebbly beaches. One of the pilots, Jim, knew Ross Hodgers from Kotzebue. As they showed us

123

around the settlement, we stopped at a soft-serve ice cream machine and our host generously offered us a cone. 'Yes, yes,' my body yelled out, that was what I needed. We gulped them down. Ice cream never tasted so good as it did that day. Jim offered us another round, we could not turn down his offer, nor could we resist asking for another round. To retain some dignity, Fanie produced a $50 note, and put in a bid to purchase the entire tank of ice cream. We were in paradise; even Derry over-indulged, gulping down bowlfuls of the creamy coils. The scene was comical; our Alaskan hosts watched in disbelief until at last we could feel our sugar-levels balancing out. The famine was over.

Now that we were back to normal physically and, to a degree at least, mentally, it was time to debate whether to fly to the end of the Colville or to continue paddling it. The flying option was more than tempting, since there were still 300 km to go. I held my ground.

'No way, guys! We can't come all this way and not finish the course – it just wouldn't be right. Come on, Frans, let's keep going; it's only another five or six days,' I said, using all my powers of persuasion, 'and at least we'll have food now.'

Fanie, however, was adamant. His job back in South Africa was on the line, and he had simply had enough. Much to our surprise, he told us that he had already organised and paid for a ticket on the first departing plane out of Umiat. François, by contrast, was still undecided and obviously locked in thought. The idea of re-entering the inhospitable, cold Colville was nightmarish to us both.

'Okay, Tim, I'll join you,' announced François finally.

'Brilliant, Frans, that's great, we'll make it.'

The time had come for Fanie to leave us. We shook hands and thanked each other. Minutes later François and I watched how the small, red floatplane banked steeply as it headed for Nuiqsut, our friend

Lunch stop with no food to eat (−25°c).

124

Fanie seated snugly on board (and my old blue kayak strapped securely to a float).

François and I were back on the trail once more. This would be a hard leg, as we were both mentally and physically drained. However, the end was now in sight.

The Last Haul

The following morning François, Derry and I made our way back to the old red canoe. We restocked with sugar, milk powder, salt, cooking oil, butter and anything greasy and fatty we could find. Three hundred kilometres stretched before us; the finishing line was within reach. The grey waters of the Colville had slowed down as they meandered in giant, snake-like coils through the tundra plains. The wind that greeted us was a headwind on one bend, and would be a tailwind on the next. We battled on through snow and sleet – a routine of early rising, 10 hours of paddling a day, pitching tent and camping, eating and sleeping.

All going well we would make it in five days. Every day we ticked off the miles, bend by bend, kilometre by kilometre, hour by hour. We were making it. Our casual cruise down the Colville had become a super challenge, one that had caught us off guard and stretched us to our limits. Howling headwinds drove sleet and rain against us and halved our speed. Each day we watched the ice growing further, winning its battle to cover the 300-m width of the Colville.

At one point, we carelessly missed a paddle stroke and were too slow to brace and correct ourselves. The overladen canoe rolled dangerously and shipped some water. We frantically braced with our paddles to avoid capsizing, shocked at how close we had come to disaster. A swim in these conditions might have been fatal – even if we managed to swim to shore, hypothermia would have set in.

'What a way to go!' the thought flashed through my mind. 'To die in the middle of a dead flat stretch of Alaskan river, so far from home, in a place so cold and barren.' I even went so far as to pray to the god (or whatever it was that had helped me off the Andes Mountains some years earlier). 'Oh God, please help us. We need to get out of this godforsaken place.'

Somehow, I saw myself as a hypocrite. Why was it that I had the gall to call out to this god on all my big trips, and yet I had never been prepared to get to know him? I had to recognise that I conveniently forgot as soon as my crisis was over, and then arrogantly blundered on until I was in a jam again. I had noticed several times Fanie reading from a small Bible, and had secretly scorned him, wondering what he was drawing from it. My mind even backtracked to the early 1970s and our Springbok tour to Denmark, where I had seen my Afrikaans teammate, Stefan Hugo, reading his Bible quietly – he was a guy I respected. Maybe there was something in this god after all.

On our fourth day out of Umiat, we noticed an abandoned Eskimo fishing hut, with an ice cellar for storing fish and a low canvas roof. Our spirits lifted; we sensed that the end of the trip was approaching. At the end of that day, we glimpsed in the distance a silvery, corrugated-iron roof.

'There it is, Frans, that must be Nuiqsut,' I called out. 'We are here, we've made it!'

The Final Twist

The sweetest sight for a person's eyes is the treasured, long-awaited goal of his dreams. This was the case as a line of low, timber-framed buildings floated into view. Then came a small deserted jetty, and alongside it some old powerboats of different sizes. Emotions welled up; we were incredibly relieved to be here, but physically and emotionally, we were on 'empty', with red lights flashing.

With no one to welcome us in we tied our boat to the jetty, hauled ourselves onto the walkway and walked towards a drab timber building. François knocked. A few seconds later the door opened with a creak and an Eskimo policeman looked us up and down.

'You're the South Africans?' he asked.

'Yes we are, sir; we've been on the river.'

'Yeah, I heard from Jim at Umiat that you would be popping in. We've been waiting for you. Like some coffee and cake? It's the first time we've heard of anyone crazy enough to canoe this ole river – especially in wintertime. You folks are lucky you didn't get snowed in. You could have perished out there you know – but, well, you're here. Well done!'

Looking down at the shivering dog, wrapped in his brightly coloured paddling vests, he remarked, 'As for this "dawg" – miracle he made it.'

'Yeah, miracle indeed,' I thought to myself.

We sat around the small desk, loudly sipping thick coffee from a tin mug. We had reached the end but had not quite completed our mission. One more small stage remained before heading for home. We wanted to taste the salt water of the Arctic Ocean, as that would really signify the end of our journey. François politely asked the policeman if he knew someone with a boat who could take us.

'Sure, I've got a young lad who can run you out; it's only one to two miles.'

Gerald was a stocky Eskimo lad who wore yellow oilskins and an amused expression. We boarded his boat, the Johnson engine kicked in, and we were off to the Arctic Ocean, the river water pounding against the hull. Now we understood why Eskimos developed that fatty pouch on their eyelids. François and I could not even raise our heads into the sleet and biting wind, whereas Gerald stood erect, staring straight ahead.

At last: the Arctic Ocean! We could make out the thin, white line of an ice cap in the distance. Large, rolling swells were sweeping in from the northwest. François and I both dipped our hands in the ocean scooping up a mouthful of water. 'Salt water, Tim,' François shouted. We laughingly slapped each other on the back, and shook hands.

Aloofly Gerald watched us and continued racing out to sea.

'That's fine, Gerald,' said François, 'you can turn back now, we're happy.'

We were a good 2 km offshore. He revved the engines and began to swing around shoreward, but immediately the motor spluttered and stalled. We tried not to look alarmed, noticing now for the first

The first sign of Eskimos ~ a fishing camp.

time that there were no paddles or life jackets on board. The small boat broached the swell and rolled dangerously. Gerald was bent over fiddling with the throttle mechanism. I moved over to see if I could help. The cable had sprung out of the worn mechanism and he was clumsily loosening a screw with a screwdriver. Suddenly the boat lurched unexpectedly and he flung his arm out to support himself. The screwdriver dropped from his hand like a stone and disappeared into the sea. That was our only tool. Helplessly I looked around: we had no paddles, no anchor or life jackets, and now the gusting wind was pushing us to the ice pack.

'Frans, we're in trouble again,' I said. No one had seen the boat leave, and we would not be missed until nightfall.

'It can't be!'

I found my Swiss army knife in my pocket, and set about carefully unscrewing the throttle mechanism. The slide was so worn that it didn't surprise me that it had failed. It did not take me long to reassemble it.

We were now 3 to 4 km out to sea and the wind was gaining in force. Gerald pulled once, pulled again, and on the third attempt the motor roared to life. Without hanging around, we sped back to Nuiqsut, wondering whether there could possibly be anything else in store for us.

The next day we boarded a plane for Anchorage. It flew over the Hudson Bay oil fields, and we stared down at the rapidly freezing Colville. It was covered with snow and was very austere.

'You know,' said François philosophically, 'you've got to hate a place a lot before you can grow to love it. I think I could still love this place. Someday I'd like to return.'

I remained silent, pondering our epic journey. I was not sure that I would return. All I knew was this: I was glad to be out of it.

Our epic trip into the Arctic Sea.

The Colville delta.

Chapter 5

THE RIVER OF LIFE

Obsessions

I've shared much so far about the thrills and spills experienced during this early, carefree and exhilarating stage of my life. I now want to share about changes that were happening to me spiritually and in my personal life. After returning from the Colville in 1983 things were happening to me that I could not fully understand, nor did I seem to have any control over them. The big rivers of the Andes and other factors had inexplicably forced me to re-examine myself and in fact my entire philosophy of life. I had reached a crisis point.

After spending my entire school career at Ixopo High School, I had spent a year in the military before studying geology at the University of Natal in Pietermaritzburg. It was here that I rekindled my love for canoeing. I had never been much of a 'girl's guy', but in that season of 1973, I fell in love – head over heels, with a sleek, slender and beautifully shaped canoe! I was stoked.

This interest developed when my older brother, David, arrived home one day with a 17-foot, red racing canoe strapped to the roof of his Mini. My family was pleased with David's interest. He had contracted severe and debilitating polio when he was only 18 months old. Now he was a hero to me. He sported a powerful upper body and a personality to match, and had taken to canoeing like a duck to water.

At about the same time, I had become friends with Rory Pennefather. Rory's passion for the sport matched my own, and his uncanny ability to read water and find the fastest line down rapids held me in awe. With his help I found my first racing canoe and together we started competing in local races,

A new dream is born.

learning the ways of rivers and of canoes. As I grew to love the sport I developed a secret dream – to reach the top in canoeing, to win races and to represent South Africa in international competitions. Over the next couple of years the fixation grew and was finally realised in 1976. I sincerely believed that this would satisfy the deep longing that had been within me as long as I could remember. With headlong abandon, I dived into my new sport with all my heart. Sadly, my professors viewed this misdirected passion with concern and wondered whether I could ever pour half as much energy into my studies.

I finally managed to break into the ranks of the old guard, those hardened athletes who had dominated South African racing for the past decade (Tony Scott, André Collins, Robbie Stewart, Sunley Uys, Pete Peacock, Paul Chalupsky and the likes). The national trials for a Springbok tour to Europe were to be held on the Berg River near Cape Town. The trials saw me finishing a close second to the country's top marathon paddler, Stefan Hugo. To my delight, my friends and teammates Rory, Clive Curson (who later joined us

on the Urubamba River) and I were selected for the six-man team. I was thrilled – one step closer to reaching my dream.

Six weeks later, we represented our country at the Gudenå marathon in Denmark, the first event of the tough European circuit. Rory and I raced in a K2 (doubles canoe) in the gruelling 120 km flat-water marathon. We paddled our hearts out, winning on the first day, but finally finishing a close second to a crack British crew. I was thrilled to experience the privilege of racing against these world-class athletes; my dream was happening – but sadly this happiness was short-lived. The reality of politics began to rear its head. Due to South Africa's policy of apartheid, our country's sportsmen were under an international sporting ban. It was not long before word leaked out that South Africans were competing, and the result was an immediate ban from the racing circuit. As we left, suitcase in hand, the same old feeling of emptiness filled me: feelings of deep disappointment, strong emotion, backed by emptiness. I had raced for four years, season in and season out, had made the national team, raced abroad, attained my degree, yet I

My friend and double's partner ~ Rory Pennefather.

130

My passion ~ the Duzi Canoe Marathon. Rob Stewart and me in K2.

felt lonelier and more unfulfilled than ever. It seemed futile – chasing after this sport which I had thought would satisfy the hunger in my soul. My dream that had held such hope and meaning, slipped out of sight like a vanishing mirage in the desert.

Something was wrong, badly wrong. I needed to try something else, to set new targets. There had to be something more fulfilling and meaningful in my life. My obsession to search for this elusive treasure was stoked more than ever before.

There was, however, one more goal to set myself before I moved on from racing, and that was to win the Duzi Canoe Marathon, South Africa's premier, most popular canoeing event. The 'Duzi' is a three-day-long marathon through 120 km of rugged terrain, following the Msunduzi and then Umgeni River from Pietermaritzburg to the mouth at Durban. Even to say that one had finished this gruelling race was the equivalent to an initiation into manhood for local sportsmen. For me, the Duzi embodied the very essence

of racing in Africa: a combination of paddling and portaging (running with one's canoe on shoulder along narrow cattle paths over rock-strewn hills) and then leaping back into the river. It had all the ingredients that I loved – rugged, competitive, exciting and adventurous. I longed to win the race, but there was one giant hurdle: a river genius called Graeme Pope-Ellis! Graeme had dominated the marathon for an astonishing 7 years! His uncanny skills and his knowledge of the river had justly made him a legend in sporting circles. Even today he is fondly referred to as 'The Pope' and is undoubtedly one of the country's greatest athletes.

It was 1977. I was completing my BSc Honours in engineering geology at Durban when I was approached by Robbie Stewart, a powerful and charismatic Springbok paddler. Rob had been pipped to the finishing post into second place by 'The Pope', for no less than six consecutive years. We were both driven by a common goal – to beat The Pope!

Duzi highlights.

'Come on, Tim,' said Robbie. 'Someone's got to dethrone him, we can do it.'

I accepted the challenge. On 22 January 1979, Robbie and I almost wept with emotion as we crossed the winning line ahead of the field at Blue Lagoon. Oh that sweet taste of success, it's so good! In 1982, I teamed up with my younger brother and close friend, Dan, for another attempt at gold. Dan was as passionate about running as I was about canoeing, and had achieved no less than five gold medals in the famous 89-km Comrades Marathon. This attempt at the Duzi was another thrilling race, and together we managed to break the tape ahead of Graeme and Tim Cornish. Although I had now managed to bag two wins in the singles section, and two wins overall in doubles, I still recognised 'The Pope' as the true king of the Duzi. I might have been slightly swifter on foot, and faster on the water, but over the course I was no match for his superior river knowledge and his uncanny ability to race through the rough terrain.

My racing season had closed, and another call, which seemed more exciting and adventurous, now drew me on.

Winning the Duzi with my brother Dan.

Carrying On

Long before our Urubamba expedition in 1981, I had become fascinated by the Andes Mountains and the steep rivers running off their slopes. Surely this was the most exciting place to explore, and the place for the ultimate adventure. Yes, this would be what would fire me up. Was life not for exploring new rivers, for pushing oneself to the limit; letting your heart run wild?

After the Urubamba I teamed up with a Polish team of river runners and explorers, Canoandes. In 1983 we ran a first descent of the Apurimac's Black Canyon, followed by a *National Geographic* backed descent of the world's deepest canyon, the Colca Canyon. Then followed the icy experience of the Colville River in Alaska, and with each new expedition came the reward of thrills, danger, fun and the emotional gala of having successfully completed another great mission. It was with alarm that I noticed that after each trip I sported a bunch more grey hairs on my head.

I was now 30 years old, pretty much in my prime physically. I had chased after my goals and hunted them down one after the other. Most of them had gone my way, a few had not. I had more trophies than I had room for and yet, uncannily, that familiar emptiness of heart still remained. I did not know what to do.

Morally I was on a downward spiral. My lifestyle had become increasingly more selfish and self-centred. I was giving less and less, wanting more and more, and depending more than ever on my ego to sustain me. In my heart, I knew that life for me was not what it was supposed to be. I had tried my hardest to chase the things that I was passionate about and I had found them. However, they had only left me unfulfilled and depression invaded my soul like a dark cloud. I could no longer spontaneously roar with laughter. Even my kayaking did not taste as sweet as it had before. The fear of drowning was beginning to stalk me – how many chances did I have left in this game?

Margie

In 1983, home from South America, I was back in my old stamping-grounds in Cape Town, where I worked for a geo-technical consulting firm. Fortunately my bosses, Tony Dick and Andy Forbes, who were both friends of mine, were tolerant of my frequent expeditions and eccentric urges, and had been willing to hold a post open for me.

It was in Cape Town in 1984 that I met someone who would change my life radically. Margie Quirke was a soft-spoken, attractive architecture student who I had met at a canoeing marathon. We took an immediate liking to each other, and from the outset I sensed that this could be a serious relationship. There was something about Margie that set her apart. I was drawn and attracted to find out more – I had never known anyone else with those qualities of warmth, strength and luring femininity. Margie provided me with some powerful input, and it was not what I wanted to hear.

She told me that she was a Christian – ouch!

My friends derived much mirth from this new development, especially as my history with girls had so far been dismal. I never seemed to have time to share my lifestyle with anyone else. Along with my fellow geologists I had made the most of Cape Town's bright lights and fine weather. We partied hard and we played even harder. Weekends were one adventure after another, pleasure upon pleasure, filled with kayaking, rock-climbing, cycling, windsurfing, racing and whatever we could find to do. I did not have space or place for anyone else – but Margie put a change to that. Our relationship developed cautiously, with weekend visits to the 'mother city' after a hard week's work in the 12-km Hex River tunnel, which was being constructed near Cape Town.

Now, suddenly, I had to work a woman into my hectic, hedonistic life. The result was a great improvement in quality of life, for now there was a gentle person joining me for a meal and someone to share

Margie

a late-night cappuccino with. Margie had a personality that radiated both warmth and strength, and a character that was underpinned by gentleness and depth.

Choices

I did not like Margie's revelation. I had always made a point of steering well clear of Christians. As a result, our relationship stalled a little because I resisted her beliefs. Margie, on the other hand, was resolute and not one to be walked over by an eccentric geologist and adventure-seeker. We were driving through Cape Town one day when we had our first clash.

'Tim, I'm feeling uncomfortable about us carrying on; we are on different paths spiritually. I can see you aren't happy about me being a Christian, something must change,' Margie challenged.

There it was. Her intentions were direct and it brought clarity to the situation. Her ultimatum knocked me back badly, and I realised just how important her beliefs were to her. I also realised how important Margie was to me. I did not want to lose her.

'What do you mean? I *am* a Christian,' I said, hoping that would settle the argument right there and then.

Margie gently held her ground, 'No, you are not, Tim, and you know it. Didn't you admit that you can't stand being with Christians?' Margie had me. She was right. While at university I had developed an irrational dislike for outspoken Christians who I had come across. They somehow 'yanked my chain', and set off a bad reaction within me. Sitting in the car, my blood started to boil, but Margie was right. Christianity was absent in my childhood – going to church at Easter and Christmas in the small village church in Ixopo certainly did not amount to anything more than a tradition.

'Okay, okay – whatever this Christianity was about, I concede – I wasn't any part of it.' My hackles rose at the thought of being tied in knots by this woman; my blood reached boiling point. The Urubamba was easier to navigate than this mess I had got myself into.

'I'm sick of you damned Christians! You think you have it all and no one else counts!' I retorted. 'What's better about you than anyone else? I can't stand it.'

Margie looked at me silently. There was no retaliation forthcoming. I struggled to compose myself – I was not used to this kind of challenge. I did not need this in my life. Who did she think she was, anyway? I dropped her off at her flat feeling upset and confused. I bade her a forced goodbye and sped off to Worcester (about an hour-and-a-half's drive away) to be in the comfortable company of my mates. At least they did not challenge me on these outrageous, embarrassing issues.

A week after our argument, I was back in Cape Town and drove to Margie's flat. I had thought a lot about it and its possible consequences and I was in a spot. I could either end the relationship, or I could give in to her uncomfortable demand and consider Christianity. As I stopped at her flat I realised that this was now my call – everything depended on my approach.

I inhaled deeply, swallowed a good dose of pride, and said: 'Okay, Margie – I'm prepared to look into this Christianity business. I'll make a final decision about us later.'

Margie responded in her usual calm way, 'Fine, Tim. It is really something you need to think about.'

'Well, what shall I do?' I challenged.

'Why don't you come to the service tonight? Frank Retief is preaching. Just come and listen.'

That was like pouring ice-cold water over me.

Into the Fire

As we walked into the large and bustling St James Church in Kenilworth, eyeing the masses of people mulling about, I hoped desperately that no one would know or recognise me. A church was hardly the stamping ground I felt at home in.

'Let's sit here,' I suggested when I spotted empty seats in the back row. After sitting down inconspicuously, I was secretly surprised at the buzz and the warm vibe in the church. People seemed happy to be there and it showed on their faces. A dark-haired, good-looking man then walked up to the pulpit.

'Who is that?' I asked.

'Frank Retief, he's the minister.'

'Oh.'

Frank introduced himself and started to preach. His passion and commitment immediately struck me. He opened the Bible and preached with fervour. He spoke about man's inherent selfishness, and resentment towards God. So far, so good, I thought; nothing too personal to get all excited about. Then he went on describing people in that church who hid from the truth by trying to fill their lives with dramatic, self-centred activities and pastimes. 'They become fanatical about self-achievement, self-ambition – themselves . . .'

Hold on a minute, I thought.

Who was this man talking about? I clicked – he had been tipped off about me. Hadn't he looked straight at me several times while preaching, and especially while saying that about pastimes? I started feeling uncomfortable at once. What would he say next? It felt as though the whole church knew that Frank was talking directly to me.

Margie must have told him about me. I looked at her from the corner of my eye but she was not letting on. I grew angry with her, with this man in the pulpit, with everyone around me. They were all in on it! Through my paranoia, Frank Retief's words continued to batter me.

'God is not a God to fool with. He will not tolerate your sin, your pride. You might think you can carry on with your little world, doing what you please, living according to your own rules, but God does not accept that. You need to come to God, repent sincerely, confess, say sorry to the people who you have wronged, and come to the foot of the cross where Jesus can take that heavy load from you. Only Jesus can take away the unhappiness, that lost feeling, that *emptiness*. Only Jesus can soften your hardened heart; He has paid the price for your sin and mine. He died for you . . .'

Then I lost it, my mind tripped out, I'd had enough of this crazy talk. Frank was talking about my life! I was as furious as could be! Strange things were going on inside me: emotions were clashing. All the while, something sinister in me was screaming: *Get out of this place; this is a trap . . . you've been caught! Get out!*

I was about to storm out, but my self-consciousness and fear of being noticed pinned me down in my seat. If I got up, everybody would see me! I decided to

Frank Retief.

stay and bolt for the door the second that Frank said 'Amen'. At last the service ended. I did not leave as planned, but watched how people streamed to the front of the church. Frank had invited people to come for prayer. These folks responded. Goodness knew what they were going to do next!

'Goodnight, Margie. See you again sometime,' I stammered angrily, still mistrusting her.

Then I fled.

Changes

Still confused after the night's haunting church experience, I got into my bakkie, and roared off into the night, eager to put as much distance between me and the church as possible. I was relieved to have escaped the ordeal without serious emotional injury. But even when I was miles away my head was still spinning, my mind still confused.

I did not like the way that the Reverend Frank Retief spoke to me.

'Who gave him the right to do that? Who does he think he is? No, Biggsie, this Christianity thing is not for you,' I said to myself all the way back to Worcester.

Strangely, the evening's happenings were not so easy to shake off. As I drove through the winding Du Toit's Kloof mountain pass with a three-quarter moon casting its silvery shadows, my mind was in turmoil. I could not understand my strong reactions to Frank's message. Usually I was tolerant of people with views that conflicted with my own. The best thing I could do was to avoid church altogether. As for my relationship with Margie, I can honestly say that I realised that the writing was on the wall.

The following weekend was action-packed and adrenaline-filled, with some hair-raising rock climbing with my friends on the vertical rock faces of Table Mountain. I decided not to see Margie at all, and certainly there would be no church. But as I headed back for home I had a last-minute change of mind and did something that took me years to understand. I decided to check out the evening service!

'I'll go on my own and slip into the back row where no one will notice me. Then I can at least say I was gentlemanly enough to have tried out this Christianity twice before I dropped it completely.'

I waited tensely in the dark shadows outside the church building like an undercover agent, until the last people had moved inside, before sneaking into the back row. Relieved that no one noticed me, I plonked down, my heart beating. Then another weird and utterly annoying thing happened. An old granny sitting next to me gave me a warm smile and touched my knee with her hand as a welcoming gesture!

I wasn't as antagonistic to Frank's sermon this time. I listened intently to his reasoning and his challenges. The content was bearable – if only he didn't speak so much about sin! Up to then, I had never considered myself a sinner. I was an honest man. I hadn't murdered anyone. Overall, I considered myself a reasonably good guy. I knew I was not perfect, but a sinner? No way! Having satisfied myself that I was not on the sinning side of things, I scanned the rows of heads to see if Margie was there. I did not see her and felt relieved.

Meanwhile the service continued, Frank pressing on with strong challenges.

'My friends, God loves you as a father loves a child. He knows your heart, your most intimate thoughts, what you do and think in private. Have you not overlooked your sinfulness, my friends? Reflect on it for a moment. Are you proud? Do you love your neighbour the wrong way? Do you tell small lies? Do lustful thoughts occupy your mind sometimes? What would Jesus Christ find if he searched your heart? Would you be ashamed to let him inside your most intimate and private thoughts? Why not ask Him tonight to search your mind and heart. Pray to Him and give Him a chance. Don't let this opportunity pass . . .'

I could not take any more. Enough was enough. I was not going to be humiliated twice in one week. What right did this man think he had to crash into my personal life like this? I rushed out the church and into the parking lot, savouring the cool touch of the southwesterly wind on my hot and sweaty face.

The drive back to Worcester was not a happy one. My life suddenly seemed fragile and frail, as though I was hanging onto it by a thin thread. My self-confidence had shrunk since I started investigating this Christianity thing. I missed the inner voice that told me that I could do it on my own, that my way was right. This rapid had shaken me to the core.

The Leap over the Waterfall

Months went by. Sunday after Sunday I was mysteriously drawn back to listen to Frank's messages. Slowly I began to recognise, to my dismay, the sin in my own life. Slowly but surely, I began to understand that sin meant disobeying God, not only in my actions, but in my thought. My heart was full of it. I felt angry and upset to find myself in this condition, far from God and lost.

The most overwhelming challenge was, however, that I had to recognise that God was real and wanted a relationship with me. I had been presented with the facts and I could not deny the truth in them. I was at the crossroads; I could either turn my back on God, or follow Him. The frightening part was that if I followed Him and accepted His claims of who He was, I would have to go the whole way. It was one or the other.

Twice I met privately with Frank to discuss and challenge him on issues that troubled me; the question of evolution; the eternal destiny of primitive tribes and groups of people who had never been exposed to the gospel; the narrowness of the Christian path. He answered me so calmly and clearly that my hostility towards him soon dissolved. To my surprise, I even started liking the guy. He was in touch with my feelings and understood them. He was open and very straightforward. My trust and respect for him lifted a notch.

Easter Sunday 1983 arrived and Margie and I attended the morning service at St James. The church was packed and vibrated with cheerful chattering and laughter. We took our usual back row seats where my granny friend passed me a warm smile. I passed her a smile in return.

Frank began preaching about John the Baptist's strong stand against sin. There it was again, that terrible word – sin. Suddenly something in my heart shifted. It was as though a stone structure in my heart collapsed. Emotion welled up in me and I fought back the tears. What was happening? I wanted to cry, but I dared not.

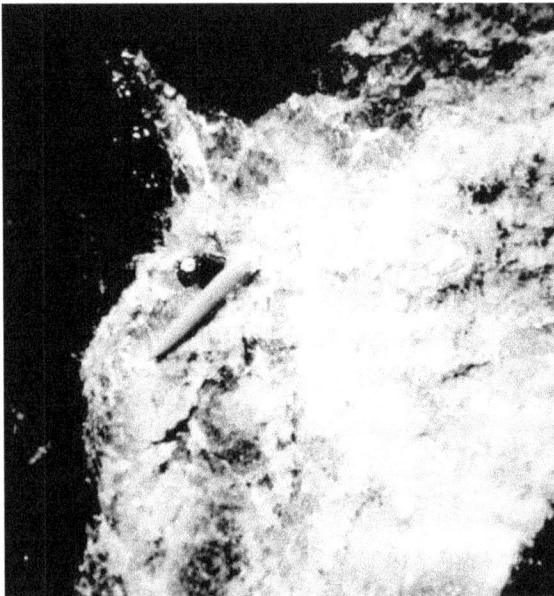

Life can be like a river – sometimes you feel out of control, sometimes it simply overwhelms you.

Something gently forced me to look within myself. The glimpse I caught was not pretty. My heart was alarmingly dark and stained, my conscience muddied and clouded. Sin after sin flashed through my mind in an endless stream: selfishness, lying, bad thoughts, pride, ego, immorality. There, for the first time, I admitted to myself that I was spiritually in need of help. It was hard – I was teetering between two worlds: the non-spiritual world where I was in charge, and a spiritual world where a radiant Jesus Christ stood as head. Surely Margie would sense the intense battle that was raging in my mind. Thinking back, it was a real showdown. An irrational hate for everyone in that building, including myself, would surge up in me.

I no longer heard Frank's sermon as the battle in my mind intensified. I was caught between two furious forces, neither of which I was the master. Sadness swamped me, sadness because of my lostness and out of control turmoil. I wanted to cry again, but fought it back.

Frank's words reached my ears again. 'There is a person, Jesus Christ, who is calling you, who loved you with such love, such a deep love that He died for you. My friends, please don't turn your back on Jesus, the Son of God. He wants you. He loves you.'

I knew that God was speaking directly to me, calling me to Him. I knew it was His Spirit speaking to me earlier. I knew it was Him, but my will kicked against it. It was as though invisible hands made a last failed attempt to keep me away from the truth. Deep in my heart I knew Jesus was the answer, that He was what I had been missing all my life. Racing canoes, adrenalin, adventures, fame, exploring had not filled this void for me – it was only Jesus that could.

An intense and weighted silence filled the church as Frank's message ended. My heart was thumping violently in my chest.

Frank gave another invitation. 'Those who feel challenged, please come and see me. We can pray together.'

I knew I had to go and waited until the churchgoers bottlenecked towards the exit before I parted from Margie without saying a word. Emotionally upside down, confused, but deeply moved, I knocked on the vestry door, hoping that no one had spotted me.

Frank smilingly greeted me and invited me to sit. 'How are you, Tim? How can I help?'

'Your message challenged me, Frank,' I choked out. 'I would like to make right with God. Today. I have to.'

'Tim, are you ready to accept Jesus as your saviour? It's not a small thing making such a commitment to God, it's the most important decision we can make in this life.'

'Frank, I'm still confused about a lot of things, but I know I want to do it.' I paused. 'Yes, I want Jesus as my saviour.' My chest was pounding and my mouth was dry.

Just then, another voice screamed inside me, a nasty, malevolent-sounding voice: 'Don't do it, you fool!'

The tension had become unbearable, not unlike the feeling I knew so well while kloofing in the Cape mountains, leaping off those waterfalls into the coffee-coloured water far below.

'Let's pray together. You may pray after me, Tim,' Frank interjected. We bowed our heads together and then Frank prayed a simple prayer.

'Lord Jesus, I have sinned against You, and You know my heart. I want to repent and change my life. Lord, You died on the cross for my sin, so that I can be a new person. I believe in You, Lord Jesus. I confess my sin. I believe that You died but rose again. I am asking You to come into my heart as my personal saviour.'

I slowly and sincerely repeated the prayer after Frank, fighting back the emotion and tears.

'Amen,' Frank ended.

'Amen,' I repeated and remained bowed for a few seconds before looking up. Emotionally I thanked Frank and he warmly shook my hand.

'Tim, come and talk about it if you can. I'd love to help you through this.'

Outside the church, I met up with Margie. 'Margs, I did it. But I need to be alone for a while.' I saw her expression of deep joy, which she suppressed.

'That's okay, Tim. Take your time, I'll be at the flat.'

I knew where I needed to be – the Rondebosch forest on the slopes of Table Mountain. It was one of those perfect autumn April mornings; a slight nip in the forest air hinted that winter was approaching and the morning sunshine filtered lazily through the leaves, gently touching the soft mat of fallen pine needles. I had been shaken to the very roots and desperately needed to be alone. My thoughts were anything but calm: they were confused, bouncing back and forth between disbelief and reality. I knew it was time to deal with the internal surgery that I had undergone earlier that day, and more specifically, its after-effects.

I lay face down on the soft mat of pine needles, ready to open up to the hidden emotions that were waiting to pour out like a flood. Uncontrolled tears of relief, confusion, sadness and joy started to flow down my face, then all broke loose. I cried and cried, sobbing until I was utterly exhausted: I was 31 years old and had never cried like this. A warmth I had never experienced crept into my heart. Something wonderful had happened. Then it dawned on me . . . That empty, lost feeling that had haunted me since my school days was gone! The confused thoughts that I had had when I entered the forest were slowly beginning to clear. I rose slowly from the bed of pine needles, with a new lightness in my heart.

A movement caught my eye. A small brown squirrel sat poised against a tree trunk, staring intently at me with a quizzical expression. For a second our eyes met – then something triggered. I began to chuckle, then laugh – I laughed until my sides ached. All my heaviness seemed to melt away and disappear.

After the Fact

I drove to Margie's flat. I still wasn't up to discussing this mammoth event with her – it was still too personal. I said a quick goodbye, and headed once again for my home behind the mountains, singing to God with all my heart, at the top of my voice. I sang to the great God who created the mountains which I loved so much, the beautiful rivers, the rocks, the trees, the birds. Somehow, everything looked more impressive and illuminated that morning.

I felt free and clean. 'Yes, God, thank You. You have shown me a new river to run. I want to run it, test its waters, run its rapids, take the most committing lines, feel its power and energy. Yes, Lord, I want to do it.'

There, on the slopes of the mountain, I prayed my first prayer as a new man. I was not sure how to go about it, but it did not matter:

'Thank you, God,
You've done something
today that I don't
understand. God, I know
You took my old heart
and gave me a new one.
Thank you, almighty
God.
I am so sorry for all my
sins against You, all my
mess-ups. Please help me
put them right. I want to
be clean.
Lord, help me.
Thank You for dying on
the cross for me —
and please forgive me.
Amen.'

Surely, I was standing at the source of a new and wonderful river. It was not a stream of ordinary flowing water, but a stream of Living Water. There had been a long struggle trying to find the source, exploring the wrong tributaries, searching in the wrong watersheds, but at last I had found that small stream of crystal clear water at the very point where it was born and ran out of the mountain, flowing from its creator. Had Jesus not said, 'I am the living water, indeed, whoever drinks from my waters will never thirst . . .'?

To me it felt like the beginning of a wonderful new adventure. I also sensed that this would be the greatest and most challenging river I had ever seen. Deep down I sensed that its rapids and canyons would be the hardest I would come across. This time, however, I had a new commander helping and guiding me. He'd be the one to tell me: 'Take that channel . . . portage here . . . mind that undercut rock face.' This would be an everlasting first descent for me, one that would take my whole life.

Jesus Christ was my new King, and walking with Him had become my new river.

Entering the River

Difficult times and tasks lay ahead after my conversion. I knew I had to tell my friends and family. The thought alone struck terror in me.

'What will they say? They will be horrified and scornful,' I thought to myself. My friends took it amazingly well. I think they had seen it coming, and they jokingly called me the 'Holy Ghoster'. I knew things would have to change between us. Sundays, for instance, would become my day of worship; canoeing had to take a backseat.

Telling my family of Jesus would be an even greater challenge. How could I tell my dear mother that I had found that great treasure that she and her family were still searching for? I hoped that Mum would rejoice with me. She surely would be glad that

her wild, adventurous son had at last found something that would settle his restless soul. I decided to tell my family in person, and not in an impersonal letter or phone call.

I drove to Murchison, our beautiful farm in the province of Natal, where a family picnic had been planned on Maxton, our winter grazing farm. After helping my dad dip and count the 350 cattle on the farm, we picnicked at our favorite spot on the shale ledges of the Ixopo River.

I waited for the moment when I was alone with Mum. 'Mum, I've become a Christian.' I paused, trying to read her reaction. 'It's a wonderful thing for me. I feel like I'm a new person, Mum. Something happened inside me when I surrendered to Jesus.'

Her response was disappointing. I had hit the first snag of my new river. After a very long silence it was as if I could feel a cold, steel curtain dropping down between us.

She replied at last, her words forced.

'Tim, I am glad for you.'

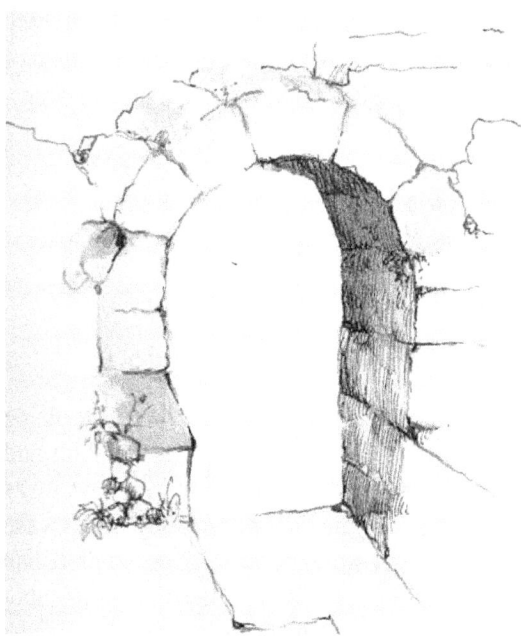

It's a narrow way.

141

That was it! I felt devastated. I stood up and walked away when it became clear that our conversation was over. I was hurt, but, thinking about it, Mum's reaction was quite understandable. I had sprung my news on her by sharing that I had parted from her sacred way, our whole family's way. I had found a new path which clashed with that of hers. Mum in her quiet way was the spiritual head in our family, and this was obviously a hurtful blow to her.

The picnic deteriorated when Dad, who followed the eastern-based ideologies of his father, also showed negative interest in my news, as did my brothers and sisters. The reality of the situation began to dawn on me. I realised how naïve I had been, expecting my beloved family to enthuse and support me over my radical meeting with Jesus. Sadly I had initiated a rift between us.

Barbara, my eldest sister, eyed me with steely, cold eyes. 'Tim, are you sure you've done the right thing?'

'Yes, Barbara, I am,' I replied. 'It's real what's happened to me.'

My dear parents have since passed away. My mother, in the final year of her life, had a change of heart. A good friend of ours, Warwick Cole-Edwardes, won my mother to the Lord with his moving preaching and caring spirit, and was able to lead her in prayer to accept the Lord Jesus Christ as her saviour. Dan, my younger brother, also came to know and accept Jesus as Lord.

Walking with Jesus

The next few months were the hardest of my life. Being a new Christian, I was still growing in my faith and making mistakes as I continued on my journey. I was in the firing line. My lifestyle was midway between the old and the new. I struggled to let go of certain habits and patterns. My old friends had understandably cooled off towards me, and I had few Christian friends, besides Margie, and her brother Steve.

Steve drew me aside one day. 'Tim, I can see you are struggling, but we're here for you, if you need help with anything, just let us know.'

'Thanks, Steve,' I replied. 'I know I made the right choice, but I'm still mixed up about some things. I guess it'll take some time to work everything out.'

'One thing I know is that God will never take you through more than you can bear. He'll always help give you the strength you need, Tim.' Steve's encouragement meant a lot to me.

Several months later, on 24 November 1984, I married the girl of my dreams in Cape Town. Frank Retief married us. The next few months were a blur of what have become heady and wonderful memories. I was in love with the lady of my dreams, and she with me. The next eight months felt like an extended honeymoon for Margie and me, until I departed for our Amazon Source to Sea Expedition (the Apurimac) in South America. This time apart only strengthened me spiritually, and reaffirmed my love for and commitment to her.

In 1985, after the family asked for assistance with running the farms, we made a radical change in careers and settled in Ixopo, KwaZulu-Natal. I

The girl of my dreams.

142

eventually tried my hand at contract-logging operations on the steep plantations in the district. The romantic novelty of living together in a rustic old cottage, without running hot water or electricity, and far from anywhere, soon wore off. Margie fell pregnant, and we were in the middle of the rainy season. We sometimes found ourselves stranded with only an old John Deere tractor – our only means of reaching Ixopo.

For 18 years we battled to build our timber business. Sadly there was a season when I struggled with depression, mourning the loss of my free and easy days when I could run my own life as I pleased.

Margie and I poured our energies into the small Methodist Church in Ixopo. She established a thriving young mothers' group, and I tried my hand at lay preaching. During this time, God blessed us with four beautiful children. First, there was Sam, then my daughter Keetah, then Ben, and finally Jonathan. The timber business also expanded steadily, but by no means smoothly. Despite opposition from just about every front, Margie and I decided to home-school our children, believing that it would ground them with a solid spiritual foundation which would see them through the difficult times and challenges ahead. Margie would also later set up a family violence crisis centre in the townships.

In the late 1980s and early 1990s, South Africa experienced an alarming number of attacks and murders on white farmers. We lost friends and neighbours, but through God's grace, we escaped harm.

A special friend and mentor during these times was Joe Newlands, a missionary from the nearby community of Donnybrook. I had felt the need to share the gospel with my workforce (200 Zulu and Xhosa people), and as Joe had a perfect command of the Zulu language, he gladly accepted the invitation to help. During the 18 years he never missed an opportunity to share the gospel with our forestry teams out in the hills. Our pews were freshly felled logs, and our church building was the lush eucalyptus canopy above us. I began a ministry with the Gideons International Bible Society, and together Joe and I would distribute tens of thousands of Bibles to the surrounding rural schools. Later Margie and I joined Joe Newlands' Kwasizabantu Missionary Church in Donnybrook. My empty days seemed behind me. It was amazing to think back to the times I had wanted to flee from St James Church in Cape Town.

In 2003, Margie and I both felt that our season in Ixopo had come to an end. The 18 years of farm life had yielded a rich harvest for us. We now had four children, timber farms, a busy timber-treating business and multitudes of happy memories. Flaxton Timbers had grown and thrived, but we felt the need to move on. Our prayers were answered when a timber farmer and friend, Pete Hayter, bought our farm and business.

We then moved to the beautiful city of Pietermaritzburg. The river of life had led us through some gruelling canyons where we had learnt invaluable lessons and were challenged to the limit. We had also gathered caskets of priceless treasures – wonderful memories and happy times. A river doesn't stop or wait for anyone, it just keeps flowing downstream, passing through one canyon to the next, always moving, heading towards its final destination – the sea.

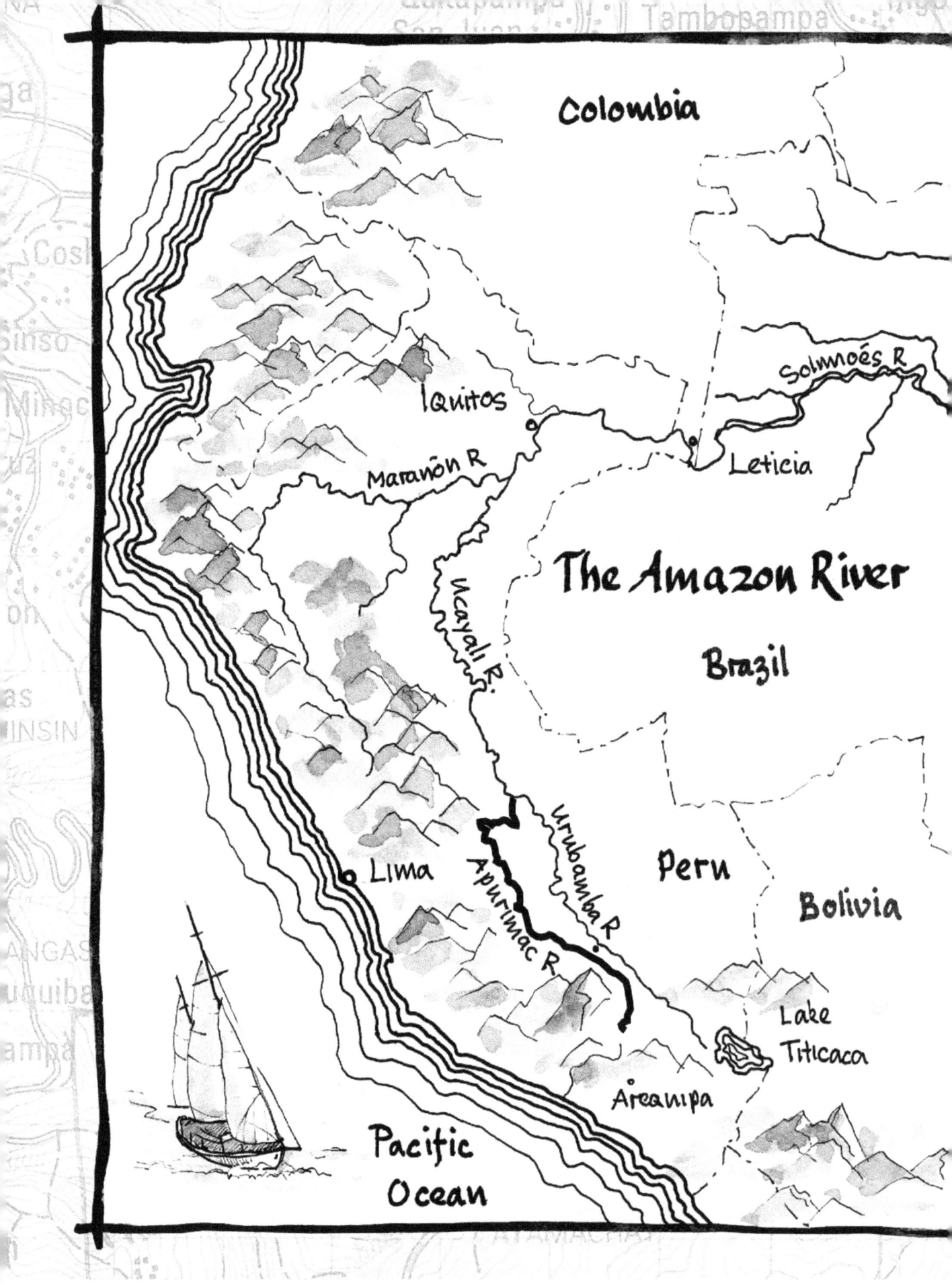

Colombia

Iquitos

Marañón R.

Solimões R.

Leticia

The Amazon River

Brazil

Ucayali R.

Lima

Apurimac R.

Urubamba R.

Peru

Bolivia

Lake Titicaca

Arequipa

Pacific Ocean

The Apurimac River
1985

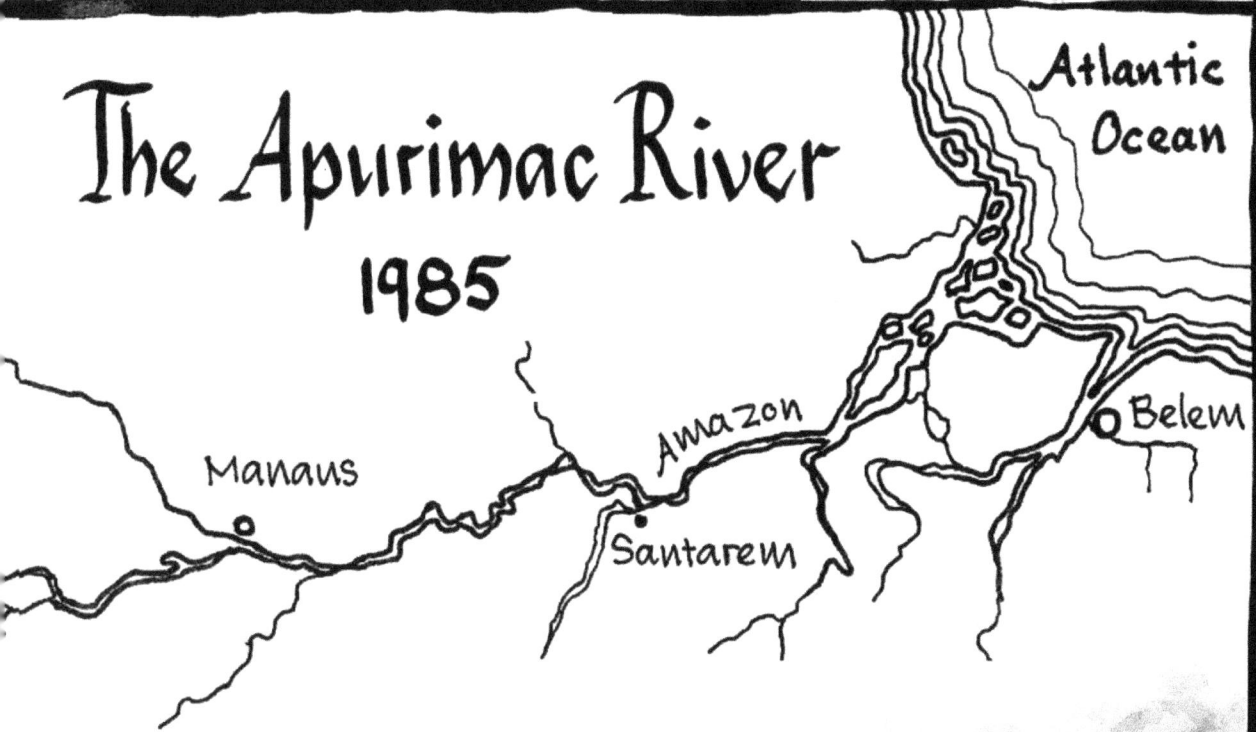

Atlantic Ocean

Manaus

Amazon

Santarem

Belem

N

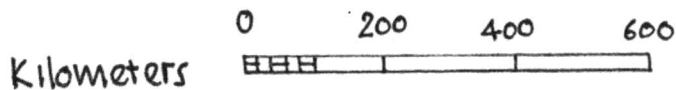

PART 2

0   200   400   600

Kilometers

Chapter 6

THE SOURCE

Restless Natives

All hell broke loose as we drove into the village of Lauri on 29 August 1985. Lauri consisted of a few ochre-coloured mud dwellings and an imposing Roman Catholic cathedral that overlooked the dusty, unpaved plaza. From here we would begin our hike over the Andes in our quest for the source of the Amazon. But the arrival of our group proved to be a rude awakening for the village. Almost at once an angry crowd of excited locals gathered about us and started a fray. Unbeknown to us, there had been bad blood recently between the villagers and a group of gringo gold prospectors. So, when our overloaded Condorita (as we affectionately called our Land Rover) bumped and bounced into the village plaza with gringos hanging out of every window, the scene was set for a major confrontation. While François and Piotr attempted to negotiate the hire of four donkeys (burros), the suspicious villagers drew their own erroneous but completely under-standable conclusions. It did not take long for them to act on their suspicions.

'Here they are again! Let's get them!' screamed someone in the crowd, and in a moment they came at us.

Leading the charge was a drunk, toothless Que-chua woman. What a sight! She yelled as she danced around us, her bare feet stamping the dusty ground as she performed her ritual. 'Filthy gringos!' she screamed as she circled our group, drooling coca-green saliva.

'She's a witch,' I thought. To my dismay she spun around and homed in on me, swaying to and fro and casting spells in witch-like fashion. Hurrying to escape, I ran into the crowd, but she persistently tracked me down. Frustrated, I eventually turned on her and re-taliated with my own hissing and wild gesticulations! It worked, and the woman withdrew, keeping a safe distance, her eyes fixed on me. The mood of the crowd, however, was approaching flashpoint, and angry shouting broke out amongst the men. Anything was possible now, anything.

Our escape route down this street with our donkeys.

'Let's get out of this place!' François shouted over the din.

We dispersed at once, but the shindig on the plaza wasn't over. Pastor and Jose, the owners who had agreed to hire us their donkeys, were set upon by the threatening villagers. Under their breath they muttered to François and Piotr that the deal must be concluded outside the village gates.

'Drive the donkeys out that way, to the gate!' shouted François.

In unison we whacked the startled donkeys on and yelled, 'sburro, sburro'. The reaction was spectacular. The four donkeys took off at a gallop, sending the bewildered crowd flying in all directions. 'Keep them running,' I shouted to Joe. 'Move it, move it!' Next to the donkeys, we ran along a narrow, cobbled roadway to the outer wall. To our relief the gates were open and we chivvied our convoy through, expecting the village mob to be in hot pursuit. Looking back we saw only our guides, Pastor and Jose, running and out of breath, and, behind them, François and Zbecek.

The Amazon expedition had truly begun!

A Little Bit of This, A Little Bit of That . . .

Our team comprised 10 men and a woman – a more diverse and eccentric group one would struggle to find anywhere. François was the expedition leader, with Piotr Chmielinski second in charge. My role was to be the 'on-the-water-leader'.

Of the eleven, there were four kayakers: Jerome Truran, Piotr, François and me. The support team consisted of two South African cameramen, Fanie van der Merwe and Pierre van Heerden; Kate Durrant, a British doctor; Sergio Leon, a Costa Rican game ranger; Zbigniew (Zbecek) Bzdak, a Polish photographer; Joe Kane, an American journalist who would document the expedition; and our sponsor Jack Jourgensen, a retired American businessman who would join us further downstream.

François had indeed put together a diverse team! This time around my surprise of including a woman (who had also never been on a river before) in the team was not as startling as I had found it four years

The team (left to right): Tim, Zbecek, Piotr, Kate, Joe, Sergio, François, Jerome & Fanie.

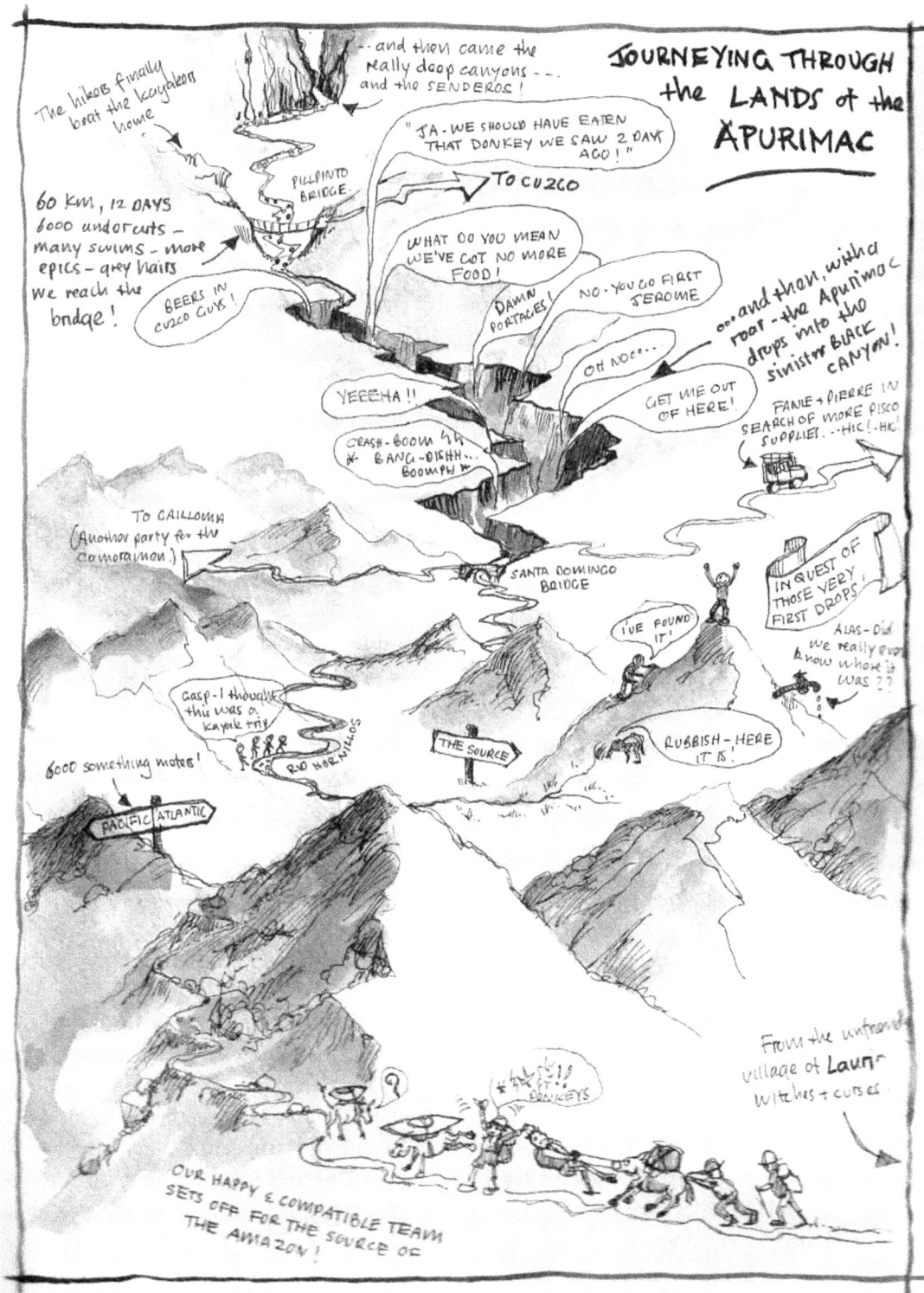

earlier. Nevertheless, the mix of one woman, 10 men, and a long, tough river trip seemed to be courting disaster. Kate was pleasant, slight, attractive with straight auburn hair, and she was obviously no walk-over. Her presence on the trip, plus the fact that we were five different nationalities and spoke four different languages, made the expedition unique. Spiritually we were even more diverse – agnostic, humanist, Christian Scientist, Buddhist, Roman Catholic, and at least one born-again Christian. An expedition chaplain was obviously out of the question!

Our motives, too, differed vastly. Some wanted to explore, others craved fame, some wanted to film the journey, another to document it in writing, and some simply to kayak white water. One or two were out for personal commercial interests but others again were quite satisfied to be part of the support team. Overall, we were a cosmopolitan cross-section of society.

At the outset of the expedition it soon became obvious that the party was too big. We could see that once the four kayakers were out on the river, the remaining back-up team simply would not fit into Condorita, our short-wheel base Land Rover. Quickly we drew up a contingency plan. There was no option but that we split the support crew. Some would travel in Condorita; the rest would hike by foot through the mountains, shadowing the river.

But before we began to navigate the river there was the small matter of finding its source! Having concluded the donkey deal with Jose and Pastor, we started up the steep trail that wound up to a pass at 5 030 m – the geographical divide between the Pacific and Atlantic Oceans. Hiking the pass were François, Piotr, Zbecek, Fanie, Joe and myself, while Pierre, Kate, Jerome and Sergio drove around to meet us at a small weather station. With two guides in front and our kayak-loaded donkeys between them, we moved in single file up the mountain. It was not long before we started to feel the effects of high altitude. Our strides became progressively more mechanical, and our breathing more laboured. We hiked hard until

Hiking over the Andes divide in search of the source.

late in the afternoon when Pastor recommended that we set up camp on a rocky ridge that would offer some grazing for the donkeys.

This would be our first camp under the Andean stars. Our campsite overlooked the spectacular Colca Canyon, where the river plunges down a spectacular chasm, far below us.

'Tim,' called out Piotr, with his heavy Polish accent, 'remember the Colca? Look, I can see where we carried our kayaks in.'

'Yeah,' I replied, leaning back on my backpack. 'That was a great trip.'

Piotr explained to the others how his 1982 team of Polish rafters (called the Canoandes) had run the first descent of the Rio Colca, supposedly the world's deepest gorge. In 1983 Piotr had invited me to join the Canoandes on a second expedition down the Colca, to document the trip for *National Geographic*.

Early Signs and Symptoms

I had recommended Piotr for the Apurimac team mainly due to the friendship that was forged between us on the 1983 trip. I was impressed by his expeditionary strengths, his courage and determination, and the leadership skills he had displayed on the Colca and in the Black Canyon of the Apurimac. François contacted Piotr in the United States and arranged to meet him to discuss his joining us.

At that stage of our planning some unsettling changes had erupted. The British film company who had first agreed to sponsor us unexpectedly dropped out, and, with only a month to go, it was touch or go whether there would be any expedition at all. Now Piotr came to the rescue. He suggested contacting Jack Jourgensen, the American businessman who had sponsored his Colca expedition. Jack showed interest, with the condition that he be a partner in the film documentary and join the team for certain sections of the river. François quickly arranged a meeting with Jack to discuss the proposal.

It transpired, however, that Piotr had already made a first move! He attempted to manipulate the deal by persuading Jack to offer the sponsorship only if he, Piotr, would become the overall leader of the expedition. François shared this disturbing news with me in a letter. I was stunned and alarmed, and immediately phoned him.

'Frans, is Piotr really trying to take over the leadership?'

'Yes, it's true,' confirmed François, and he explained to me the sequence of events and the resulting politics. 'Piotr,' he added, 'is not as straightforward a person as he appears – not by any means!'

'Frans, listen to me. If Piotr is doing this sort of thing before we've even started, what will happen out there on the river? He must not come! Unless this thing is sorted out, count me out!'

'Tim, it's okay,' François reassured me. 'I will deal with Piotr. Don't worry about it, my friend.'

I hung up, nonplussed and disillusioned by Piotr's uncharacteristic behaviour. These alleged actions did not correspond with the man I knew.

Anyway, the ball was now in François's court. Soon after this, he met with Jack and worked out a deal whereby Jack would be partner in the film project, François the expedition leader, and Piotr second in command. This latter decision again surprised me. How could François give a leading position to one whose motives were under suspicion? How could he trust someone who had attempted a pre-expedition 'coup d'état'?

François justified his decision by saying that he needed Piotr's expertise to run the expedition. I questioned this, arguing that, after all, we had managed fine on the Urubamba, and could manage the Apurimac without Piotr's know-how. I kept to myself, however, the premonition that we might be building up for a disaster – one that would have nothing to do with the river's treacherous waters.

The Source

Our first night under the stars was, for me, a night of mixed emotions. We were at the start of a 6 700 km journey that, from west to east, would practically span the South American continent. It was a tall order for any group of people, let alone one that showed the first hints of personality conflict. Our leader had already shown signs of compromise, and our 'deputy' had apparently tried – even before a paddle touched the water – to seize the leadership. 'This is crazy, crazy,' I thought to myself before rolling onto my back on an uncomfortable sleeping mat. I looked for sleep, but found something else instead.

The Southern Cross, Orion's Belt, and galaxies of stars hung above me in the sky, breathtakingly bright in the crisp night. Towering above us was the 6 000-m high Mount Hualca, eerily white, and illuminated by a silvery half-moon. I lay gazing upwards, wondering what this exploit would bring in the coming weeks and months.

UCAYALI R
Perene R
ATALAYA
URUBAMBA R
ENE R
FINISH
TAMBO R

Mantaro R

APURIMAC
RIVER

Santiago

Luisiana

APURIMAC R

Sandero Red Zone

Nevada Salcantay 6949 m
Acobamba Abyss

Pampas R

ABANCAY

Cunyac Bridge

To Lima

Military Br.

CUZCO

2800 m

Pillpinto

Surinama

Black Canyon

Hanging Br.

3875 m

N

4000 m

YAURI

La Angostura

Mt. Mismi

START

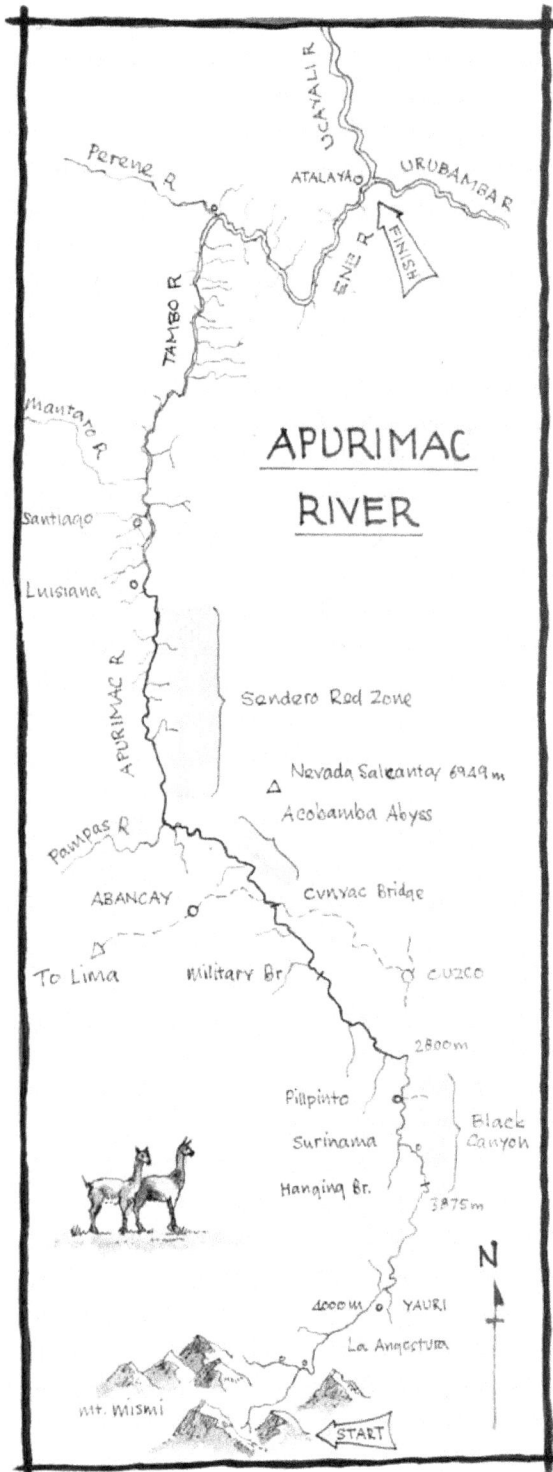

We woke to the bustling sounds of our guides attending to the donkeys. Clouds had moved in overnight and the weather looked threatening. Yesterday's high spirits had evaporated. We all had headaches and the slight nausea that is symptomatic of *soroche* (altitude sickness). Even the donkeys were irritable, the mare refusing to move from her spot, much to Pastor's frustration. We set off, but, not being sufficiently acclimatised, laboured slowly up the grade: first 4 500, then 5 000, then 5 500 m. The weather turned ominously grey. Dark turquoise clouds chased in sleet and snow from the northeast.

'Time to camp before this weather really sets in,' advised Fanie. 'We are at the base of the snow line. Any higher and we'll be in thick snow.' Fanie, our cameraman and age-wise the senior member of the expedition, was a tall, dark and good-looking Afrikaner. He had led ice climbs in Patagonia and on Baffin Island. Our Colville expedition, in particular, had taught François and me to respect his judgement. The man simply had the knack!

We began to look for a campsite, but Pastor, Jose and Piotr overrode Fanie's suggestion, arguing that we should push on for the summit. The potential for an argument was imminent. It was up to François to make the call.

'Okay then, if you insist, although I tend to agree with Fanie,' François consented.

Grudgingly the rest of us agreed, pulled on extra clothing, and, leaning into the headwind, plodded on, one foot at a time. The steep trail eased at last, and at the ridge Piotr stopped, half-stooped, with a stick in his hand.

'Ten soles (Peruvian money) please, now crossing continental divide,' he rasped.

We managed a laugh, stepped over the line, and threw down our backpacks. It was time to savour the moment and rest our aching legs. This was indeed a landmark, the line dividing watersheds that stretched away to the Pacific and Atlantic Oceans.

François, who was last over the crest, looked ashen and fatigued.

'You okay, Frans?' I wheezed, not feeling all that well myself. François did not answer, but simply slumped to the ground and closed his eyes.

Joe Kane had been quiet all day and he, too, was clearly struggling with nausea and a headache. He managed a smile and sat on his own, absorbed in his thoughts. Joe was a San Francisco journalist who had been invited by François to write up the expedition, it being understood that he would pay his own way. Of average height and build, Joe seemed to be a pleasant person, but at this moment, he was still adjusting to the enormity of the situation. He was neither a kayaker nor a rafter; he was surrounded by a multinational group of people that he did not know, and it was his business to document one of the longest river expeditions ever attempted. No wonder he was a little reflective at times!

Surrounding us were the snow-covered giants that guarded the Amazon's source: Quehuisha, Mount Mismi, Chayco, Huillcayo. Darkness was almost on us; we had cut things fine. Certainly we were underdressed for sub-zero temperatures, as we realised while we tramped down the snowy slope, edging closer and closer to the source.

'All down hill from here,' called Joe.

We found a decent spot and pitched our tents as fast as we could with fumbling, frozen hands. It was my turn to cook supper, the weather being so cold I prepared the meal in the cramped two-man tent that I shared with François.

'What's for supper, Zulu?' Zbecek asked, pushing his head into the tent and letting in an icy draught. (Hailing from Natal, the traditional Zulu Kingdom in South Africa, the nickname 'Zulu' was inevitable!)

'Zbecek, come inside and close the bloomin' tent!' I scolded. 'Okay, what shall we have – beef Stroganoff, savoury mince, or chicken á la king?'

'Anything, as long as it is hot!' came the wolf-hungry reply.

Delicious pre-cooked dishes had been supplied to us by our food sponsor Eureka (now Johnson Camping), a Canadian company. Each meal was vacuum-packed and sealed in aluminium foil, complete with gravy! Eating in a tent was always a loud, hectic, team event with the clinking of pots, the clanking of mugs and plates, and the smell of kerosene. When the meal eventually ended, I pushed the unwashed dishes outside the tent and curled up in my sleeping bag.

There was silence around us. The sound of voices quietened. I lay back thinking, trying not to focus on the throbbing headache that pounded my temples. 'Where was my sweetheart tonight? Can't say I'm not missing her terribly,' I thought, before dropping off in a deep sleep.

Zbecek, a 33-year-old Pole, was squarely built with a balding head and wild flowing reddish beard.

François (left) Tim and Piotr at the source.

Although resembling a Viking from a distance, he had a warm and easy-going personality. A nuclear physics and photography student at Cracow University in Poland, Zbecek had been invited by his friend Piotr to join a group of nine students on a six-month kayak tour of Latin America. They left Poland in 1980 with 20 fibreglass kayaks, and, five years later had still not returned home!

'First river we run is Pescados, Mexico; we put in seven kayaks in river and in fifteen minutes we lose six of them. River just takes them away. Big Polish joke.'

I had enjoyed the company of this ever-jovial Pole on the Colca, and I had recommended him to François as a solid river man and a top-class photographer.

Sergio was the only native Spanish speaker in the group. He was short and wiry, with the typical high cheekbones of his Indian ancestry. He sported a thick moustache and a mop of black hair. François had befriended him while doing research in the Costa Rican National Park and had invited him to join our team as the 'jungle expert'. Sergio was director of the Corcovado National Park in Costa Rica and had had to take leave to join the expedition. He was a devout Christian Scientist – a quietly spoken man with strong convictions.

The next morning we hiked back toward the summit to search for – and film – the source of the Amazon. The maps from the Instituto Geographico Militer seemed to indicate that the stream Apacheta was the longest of the Apurimac's tributaries, and thus qualified to be the source of the Amazon. Over the years several studies had been carried out to determine the true source – research was published by Loren McIntyre in 1971 and Nicholas Asheshov in 1979. They had looked for the longest of the tributaries between Quebrado Calomoroco and Ccaccansa, the sister streams of the Apacheta.

We decided to follow the course of the Apacheta. On our 1:100 000 map the Apacheta seemed to be the longest of the feeder streams, narrowing then widening, disappearing then re-emerging. This was what was happening before our eyes, and eventually, at an altitude of 5 240 m, we came to a point where the water trickled miraculously from the spongy ground.

'This must be it!' a cry went up.

We were fascinated and knelt down to observe the phenomenon. I scooped up some of the freezing, crystal-clear water in my cupped hands and drank. It was sweet to the palate.

'It tastes good,' I declared, wiping my mouth. Then I looked around at the endless spurs and ridges, each with its own small stream; each oozing a trickle of water from the mountain bedrock and the marshy soils. Suddenly it struck me . . . how could we be sure that we had found the real source? Finding a source in this terrain could only be a subjective affair. How did we know which of these streams were seasonal, and which were permanent? The Andes is a relatively young mountain range, still in the process of buckling and folding. For all we knew the cartographer had an off-day when he squinted through his stereoscope at the scores of similar-looking streams. Could he perhaps have erred on that day, even by a few millimetres? Maybe this wasn't the true source at all!

Above us, an impressive vertical ice-flow hung from the black rock face. Piotr suggested that we move all our equipment to the site and film it. The two Perception kayaks that we had hauled across the continental divide to be photographed here were now being filmed from every possible angle! Finally, Piotr performed a ceremony. A small metal plaque bearing the expedition's name was attached to the rock face at the source – or what we assumed was the source! For me, the hype and the commotion at our 'discovery' struck a false note. I realised how much my sentiments differed from Piotr's. It was surely almost irreverent to claim that we had located the origin of the mighty Amazon. Instead I felt a deep empathy, a sort of spiritual connection, with this almost sacred birthplace in the Andes. It was from

Vicunas looking at home in the snow.

here that the smallest of trickles grew to become the greatest river on the planet. I wandered off to be on my own, stepping carefully over spongy mosses and fragile Altiplano plants. Eventually I found an outcropping ledge where I could sit and marvel at the magnificent scenery.

Even as I watched, the heavy cloud that veiled the eastern slopes rolled away to display the full panorama of what lay ahead of us. A thousand interlocking mountains spread without end. In the

distance a small flash caught my eye. What was it? A delicate silver thread, created by pulsating flashes of white water, appeared between towering walls of rock. Instantly a rush of adrenalin raced through my veins – would we be going into that faraway chasm? It looked wild and inhospitable, yet luring and exciting. The Apurimac was calling me, beckoning me on. The mysterious door to the Apurimac which I had peered through so many years ago was now spread out before me.

The First Prayer

We were supposed to meet the rest of the team at a weather station some 30 km from the source. Late that afternoon, as we struggled downstream with our kayaks and our cameras, a light snow set in. To aggravate the situation the light began to fade and an icy wind drove the temperature down to minus 15 degrees Celsius. There was very little chance of reaching the weather station before nightfall. As if things were not bad enough, we now realised, with trepidation, that we were lost. Joe had decided to make an early start and join the donkey team on their hike to the station. Our camping equipment was with them, which meant we were left with two

Our rendezvous with Condorita near Angostura.

options: either keep walking to find our friends, or spend the night in the elements with no gear for sleeping or camping.

Nine o'clock found us stumbling exhausted along the rocky Altiplano mountainside with only two dying flashlights to light our way.

'Isn't that a light?' came a shout from François. 'I'm sure I saw a light flash.'

Out of sheer desperation, and taking a real shot in the dark, he called out, 'Fanie, Pierre, are you there?'

To our astonishment Fanie's voice drifted faintly down: 'Come this way, we're all up here.' With immense relief, we hurried up the rocky path to the weather station and met up with our friends. Missing the station would have meant a gruelling survival night out in the cold. Ravenously we wolfed down bowls of soup and hot food.

Our next meeting point was Angostura, the small village on the Hornillos River where the kayaks would at last be launched. We couldn't wait for the moment. The effects of having spent almost three weeks in Peru without a river to kayak on had demoralised me.

The following morning we assembled outside the rustic weather station, stamping our feet and breathing steam into the crisp, cold air. After waking up early, I had felt strongly that we should pray together before splitting up into different groups. It took me all breakfast to pluck up the courage to ask whether I could say a prayer before our group parted. Knowing that my gesture would not necessarily be well received, I took several deep breaths and stepped forward.

'Guys,' I called, 'it's Sunday and we probably won't see each other for some time. Do you mind if we pray before setting off? I've been thinking . . . it would be good if we could also pray before meals on Sundays.'

My request caught everyone off guard, and after a few awkward moments of silence, Fanie, Pierre, Sergio and François responded positively.

'Yes, we'd like it,' the four of them agreed.

I began the prayer in a shaky voice: 'Lord, we thank You for getting us here so far. We are now splitting up. Please be with us – protect us as we go, and thank You for this beautiful place, Father. Amen,' I stammered to a close, my knees weak and shaking.

We split up – Jerome, François, Piotr and I following the river; Joe, Sergio and Zbecek hiking along a short cut, and Fanie, Pierre and Kate travelling in Condorita. It took two full days to hike down the Hornillos River to its confluence with the Apurimac, and where we found the small village of La Angostura. We hoped that here we would find water deep enough to float our kayaks. We all met for a meal in a primitive 'restaurant' where it became noticeable that certain 'alterations of relations' had occurred within the team. Joe, Zbecek and Sergio had bonded and were getting on well, but the Condorita team was showing signs of discord, with Kate unhappy about the treatment that she had received from Fanie and Pierre.

'These guys just won't leave me alone,' she complained. 'There has been nothing but crude jokes all the way. I've had enough – damn male chauvinists!'

Joe was quick to suggest that she join their hiking team. After discussing the matter with François, Kate was game to try, and was warmly welcomed by the hikers.

Hitting the Water

The moment for the kayakers had at last arrived when we would begin our journey down this small river to the Atlantic. We spent the morning waiting for the frost to thaw, using the time to cram our tents, sleeping bags and provisions into the cramped interiors of our kayaks. Then to the enthusiastic cheering of our friends, and with cameras rolling, we waved goodbye. Our grand departure was, however, short-lived as we embarrassingly found ourselves beached on a gravel bar after just 100 m! Roars of

Jerome straddling the Amazon.

laughter and loud jeers erupted from our support team as we sheepishly waded through the ankle-deep water, dragging our kayaks to a deeper channel!

The day was clear and warm, and we joked and laughed as we manoeuvred our craft through the shallow channels of the Hornillos. A river, however, never stays the same for long. After we passed the pre-Inca stone ruins at Macallokta, we entered a small canyon between 15 m volcanic sides. A Quechua fisherman, casting his net into the river from cliffs above, stopped and observed us suspiciously. Further downstream a lone 'goldpanner' squatted in a small patch of sun, patiently sifting the gold dust that, if he struck it lucky, would fetch him $3 a gram in Cuzco – enough to feed his family for another few months. Spotting us he stiffly rose to his feet.

Stone bridge at Santa Domingo.

Plaza doorway ~ Santa Domingo.

A folk dancing gathering in the hills.

'Where are you going to?' he called out.

'To the sea.'

'When will you get there?'

'Next year!'

The man fell silent, wondering whether to take us seriously. Then, with the faintest trace of a smile, he raised his arm in a salute.

Three easy days on the river brought us to Santa Domingo Bridge and the village of Yauri where we were reunited with the rest of the team. To our surprise the locals quizzed us as to whether we were part of a team that had passed through two weeks earlier. Two Swedish kayakers, heading – so they said – for the Atlantic Ocean, had spent a night in the village. They carried all their food and equipment in their boats and had no one supporting them.

I grew as cold as ice. Had we come all this way only to be pipped at the post by these two Swedes? Would our expedition now become a long, long race to the finish? Only time would tell.

The hiking team had arrived before us and were having blisters and infected scratches attended to by Kate. For entertainment, we chose to eat at a jolly restaurant that featured wild Peruvian music. After the meal we retired to the Parochial House (hostel) where we collapsed on our beds, exhausted.

A low-grade fever had been troubling me over the past two days and I was worried lest a recent bout of glandular fever should re-occur. I needed rest, and was immensely relieved when François announced that we would spend a full day filming at Yauri. In 1981 I had contracted severe brucellosis from eating goats' cheese and had suffered incessant attacks over the next four years. Was I in for a similar sickness?

Our next rendezvous would be the Hanging Bridge where Fanie and Pierre would film the arrival of the hikers and kayakers. We were apprehensive about entering this dangerous gorge. Floods, rock slides and tectonic upheaval in these high-altitude Andean rivers can completely change the river's course from season to season.

A Dog's Life
(Puenta Domingo to the
Hanging Bridge)

Kayaking downstream from Puenta Domingo, we passed through a series of small gorges, displaying three familiar Andean colours: bluish-grey rocks, ochre-yellow ichu grass, and turquoise-green water. A fourth colour was the endless backdrop of cloudless, azure blue sky. The river level of the Apurimac was higher this year than in 1983 when Piotr, Andrej and I ran the same section to the Pillpinto Bridge.

The canyon sides grew steeper, with the result that the number of blockages increased. At some places entire sections of the mountainside had become dislodged and crashed into the river. This forced the river to flow under gigantic house-sized rocks for distances of up to 1 km. This phenomenon certainly introduced a new dynamic into our river-running. We would round a sharp bend, see the obstacle ahead, and then paddle frantically for the side to avoid being sucked into a deadly siphon. Jerome was a 'natural' when it came to naming rapids, and soon we had a list of them, such as 'Sneezebox', 'Russian Roulette' and 'Insomnia'.

At 'Sneezebox' we had our first near mishap. The river dropped steeply through a rock-choked chute and slammed headlong into an enormous boulder. From here, the current siphoned underneath the boulder before it turned right and rushed through a series of drops. Entering first, I managed to get clear of the siphoning boulder, but my kayak's overloaded stern bumped a submerged rock and threw me off line. Instantly I was wedged sideways across the current, water crashing over my body. Jerome, coming close behind, made a desperate lunge for my kayak's nose as he sped past. Yanking it forward, he managed to dislodge the stern from the rock. The tail of my kayak swung around, forcing me to run the rest of the rapid backwards. Looking upstream, I glimpsed Piotr's kayak jamming at the same spot. I began

The river goes underground.

Siphons - you don't want to go in there.

Whooa -- what's around the corner?

Sneeze Box Rapid.

Lost among the rocks.

racing for the side to pull him out, but luckily he freed himself and also came crashing down the rapid backwards. We managed a quick grin as we passed each other.

'Things are looking up, guys – we won't be bored on this trip,' I laughed.

'Well, man, this is what we came for – to see some action!' whooped Jerome.

Incidents like this got the adrenalin flowing, and we were ready for more.

'We will have to repack our boats tonight,' said Jerome, 'we have too much gear in the back. We need more weight in the nose.'

'Yeah,' I answered, 'we can chuck all the veggies and tinned food forward of the footrest.' Our kayaks were loaded with some 20 kg of food and gear and wallowed sluggishly in the water, making nippy turns almost impossible.

'Where's François?' I called, suddenly realising that he hadn't come through yet. 'We've got another good rapid ahead.'

Sixty metres above us, clinging to the side of the cliff, François was making his way down to us, struggling to carry his heavy kayak. He had decided wisely to portage the section that had caused me such trouble. I beckoned to him and pointed out a line through the rocks whereby he could re-enter the river. Thirty long minutes passed before he at last lowered his kayak through a narrow crack and climbed into the cockpit. Unfortunately for him, his kayak faced backwards so that his first move was a tricky reverse ferry across a turbulent channel. The move fazed him, but there was no option but to go through with it.

'Come on, Frans, do it, you'll be fine!' I called out encouragingly.

At first I sympathised with him. Being the weakest paddler in the group was no fun, especially when your confidence was already low. I waited patiently, but became concerned at his reluctance to run something that was not particularly difficult. How would

Are these blockages ever going to end?

he fare when the real challenges came? Along with my sympathy certain resentment welled up. I thought of the Urubamba trip of 1981, and how he had jeopardised the safety of the team with his poor river skills. All year, prior to this trip, I had begged him to train and practise so that we would avoid situations like these. But he hadn't done his 'homework' and that frustrated me. Meanwhile, downstream, Jerome and Piotr waited patiently in an eddy, watching us work through the section.

They had found a campsite on a raised rock shelf some 3 m above the river. This would be our camp-site for the night. It was Piotr's turn to cook and we enjoyed a tasty Eureka stew with garlic potatoes, washed down with tea.

We were still well above the tree line, and so we were without the luxury of a blazing campfire. Instead we entertained ourselves by setting fire to long tufts of tinder-dry ichu grass which emulated a mini fireworks show, with multi-coloured flames flaring up and

161

Choosing the right campsite is an art.

Writing my diary by candlelight.

dancing against the black night. Having set alight all the grass within a 50 m radius of our camp, we each drifted off to our private, carefully selected sleeping spots. Selecting the right spot to lay one's sleeping mat requires a combination of skill and instinct; it's half a science, half an art. Firstly, and of utmost importance, the spot must feel right and have the right atmosphere. This is directly related to your own mood on the day, and of course the moods and general vibes of the teammembers. If you've ever watched a dog searching out the best spot to curl up in, you'd have noticed how it will walk in ever-decreasing circles, sniffing at the ground, lifting its hind leg against a rock or object to mark its territory, and sniff the air for any signs of danger. The four of us didn't look too different to this. Of lesser importance, the site should also be reasonably level and comfortable, and if possible have a sand or grass covering where a small hole can be dug out to fit the profile of your hips and shoulders. Wind direction, closeness to the camp fire (and to your friends), aspect and river view must all be entered into the complicated equation. Sometimes like a dog, a challenging growl at your neighbour if he has intruded on your territory, or discovered the ultimate spot before you have, is necessary.

The next morning, our fifth day on the river, a clattering, busy sound rudely woke me up. 'This is nice! One of my teammates has decided to surprise us with an early brew of tea,' I thought, but was it necessary to make such a song and dance about it? I stuck my head out of the sleeping bag, only to discover a short, stocky, coca-chewing Quechua man rummaging through our belongings.

'Hey, what do you want? Que pasa?' I yelled, leaping up. There was no response from the mountain man, who calmly stepped off our rock ledge, strode along the river's edge and disappeared among the boulders.

By now the others were up, aroused by the commotion. 'What's going on, Tim?' asked Jerome.

I told them the story, and how I had thought it was one of them making tea.

'Strange to see someone by the river at this time of the day,' said Piotr.

'Maybe he is "not all there" in the head,' I said. 'He didn't even look at me.'

As far as we could see nothing was missing, so we forgot the incident and began to prepare our Jungle Oats breakfast.

That day we pushed hard to reach Hanging Bridge where Fanie and Pierre would be waiting for us. The idea was to film the long portage that lay upstream of the bridge. Before arriving, however, two strenuous portages saw us roping our kayaks to the wall of the canyon as we skirted the enormous chunks of mountainside that had crashed down, burying the river-course for hundreds of metres. This delayed our schedule, and although we paddled hard (Jerome almost paying the penalty for our haste by getting stuck in a chute), darkness overtook us and we had to spend another night under the stars. Our camp was in a small, sandy cleft, wedged uncomfortably between polished black rocks. Everyone was grumpy and irritable, and François was not at all happy that we had had to paddle the rapids in the semi-dark.

The Hanging Inca Bridge where we were summonsed to a people's court.

163

Hung Jury

The magnificent Hanging Bridge came into view after we had negotiated some tight and difficult rapids. It was a beautifully designed structure, with grass ropes plaited in a graceful arc between the two buttresses of rock. As we clambered out of our kayaks, two stick-wielding Quechua men shouted angrily at us from the bridge and came sliding down the steep bank towards us.

'These guys look hostile. Seems like they've got something on their minds,' remarked François dryly.

As if a sign, a loose boulder crashed into the river a few metres away from us. Meanwhile our friendly 'neighbourhood watchers' approached.

'They look drunk; we'd better look sharp,' I warned, clutching my paddle just in case.

'Señores,' shouted the solidly-built man in poor Spanish, 'the Principal of our village has sent for you. You must come with us immediately.'

'Why, señor?' François asked. 'What have we done that you should be so angry with us?'

'Señor, you need permission to pass under this bridge,' answered the man. 'Also your friends make a film with cameras. You must pay for this – we have come to charge you.'

'Where are our friends?' asked Piotr, stepping forward.

'There, along the road.' The drunk spokesman pointed to the top of the ridge where we spotted the parked Land Rover. Fanie and Pierre had seen us and came down to meet us. Apparently two drunk men had threatened them during the night, and the Land Rover had been stoned in the early hours of the morning.

An argument broke out between François and Piotr as to how best to respond to the persistent demands. François wanted to go the diplomatic route: 'Yes, we'd love to meet the Principal. We'll gladly drive up to the village and explain to him what we are doing.' Piotr, on the other hand, was all for an

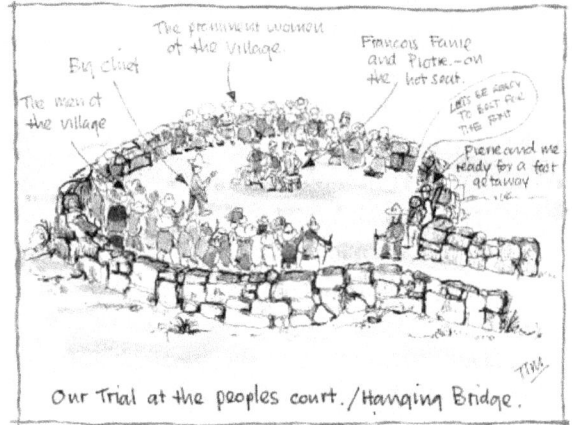

Our Trial at the peoples court. / Hanging Bridge.

aggressive line: 'Tell your chief to come down to us if he wants to speak to us.'

'They only want money from us for filming the bridge,' Piotr explained to us.

But François had handled more delicate situations than this. He assured us that all we had to do was to be decent to the people and show respect.

In 1983, when the Poles and I passed the Hanging Bridge, we discovered that the Incas rebuilt it every year as a co-operative project between the citizens of Chumbivilcas province to the west of the canyon, and of Canas province to the east. Woven entirely from ichu grass, its purpose is entirely ceremonial and it stands as a beautiful and graceful structure.

According to the villagers at Huinchirian, an American film crew, which had once arrived to film the bridge, had refused to pay the fee, and the villagers had burned down the bridge in anger. We certainly did not want to provoke anything like this. So when, years later, Condorita came chugging into view laden with cameras and gringos, the villagers understandably jumped to conclusions and prepared for war. This explained the tense atmosphere that we now drove into. We immediately became the centre of attention and soon the small plaza was swarming with hostile villagers surrounding us.

The leader of the village – a small, wiry, sharp-featured Quechua man, dressed in traditional hessian shirt and trousers, and wearing car-tyre sandals and a woollen alpaca hat – introduced himself to us. We were ushered into a circular enclosure with a hand-hewn stone bench in the middle. François, Piotr and Fanie (our spokesmen), were ordered to sit on the bench, while Pierre, Jerome and I (the plebs) sat far back in the cheap seats.

'Good thing we are sitting here,' I whispered to Pierre. 'From here we can make a quick getaway should we need to.'

The prominent men and coca-chewing women-folk of the village streamed into the arena and formed a tight circle around us. The 'jury' – two village elders and the Principal himself – made three imposing figures as they faced the accused. A silence fell over the arena, and the tension levels nearly went off the charts.

Fanie leaned across to François. 'This reminds me of the Dingaan's kraal massacre,' he muttered in Afrikaans. (In 1838, Dingaan, a Zulu chief, lured a party of Boers into his kraal under false pretences and murdered them.)

I prayed a quick prayer, 'Lord, we're in trouble, please help us – You know best how.'

The Principal began his interrogation in a Quechua dialect and an interpreter translated it into Spanish.

Fanie growled in Afrikaans, 'The interpreter, he's the one who was drunk and threw stones at us last night! I'd like to bliksem him properly!' (Bliksem is an Afrikaans word meaning 'to work over thoroughly with the fists'.)

Piotr was first to respond to the Principal's interrogation. He stood up and began his well-rehearsed presentation, displaying letters from the Peruvian Tourism Organisation, the Peruvian Police Commissioner, and newspaper clippings showing photographs of our team. (Luckily, we had persuaded Piotr to remove his 10-inch dagger before the 'trial' began.)

'We are not just ordinary tourists making a film,' he announced. 'We have been commissioned by the Prime Minister himself to explore the Amazonas; to help make Peru the greatest nation on earth! How could we be asked to pay for passing under the bridge? Would not the honourable Prime Minister be offended if he heard how badly we are being treated by your village?'

Piotr's outrageous, overacted story was embarrassing, but it completely took in the audience who were impressed and silent.

François followed with another diplomatic volley, explaining our goals and our itinerary and even offering free medical care from our team doctor, Kate. After an hour of grilling, and much debate between the three wise men, the tension started to lift. Maybe we would not be beheaded after all! To our relief we were finally dismissed without having to pay a cent. We hurried back to the river hoping that the jury would not change their minds and call us back.

Now the hiking team arrived, bedraggled and exhausted. Kate had infected blisters, Zbecek had a pain in his chest and Joe struggled with a strained knee. François, too, was showing signs of stress. The effort of leading such a diverse group, each member with his or her own demands, was testing him to his limits. A volatile situation flared up when François asked Joe to assist with the carting of camera gear back upstream to the blockage. When Joe had refused, appealing that he needed to rest, an intense argument broke out between the two of them. The dispute was only resolved when François consented to Joe staying behind to assist Kate with the medical treatment of the villagers.

At Hanging Bridge we once again split up into three groups. The plan was to meet downstream in approximately five days at the village of Surinama, situated at the end of the notorious Black Canyon. This would be the crux section for the kayakers, and would demand all our skills and boldness.

Chapter 7

THE BLACK CANYON

Infighting

After it passes the Hanging Bridge, the Apurimac plunges into a steep-sided gorge called the Black Canyon. In 1974 Calvin Giddings, a chemistry professor from Idaho, led the first US team to attempt the gorge, which he described as 'a place where enormous rocks covered the valley floor. The water charged in frenzy at these giants, boiling beneath and between them in search of a distant sea.' The American team soon abandoned the attempt, claiming that a navigation of the canyon 'would be suicidal' (*Demon River Apurimac*, J. Calvin Giddings, 1974–1975).

The Apurimac crashes through 60 km of winding, volcanic canyon, and drops, as it does so, more than a vertical kilometre – that is, a fall of 20 m a kilometre – before Pillpinto Bridge. In 1983 I had, with Piotr and Andrej Pietowski, run a descent of the gorge, reaching Pillpinto 10 days after setting out, battered and out of food. The river had stretched our skills to the utmost, and the experience had forged strong bonds of friendship between us.

After paddling a few kilometres we found ourselves in familiar territory – blockages, blockages and more blockages! Colossal house-sized rocks split the river, creating a complex of siphons, sieves and blockages that made up to a lethal stretch. I was worried about François's deteriorating self-confidence, which would surely have a negative impact on the whole expedition. It was critical that he regain self-assurance before we got to the walled-in sections of river. Gradually, by coaching him and encouraging him through the easier rapids, his self-confidence grew, and he improved steadily. But he still did not want to run the more difficult rapids, and made slow progress through the strenuous portages and over the giant rocks.

We only had food for four days in our kayaks, and so our speed of travel was critical. At one point we emerged after taking more than four hours to negotiate a mere 800 or 900 m. Both François and Piotr had already taken bad swims and had on more than one occasion narrowly missed being sucked under the rocks. While I was assisting François, I found myself beginning to negotiate the rapids through his eyes, feeling his fear and insecurity.

'No. This can't go on,' I told myself. 'Someone is going to come adrift or drown at this rate.' I had already warned François that I might have to ask him to leave the river. The time for that was getting near.

To complicate matters further, François and Piotr were engaged in an unspoken psychological tussle to see who notched up the least swims. François had had four gruelling swims since Hanging Bridge; Piotr only three. On our third morning the canyon unexpectedly opened out, and François's paddling immediately improved. I led the way through a tricky class 4 rapid, and, reaching the bottom, looked back to see Piotr's upturned boat and Piotr being 'pinballed' as he swam through the steep drops and rocky channels. François completed the run in fine style, whooping at the bottom of the rapid. I could read his mind. 'See that, Tim? Why should I leave the river and not Piotr?' The score in their game was four all!

We finally arrived at the rickety Chaca Bridge, deep within the canyon, where our maps indicated a possible take-out point. I was sure that the wisest thing to do was for François to portage this section. I approached the expedition leader.

'Frans, old chap, I'd like you to walk from here. The river's getting worse and I can see you're taking strain. I'm also stressing just looking after you . . . Frans, I'd really like you to walk. It seems there's a footpath to Pillpinto, along the right bank.'

Disappointment swept across François's face. He was struggling. He had so badly wanted to run the whole river and being asked to leave came as a hard blow.

'Tim, don't you think I'll be all right? I'll portage anything that looks difficult. I won't hold you guys up.'

'No, Frans, I've given it a lot of thought and I'm worried about you. Besides, we're really short on time and our food is low. We've just got to maintain pace in the next section if we're to get back on track.'

François argued against my proposal, but I stood my ground.

'Frans, remember our discussion? We agreed that I could and would ask you to leave the river if you weren't coping. Well, the time has come. I'd like you to set off tomorrow at first light – we'll meet you at Pillpinto Bridge.'

At last he gave in.

That evening the atmosphere was tense. Little was said. We sat around the smouldering fire until a cold, steady drizzle set in, and drove us to our sleeping bags.

The Sieve

François set off early in search of helpers to carry his kayak. Two hours later he was back with two sturdy Quechua men who effortlessly hoisted the loaded boat onto their shoulders and set off into the hills at a cracking pace, François tagging on behind.

Jerome, Piotr and I continued downstream, into a sheer-walled section of canyon where the high-water mark was a sobering 186 m above water level. The section began with big drops and tight turns. Bend by bend, we worked our way down the river until eventually we arrived at a steep, confusing rapid that Jerome volunteered to scout. The rapid began with a 2-m drop into a pool, and all I could see from the top was mushrooming water in the pool below. I watched Jerome intently as he 'acted out' the run. Our years of kayaking had developed an almost telepathic rapport between us. By watching his expressions, his hand movements, and his body language I could form a pretty good idea as to how involved or how easy a rapid was. If Jerome walked to his boat to take out his throw-line, that was the signal for me to climb out and look at the rapid for myself. If Jerome said 'Go' I would run the rapid blind, remembering his directions and hand signals and working out the rapid as I went. This time, however, Jerome turned towards me, raised his arms in a paddling motion (describing a fast entry), and then, with his right hand, indicated a 'boofing' move (where the kayak lands flat on the water) followed by a hard sweep, directing me to an exit drop on the left side of the pool. Apparently it was that simple. From the small eddy where I was parked against the cliff face I peered over my shoulder, feeling a strange uneasiness about the run. Jerome's thumb went up. 'Okay, I'll do it,' I said, trying to convince myself. I nodded to Jerome that I was going in.

There was time for three hard forward strokes before I launched over the drop. As I approached a ghastly recollection exploded in my mind. This was the place where I had almost drowned in 1983! In disbelief

I stopped paddling for a moment, but it was too late – I was committed. From my 1983 experience, I knew what was waiting. There would be water mushrooming up, followed by a flood sucking beneath the large undercut rock – a sieve, a one-way ticket to nowhere! (Where the water washes under a rock, there is no way out if a kayaker is dragged underneath.)

I heard Jerome scream 'Paddle, Tim, paddle!' but I had lost my momentum. The kayak dropped far too slowly over the chute; water forced my stern down, and my kayak reared up in a vertical 'endo'. I braced myself, keeping upright, but I had lost my line to the left where the exit chute washed through. Within seconds, I was re-enacting the 1983 episode. What were the odds of this happening? Almost immediately my kayak was washed sideways against the opposite wall where the flood of water rushed under the rock. Shock overtook me; adrenalin pumped furiously through my system. I threw myself against the rock to hold myself away and avoid being flipped by the powerful current. Then, as if this was all part of a sick joke, the dreaded event happened – while I was broadside against the rock a violent surge flipped me upside down. I struck out with my right blade, trying to 'Eskimo roll' against the current, but without success. My boat slammed against the rock wall and it was only its buoyancy that kept me afloat and away from a black, watery grave. I began to set up for another roll, leaning forward and striking with all my strength. 'I must roll or I'm dead,' flickered through my consciousness. I struck with my paddle and broke the surface just long enough for a gasp of air before going down again. Then I was out of breath – was this the end? As a last resort, I reached for the spraydeck handle, yanking it as hard as I could. In an instant I was sucked out of the kayak and into darkness . . .

Another day in the canyons.

169

Touch and Go

Strange things can happen in life-threatening situations; I felt a calmness sweep over me, as though I were watching myself in a slow-motion movie. In a last bid for survival I grabbed the rim of my cockpit and let go of the paddle. My legs were being sucked horizontally under the rock, while my head and shoulders slammed against the undercut rock roof. I had to get air, but my own boat blocked my escape route. I could feel my outstretched arm tearing at my shoulder as I fought to hold myself against the powerful current.

'Hold on, hold on. Lord God, I can't last anymore. Please help me; I'm finished.'

I can't remember how long I held on. Then an unexpected jerk yanked me sideways along the rock. The current slightly weakened its grip. I kicked out with my legs, hunting for any type of foothold; 'there – a slight crack in the rock roof'. Cautiously I pushed against the rock with my feet so that, using all my strength, I could force the hull of the kayak away with my head. It moved and I broke through, drawing a huge lungful of air. Then my foot slipped off the crack, and once again I found myself mauled by the undercurrent. The kayak was dragging me along the rock face. Gradually the pull of the current eased and allowed me to wrench my head out from the water. I found myself a handhold on the rock face with my one arm, but my boat refused to follow. I had to either let go of the rock or the boat. A violent surge made the decision for me. It yanked the kayak from my grip and forced it back into the siphon. Fortunately my handhold held, giving me a breathing space to find another hold for my left hand. I lifted my legs

The same siphon rapid I was caught in 2 yrs earlier (picture taken in 1983).

out of the siphon, but my fingers began losing grip, and I was about to fall back into the siphon. Suddenly a hard object shoved against my back, pinning me momentarily against the rock face and allowing me to frantically lunge for another handhold. To my amazement I realised it was my kayak, which had projected out of the water and given me a shove before it slipped back again.

Hanging on to the rock, and with the current still pulling at my legs, I inched away from the siphon. With my left foot I found a small foothold – at last I could rest my arms. But I was still flat against the slippery rock face, completely stuck, unless – unless . . . Glancing sideways at the polished rock I noticed occasional small fingerholds. Would these give me a way out? There was no other option.

Over the roar of the water I heard frantic yells from Piotr and Jerome. In the corner of my eye I could see, in arm's reach, a throw-bag, bobbing in the turbulence. It was one of those 'so near yet so far' situations. I dared not lose my grip by grabbing at it, or even by looking around. If I did, I'd be under the rock in a second, headed to one destiny – death by drowning! Gone, 'married with no children . . .'

'Climb, Biggs, climb! Climb like you've never climbed before.' The smooth rock offered no favours, just small dents and nubs for fingerholds. Sideways I caught a glimpse of the kayak, still battering against the wall of rock. A new fighting spirit overtook me: 'No, forget it, I'm not going back in there again. Not for anything!'

Hanging in There

Jerome described the final moments of the drama in his journal: '. . . Tim pulls himself up a little, but sinks down. He makes a quick grab and sticks a hold. Pulling his legs away from the current, he slowly gains ground, working his way to the side where the rock eases its angle. More of his life jacket appears above the water, then the neoprene spray skirt, and

Our campsite after my bad swim - I was ready to go home!

then he stops. He clings, having to hold up the weight of his own body. He doesn't move for a while, his hands constantly adjusting his grip on the same holds, trying just to hang on. I think we (Piotr and I) were silent. Slowly he gets a leg up where he can place a foot against some slightly favourable slope. A hand moves, then the other foot. He eases up and finally gets hold of something, then moves on to better holds around and up to the side and pauses. After a while he finishes the moves, climbing out onto a sloping ledge where he slumps down with his head on his arms . . .'

'Thank You, oh my God. You saved me. I was done,' I gasped. Jerome had paddled across the river to my rock island to join me.

'Tim, well done, man, that was amazing . . . how did you do it? I thought you were gone,' Jerome said, kneeling next to me.

'That's the place I told you about. Exactly the same thing happened in 1983, but I only recognised it as I went over the drop.'

We stopped for a while to hook and haul my boat out of the siphon rip and brew some tea. My paddles and sandals now belonged to the Apurimac, but it was a small price to pay. 'That's all you're getting from me this time, old river,' I quipped, hoping indeed that it would be so.

Trying to look confident, I climbed back into the kayak's cockpit, fighting my fear and unstable emotions. When one has been thrown by a horse, the best thing is to jump back into the saddle. But it was not easy: part of me cried out, 'Enough, enough,' while another shouted, 'Come on, Biggs; pull yourself together. Don't "psyche" yourself out now; you can do it.'

I slipped back into the fast, green current, pushing ahead of Jerome. Jerome knew me well and held back, allowing me to take the lead and restore my battered confidence.

'Careful, Tim, looks like the water goes hard right after that blockage,' he warned.

It was a difficult class 4 rapid with another bad siphon. I charged at it and fought my way down, terrified, but high on adrenalin and false bravado. The other two followed without mishap.

'Good one, Timmo, good line,' came Jerome's opportune encouragement. 'Let's call it a day. We need a break.'

Piotr knocked up a fire and had a brew of strong coffee going within minutes. I shed my wet kayaking gear, sponged out my kayak, dragged it up to a small patch of sand, and then returned for some hot, sweet coffee.

That night I lay gazing up at the stars, graphic flashbacks of my epic swim playing through my mind. In the flickering light of a candle I hauled out my pocket Gideons Bible which I had received during my military service and soaked up its comforting words from the Book of Psalms: '"Because he loves me," says the LORD, "I will rescue him; I will protect him, for he acknowledges my name."' A sense of deep comfort and gratitude came over me. 'Hey Lord,' I mused, 'today you saved me all right, you sure did and Lord – I just want to follow you!' I rolled over and slept deeply.

Close Shaves

With my close shave behind me I started the new day with a positive approach. I was determined to win back my confidence, and face my fears head on. We were at a section where the Apurimac charged between the 600-m walls in continuous class 3 to 5 rapids. The gradient had increased to 28 m/km, with a volume of 60 m³/sec (2 000 cfs).

Piotr woke feeling nauseous, so we waited until the sun's rays crept into the narrow gorge to warm us before we set off. Piotr had paddled courageously and had suffered more than his fair share of swims. Now his body was a mass of cuts and bruises. He was a superb expeditioner and I enjoyed paddling with him. Out on the water it felt like the old days again. If it were not for the cloud of suspicion that hung over him after he had tried to take over the expedition, he would have been the perfect man for the job. Would his game plan change when he transferred to the raft team, and he had his own power-base? Once again, time would tell.

I was paddling behind Jerome, with Piotr some way behind me, when we approached a steep rapid. The whole river flowed into an obvious siphon, the water visibly sucking under an enormous 6-m boulder. It would take some nifty paddling to work ourselves to the right-hand side and avoid the rock undercut.

Jerome went through first, and as I began my run, my boat glanced off a submerged rock, sending me directly towards the undercut. I desperately cranked a left sweep, but there was no time and I crashed headlong into the rock wall. My kayak's nose wedged under the rock; the stern swung around broadside against the rock – an almost identical situation to the day before! My blood turned cold and I threw myself against the rock with such force that the paddles clanged with the impact. Five long seconds dragged by as I wrestled to keep the boat upright. There was no way I was going to flip again! At last the kayak edged forward, finding enough moving water to swing into the main current. I was free and gasped with relief.

We pushed ourselves hard that day, and after seven hours on the water, we pitched camp. It was Piotr's turn to cook and we wolfed down the large pot of supper.

'Excellent food, Piotr. Your mother taught you well,' teased Jerome. We sat around our little fire, chatting and edging as close as possible to the flames to warm ourselves. Looking across the fire at Piotr I couldn't help wondering whether he was still planning another leadership challenge or not. On the water he was 'as good as gold' and a pleasure to be with; however, I still felt I had to watch him.

The following day (day five since our 'trial' at the Hanging Bridge), as we were working our way through the continuous rapids and boulders, we heard distant yells from the cliffs above us.

'It's François,' Piotr shouted. 'Look, up to the right.'

François and his two Quechua guides were perched on a narrow traversing ledge, 100 m above us. With the help of a throw-line, François began climbing down towards us, holding the kayak which the guides lowered from ledge to ledge. At the final vertical drop François was left dangling some 3 m above ground with no rope to spare.

'Drop, Frans, drop,' we shouted. 'There's grass below you.'

Jerome taming the Apurimac.

François let the rope go and thumped to the ground in a heap, fortunately without injury. We greeted each other heartily, exchanging tales and war stories, and then pushed on hurriedly downstream. We had passed through the most difficult section and could make good time on the water. Surimana Bridge came into view shortly before nightfall, and a volley of cheers went up from our waiting support team of Fanie and Pierre as we paddled under the bridge. Joe, Zbecek, Sergio and Kate were still on the trail, and we would have to wait for them before moving downstream. Jack Jourgensen had arrived to join us. Jack and I were old friends; we had been on the Colca expedition together in 1983.

'Hey, Zulu, you've got yourself a beard,' he laughed. 'You look like a shortened version of Abe Lincoln.'

'Thanks, Jack, that's a compliment; you're looking more like a Viking than ever.'

We couldn't find a campsite by nightfall, & had to sleep on the rocks.

Jack beamed at us and looked comfortable amongst the team. Fanie, Pierre and François brought out their brandy and we celebrated our running of the Pillpinto gorge sitting around a large fire, spinning tall stories of the past day's adventuring.

Fanie's time was up. He was to head back to South Africa, leaving Pierre to continue with the filming. Pierre had so far kept out of the limelight – except when there was a party in progress and then he would join Fanie and François in sinking a few bottles of brandy. Meanwhile a report on the Swedish

team that had preceded us was disturbing. Apparently they were a week ahead of us, and had spent two days in Cuzco before continuing downstream. Well, at least we had gained a few days on them during this last run.

The Swedish issue had rattled us. Knowing we were trailing in the quest placed pressure on us to speed up our progress. Other developments also raised the tension level within the group. François and Joe were clashing frequently over team issues and over the terms of the contract between them. The shockwaves from these scuffles began to have a polarising effect on François and the hikers, with Zbecek and Kate showing a degree of antagonism towards François.

That night was my turn to cook. 'Tonight we are going to eat basketfuls of grilled trout,' I had unwisely boasted. I had spotted a Quechua fisherman with a dozen or so fat trout close to our camp. 'Surely I can do the same,' I thought. I spent the whole afternoon fishing, but – to the hoots and jeering mirth of my peers – I crept sheepishly back to camp with my trophy, only one mingy 3-inch trout!

We celebrated our reunion late into the night and left early the following morning on the final five-day stretch of the canyon to Pillpinto itself. The next few days were slow and difficult. We picked our way, eddy by eddy, through a maelstrom of rocks, drops and blockages. On the third day we paddled till dark, covering only 7 km. The river was unfriendly towards us and we were unable to find a camping site along the steep sides. At last in the semi-darkness we could make out a cable spanning the river with its small carriage (oroya) on rollers hanging high above us.

'Let's try that rock shelf,' I called. 'The river might get worse and then we'll be in a real pickle.'

Everyone agreed. We hauled our kayaks on to the uneven shelf and fastened them with the equipment and sleeping bags to the rock. A narrow slit of sky above us with a few bright stars indicated another clear, beautiful night. The moon had cast a golden light over the western slopes of the canyon walls. I wondered how my Margie was bearing up back in South Africa. I had posted a letter at Yauri but whether it would ever reach Africa was anyone's guess.

We woke early after an uncomfortable and sleepless night. Clinging to the sloping rock all night had been no fun at all. At midday on our fourth day Jerome, François, Piotr and I finally sighted the Pillpinto bridge ahead. With hearty backslapping, whooping and shouting we paddled under the bridge. We were through the Black Canyon.

Chapter 8

THE LOWER CANYONS

Pillpinto – Puente Militar

The next stage of our journey was the 110-km section from Pillpinto to Puente Militar. Each bend we rounded unveiled another perspective on the spectacular river wilderness through which we were travelling. Each canyon revealed a unique, contorted geological story – giant art pieces for us to see and admire. We gazed in awe as nature's sculptured ramparts towered majestically above us – polished black columns reaching up thousands of feet, gnarled and folded metamorphic arches and multi-coloured tooth-shaped schists.

This five-day stretch would be the last we would navigate by kayak alone. After Puente Militar the raft would join us. Dr Calvin Giddings described the section, with its two canyons and excellent white water, as 'easier to run' than the Black Canyon. This proved to be true; there were endless kilometres of continuous rapids for us to revel in.

We were operating as a team, moving easily with François, who, happily, was back on the river, and making quick portages whenever we scouted. During one long, difficult rapid François missed his roll and came up with a bloodied face and a gash under his chin, shouting, 'I'm hurt . . . it's bad!' We rushed to help him and to assess the damage – it was the team's first blood donation to the Apurimac. We were within a day of the bridge at Puente Militar. As Kate was with the land party, and much to François's relief, we decided not to do the suturing on the riverbank but to push hard for the bridge. We could hitch a ride to Cuzco and hopefully meet up with Kate there. Within an hour of François's injury, Piotr also capsized in the thundering rapid that he had named 'The Big One'. Hurled against rocks and swept down two steep drops, he finally managed to cling to a rock from which Jerome ferried him to the bank. He was bleeding profusely as he dragged himself on to land. Apart from a bashed knee, there were deep lacerations across his nose and lip.

Piotr in a tight spot – left's terrible – right's worse – what do I do?

We arrived at the rusted steel bridge, Puente Militar, at 3:00 p.m., battered but exhilarated. Our trip was acquiring the timeless quality of a long expedition – our month on the river felt like half a lifetime. We hauled our kayaks and equipment up onto the bridge and waited for a truck travelling to Cuzco. Once at Cuzco the team would regroup and restock provisions. Several trucks passed, each overloaded and crawling painstakingly slowly along the rutted road. Finally, a dilapidated red Ford rattled across and pulled over. Piotr led the negotiations and persuaded the Quechua driver to load us onto his already overloaded truck. The kayaks went on top of the cab and we hoisted ourselves onto the open back.

Our fellow passengers – four sheep and half a dozen leg-bound roosters – accepted us without a bleat or cackle, and we returned their tolerance by edging unobtrusively into the corners. What we hoped would be a two-hour journey ended predictably as an eight-hour marathon. We had our fair share of punctures and an overheated engine. In the freezing Andean night, a puncture was no picnic. Our likeable driver, Jose, had no jack, so the male passengers had to dig a hole in the rock-hard road, deep enough for him to remove the wheel, patch the tube, and continue until the next disaster! All the while the truck laboured through an endless series of hairpin switchbacks. At one point I looked at the snoring François, lying with his head back and his mouth slightly open. Two large ewes, their faces only inches from his, gazed 'lovingly' at his sleeping countenance.

We arrived at Cuzco at 3:00 a.m., exhausted, frozen and suffering from fleabites. Cuzco was my old stamping ground. Confidently I led my friends through the cobbled streets to the old señora's court-yarded pensione which had been my home and refuge for many a night. The next morning we met up with the rest of the team. François's and Piotr's battle injuries were attended to, and we celebrated in the festive restaurants of Cuzco town. We were informed that the two Swedish paddlers had decided to pull out from their expedition after one of them had sustained a serious shoulder injury. Although we were relieved that the race had now ended we saluted them for their courageous achievement.

Developments
(Puente Militar – Puente Cunyac)

Puente Militar marked the point where the dynamics of the expedition would change completely. Here the kayakers would merge with the hiking team, and two rafts would be with us on the river. I felt uneasy about

shopping centre at 9-10-85
Puenta Cunyac. TIM

this set-up. Was I being selfish, reluctant to sacrifice our fast and easy-moving kayak team in order to include the rafts? I had little doubt that the rafts would slow things down significantly.

The hiking team had arrived at Puente Militar a day before we did and hitched a ride into Cuzco. They had done amazingly well, following the Apurimac through endless ravines and mountains, and reaching the most isolated Quechua communities. Kate, Zbecek, Joe and Sergio gelled together well, with Joe emerging as the leader.

The hiking team came down from the mountains with rather more than good team spirit. It was soon evident that Kate and Zbecek were engaged in an Andean romance. No one spoke openly about it, but the gossip spread quickly through the camp. I felt uncomfortable with developments. A romantic affair between teammates was worrying. We weren't even a quarter of the way through the journey, and this affair would surely create tension and complications amongst us. Both François and Piotr were unhappy with the development, but there was not much they could do as they had both had similar track records on previous trips. Any objection from their side would have been unfounded. Jerome, on the other hand, found the whole thing amusing, while Pierre cashed in on the juicy news. Politically, a strengthened unity between Zbecek, Kate, Joe and Piotr was consolidated.

For Piotr the excitement of the hour was that he could at last dominate team dynamics from his raft. His adventure business, Canoandes, would run uncharted waters and so gain exposure. There were now seven people (Jack, Joe, Sergio, Kate, Zbecek, François and Pierre) who would experience the river adventure on rafts. This would require two fully manned rafts and hence two raft captains. Piotr would obviously captain his own raft, and the other would either be François, who had little rafting experience, or Jack, who had done some rafting in the United States. These two options floated round the campfire, and eventually François was nominated.

This gorge had us worried!

Again I bit my lip in frustration. Half the team had never really been essential for the functioning of the trip. I was sympathetic to the fact that they had made an enormous effort to reach the river. But now the expedition had become clumsy and unwieldy. Jerome and I were given the task of guiding the rafts down the river. This meant a reversal of roles. The kayaking expedition had become a rafting expedition, the kayaks only there to support the rafts. I sulked quietly for the afternoon and took myself for a hike downstream to escape the politicking and jostling in the camp.

François's raft was now officially 'full' but he agreed to take on one more member – a Peruvian river man, Guiyermo, from Cuzco. Guiyermo had rafted this

179

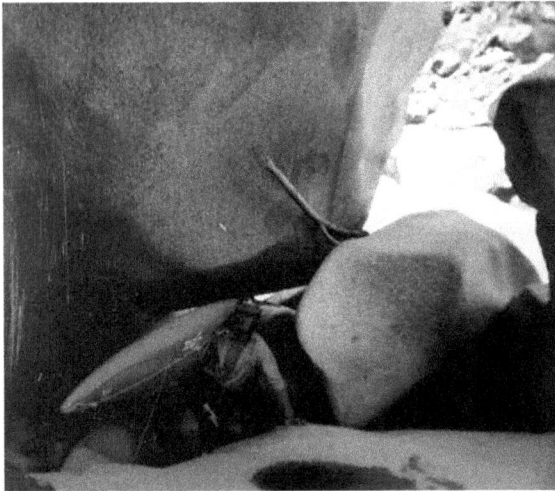

Jerome climbing through the rocks.

section before and agreed to accompany us for the four-day run to Cunyac Bridge. (By coincidence, Guiyermo was the guide I met up with when I had hiked the Inca trail alone in 1981.) He was adamant that Cunyac would be his final destination.

'Past Cunyac, no, we cannot do that stretch,' he said. 'The Senderos will kill us. Some tourists were killed there only weeks ago. Better we leapfrog that section and put in at Luisiana.'

We had no option but to respect his recommendation.

Even now as we prepared to take to the water, there were undercurrents of discontent. François, for instance, was still not seeing eye to eye with Joe. Their relationship had deteriorated steadily and we watched from a distance as the two of them clashed regularly.

'What's going on between you guys?' I eventually asked François. 'You seem to be at each other's throats whenever I see you.'

'Joe isn't playing the game, Tim,' was the brief reply. 'He's going back on our agreement, but don't worry, we are sorting things out.'

'Frans, I'm not comfortable with things here. Since the rafts came on, things have gone crazy.

Piotr is obviously trying to seize control. Kate has sided with Piotr because of Zbecek, and Joe and even Jerome are moving to Piotr's side. I'm fighting with Piotr about his choices on the river and you're fighting with him and Joe. Only Sergio is probably neutral. There's a bad vibe amongst us. We're setting up for a major run-in.'

On a more personal level we were aware that the tension between the two of us was dangerously high. My assisting him down the river had taken its toll on our relationship.

The river trip that followed was fraught with tension, as I had feared. Piotr and I had our first real head-on confrontation over a river-running decision. Being captain of the raft (his own raft at that), he obviously had the right to decide what to run and what to portage. However, he was becoming reckless and his crew were starting to question his judgement and worry about their safety. The issue came to a head at a dangerous 600-m class 5 rapid.

'Shouldn't you miss this one, Piotr?' I prompted. 'Jack's not coping and your team looks as scared as hell. I reckon you should portage this one. It's big and dangerous. Jerome and I are both portaging.'

'No, Tim, no problem this rapid. We run it, I see the line.'

'Piotr, I disagree,' I said. 'Jerome and I both think you should give it a miss. We'll help you with the portage.'

Seldom in my river-running career had I found it necessary to make such a strong stand. This was someone who I had kayaked with for some years and who I highly respected. Our eyes locked. I could see Piotr's rage, but I held my ground – and my stare.

'No, Tim, I'll do it.'

'Piotr! You don't understand: I'm telling you not to. Don't run it – you must portage here!' It was as though he disregarded not only my advice but also my position in the team, let alone the safety of his crew.

Without a word further, he spun around and scrambled back over the boulders to the raft. Jerome, who had been listening intently, flashed me a look of concern. This was a make-or-break moment.

'Hey, Jerome, Piotr's got to listen if I ask him not to run,' I said. 'He's not alone in a kayak now; he's got a whole team with him. He must be prepared to be accountable, otherwise this trip is a shambles.'

I was the on-the-water leader: that was the deal. We could not allow everyone to follow his own head, especially in the sort of dangerous place where we now found ourselves.

I was about to go to the raft to help with the portage, when François shouted, 'Hey, look. They're running it!'

We kayakers leapt onto boulders to find a vantage point from which to view the run. The raft was already well into the approaches – it was too late to set up any sort of safety plan. We watched transfixed. The line looked good as the raft ploughed through three enormous waves. Then it plunged over a 3-m drop, crashed into the stopper at the bottom and swung 180 degrees before being dragged back into the thrashing hole. The entire team were laid flat by the impact. Jack was catapulted overboard and landed metres from the raft. He was now being swept helplessly toward the next drop. We groaned as we witnessed the spectacle. Disaster was a heartbeat away. Then, amazingly, the hole released the raft and it charged forward in spectacular style. Zbecek lunged out at Jack as the raft overtook him, gripped him by his life jacket, and in one powerful movement hoisted the 90-kg man back on board. The raft steadied, straightened and miraculously sailed through.

I was relieved that the raft had got through, but I was also angry and upset. I had been patient and reasonable with Piotr, but now he had blatantly defied and undermined my authority as on-the-water leader. Had I not often seen him order someone off the water when he thought the team's safety was in jeopardy? Now the tables were turned, but he was too arrogant to be on the receiving end. This latest incident only widened the split between us. Piotr was

testing me at every point, deliberately pushing me to the limits. The team could not afford defiance like this – not with the Sendero threat still hanging over us like a dark cloud. The situation needed fixing. Quickly.

François and Jack approached me that evening and shared their concern over Piotr's reckless behaviour. They, too, felt he was running a 'one man band'. The team itself was afraid that, at the rate and the way things were going, someone might pay the ultimate price. We decided to approach Piotr that evening when we had all cooled down.

That night I found Piotr in a subdued and quiet mood. I drew alongside him.

'Piotr, what's going on, man? Why are you fighting me? I invited you on this trip as a team member, in good faith. Why are you behaving like this? Are you trying to take over or what . . . what's going on?'

Seconds of silence followed before he looked at me with his steely blue eyes.

'Tim, leave me a while. I need some time,' he said, and walked away.

I could sense a struggle in his mind and I backed off, watching as he made his way despondently across a small beach.

Incan terraced slopes.

Days later we arrived at Puente Cunyac. Although the general atmosphere had calmed, tensions among the team still brewed. We camped on a large open playa below the bridge where a great deal of filming, talking and more talking took place. From our camp we could clearly see the ancient ruins and abutments of the largest of the Inca hanging bridges in the Andes. It features in Thornton Wilder's book *The Bridge of San Luis Rey* (1927). The Incas burned the woven grass bridge in a last desperate attempt to halt the Spaniards on their march inland. Ironically, at this point, where the Spaniards met fierce opposition, we would now venture into hostile Sendero Luminoso territory.

We certainly could not pretend that we hadn't been warned of the potential dangers in this territory. The locals, the police, and the military had all ordered us not to proceed past Puente Cunyac. The Maoist revolutionary guerrillas had wrought terror and havoc in Peru during the past decade and were active and operational. But, needless to say, our stubbornness, and the desire to travel some of the Apurimac's most formidable waters, got the better of us. We were determined to keep going, even if it meant cutting down to one raft and three kayaks. We made our decision before we left home: we would do what it took to run the river. Guiyermo left the river; we carried on.

Guerrillas with machine guns were not going to stop us.

A mood of quiet introspection hung over our team, not unlike the mood among a platoon of paratroopers before setting out on a dangerous mission. I felt a deep longing to see and hold Margie before entering these badlands. I was missing her. Maybe some of us would not make it through this stage. 'Should I volunteer to pull out and skip this stage along with Kate, Jack, Guiyermo, Pierre and Sergio – for Margie's sake?' I thought. All my teammates were still single and independent; was I being reckless and irresponsible by pushing on? I spent a few hours on my own praying and contemplating the decision. I had another half hour to decide before the support team began their walk out. Then my mind cleared and I knew the answer. 'Stick to it, Tim, this is what you came for – you'll be looked after.' The voice that spoke rang true – I was on!

Sitting Ducks

On 12 September we set off with one raft, four kayaks and enough provisions for an eight-day journey. Our next destination was Cachora, where Kate and Sergio would meet us with new provisions. We were now in a military zone with no maps available, and were soft targets to the Sendero Luminoso guerrillas. Past reports forewarned us that apart from the Sendero threat, the river itself would be the most challenging we would yet encounter, with long walled-in sections and no access out of the canyon.

Anyone's guess what's around the next corner.

Over the last half-century various groups had attempted the gorge but none had been entirely successful. The most recent was that led by Dr Calvin Giddings in 1974. When his party reached an impassable section with vertical sides, they walked out, carrying their kayaks for five days before they found a village and a road back to the river.

The canyon sides rose up a staggering 2 000 m on both sides of us. The spectacular snow-capped Nevado Salcantay peak, some 6 200 m high, completed the surreal setting. The first day's paddling was relatively easy, and we worked our way through long uninterrupted sections of class 3 rapids. Suddenly Piotr, on the raft behind me, hollered a command: 'Paddle, paddle hard!' The rapid seemed straightforward and I did not understand why he was getting excited. The next moment I reeled as my kayak was struck from behind by the raft. I immediately capsized and ended up under the raft where I was held, jammed against the underside of the hull. Realising my predicament, I desperately tried to roll up when a massive blow to my helmet knocked me back. I was dragged upside down over shallow rocks suffering two more blows to my head in quick succession. After getting a final huge knock to my shoulder I decided to bail out of my kayak. I fought my way out of the cockpit and emerged behind the raft, spluttering and badly beaten up. Jerome had seen me disappear under the raft and was waiting for me. He towed me to the bank where I lay, shaken and hurt.

'You okay, Tim? That looked bad. I don't know what Piotr thought he was doing,' Jerome muttered angrily.

The raft retrieved my boat and paddle and pulled in to the bank, several hundred metres downstream. I sat on the rock, in my dazed state, trying to work out what had happened. Slowly it came back to me.

'Piotr, that was a dirty move. You ran me down, you bastard!' I cursed, under my breath. I hobbled down to the raft, my emotions seething, but determined to exercise self-control.

Not always a friendly river.

'What's up, guys?' I asked quietly. 'Piotr, are you trying to kill me? What was that all about?' Our eyes clashed.

'Sorry, Tim, we didn't see you,' said Piotr, trying to justify his action. 'You were too close to the raft.'

'Pathetic,' I muttered under my breath. I picked up my kayak and paddles and walked off, not staying to argue the point. What was the use? I got back into my kayak and floated downstream. I badly needed some time alone.

Piotr had changed since taking over the raft. He was a different person to the Piotr I had known on the Colca River.

Three days from Puente Cunyac we entered a steep, difficult section of white water where the river swelled to 100m³/sec (3 500 cf/s). By afternoon the canyon width had narrowed to a mere 15 m with grey rock sidewalls rising 100 m above us.

A blasting headwind carried clouds of fine dust that reduced visibility to the point where paddling became virtually impossible. Even with the strong downstream current the wind made it difficult for the raft to make headway. Admitting defeat, we decided to camp early, and after a long search we found a spot with just enough sand between the boulders to pitch our tents. Opposite us a 200-m waterfall cascaded down between travertine coated walls of rock. Immediately beneath us roared a fierce class 4 rapid. The wind eventually died down and a soft rain that had begun to fall during supper soon became a hard downpour, sending us scuttling for our tents.

François and I dashed inside our tent in time to see small rivulets of water trickling into the sleeping bags. Our attention, however, was quickly diverted by the giant splashes and explosions made by falling rocks that had dislodged from the sheer cliffs above us. We bolted for cover under a nearby cliff overhang where Pierre and Jack already sat huddled against the cliff face. Jerome, Zbecek and Joe risked sticking it out in the dry tents. Jerome went through the incident lying on his side in the tent because 'there is less chance of being hit if I lie on my side'. Joe opted to sleep with his crash helmet on. Zbecek, however, took the cake, reasoning in his Polish accent that 'I stay here, maybe I get hit by rock. I go outside maybe I get hit by rock, but for sure I get soaked. So I stay here.'

After some time under the cliff overhang, the rock fall subsided and we returned to our tents. 'We saw a lot of this on the Colca,' I remarked to François, thinking of the falling rocks cascading off the walls and sending showers of sparks into the darkness. 'Once, while we were scouting a rapid, one of the guys left his wooden paddles on the rocks. Just as he was about to pick them up, a rock the size of a rugby ball hit them, bull's eye! They simply disintegrated before his eyes – lucky it wasn't his head.'

'Ja, I hope we don't have one of those on our tent tonight,' said François sleepily. 'Anyway, I'm off to sleep. Goodnight.'

This was the only beach we could find for our lunch stop.

'Goodnight, sleep well.' I lay for some hours listening to the sporadic bombardments around us, thinking and praying about our journey. 'This sure is turning into one strange trip. It's not a cheerful affair like the other expeditions. It's as though there are sinister undercurrents at work, undermining our team and sabotaging our relationships. I sense trouble ahead, big trouble.' Negative thoughts sabotaged my mind, keeping me awake late into the night.

I moved the short stump of candle closer to my sleeping bag to read from my Bible. I turned to the Book of Psalms (my favourite book) and paged through it. I read the first two verses of Psalm 121: 'I lift my eyes to the hills, where does my help come from? My help comes from the LORD, the Maker of heaven and earth.'

I also read another Psalm that encouraged and comforted me: 'The Lord is my strength, He is the rock of my salvation, my refuge . . .'

'Yes, Lord,' I started to pray, 'I'm not up to this on my own. Please come and take over. I need You, Lord; I've put my trust in You. I need your help. I'm not happy about the state of affairs around here. Please give me the wisdom to deal with all these crazy relationships. Amen.'

The tension that, consciously or subconsciously, was simmering in all of us came to the fore that very night. While I lay deep in the land of dreams, frantic yells and shouts interrupted my sleep. I leapt to my feet, expecting to find a rock through the tent, or a hole in François's head! François was screaming incoherently.

'Frans, what's wrong? Are you okay?' I groped around in the dark for a torch. The next moment the tent broke loose from its pegs and I was being dragged along on my back.

'Frans, Frans, stop, it's okay! Frans, you're having a nightmare. It's okay, nothing's wrong!'

The tent stopped moving, followed by a moment of silence while François regained his composure.

'Hey, sorry man, Tim. I had a terrible dream. Sorry, man.' We laughed and re-erected the tent.

Me running a drop.

Pierre came to investigate. 'Wat gaan aan, mense?' he inquired in Afrikaans. 'Hoekom al die geraas?'

We laughed again, and tried to snatch an hour or two's sleep before dawn.

Lonesome Zulu

The rapid we had listened to all night from our tents looked far scarier in the morning. The Apurimac had risen a foot and was pushing huge stopper waves that spanned the river, pumping out plumes of spray. Cold and wet, we stood on the bank analysing the best line for running the rapid. Jerome, who had been kayaking brilliantly thus far, was confident.

'We punch through both holes, then hard left to miss that pour-over, and we're through. It'll be fine. I'll go first,' he added.

I was scared today. I had had enough of rapids and white water for a season, and my shoulder was painful. I wanted to go home; home to my sweetheart. What on earth was I doing here when I should have been lying in a warm bed with my beautiful wife?

'Oh, no, this must all be a huge mistake! I'm crazy to be here,' I scolded myself.

'Zulu, why you so quiet today? No joking this morning. What's wrong, Zulu?' teased Zbecek, sidling up to me, and sensing that I wasn't myself.

'You miss your Margie, hey Zulu? No worry, you see her again one day, not too long.'

'Hey, Zbecek – you know what I'm thinking. How do you know so much?' We caught each other's eye and laughed together. I liked this big Polish friend.

The first hole was massive, bigger than it had looked from the bank. It totally buried Jerome, after which he fought his way through the second. Then the raft followed, hovering for seconds in the turbulent pullback before the paddlers managed to claw their way through. Finally it was my turn, and with my heart in my mouth I sprinted towards it. Cold water crashed over me and took my breath away. I strained at my paddle and narrowly fought my way through. 'Two strokes and I'm into the next hole . . .' The stretch had started in earnest, another day at the office.

The gradient was picking up. As I made my way down a long, fast rapid, floating sideways, I dropped obliquely into an enormous 20-m-wide hole. It took me completely by surprise. I bounced and braced against the wall of water, hanging in for dear life. Gradually I edged my way to the side when, suddenly, a huge surge whipped me upside down. Two violent cartwheels later my kayak and I catapulted out of the hole and swept through a procession of roller-coaster waves.

Meanwhile the raft's progress became slower and slower. Jerome and I often had to wait 30 minutes below a rapid for the rafters to make their run. Portaging the raft itself was an exhausting and difficult operation. First we would haul out the gear and then, staggering between boulders, some as big as houses, we would carry the unwieldy raft. This often meant arriving at the bottom of a rapid several hours later. After a full day's river running, we had only travelled 1.5 km! At this speed we would only reach the sea next century.

Entering the Acobamba Abyss

Four days into this section, the river narrowed before veering west. Rock walls reared upwards, virtually closing out the sky above us. This was surely the most ominous chasm any of us had ever seen. It could only be the Acobamba Abyss, appropriately named by Dr Calvin Giddings's team. It was here that they had abandoned the river to make an exhausting, five-day portage through the mountains.

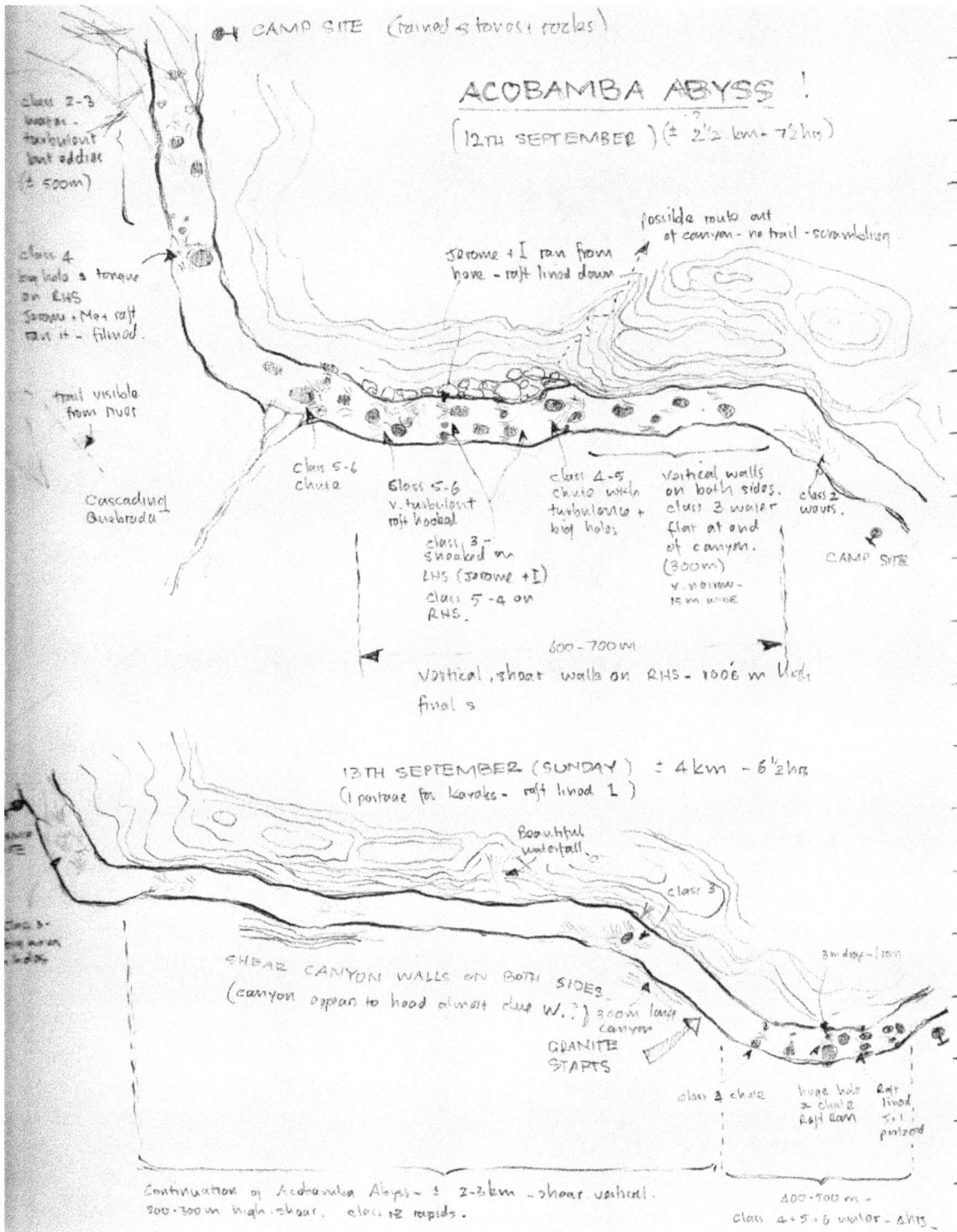

My journal notes of the Acobamba Abyss.

The rope snapped, & away went the raft - with our gear.

The entire Apurimac plunged into the 20-m-wide chasm and then rushed on through a series of class 5 rapids and chutes. The crazed brown waters crashed wildly through the constricted channel. Clambering up the rock sides we realised that there was only one option: go downstream! We could not camp, for fear of being bombarded by rocks from above; we could not portage along the vertical sides, and looking back for a way out was unpractical and out of the question. We had to run the rapids; that was it. A difficult, highly turbulent section of class 4 and 5 water cascaded between the cliffs. Some hundreds of metres on, the river calmed slightly before it disappeared out of sight, still confined by the sheer walls. What lay around that bend? Waterfalls? Cascades? It was anyone's guess. We elected to line the raft; three of us holding the 150-m rope while Joe pushed the vessel into the mainstream. Immediately the current

swept it to the middle of the river. As the raft plunged over the first drop it reared as it struck the foaming water and then ejected forward, heading for the next rapid. We were glad nobody was on board. We hauled it back towards us with all our might, but the line snagged on a protruding rock and the raft's nose was instantly dragged under the torrent. In vain we tried to release the snagged line, but the water pressure strained the one-ton line to breaking point. With a 'twang' the two ends whipped apart, and the unattached raft raced downstream. We held our breath as it sped away. Would we now be stranded in the abyss without our raft? Jerome, who was already some way downstream, saw the runaway raft speeding towards him. Diving into the current, he swam powerfully to it, hauled himself up, coiled the front bowline, and hurled it in my direction. Catching the line, we pulled the raft back only seconds before it

188

would have careered over the next chute with Jerome on board. Jerome secured the raft and leapt ashore, the undisputed hero of the day. What a relief it was that our supplies hadn't disappeared down the hungry throat of the Apurimac.

Another difficult manoeuvre now awaited the rafters. They had to line the raft around yet another dangerous chute. One by one they inched their way along a narrow ledge, traversed the cliff and then jumped 2 m down on to the raft that Zbecek was holding against the surging current. Jerome and I decided to run the next rapid and wait below for any 'swimmers'. We skirted the first dangerous hole, and then dropped through two more enormous holes before eddying behind a boulder. We had a breathing space in which to marvel at our dramatic surroundings. We were now in the deepest, most walled-in section of the Acobamba Abyss. Some 500 m above us, the converging walls virtually blocked out the sky,

Dodging holes.

allowing only a thin sliver of light to filter through the chasm. Short of breath, we sat tucked into the small, surging eddy.

'I've never seen anything like this,' I gasped, feeling small in the awesomeness of the place. 'I just can't believe it's so sheer and so walled in.'

Class 5 rapids in the Acobamba Abyss.

189

'Yeah, I just hope it lets us out,' answered Jerome. 'I don't get a good feel of what's around the corner – could be anything.'

'Ay, well – isn't this what we came for, Jerome?' I laughed. 'Can't get much better than this, hey?' We waited 20 minutes for the raft to appear, and just as we were beginning to worry, the craft burst into sight, careering broadside down the chute. The overloaded raft was barely under control! To top it all François was also on board, hanging on to his kayak. The wild expressions on the rafters' faces told the story of a harrowing run! They pulled into an eddy and offloaded François on to a ledge, obviously not wanting to risk another rapid with him on board. François climbed along the cliff face until he was

blocked. His only option was to swim the remaining section of the rapid and link up with his kayak. His nerves were already jaded, and the prospect of a torrid swim did not lighten his day. He stood frozen against the cliff, wrestling with his fear and wavering.

'Come on, Frans,' I thought, 'you can do this. Jump man, just jump. You won't drown. We can't get to you, anyway, so you have no choice.'

I understood our leader as though he were my brother – perhaps too well. The trip had reached a point where I would stress when I saw him stress.

Right now, however, he needed some encouragement, otherwise we would be at this same spot come tomorrow.

'Swim, Frans, swim,' I yelled above the roar of the river while imitating a swimming action.

The splash of a rock striking the water only metres away brought us back to reality. We squinted up at the thin crack between the vertical walls from where loosened rocks were beginning their daily bombardment of the river. The rock had cooled and contracted, sending missiles whistling down towards us. Two more rocks narrowly missed the raft. As tension levels spiked, we decided this was not the time to wait for François to make up his mind. A volley of shouts and yells followed. Five minutes became ten, until, at last, François plunged into the fierce water, disappearing under the turbulence. I paddled across and ferried him to the raft, where he received an icy welcome.

'Let's go, let's go,' shouted Piotr impatiently, 'before more rocks come down!'

As he spoke, another one whistled past, exploding like shrapnel as it struck a boulder nearby. We sped off downstream, feeling that we were 'running the gauntlet'. The sharp bend around which we had seen the river disappear now approached fast. The cliffs were still sheer and we prayed we would not find yet another waterfall or cataract. We paddled ahead of the raft searching for the first glimpse of what lay around the unknown bend.

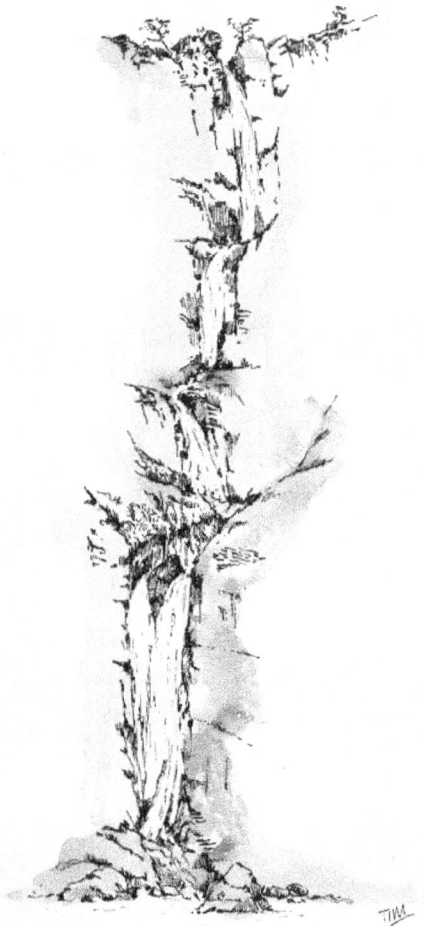

Escaped convicts - (Jerome & I on cooking duty).

'Look – there's a beach on the left,' François called excitedly. The river looked calmer and the vertical walls were less walled in, and a waterfall cascaded down the side. Emotionally exhausted by the day's dramas, and famished (we had not eaten since breakfast), we sighed a collective sigh of relief. It had been a disastrously slow day – one lousy kilometre in eight hours!

Big Rapids, Bad Politics

The following morning our hopes that we were out of the Acobamba Abyss were dashed. We floated straight into another 3-km canyon with sides, some 500 m high. Ready for anything and on high alert, we cautiously passed through a series of class 3 rapids that punctuated the racing current. Were we the first ever to venture into these austere depths of the earth?

Then, as we rounded a bend, the sides parted and the river opened wide, showing an horizon line of white crests spanning the river. River-running instils a 'gut feel' for when a waterfall or steep section approaches.

'Looks like we may have to scout this one,' called Jerome as we approached the crests. 'Feels like good gradient ahead.'

The dark gneisses and schists we had become familiar with changed abruptly to a lighter, coarse-grained granitic rock. The Apurimac plunged fiercely into yet another boulder-ridden gorge. Jerome and I ran half of the 600-m rapid before we eddied out and waited to support the raft. An hour later there was still no sign of it. Frustrated, we climbed the steep sides only to find the rafters working on Pierre's jammed camera! Blimmin' hell!

The river worsened and grew more demanding. Long, tedious portages became the order of the day. This meant hauling out the raft and then hoisting it and the gear over and between house-size boulders. Our progress for the day was 2 km.

'Our food is down; we must eat less,' was Zbecek's brief assessment on our fifth evening after leaving Puente Cunyac. There was a silence in the camp. We all looked at him.

'Zulu,' Zbecek went on, 'you must eat only half what I eat because you half my size.'

'Zbecek, next time you're in the river swimming I'll only rescue you if you give me your supper,' I replied, returning the friendly fire. The subsequent laughter was a pleasant relief.

'How long until Cachora do you think?' asked Jerome.

'Five days, maybe six,' answered Piotr, looking serious. 'Who knows?'

'I went scouting downstream yesterday afternoon,' I butted in, 'and for the next kilometre or so it's still really heavy going.'

'Well, we've no choice but to halve our rations,' François announced. 'Zbecek, could you and Joe work that out? You're in charge of supplies.'

Joe lay reclining against a rock, silent. It was anyone's guess what he was thinking. Zbecek nodded, twiddling his red 'Viking' beard with one finger.

'Okay, we do it,' he replied.

We all knew what that meant – our daily ration halved, and diluted with twice as much water to make a tasteless gruel. Yippee.

That night sheets of rain poured down and drenched us. The rainy season had begun in earnest. We needed to get out of this canyon before the river became impossible to run and too dangerous. By the next morning the river had swollen to a swirling 140m3/sec (5 000 cf/s), and was chocolate brown and turbulent. The rapids were relentless and grew worse as the day progressed. The raft capsized a couple of times and at one point Jerome had to chase after Joe and rescue him from a possible drowning.

'Where's Pierre?' someone shouted. In the commotion Pierre had simply disappeared.

A miserable campsite. 'Half rations from now,' announced Zbecek.

'I think I saw him being washed into the next rapid,' Piotr shouted back. Jerome and I ran the rapid blind and found an exhausted Pierre sprawled out on the beach.

'I thought I was finished,' blurted out Pierre, whilst retching up water. 'I was trapped under an undercut. Then, somehow, I got washed out.'

We were all taking an emotional and physical beating on this section. Everyone suffered from infected cuts and bruises caused mainly by the man-handling of the raft over slippery rocks. Zbecek had a badly injured knee and Piotr a crushed hand. Emotionally, we were frazzled from the constant tensions and scuffles between members. That night the camp was silent and restrained. Each of us sat engrossed in our own thoughts. We had only covered 2.5 km in nine hours on the river.

Whilst we lay in our sleeping bags, gazing at the slit of sky above us, François privately confided in Pierre and me that he wanted to take the raft off the river at Cachora. I agreed fully. I had been against the raft joining us from Cunyac; it was too slow and too dangerous to the crew (a point that had now been proven over and over).

The next morning the atmosphere in the camp was electric. I learned later that Joe had overheard François's conversation and had reported the matter to Piotr and the rest of the raft team. The rafters looked like an angry hornet's nest and I knew that a showdown – in true spaghetti western style – was only a few six-shooters away.

The original contract – that the raft team act as a support crew to the kayakers – was about to be reconstituted.

Piotr drew first: 'No ways am I taking the raft off the river. I am going on, even if it splits the team.' A murmur of support rumbled from Piotr's camp.

'Piotr, the raft is moving too slowly,' François replied, returning fire. 'It has become a risk. The raft must go; from Cachora we go with kayaks.'

Then Jerome dropped a bombshell.

Only 2½ km in 9 hours!

Jerome rescuing Joe.

'François, the way I see it, we've got two options. We either slow this whole trip down and let it go at its natural pace, even though we will probably miss our deadlines, or we go flat out and turn this trip into a race. If we go flat out, you are the first one who must leave the river – you are the slowest in the team.'

Jerome's broadside, obviously personal, cut deep and took us by surprise.

François was silent, and then he looked up from the fire. 'That's interesting,' he responded calmly. 'We can talk about that.'

Piotr hotly flew in and joined the argument – which was by now more a free-for-all – his voice thick with emotion.

'We agreed that the raft comes – agreed long time ago. Many of us risked our lives to get raft down. There is no question,' he went on, shaking slightly. 'The raft is staying on the river.'

François was in a spot. It was a lose-lose situation. If he insisted that the raft be taken off the river, a mutiny looked inevitable. But if he buckled under pressure he would lose face and his authority-base would be further eroded. From where I stood, I could see no escape route for my friend.

We dared not dismiss Jerome's attack lightly. Jerome held our respect as the most skilled kayaker in the team. When he weighed in with an opinion, we listened. His criticism of François, albeit personal, had some truth in it. On the other hand, although François was the slowest of the kayakers, he was still faster than the raft. Jerome's resentment of, and dislike for, François was now no secret and his long festering resentment of François, stemming back 10 years to the Limpopo, was still alive and well.

Piotr's charge also held water. François had agreed, before the trip, that a raft could accompany us, provided that it conformed to the kayak expedition needs. After all, there was no way François could have foreseen river conditions in their entirety.

As a gesture of goodwill we agreed to discuss the matter further when we reached Cachora. With tension levels tightly strained, we packed our crafts and plunged into the rapids. Towards the end of the day – after running one particularly difficult 300-m rapid – some movement on the rocks caught our attention. Squinting into the glare, we recognised the frantically waving figures of Sergio and Kate. A huge relief flooded through us: we realised that we had made it – yes, made it to Cachora! We cheered, laughing and whooping like teenagers, our self-imposed troubles temporarily forgotten.

The Cachora Conference

A single *oroya* spanned the river, linking two ancient Inca footpaths. One wound eastwards through the arid mountains towards Cuzco, and the other made for Abancay and the Pacific Ocean. It was along the Abancay trail that Kate and Sergio trekked in with a pack of hired donkeys to supply us. Sadly disaster struck along the way when one of the donkeys missed its footing and plunged hundreds of feet down an almost vertical slope. The ass somehow survived, and our friends managed to recover a great deal of our precious supplies.

A sequel to this was an accident due to my own clumsiness. I was carrying my kayak up the steep bank from the river, when, as I crested the top, my foot slipped on a loose rock. Waiting to greet us at the top was an old man, Feliciano, who lived like a hermit on the riverbank. As I fell forward, my kayak swung around and struck Feliciano squarely on the mouth. I scrambled to my feet to find the old man buckled over, holding his bloodied mouth. Then, to my amazement, he straightened up – and with blood flowing – presented me with a charming but toothless grin.

'Oh, no!' I groaned, 'I've knocked all his teeth out. Señor, señor, lociento, lociento . . .' I stammered in poor Spanish.

Sergio came to the rescue and comforted the still smiling old man.

'It's not so bad, Tim. You didn't knock his teeth out. He didn't have any!' said Sergio,

Our able doctor quickly stitched up the cut lip and peace was restored.

Feliciano lived in a unique riverside bachelor flat. His lifestyle might be the envy of any lone bachelor. His 'designer' house was constructed around an enormous tree trunk, with walls 1.5 m high and made of carefully selected stone and mud. It was ingenious; a creative jewel in a primitive environment. His cash flow came from trading a few basic essentials from his garden to those who occasionally crossed the *oroya*. We marveled at the simplicity of his lifestyle – so remote, so uncluttered.

We pitched camp under a canopy of acacia trees, purchased the complete stock of Feliciano's vegetables and fruit, and relished the prospect of a whole day to rest, eat, and relax – soothing balm for sore bodies.

I desperately needed time to be on my own. I had to think clearly, digest and see things in perspective, work out why things were going wrong, why our relationships were breaking down, and why there were

Feliciano
~ after my kayak hit him in the teeth.

Hand made plough
at Feliciano's house
18 Sept 85. Tim

Feliciano Pancurma's casa
at Cachora crossing.
18 Sept 85. Tim

195

such dark undercurrents to our expedition. I unpacked my waterproof bags from the kayak, took out my small Bible and sleeping mat, and climbed to a point that looked over the Apurimac far below. With the soothing, cool breeze on my face, I began unraveling the situation in my mind – working through each relationship, jotting down what I saw as the main dynamics, the possible solutions, and praying for help and wisdom from One who understands every heart and every mind.

Sitting there, the role that I had to play became even clearer. It was to try to keep the team together, to prevent a split. All the arguments and mistakes we had made, all the angry things we had said to each other, must now be forgotten and forgiven. Whether or not François had made mistakes did not justify a mutiny. We had all agreed to accept him as leader. If Piotr felt like running his own show, now that he had a support base, he still had no right to threaten the group's unity as he had been doing. I was not prepared to allow him to waltz in and take over. He must honour his original commitment to François as leader or, sadly, leave the river. Tomorrow we would meet for the showdown.

As the emotional exhaustion began flooding through me, a need for sleep – for days if necessary – overwhelmed me. The afternoon sun shone bright as I drifted off into a long, deep sleep. I woke with a start. The sun was not yet down. I lay back again, gazing into the evening sky. Refreshed, I wandered back to the camp. The tents were up and the mosquitoes hard at work. Our team had separated into two groups

Mutiny! – the worst day of the trip.

and sat bent over their bowls, a pile of coals glowing between the rocks. François spotted me and called out: 'Hey, Tim, where have you been? We almost came looking for you. Come, we kept some food for you.'

I was ravenous and gulped down a huge bowl of vegetable stew. That night we all avoided discussing the charged issues that lay dormant between us.

Then D-day arrived and Jack, François, Piotr and I held a meeting. We sat a few hundred metres away from the rest of the group, under some scrawny thorn trees. We all understood the situation and were fresh after a good night's sleep.

'Well, guys,' François began, 'we have some decisions to make. I would like the raft to leave the river for this stretch. We still have big water ahead, and we can move faster – and more safely – using only kayaks. Piotr is refusing point-blank to leave the raft in favour of a kayak, even if it means splitting the group. As leader I cannot accept this. Imagine this newspaper heading: "Mutiny in Amazon Expedition". We also have the dangerous Red Zone (a stretch of river renowned for guerrilla activity) ahead. Four kayaks will be safer and less conspicuous than a big raft . . . What do you think, Jack?'

François came into his own in this type of situation. It was what he was good at. Jack had aged visibly over the past eight days and puffed on his pipe before speaking. Wearing his Wyoming hat and sporting a full white beard, he looked more like an out of shape cowboy than a river runner.

'Yeah, François,' he drawled. 'I guess I can go along with that. My concern is that we are miles over budget. We need to speed things up or we just won't make it. I'm also feeling that I've had enough rapids for a lifetime. Too many close shaves for my liking! I don't know how many more I can put under my belt before this ole river gets me for good.'

I was fond of this old Viking, as he liked to think of himself. Considering his poor shape, we were amazed that he had lasted so long. It was no secret that he was on the water because he held the purse strings. Whomever he handed the money to when he left the river would have the final say in the future of the expedition. Both Piotr and François were more than aware of this. I had cynically observed both of them currying favour with Jack in the past few weeks, trying to ensure that the purse would be handed their way. During the last few days François and Jack had spent more time together and were getting on well. I guessed who had won this round.

I expected it would be my turn to speak next and the adrenalin started pumping. But François caught me off guard.

'What do you say, Piotr? Do you still think it's the right thing to break away from the team and proceed on your own with the raft?'

Piotr looked gaunt and drawn, with the wild look of a trapped animal. For a moment I pitied him.

'François,' he said, 'I've told you already. Why you take raft off now? I think you just do it because you

197

want Joe and Kate off the river. We risk our lives to get raft down, to bring it so far, and why now take it off? No, I stay with raft and my team, no matter what.'

'Tim, what about you?' asked François, turning to me. 'What do you think?'

I paused for half a minute.

'Hey, guys, I've thought a lot about what's happened. I know there's been a lot of tension in the team, and a lot of it I understand. I can see Joe's and Kate's and Zbecek's point of view, wanting to stay on the river. The only thing I want to make a stand on is that I feel it is wrong, Piotr, for you to split the team at this point. What right have you to hijack the expedition's integrity just because you and Frans can't get on? Of course Frans has made mistakes and has weaknesses, but we all have – you as well. You've also been reckless, and refused to listen to anyone. What you are doing is wrong. Would you have allowed anything like this to arise in one of your expeditions? I know you and you know me. We've spent months on rivers together, we've saved each other's lives, and I know you would not have allowed this situation to arise. You've always been a man of your word, yet now you suddenly forget about the contract you signed and agreed on before the trip started. You agreed to accept François as leader in all major decisions. Come on, Piotr, this isn't right. You either agree not to split the team and sign that you accept Frans as leader, or you get off this river right here.'

There was a heavy silence. No one responded. My teammates were obviously unprepared for such an emotional and radical stand.

Jack moved first. 'Who is for a brew of coffee, gentlemen?'

'Thanks, Jack, that sounds good,' we replied, grateful for a small break.

Piotr rose, stretched, and moved away from the group to be on his own. François and I remained sitting, watching as Jack poured out four mugs of steaming coffee. No one spoke.

Piotr then turned to face us. 'No, I will not sign,' he said, in a clipped manner.

Jack and François glanced at me uncomfortably. Jack answered before I had any chance to make a heated reply.

'François, what if we do take the raft, but still insist that Piotr signs?' Jack suggested, his years of experience as a negotiator paying off. Another silence followed. François knew he would be forced into a compromised position. His camp would now be in the minority, two against five.

Another day ~ another gorge.

'Jack,' he asked, 'if you leave the river now, what will the financial situation be?'

We all knew exactly what he meant. This was the telling moment.

'Frans,' said Jack, 'I will leave it with you. You are the leader.'

One could have cut the silence with a knife. Piotr looked shattered. This had been the big underlying issue.

'Okay,' said François, 'I think I can live with that. I'm prepared to give it a go – that is, of course, if Piotr signs.'

Minutes passed in which nobody moved or said anything.

'All right, give me this paper,' snapped Piotr at last. 'I sign.' An unrecognisable squiggle, quite unlike Piotr's normal immaculate signature, was duly scribbled below the hand-written agreement.

The rest of the team were now beckoned over and sauntered across to join us. Once they were seated François announced: 'Okay, guys, this is what we are doing. We will continue with the raft, depending on river conditions, but we will stay together.'

This announcement was met with a chilly response.

'We have discussed the leadership issue,' François continued. 'I will still remain leader of the expedition. Piotr has actually signed that he will not attempt to split the team again. Are there any questions?'

No questions; still silence.

'Good. Let's have lunch and then head on.'

Triunfo

The river at last opened out into a 3-km deep, V-shaped valley, displaying three distinct vegetational and climatic zones on its towering slopes. The dark and narrow canyons had receded behind us into the Andes, and it was wonderful to experience a full sky of stars at night again. How we had missed them! – particularly the Southern Cross, always behind us, cheering us on, watching our daily progress.

View of Salcantay ice peaks from Triunfo.

Our food supply was finished after the five-day stretch from Cachora and we planned to hike out to Triunfo to be restocked by Pierre and Sergio. This would carry us through the Red Zone section to the village of Luisiana. We had now been on the river for a full month and had covered some 500 km of canyons. Surely we had broken the back of the white water section of the Apurimac.

The final rapid before our take-out point was one I will never forget. The full flow of the Apurimac charged at the vertical cliff face. The force of the descending torrent collided head-on with the cliff with such force that a rebounding wave, 40 m wide, formed a corridor of exploding waves.

As I entered the rapid, I realised to my dismay that my approach was too far left. Frantically signalling to François and Jerome to keep right, I was swept into the maul and was buried in the violent collision of

199

The spooky banana-thatched hut.

meeting waters. After a few battering seconds, the river lifted me and hurled me over into the crashing cross currents. I tried to roll – one, two, three times – and eventually dragged myself up, gasping for air. Before I could focus, I was hurled over again. At last, the river released me and I righted myself, gasping for breath. Talk about a ducking! Jerome and François paddled through the left run, calling out with amused expressions: 'Thanks for the warning, Tim. Glad we didn't follow you through that lot!'

'It sure took me by surprise,' I laughed. 'Cleared out my sinuses.'

Shortly after 'washing machine rapid', we arrived at a bend which, we decided, must be our take-out point for Triunfo. A high mud bank on the left side prevented us camping there, so we pushed up onto a sandbar on the right and set up our camp. There was no sign of Pierre or Sergio (our support team who

had left Cachora by foot). We cooked up a meal, and waited.

'I'm going across the river to look around,' I volunteered. 'Maybe I'll find them. Don't worry if I'm back late.'

Besides worrying about Pierre and Sergio, I also needed some time alone. I ferry-glided across the river, dragged my boat well up from the water and began exploring a route up the loose and slippery 50-m bank, knotting long sheaves of grass to mark my route. Up on the terrace the vegetation changed to lush, subtropical forest. Soon I came across signs of cultivation and, thinking there might be someone around, kept walking. I found a few breaks in the vegetation and came across a very slight footpath. Spotting some banana trees in the distance I worked my way towards them, hoping to find some activity. All I found was an abandoned banana-thatched hut, with timber and cane sides. Peering into the hut I immediately sensed in the eerie silence that eyes were watching me. I quickly moved back into the cane, scanning for any signs of life around the hut. Nothing moved, so I continued upwards, hoping to find someone who could give me word on Pierre and Sergio. At last I found a stronger footpath and picked up the pace to a run.

Drawn on by the excitement of exploring new territory I ran on, knowing I might not make it back to the camp by nightfall, and that my friends would not be impressed at my pushing on alone. The vistas of the river and the valley became more magnificent and spectacular every time I looked. I was now in full stride and exploring mode. I loved this type of adventure – running through uncharted country, free as a lark, energised by what was spread out before me. I was now almost halfway up the mountainside. Dark grey clouds, heavy with rain, mantled the summit, and tell-tale vertical wisps of rain-mist warned of an impending storm. I ran hard for another 30 minutes before sitting down on a flat rock to drink in the spectacular scenery. In the distance, the snow-capped peaks of Huascarán – 6 800 m high – protruded through low clouds. Far below, the Apurimac wound like an uncoiled snake; twisting around sheer cliffs and steep spurs until it became a thin thread, speckled with silver streaks of white water. I took two photos with my old camera, hoping to capture the magic of the moment.

Spending Time with God

Finishing off my last two biscuits from yesterday's lunch, I sat marvelling at what lay before me. It was magnificent, majestic. An urge to thank and praise my creator for this beautiful wilderness overwhelmed me. I felt so close to God out here; it was almost as if I could feel his tangible presence around me.

'Father, I love this place of yours. Thank You for it; it's so good to be here,' I prayed.

A desert canyon indeed.

Oh – to soar like a condor.

201

Bible verses reeled through my head, drawing me closer to him. It was as though he gently confirmed that he was indeed the owner of the cattle of a thousand hills, knew each sparrow, commanded the moon and stars, and created these rivers and mountains. I felt an intense closeness, and prayed for my dear wife Margie; for our future together. A rough-edged soul like me did not deserve such a woman. I thanked God for saving me from the siphon, and for protecting us all so far. I could easily relate to the young David of the Bible, a wild shepherd boy who loved God, but whose adventurous spirit God loved in him. Moments such as these were priceless to me.

A Huff and a Puff, There Goes my House

Ominous green-grey storm clouds gathered on the far hills, sending down occasional flashes of lightning and dropping vertical pillars of rain. Time was up. I had found what I came for. 'Now I must get moving and race the monster down the hill,' I reminded myself. I quickly packed my small bag and began the run back down the mountain. Again I felt the exhilaration of half floating, half flying down the Andes mountainside. Long before I reached the hut, the rain overtook me, first in large cold drops, then in a thundering deluge. I tried to keep moving but soon hailstones drove me to the shelter of a boulder. I crouched under it for half an hour until the rain stopped and a misty drizzle, giving only a few metres' visibility, took its place.

I chuckled to myself. 'Biggs, you silly clot, you asked for this. There's no way you'll make it back to the camp now. You are "benighted", old chap.'

The mist did not let up, and I cautiously made my way down to where I thought the hut was. It was 6:30 p.m. and darkness was spreading over the mountains and the Apurimac! Without applause or indication, the mist suddenly rolled away and presented to me the next performer in this fascinating Andean concert: an enormous yellow moon, hung quietly and perfectly over the rugged skyline. The transition from rain to hail to mist to moonshine was dramatic and exciting – in my mind, I applauded loudly.

Forty minutes later I stumbled across the hut with its banana-leaf roof. My anorak had proved to be less than waterproof. I was wet, frozen to the bone, and starving.

'Well, Biggs, you deserve it, so accept it. A cold night without fire or food – yippee!'

Then it happened again, this time sending shivers down my spine, making the hair at the nape of my neck stand on end. Someone was watching me. I had felt it that afternoon and I felt it now. There was a strange, uncanny vibe in and around the hut. What was it? Ghosts? Ancestral spirits? Demons? Was there somebody in there that I could not see? I was convinced I was not imagining things; it was all too similar to a night that I had spent in a deserted Zulu hut back in

--- In the middle of the night - without warning – the banana hut collapsed ontop of me !

South Africa. That same uncomfortable, unearthly vibe was present in both situations. Something was near, I was certain. I prayed to God for protection.

I crawled through a small doorway in the hut and, using some large banana leaves as a ground-sheet, found a suitable place to lie down and rest. Gazing through the doorway I watched the moon as it climbed through the stars, shining its luminous sheen across the hills. At my side lay a weighty 'club' which I had cut from the branch of a tree, in case intruders paid me a physical visit. Minutes later I passed out, too tired to worry about the cold.

Some time later, a crashing roar broke the raw night. I yelled out in fright, leapt to my feet, and was immediately struck down and sent sprawling by something hard and solid. As the roar continued I dived for the doorway and scrambled out, terrified and shaking. Seconds later it was over. Silence reigned; not even a cricket chirped. A cloud of dust slowly settled to reveal the moonlit wooden structure, my 'Andean Inn', collapsed in a heap. I stood there with my mouth open, gasping, and shaking in total disbelief and raw fright. Was this a bad dream? I could not fathom what had happened, and an odd disorientation filled me.

'What the heck just happened?'

I found myself gripping a pole to defend myself, ready for anything. With the entire hut now demolished, silence returned, but it was now scary and unnatural. I could hear nothing: no footsteps, no hooves galloping away, no rustling, nothing. It was 3:00 a.m. and there was no sign of a wind that could have blown the hut down, nor anything in the vicinity that could explain the macabre roar. The big bad wolf had blown my house down and that was that. Shady Pines Asylum, room 110 (the windowless one), here I come!

In the meantime, the moon had crossed the sky and was dropping behind the mountains in the west. I crawled into a thicket of banana trees and waited out the darkness. Two hours later, dawn's welcome soft rays pushed darkness and its nocturnal abnormalities thankfully out of sight. I rose, sore and stiff; with my head throbbing from the wooden beam that had struck me. I examined the area for footprints or other clues as to why the hut had spontaneously collapsed in the night. Apart from my own, I found no other footprints, and no other clues. It was indeed a mystery.

I did not want to spend another minute there and made my way back through wet, dripping vegetation to the cliff. The descent was more testing than the climb up – several times my foot slipped in the mud, and I slid several metres at a time. The river had risen with the storm and was almost lapping at my kayak. I scrambled in and paddled across the river. 'Una mas experience,' (One more experience) I said to myself, relieved to reach home base.

Finding the Hikers

The campfire crackled into life, helped along by a healthy dose of kerosene and a match. I made tea and started breakfast (our last cups of oatmeal). Despite our internal struggles and clashes, I was glad to be back among our team. Now if we could only find Pierre and Sergio.

'Where were you, Tim?' François scolded me, as he crawled out of his tent. 'You had us worried. We didn't know whether to go looking for you or not. What happened?'

'Guys, I'm sorry, my fault. I got carried away and went too far before turning back, then I got caught in the thunderstorm and had to sleep out.'

I went on to share the story of the collapsing hut. Everyone listened in awe, and when I got to the mysterious bits, we all roared with laughter.

'Biggs,' they teased, 'are you sure you weren't dreaming, or on some strong Andean weed?'

The next morning François and I set off to look for the hikers. We followed the route I had taken, and stopped briefly at the collapsed hut. There were still no signs of life. We climbed until midday before we reached the ridge, a good 3-km climb. Following the path, we came across the lone figure of an elderly Quechua man, trudging along.

'Have you seen any gringos, señor?'

'No.'

'Where is the village of Triunfo?'

The old man pointed in the direction that we were hiking, and then simply carried on walking. We continued along the ridge until the landscape fell away thousands of metres on each side of us. In the clear, blue sky we felt as though we were on top of the world. But we could not linger; we had to establish the whereabouts of our hikers.

Late that afternoon we arrived at the two-house village of Triunfo. What an anticlimax! We had hoped for a thriving village with a restaurant and accommodation. Instead we had stumbled on a ghost town, originally an old sugar mill. The two resident families treated us with suspicion, unsure about our mission. Neither of them had seen or heard of any gringos. Disappointed we walked on, unsure where to start looking for our friends. The sun dropped behind the

Primitive sugar mill at Chaquaquirao 19 Sept 85.

TIM

purple skyline, leaving a blaze of colours and gilt-edged clouds.

We were in a spot of trouble. If Sergio and Pierre had been held up and were not going to arrive we had no choice but to head on downstream into the Red Zone, scrounging what food we could from the locals. With those thoughts on our minds, we continued on our way. Soon the shadows started to stretch and the icy mountain air began to move in. This was no place to get caught out in the cold. A second night out did not appeal to me! Providentially, a small Quechua hut came into view.

'Let's see if we can sleep here,' I suggested.

The small family understood our plea and invited us into their humble home without hesitation. Apart from three young ones, the family unit also comprised seven guinea pigs, three hens, a rooster, and a small dog. We made ourselves as comfortable as we could in a corner against two unplastered stone walls. Two llama skins were generously lent to us as blankets, and we shared our meagre rations with the family. Our hostess later offered us a plate of potatoes and watery soup which we gratefully accepted.

During the night, the temperature dropped to minus ten degrees, and when the first rays of dawn beamed through the open door, we were freezing and miserably covered in fleabites. Outside the ground was white with frost; inside we huddled around the warm dung fire, eating boiled potatoes and gruel from a bowl. We settled with our hostess by chipping in with some tins of tuna and dried fruit. At 9:00 a.m., with still no sign of our hikers, we decided to walk on for half an hour and then turn back.

After 20 minutes we came to a fork where, in the large path that joined ours, we noticed some boot prints. Did Sergio and Pierre pass this way? How

Tim
Jerome on his
birthday - FRI 13th sep.!
Triumfo.

Pierre - doing admin
at Triumfo sep 85

would we know if they did? We played 'detective' and meticulously worked through a process of elimination that merely got us back where we started from – 'Did they pass this way?' As we sat on a big round boulder, contemplating our next move, a donkey pushed its head over a distant rise, followed by the familiar figures of . . . Sergio and Pierre! Elated we jumped up, shouting and waving.

It was a great reunion.

Chapter 9

SENDERO COUNTRY

Jerome's Revelations

Had the Apurimac lost its sting? In two months we had not seen the river so well behaved. As if in agreement, the valley sides began to open up and all traces of a canyon disappeared. Even the water was warm enough to swim in. The changes seemed too good to be true. However, 10 km further along the 'tame' Apurimac, we rounded a bend and entered another world! The Apurimac had dealt us another card. Gone was the lush vegetation and in its place were wind-blasted cacti, an occasional scrub thorn tree, and general desolation. We had entered a pastel-painted desert where ochres, browns, reds and mauves composed a giant canvas.

Despite its barren beauty, this harsh, arid region was now part of the territory that the Maoist group, Sendero Luminoso, had occupied during their bloody eight-year revolution in Peru. Symbolic of the unfriendly surroundings, a howling 40 km/h headwind met us. When Joe looked up from paddling that afternoon and saw the river's rocky sides moving forward past him, he shouted out, 'Guys – we're been blown back upstream!' Wisely, we decided to camp early.

The campsite, partly sheltered from the gusting wind, was pleasant enough with its clean sand and boulders. There were ample supplies of firewood, and the beautiful surfing waves enticed Jerome and me to take our empty kayaks into the water and attempt some surfing – something we hadn't been able to do anywhere else on the trip. Although Jerome and I still got on well, and combined well as a team, this expedition, now in its second month, had eroded our friendship. We enjoyed the water, but we carefully avoided the topic of the split in the team. Approaching

Jerome lets it all out.

the camp, however, after an hour of carefree surfing, Jerome suddenly stopped.

'Tim, I suppose you must be wondering why I've joined Piotr's side, and left you guys,' said Jerome, getting straight to the point.

'Yeah, I guess I am,' I replied.

Our friendship had started in the early 1970s at university, and we had done a lot of kayaking together, including the Limpopo Expedition from which François, as leader, had pulled out while we were still on the river.

'I just cannot get along with François anymore. I don't like his style. I suppose I'm still carrying baggage from the Limpopo business. The bottom line is that I'd rather be with Piotr. I appreciate your situation though, Tim. I respect your standing up for him, and the way you've looked after him on the river.

But, as far as I'm concerned, I can't see that anything has changed since the Limpopo.'

I was surprised, but not rattled by Jerome's revelation.

'Whew, Jerome, the Limpopo was years ago!' I replied. 'You've got to move on from that stuff.'

'Yeah, you're right. But it's easier said than done.'

'I'm upset,' I went on, 'about how our expedition will be viewed back home and abroad. We're really dragging South Africa's kayaking reputation through the mud.'

We paused for a while, and then I probed: 'How do Joe and Kate and Zbecek feel after our indaba at Cachora?'

'They all want François off the river,' came Jerome's reply.

'Gee, that's heavy stuff.'

A geologist's paradise

We walked silently back to camp, carrying our kayaks. A stiff breeze fanned the smoky fire, and the battered pitch-black pot, perched between two rocks, puffed out steam rhythmically. Since our re-stocking, we were relishing full meals and a nice variety in our menu. We said goodnight to each other and trundled off to our separate sleeping mats, disappointed in the slow progress of the last three days. At Cachora the raft team had been reshuffled and comprised Piotr, Joe, Zbecek and Kate, with Pierre and Jack hiking out of the canyon and heading back home. The romance between Zbecek and Kate was obviously flourishing under the harsh Andean conditions, and they would take every opportunity to spend time alone.

I lay thinking about my chat with Jerome. At least it was clear who he would support if it came to a split.

Soft Targets in Sendero Country

The soft pinks and mauves of a cloudless dawn unveiled the desert landscape. We were starting to prepare for breakfast when the unmistakable 'crack' of rifle fire riveted our attention.

'Look across the river!' someone shouted.

High on the opposite bank, a row of six small-silhouetted figures moved along the rim of the canyon. With their sombreros, they painted a typical western movie scene.

'Move, move!' Piotr shouted to his crew. 'They've got guns!'

Pandemonium broke loose as we rushed about the camp grabbing our gear and equipment. The unmistakable 'crack, crack' of gunshots rang out, together with high-pitched whistling as the bullets ricocheted around us. Still reeling with the shock of being shot at we hurled our gear into the raft. It was time to move out!

With the raft about to be launched, I paddled hard into the current. François was close behind me and Jerome was still on the bank. Glancing up, I saw to my horror that one of our assailants was crouched halfway down the slope, rifle to his shoulder, and aiming at us. Whipping into an eddy behind a rock, I screamed back at Jerome, 'Jerome, look out!'

At that moment the raft swept past me, followed by François. They were all paddling furiously, keeping their heads down. I waited for Jerome who had still been on the bank when the shots started but could not see him. Was he okay, or had he been wounded? Would we have to transport a wounded Jerome hundreds of miles to some first-aid post? Meanwhile, the band of Sendero had split up. Some were running downstream along the rim while the rest ran down the slope towards us.

One minute passed, then two. Where was Jerome, what was keeping him? Was he still alive? With a pounding heart I prepared to dash back upstream when Jerome's blue kayak appeared, crashing through the waves. With relief sweeping over me, I peeled out into the current and together we sprinted after our teammates, our shoulder blades flinching for fear of a bullet in the back. We caught up with the raft and François, and dived headlong into the next steep rapid. There was no time to scout. A white stream of water on the extreme right indicated the most likely line.

'Go for the right!' Jerome yelled.

I followed closely as he disappeared over a 2 m drop. As I plunged over the lip, I saw him buried in the hole below, struggling to edge out of its grip. I swerved to miss him, plunged in deep, and came out tail-walking. We raced for an eddy, signalling to the raft and to François to avoid the danger. The raft careered over the lip, collided with the foaming turbulence, turned sideways, and began sliding back into the hole.

'Paddle, paddle!' Piotr screamed, but it was too late. The raft's left rail dug into the current, rose vertically, and catapulted the crew and the loose gear in all directions. We groaned. There could not have been a worse moment to flip. I sprinted across to

Whoops! ~ that was bigger than I thought.

Running rapids with Senderos firing at you is an adrenalin rush.

rescue Joe; Jerome rescued Kate, and François swept up all the flotsam. I never saw four rafters climb back aboard faster than they did that morning! Once they were up, we glanced nervously up at the cliffs for any sign of our 'friends'. There was no one in sight. We quickly regrouped, repacked our gear, and rushed on downstream.

'That was close,' François remarked, obviously relieved. 'We just don't know if they have radio contact with each other. If they have, we can only hope that they haven't notified their buddies downstream.'

'Those guys were either useless shots, or they weren't trying to hit us,' I reflected.

'Well, I don't know about that!' chuckled Jerome. 'While I was packing my boat, a bullet struck the sand just a few feet from me.'

'Ja, maybe they had a big party last night – too much pisco,' I laughed.

We could laugh now, but we had no doubt that we had had a close shave.

'Hey, Piotr, we voted you the "fastest raft-righting" team in the world,' Jerome joked.

'Yes, world champs next year!' grinned Piotr.

'Hey, Zulu, why you no tell us about big hole in last rapid,' Zbecek scolded, with a dry laugh. 'I fly ten feet in the air – like a low-flying duck. Maybe I should just keep flying.'

Captured

An enormous rapid (resembling a weir) brought us to a halt as the entire Apurimac surged over a bank-to-bank outcrop of rock, forming, as it did so, a deadly recycling hole. Wasting no time, we portaged the gear and then the raft around the left bank and were soon on our way again. Shortly after the portage, we found a hidden spot on the left bank and hungrily devoured our lunch, having had no time for breakfast.

'How about paddling into the night?' François tested. 'It'll be good to get out of this zone as soon as we can.'

'Of course, that goes without saying,' responded Piotr coldly. With his continual barrage of undermining digs, Piotr had been trying to make life as difficult as possible for François.

On we voyaged, following the Apurimac as it turned sharply north. Once again, it took just one bend to perform an instant transformation. In front of our eyes, as deftly as a chameleon, the vegetation and scenery changed colour. Back came the green forest vegetation and we knew that the jungle was drawing closer. We had settled into a good pace, with Jerome, François and me some hundred metres ahead of the raft. We were all on high alert, keeping an active look-out for Senderistas (members of Sendero Luminoso).

Suddenly François called out, 'Sendero, there, right bank.'

We squinted into the thick, shaded canopy. True, there they were . . . figures with guns, moving slowly.

'Keep moving, they haven't seen us,' whispered François.

We slid silently past, and then realised we had to warn the raft. With frantic signalling of paddles and hands, we beckoned to the team on the raft to keep paddling and keep to the left bank. Suddenly a shout of alarm broke the silence. We had been spotted!

The figures in the forest sprang to life like a prodded hornet's nest. There was no need to whisper anymore and we screamed at the raft to keep paddling. The guerrillas had been caught off guard and were running for cover. We only had a minute to escape before they regrouped – that was all we needed to escape. To our horror, we saw that the rafters weren't responding to our screams. We yelled again, 'Come on – paddle!'

Then the most bizarre thing happened: Piotr stood up, head held high, and ordered the team to paddle directly for the terrorist camp! Dumbstruck, we scarcely managed to yell, 'Piotr, Piotr, keep paddling, you'll get past them. Paddle!'

A paralysing fear seized me. Watching the raft approaching the bank was like watching a vehicle

The whole Apurimac poured over a rock ledge.
We had a rushed lunch stop
~ would they shoot at us again?

stalled on a railway line with a locomotive bearing down. The Senderistas were still in a state of confusion, but they wouldn't be for long. The raft moved to the right bank. Piotr had apparently invited himself for a friendly little chat. As we watched, armed men leapt forward, aggressively grabbed the raft, and pulled it on to the rocks.

'Let's go! They've been caught,' called François. We turned our kayaks into the current, trying to look calm and unruffled. Inside, however, we panicked. We paddled as fast as we could, bracing ourselves for the rattle of automatic rifle fire, but nothing happened. We slipped behind an outcrop of rocks in the river and tried to compose ourselves. From here we could observe the scene from a distance and take the escape route down the long rapid below us if we needed to. This would carry us a safe distance from the camp. To our utter dismay, we watched as armed, agitated-looking men led our four teammates off into the bush. Our hearts sank.

'Why on earth did Piotr paddle to the bank? He would easily have made it past them,' exclaimed François, letting off steam. The three of us were in shock at what Piotr had let them into.

'I must go back and help. I can't leave them there. My Spanish is good and I've had experience with communist groups,' said François after a few minutes of hearing and seeing nothing. 'You guys paddle on down for one hour, then wait for two hours. Then paddle another hour and wait on the left bank until six o'clock tonight. If we haven't come back by then, race on down to Luisiana and try to get the military to rescue us. They have a base there.'

François's plan sounded practical and clear, and we accepted his strong leadership.

'Okay, François, we'll do that. Take care, and good luck.'

With that, François, using eddies, paddled upstream along the bank.

I prayed a desperate, silent prayer for our group: 'Please, Lord, don't let them get shot. Give wisdom to François.'

Jerome and I turned and slipped into the fast-flowing waves. Relieved at seeing no one following us, we pulled into one last eddy for a final assessment.

'I'm amazed they haven't chased after us,' I commented.

'Same here. I would have sent a party after us if I was their commander.'

'Wow – I take my hat off to François; there's no way I would have wanted to go back in there. That took raw courage.'

'Sure did,' Jerome agreed. 'He's not great on the water, but he certainly has guts.'

'I reckon it's time to head off,' I said.

'Yep, let's go.'

With eyes in the back of our heads, and uncertainty about what lay ahead of us, we hauled hard downstream. Not a single shot was fired, and nobody came after us. We breathed sighs of relief, paddled hard for an hour, and then hid our kayaks in the dense green forest. Then we sat at a vantage point between the rocks overlooking the opposite bank.

'Let's eat now, Jerome,' I suggested. 'We may be paddling tonight!'

We had our customary tin of tuna, biscuits and a chocolate each. Together we pondered all the possible lines of action, and what the Sendero might do or might not do. I kept praying.

The long hour passed in which we had hoped the rest of the team would appear, but, no sign of them. We had to move on. Slipping into the water we paddled in silence. The rapids were now few and far between, and a noticeable transition was taking place on the bank from semi-desert to jungle. Enormous trees reached to the skies, their branches leaning across dangling plaited vines and creepers in the water. We paddled steadily until we found a protected hideaway on the left bank. It was 4:00 p.m. Would our friends show up?

We had only heard bad things about the Sendero's bloody and merciless encounters with their enemies. For all we knew our four friends were already dead! It was an unbelievable thought, but a possibility. During the past months there had been some gruesome murders and executions involving tourists. Why had Piotr paddled ashore? Why?

There was a good three-quarter moon, and with the flattening rapids we would be able to paddle through the night to Luisiana. Time dragged – with every hour we lost hope that we would soon see our friends. At 5:45 p.m. we began pulling on our anoraks, life jackets and helmets for the night's paddling. The sun had set and tropical clouds, gilded with a bright thread, decorated a grey sky. Jungle birds were calling and a distant troop of monkeys were roaring and hooting as they settled in for the night.

'There they are!' Jerome exclaimed. 'I'm sure it's them.'

We squinted into the dusk. Yes, there was some movement at the edge of our vision, and an occasional splash of water. It was them! We saw the raft, with François paddling ahead and welcomed them as if we hadn't seen them for years – as though they had returned from a war. Most of all we were overjoyed that they were all fine. Jerome and I were obviously dying to know what had happened, and how they had managed to escape unscathed.

'Tell us what happened, Frans,' I asked, as Jerome, François and I paddled together alongside the raft.

In the Lion's Den

'As I arrived on the scene,' François started, 'they were very aggressive, prodding our guys, but they also appeared scared. I think they suspected we were a military group and that more of us were to follow. Joe, Kate and Zbecek were held under watch near the raft. Kate had attracted the women of the camp, who soon befriended her. The women had been fascinated by what she was doing in these godforsaken parts; one of them apparently felt her breasts to check whether she really was a woman.'

The Sendero, who were in a difficult position as their commander was upstream on patrol, then began interrogating François and Piotr, determined to uncover the real purpose of their mission. The guerrillas understandably wanted to wait until their commander returned before they did anything drastic. According to François, he immediately realised the guys on patrol were probably the ones who had fired at us earlier. He then explained that the two kayaks which had raced on downstream, would soon reach the military camp at Luisiana where they would request assistance. François pushed this point further by saying that if they were released, it would prevent a reprisal by the military. Both François and Piotr persuaded them that they would not divulge their position once free, and that the incident would not be reported to the military.

The guerrillas were not convinced, and François decided to switch the conversation to the capturers' own dire situation. It was obvious that they struggled, especially having women and children to care for. They visibly relaxed their guard and lowered their

The negotiations had broken down, and they were back where they had started. The Sendero were still unsettled. François again requested that they release the group, and in return, he would stay with them for a few days enabling them to relocate in order to escape a possible military attack. Although flawed, this proposal seemed to calm them down.

François and the men continued chatting about the basic tenets of Marxism. The men listened intently as François described his involvement and contact with other so-called liberation movements, such as SWAPO in the then South-West Africa (Namibia today). The men listened with fascination and interest. Negotiations were back on track and the guerrillas sent a child to bring some kernels of corn that they passed around and chewed together.

After a while, the guerrillas walked away from François and Piotr and privately discussed the matter. Upon their return, they sat on the rocks and announced, 'You may go.' The impasse had been broken, their respect had been won, and they presented François with a poster of the Peruvian Communist Party as a seal of their 'friendship'.

'Carry our message to the world,' they asked. 'Tell them about our struggle.'

Before our group left, the guerrillas asked for some provisions. Piotr arranged a donation of tins of tuna, a fishing net, and some trinkets to further pacify the Sendero, while Kate had worked wonders with the women and had already exchanged earrings and some toiletries. With half-raised firearms the group watched as the raft and kayak launched into the swift current.

After a quick meal, we decided to stand watch through the night in two-hour shifts. That same evening while François and I were setting up our sleeping mats, Piotr approached François, shook him by the hand, and thanked him. 'I would not have known how to get us out of that one,' Piotr acknowledged.

I appreciated Piotr's gesture, considering his open dislike for François. As yet I had not questioned him as to why he had pulled the raft in, but this was not

Kate ~ the day before being captured.

firearms until Piotr made the unfortunate slip of asking them if they knew that the Pope was presently visiting Peru. Their reaction was immediate, both men shouted at Piotr that religion meant nothing to them, and that they did not need the Pope. To cover the blunder, Piotr then asked them if they knew who had won the soccer match between Chile and Argentina. Unknowingly, Piotr had put his foot in it again, outraging the capturers. Screaming, one man leapt to his feet and threatened to cut off Piotr's ear. 'Soccer is for the bourgeois!' the man yelled as rifles were yet again raised and aimed.

214

the best moment. The night was long and tense – all sorts of ideas came knocking. One of them was that the guerrillas' commanding officer would radio other camps along the river to be on the lookout for an all-gringo expedition, and pull us in when we were spotted. The night also brought with it new sounds and smells. There were bird calls, animal sounds, and the organic, slightly musty odour of the jungle. We were now almost out of the Andean mountains.

We lit no fires when we woke, and speedily packed our gear and bags in the raft before slipping silently into the river. Swept along by the swift current, we listened in awe to the crescendo of bird calls and the roaring and howling from the monkey kingdom. A flock of green parrots, with striking red beaks and capes, chattered and sang as they followed us, flying from tree to tree. No one had slept much and conversation was low. We all shared a common goal – to reach Luisiana as soon as possible, and be clear of Sendero territory.

We came across two men in an old dugout. Paddling rhythmically upstream, they hugged the bank to keep out of the current.

'Donde de Luisiana?' we called out.

Without saying a word, they pointed downstream. We rounded a bend and saw a line of banana-thatched dwellings along the riverbank. It was Luisiana. We had crossed one more hurdle.

A Sewer Runs Through It

The main street of Luisiana was lined with untidy buildings, some with banana-leaf roofs, some with rusted corrugated iron. It did not take the military long to spot us, and soon a group of uniformed, rifle-bearing soldiers apprehended us.

'Come with us,' they ordered, and then they escorted us into their headquarters, which was enclosed with some mean-looking razor wire. A young, stern-faced captain met us and looked us up and down, probably trying to derive some sort of conclusion. 'So many gringos at one time!' his face seemed to say. The captain was tough and hardened, but exuded an intelligence that was unmatched by his colleagues. He listened to our stories quietly, read our letters of introduction, and scrutinised our documents. When he finished, he looked down at the floor for a few moments before he spoke. We had not told him that the Sendero had captured some of our group. François and Piotr had given our captors their word and we were determined to honour the agreement.

'You must have had God looking after you. Just four days ago four gringo tourists were found dead, hanging from a tree, in the vicinity where you were travelling. You have passed through a bad area – you were lucky not to have been killed. There are numerous Sendero camps along the river. Were you not worried about travelling through this region?'

François was honest in his reply, 'Sir, we were warned, but we have a mission and we could not complete our expedition without passing through their territory.'

The captain did not reply immediately. Perhaps it was my imagination, but I detected the slightest of smiles at the corners of his lips.

'From here on downstream things improve. You should be okay; just be very careful. Oh, there is a strict curfew in the village; we do not want to see you out after dark.'

We thanked him, and two soldiers escorted us out of town. On the way out we bought provisions at street-side stalls.

An attractive and suitable beach became visible a few hundred metres downstream and we paddled across to it. We unloaded our gear and only then discovered that an open village sewer (a bubbling stream) flowed merrily through our camp! Its smell tainted the beautiful evening on the Apurimac. The last two days had been strenuous and emotionally draining and the thought of searching for a new site so late in the day was more than we could endure. We pitched the tents, contented to be where we were.

Vote of No Confidence

The first day of November 1985 would be another watershed day in the life of our expedition. Seated around a mound of glowing coals in our smelly camp-site, François had called us together to discuss our plans for the next stage from Atalaya downstream. After the Cachora showdown the atmosphere in the group had never quite recovered. Tonight was no exception, and the tension levels were almost tangible.

'Sergio will be flying in with four sea kayaks, which we will use on the long flat-water section,' announced François, with a clipped, matter-of-fact expression. 'From Atalaya, the raft is taken out, and Jerome returns to the UK to train for the world championships with the British team. Piotr, Tim and I will then continue down to Belém – that is, if we eventually get our Brazilian visas. Kate, Sergio, Zbecek and Joe can follow in a support boat, and Joe can paddle from Pucallpa, if he wants to.'

'Why can't Joe paddle from Atalaya?' Jerome queried. 'If he does, he won't have to interrupt his trip.'

'No. We're already more than a month behind schedule, and he can start from Pucallpa,' insisted François.

I winced at François's unreasonable argument. What was he up to? Why should Joe not be able to paddle if he wanted to? If Joe succeeded in reaching the sea, he would be the first American to travel the Amazon on his own steam, by river and by foot.

'Hey, François, that's not on!' I objected. 'You can't deny Joe his chance. That's unreasonable!'

The barrage that followed was predictable and ugly, and had obviously been well rehearsed in Piotr's camp.

'François, speed's not the issue. You're the slowest of the whole group, and the worst paddler,' Kate threw in – fairly drunk, and becoming very vocal. Then she sauntered 10 m away from the bright fire, squatted down, and, still talking, relieved herself. We were all embarrassed. Zbecek giggled weakly.

Jerome then dropped another bombshell. 'François, the real issue here is not about who can paddle or not, but whether you are capable of leading an expedition.'

François, already too emotional, responded angrily. 'So you have no confidence in me as leader, Jerome?'

'No, I don't,' replied Jerome caustically.

François leapt up, furious. 'Okay, I hear you, Jerome. I'd like a vote, now, from all of you. Let's get this straightened out, once and for all.'

'François,' I broke in, 'you can't just suddenly demand a vote of confidence like this. You need at least to consult with Piotr and me about it. We're also part of the leadership. Besides, everyone is too tired and emotional to go through this sort of stuff right now. We've had a rough day. Let's have a good sleep, and talk about it again tomorrow.'

I was angry at François's untimely explosion. As it was he was on shaky ground, and an outburst like this was not going to count in his favour.

'No, I demand a vote right now,' François exploded, and then shouted a challenge, 'Jerome!'

'No confidence,' Jerome angrily shouted back.

'Joe!'

'No confidence.'

'Zbecek!'

'I vote no.'

'Kate!'

'François, you're being unreasonable, but, if you insist, I vote no confidence.'

'Piotr!'

'François, you don't know what you are doing,' Piotr responded.

'Frans, Piotr is right,' I interjected. 'We are also part of the leadership. You have no right to throw this on us without first discussing it with Piotr and me. Tomorrow, guys! – let's talk again tomorrow.'

The group agreed and disbanded. Everyone was drained and tired of this never-ending bickering and fighting. I lay in my tent for an hour, thinking and praying.

The results of the poll did not surprise me.

Back Against the Wall

I woke François early the next morning with some coffee. It was my turn to prepare breakfast but I made time for an earnest word with my old friend. Things had not gone down well last night – not only for him, but also for the rest of us.

'Frans,' I called to him, 'I need to talk when you are ready.'

A few minutes later we sat on the rocks, sipping the steaming coffee.

'Frans, I've spent last night mulling over everything. I'd like you to rethink this vote of no confidence thing. You must withdraw it, otherwise I'm afraid you'll be voted out. As I said, you didn't have the right to demand such a vote without first passing it by Piotr and me. Besides all of that, it will put a smear on this whole expedition – I don't want to be any part of it.'

I again questioned him about the issue with Joe – his being sidelined from the paddle from Atalaya – and for the way he managed it. François was doing now what he resented when Piotr took the Canoandes raft down the river. Now he was putting his own interests first. But François would not budge from his decision. In a way I could understand his fear of paddling the 5 600 km with someone he could not stand. That, however, did not justify his action.

Piotr saw us in deep discussion and walked over.

'Morning, Piotr,' I greeted him. 'Come and join us.'

'Morning, guys.'

I marvelled at the man's self-discipline. He was carefully groomed, hair combed and clothes neatly pressed. Next to him, François and I looked like a couple of river tramps.

'Piotr, we're talking about last night's vote of no confidence. I don't think it was right the way François did it. He should have talked it over first with us.'

'Yes, you are right, Tim. It would have been better. Problem though – it's hard to go back now.'

Piotr was in a tricky position. Although he badly wanted François off the trip, he couldn't say so openly. Things were heating up on this expedition. But before we could dwell on the subject, breakfast was ready.

Everyone gathered around eyeing out what I had prepared to eat. The tension was high. When was the last time it wasn't?

'Morning, guys,' I greeted. 'It's Sunday; may I pray before we eat? If ever we needed help from God, it's now.'

'Sorry, Tim, it's Saturday, not Sunday,' Jerome chipped in with a grin.

We all laughed, but I said my prayer anyway. My request to say a prayer on Sundays was meeting with more and more passive resistance.

The muddy beach we camped on was perhaps the worst of the trip and besides the village sewer draining into the Apurimac, we were attacked by swarms of mosquitoes. The foul campsite smell was, however, eclipsed by our diseased attitudes and low morale. I could not wait to move on downstream.

François spoke at last. 'I've spoken with my co-leaders, and they are unhappy that I didn't consult them about the confidence vote. I can see I was wrong. I'm sorry. I would, however, like to remain as leader. When we get to Atalaya, we can hold a referendum, if it's needed. I've also thought about Joe,' he said and faced Joe.

'Joe, you can join us in the kayaks from Atalaya if you would like to. I apologise to you all for last night.'

Everyone was silenced, if not totally shocked, by François's sudden change. The rafters were visibly disappointed that he wasn't removing himself from the team. Joe was the only one who appeared to be moved by François's gesture. That impressed me.

'Is that okay with you all?' François asked.

We all turned to Joe, sensing that he had the most to lose. 'That's fine with me,' said Joe, 'having you call yourself leader. Just so long as we can have an open and simple majority vote on your decisions, if we need to.'

'Whatever you want,' a tired François replied.

'Could we have it in writing?' asked Joe.

We drew up a quick handwritten agreement that François signed. François then walked across to Joe and shook his hand in a gesture of goodwill. Joe almost fell over.

'One day we'll laugh at all of this,' said François, with a dry smile.

'I hope so,' Joe replied, not looking too convinced.

François stood up and walked away from the camp.

Letting it Out

Although François had left, I was not quite finished. The time had come, I felt, to have my final say – to make my stand clear before we parted ways. François and I wouldn't see the rest of the team again until Atalaya. We needed to push ahead to establish whether we had our Brazilian visas yet. I stood up, took a deep breath, and began.

'Guys, I've thought about what's gone on these past few weeks, and I just want to share with you what I feel. You know, François and I spent four months together on the Urubamba, and another few months on the Colville – both difficult trips, but both successful. It was a year-and-a-half ago that François dreamed up and initiated this trip. It was his idea – François did almost all the organising and the raising of sponsorship. All of you were invited on it in good faith. From the start, he knew his weaknesses, so he chose people to take responsibility for various roles. Much has been said on this trip, but we must remember that none of us would be here if he hadn't dreamed this trip up and put it together.

'When our initial sponsorship fell away, I was upset to hear that Piotr had tried to hijack the leadership. He had asked Jack secretly to hand him leadership of the expedition if he sponsored us. Sadly, from day one Piotr has been determined to undermine the authority of both François and me.

Now I know Piotr is a capable leader – I paddled with him on the Colca, but on this trip, he is not the leader. At the start of this expedition he committed himself in writing, like the rest of us, to uphold François as leader. What's happened to that commitment we made, guys?

'You know yourselves how François and I fight and argue more than all of you. That does not mean I want to oust him from the team. From what I've seen, you have only tried to break him down. The way I see it, that's not good teamwork.

'Here we are now. We have finally reached the flat water after nearly two-and-a-half months. We are at last through the difficult parts, and the end is in sight. All we've got to do is to put our heads down and paddle for the sea. I think we must keep François as leader, stop destroying each other with this negative stuff, forget our differences and get on with finishing this trip. Let's make it a success.'

I sat down. There was silence. My throat was dry. I just had to get these things off my chest. My words went uncontested. No one denied anything until Joe finally spoke up.

'Thanks, Tim,' he said, 'I can see you spoke from the heart and meant it.'

Evidently, none of this carried much weight for the rest of the group. Piotr's dedicated lobbying had solidified the general defiant revolt. His daily crusade had worn down all resistance. I thought of all the times he had insisted on his little power plays. Everyone sat gazing into the smouldering fire, deep in thought. I stood up disgusted and walked to my old yellow kayak on the riverbank, bent over it, and began packing for the long paddle to Atalaya.

Of Dogs and Things

It was with mixed emotions that François and I set off for Atalaya. Although it felt wrong going on ahead of the raft, I knew that paddling with François would be 10 times more peaceful than being with the group.

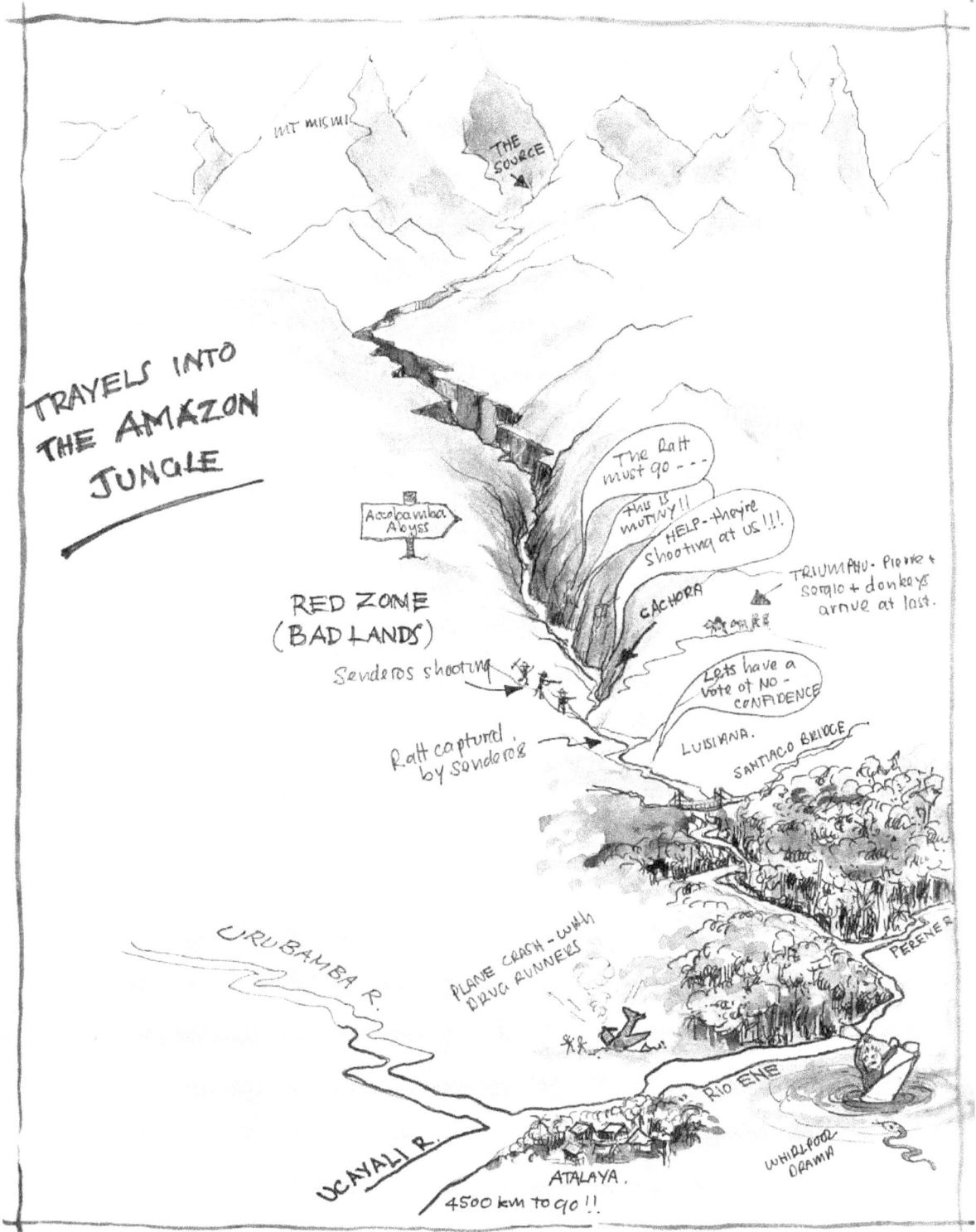

The sun was already high when François and I said our goodbyes.

'See you all in Atalaya,' I called out as I paddled into the current.

'Have a safe trip,' someone called back.

Then we were off.

The Ene was flowing strongly after the recent mountain rains. Brown masses of water poured in from every new tributary. (Through the course of the Apurimac, the river changes name several times – from Apachete, to Hornillos, to Apurimac, Ene, and finally Tambo. The Ene begins after its confluence with the Rio Mantaro.)

We paddled in silence, passing San Francisco – an ugly, untidy town with a huge rusted, steel bridge

Confluence with the Mantaro.

220

spanning the river. This monstrosity would be the last bridge spanning the river before it flowed into the Atlantic. We camped early on an island, sitting around the fire and keeping to our thoughts. François produced a bottle of Kanyasa that lifted the mood and sleep came easily that night.

'I almost hope the visas don't come through,' I mused to myself, thinking of the prospect of the remaining 5 600 km which, especially paddling with my friend Piotr, would be a trial 'de speciale'.

The next day we paddled through a sheer-sided pongo where the waters raced and surged between dark, restricting walls. Locals told us that this was the Pongo of the Seven Devils, each devil represented by a deadly whirlpool in flood season. After that, and to our left (northwest) rose the mist-covered hills of the Gran Pajonal highlands, which reach an altitude of 1 530 m. These parts are recognised as some of the wildest, most isolated areas of Peru – the hunting grounds of the Asháninka and Campa Indians.

That night bad diarrhoea plagued François, keeping him up most of the night so that he moved into the new day feeling fragile and unwell. The sun burned down hot and humid, and François spent the morning head down, passively carried along by the swirling current. By midday we were both weary and sunburnt, and found ourselves breaking the golden rule: 'Don't start any bickering when you are tired and bored.' Soon our bickering was fanned into arguing, and – to our shame – a beautiful afternoon's boating in tropical jungle was completely ruined. We were old friends, but, when we spent too much time together, we could not get on. It surely was a poor reflection on both of us.

We broke for lunch by pulling up on an island, where we rested in the shade. Jungle vegetation and creepers hung like ropes from the 60-m forest giants. A movement from the thick undergrowth caught my eye. I swung around to see a dog – a small, brownish mongrel. It was the thinnest, saddest-looking dog I ever encountered. We whistled and called it, but it withdrew into the forest. The emaciated animal had obviously been stranded on this island and was unable to swim back to the mainland. It was in the final stages of starvation – a scene I found most pathetic and tragic. We left some food for it, launched our kayaks and drifted off with the current. The hapless creature reappeared and watched us intently, sensing perhaps that we were its last hope of getting off the island. Heartbreaking wails and whimpering drifted across the water. With its last strength, the dog staggered into the hot sun and collapsed on the mud bank. I will never forget those few moments. I prayed that I would never reach such a point of hopelessness in this world.

Jungle giants.

Hunger,the Universal Language

We were low on food, and without fresh fruit or vegetables. We noticed a dugout clinging to a muddy bank, and a small footpath ascending the grassy bank into the jungle.

'Let's try this place, we need food pretty badly,' called François. We paddled across to the small beach.

'Yep, it looks good to me,' I replied. 'Maybe there's a McDonald's tucked away here somewhere. I'll have a vanilla milkshake and some French fries.'

As we climbed the steps cut into the clay bank, the unmistakable sense of being watched by scores of hidden eyes weighed on us. Walking carefully along the narrow path we came to a clearing where we found a circle of banana-thatched Campa homesteads.

'Hola, hola, bueños dias,' we called as we approached, trying not to surprise anyone who might put a dozen poisoned arrows through us. There was, however, no movement in the village – even our feathered friends fell silent. Standing in the middle of the clearing, we called again, waited a few minutes, and were just about to head back to the river when two men in traditional Campa dress, armed with traditional Campa bows and arrows, emerged noiselessly from the dense vegetation. All four of us stood motionless, eyes locked on one another, watching and assessing like wild animals, waiting for the first move.

François stepped forward. 'Bueños tardes, señores,' he called out, waiting for them to respond to his greeting. Their faces remained expressionless, and they kept silent.

'Maybe they don't speak Spanish,' I suggested, after another long and awkward silence. I raised my hands to my mouth, then to my stomach, miming that I was hungry.

'Hey, guys,' I tried, 'we're hungry – no food, empty stomach, far from home, missing my mother . . . '

François joined the mime, improving on my attempts. Our hosts were unmoved. The older, thicker-set man appeared to relax, lowered his weapon, and put his hand to his mouth as we had done.

We nodded enthusiastically, and the man rattled a few words to his younger companion, who at once walked to one of the raised houses and climbed the rickety steps. Seconds later we heard the excited voice of a woman. The younger man appeared and beckoned us to join them. He waved his arm up and down in a vertical motion, intending us to follow him. We obediently climbed the steps. Once in the house, our hosts gestured to us to sit on the cane floor. A small woman in a woven Campa cushma scuttled busily about the hut, preparing food. Meanwhile François and I tried to explain our mission in our best sign language. I was not completely sure whether they understood.

Thirty minutes later, the woman placed two calabashes before us containing a thin mustard-coloured gruel with chunks of unidentifiable solids floating in it. 'Chief' (as we had dubbed the older man) stood watching while his friend beckoned to us to eat from the gourds. Flashbacks of the monkey-hand soup on the Urubamba returned to me, but I decided to dig in. The soup, greasy and without salt, was not easy to finish, but we dared not insult our hosts. Eventually, after working through slimy lumps that resembled frog flesh, we finished the meal and graciously thanked all concerned.

Then François pulled out his party trick. He flicked his cigarette lighter, sending out a bluish flame that had both men grunting with approval. 'Chief' then took the lighter and tried it. After his fourth

Our Campa hosts.

After our hostile welcome
- we were invited for an unforgettable meal.

222

attempt he managed to trigger the blue flame and raised exclamations of approval from his wife and companion. Our hosts were suitably impressed and took us on a guided tour of the village. They obviously signalled that we were 'safe' as suddenly children appeared from every house and tree to witness these strange, bearded white men. What a sight we must have been! François and I shook our new friends' hands, crammed our kayaks with bananas and yucca, and headed on downstream towards Atalaya.

This Campa experience, strange as it was, was a welcome break from the monotony of long days of paddling in the hot sun.

Display of Power

We were approaching another major landmark, the confluence of the Ene and the Perené rivers – the point where the Ene becomes the Rio Tambo.

'Look, look at that! It must be the Perené. It's in full flood!' I shouted to François. 'Oh, no! Have you seen anything like it? It's just crazy!'

We gaped in amazement at what lay ahead of us – the Perené in full flood. A chocolate-brown roller coaster charged towards us, its exploding waves roaring and hissing as they slammed into the tranquil waters of the Ene. Along with this flood came a flotilla of uprooted trees and debris, plunging and rising through the swells and whirlpools. Several hundred metres downstream, where the Perené charged headlong into the left bank of the Ene, long slithers of unconsolidated riverbank were silently collapsing so that not only towering trees but hundreds of tons of soil fell into the boiling waters. In a moment we jolted into action. We were being swept towards the maelstrom and were about to become part of the river flotsam.

'Paddle, Tim, paddle!' warned François.

I had woken up to the situation too late, and found myself in the grip of a devouring whirlpool that careered up from behind me. My stern was sucked downwards in a spiralling vortex, leaving my bow pointing dangerously skyward. Before I knew what had hit me I was enveloped in darkness, the unseen force dragging me downwards, its merciless pressure throbbing in my ears. I had been in whirlpools before and feared their unforgiving, unpredictable grip. This was a particularly nasty one. When would it let me go? Something hard nudged my kayak. What was it: a log, a tree?

Seconds passed, and then, as fast as I had been sucked down, I was rocketed back into the sunlight, shaken and gasping for air. An enormous tree trunk floated alongside, a four-foot-long green snake clinging to one of its branches, not more than two feet from me. Another whirlpool began to form behind me, ready to suck me in. Madly, I sprinted away, but again I felt my stern go down – and stay down. I strained at my paddles, slowly edging out of its orbit, and then became free. I spotted François some distance away, observing me with alarm.

'You okay, Tim? Hell, man, you disappeared completely! Lucky you didn't get hooked up in that tree.'

'Phew, that was close – it caught me sleeping, I guess. Just as well that my spraydeck was on, or I'd still be down there somewhere.'

'Just shows, you can never relax too much on a river – it'll catch you off guard every time.'

'Yeah, every time. Thank goodness we're out of the canyons. With that sort of water around we wouldn't stand a chance.'

Almost immediately, the Rio Tambo swung hard east, powering us along in the wake of the flood. We paddled through the obstacle watercourse on high alert, avoiding driftwood, trees, and islands of brown foam and debris. Reptiles of every description, along with monkeys, armadillos, and injured birds clung to the flotsam, apparently unafraid of each other, united in their quest for survival. The animals were showing our human expedition how it could be done!

Soon the whirlpools lost their fury, and I flirted playfully with the spiralling currents. Now the river swung dramatically through 120 degrees and headed due north. The peaks of the Andes faded to a mere purple shadow on the skyline behind us, and to our left low clouds covered the disappearing mountains of the Gran Pajonal. We were slipping into a new world of jungle and water; our desert canyons and mountain ramparts would soon be a faded memory.

'Atalaya must be close now,' I called out to my friend.

He remained silent, and I realised that I had probably repeated that line half a dozen times in the last hour. It was obvious we both needed a break from the river.

Atalaya

I climbed out of my cockpit and sat on the rear deck, enjoying the more relaxed paddling position. A strange smell wafted in from upstream, and minutes later the first glint of corrugated iron roofs appeared on the left.

'Yes, yes!' I whooped. 'I can't tell you how sweet that sight is.'

Surely there would be letters waiting from my sweetheart, surely. We paddled up to a beach strewn with a flotilla of dugouts, balsawood rafts, and battered flat-bottom skiffs. A group of excited children surrounded us, touching us and prodding our unusual plastic craft. We climbed onto the bank, stiff and sore, and shook hands.

'Well done, François – we've made it this far. Well done.'

'You too, Tim, well done. Thanks for the paddle – for all your help.'

We looked at the rickety shanty buildings above us on their long spindly stilts. This place was a special landmark – it occupied an emotional place in our lives as it was four years ago (1981) that the two of us had arrived here after running the Urubamba. Where the two great rivers – the Apurimac and the Urubamba – met and mingled to become the Ucayali, we had abandoned *Berty*, our old balsawood raft. Soon after that we had caught a peci-peci ride upstream to Atalaya. Standing here now old memories

Nov. 1985.
Riverside homes along
Apurimac at Atalaya.
TIM

224

Four years earlier we shook hands on the same spot, after completing the Urubamba.

flooded back, as if 1981 was a lifetime ago. It was a nostalgic moment.

'Well, I don't know what to think about this trip,' reflected François. 'It hasn't been a good or a happy one, but here we are back again.'

'Yeah, lots has gone wrong, but at least we've made it this far,' I said, trying to sound encouraging.

'Now we've got to see what happens about our visas,' said François, bringing us back to reality. 'That will determine whether we finish here or carry on.'

With the help of some village boys, we toiled up the slippery steps of the bank, dodging open drainpipes that spewed out effluent from the dwellings above into the murky waters. A rickety 'restaurante' sign welcomed us, and we sat down at a table that overlooked the great Tambo River. François ordered a beer, me a cola. We clinked bottles, saluted each other and drank deeply.

François would now fly to Lima on the weekly flight in a last bid to secure our Brazilian visas. If all went well, he would return with Sergio and the sea kayaks. I booked into a cheap hotel and got a small room with a river view. Here I would wait for the raft to arrive.

ATALAYA & THE URUBAMBA / TAMBO CONFLUENCE.
11. NOV. 85.

225

During this time of waiting, uncertainty haunted me nightly. What would be the outcome of the visa saga? Was Atalaya going to be the end of the river for me, or only a halfway stop? On the one hand, the very thought of paddling another 5 600 km of monotonous flat water, accompanied by someone who had done his best to sabotage and split the expedition, seemed inconceivable. Then again, I knew that if my visa came through I would dedicate myself to paddling the distance, no matter what. However, I was sure that Piotr had more tricks up his sleeve. Would I be the next one they'd try to vote off the river? Anything seemed possible. I decided that if it ended up with only Piotr and me on the river, and he started his nonsense again, I would break away and go it on my own. Two factors made this last (and somewhat desperate) option acceptable. There was Margie – ready at any time to fly out and meet me along the river at a strategic point. That alone fanned my desire. Then, secondly, I could not deny that the prospect of becoming the first person to navigate the entire Amazon by kayak tickled my competitive nature.

The raft arrived in Atalaya two days later. The rafters dragged themselves up the steep bank, tired and irritable. I walked down to the water's edge to welcome them, but received a rather chilly welcome. It turned out that they had experienced some drama on the river when, the day before, an aeroplane, loaded with cocaine and other drugs, crashed near them on take-off. The team, flustered and excited, had rushed ashore to witness the police chase.

Such was life on the river.

Journey's End

A military Dakota flew in François and Sergio, bringing with them dismal news. The Brazilians remained unflinching in their resolve to ban South Africans from entering their country. Sadly, politics determined the final decision, and the journey for François and me had ended.

Of course I felt disappointed. Not one to give up easily, the news came as a blow. I had no alternative but to accept it and move on. I sent urgent telegrams to Margie, asking her to cancel her flight to join me and telling her I would be with her in South Africa in four days. With that thought my heart pounded! Piotr and Joe would now kayak to the sea, Kate and Zbecek following in a hired riverboat. François would leave whatever funds were available with Piotr and Joe. I took my hat off to them – they showed courage and determination in accepting the challenge.

Jerome's and Sergio's journey also ended here in Atalaya. They boarded the next plane to Lima, Jerome being keen to join the British white water team in the UK, and Sergio returning to his home in Costa Rica. Pierre, who had helped get the sea kayaks to Atalaya,

Tim
Catching a plane out
of Atalaya

ATALAYA.
THE "IRENE ISABEL"

would also end his time here once he had wound up the film project.

Piotr and Joe were busy packing and testing their sea kayaks at the riverside when I walked up to them to wish them well. They had a marathon ahead of them and needed encouragement.

'Cheers, Joe, cheers, Piotr. I hope your trip goes well – look after yourselves. God's speed.'

We shook hands. François and I watched as the two boats slowly paddled out of sight in the direction of the Atlantic. That was the last time I saw them. Three months later, on 19 February 1986, the two of them reached the Atlantic Ocean.

Shortly after it was my time to go – not by kayak, alas, but by plane. François would stay a day or so longer to wrap up business in Atalaya. We shook hands and bade each other farewell. I loaded my gear into the military plane, and, 10 minutes later the Dakota's engines roared as we charged over the uneven runway, bouncing twice before becoming airborne. I gazed out at the endless jungle, spanning from horizon to horizon and at the thin golden thread of the Apurimac meandering eastward toward the Atlantic. I sat back and closed my eyes. The journey for me had finally ended.

'Thank you, Lord,' I prayed.

Afterword

A while later in South Africa Margie and I were amused to receive a copy of the *Guinness Book of Records* in which Piotr and Joe claimed to be the first to navigate the entire Amazon. No other names were mentioned in the entire account. A year later a copy of *National Geographic* published an article about the trip written by Piotr. Once again we were not mentioned. A handwritten message, however, was on the inner cover. It read, 'Thank you for the trip, Tim. Without you it would not have been possible. Piotr.'

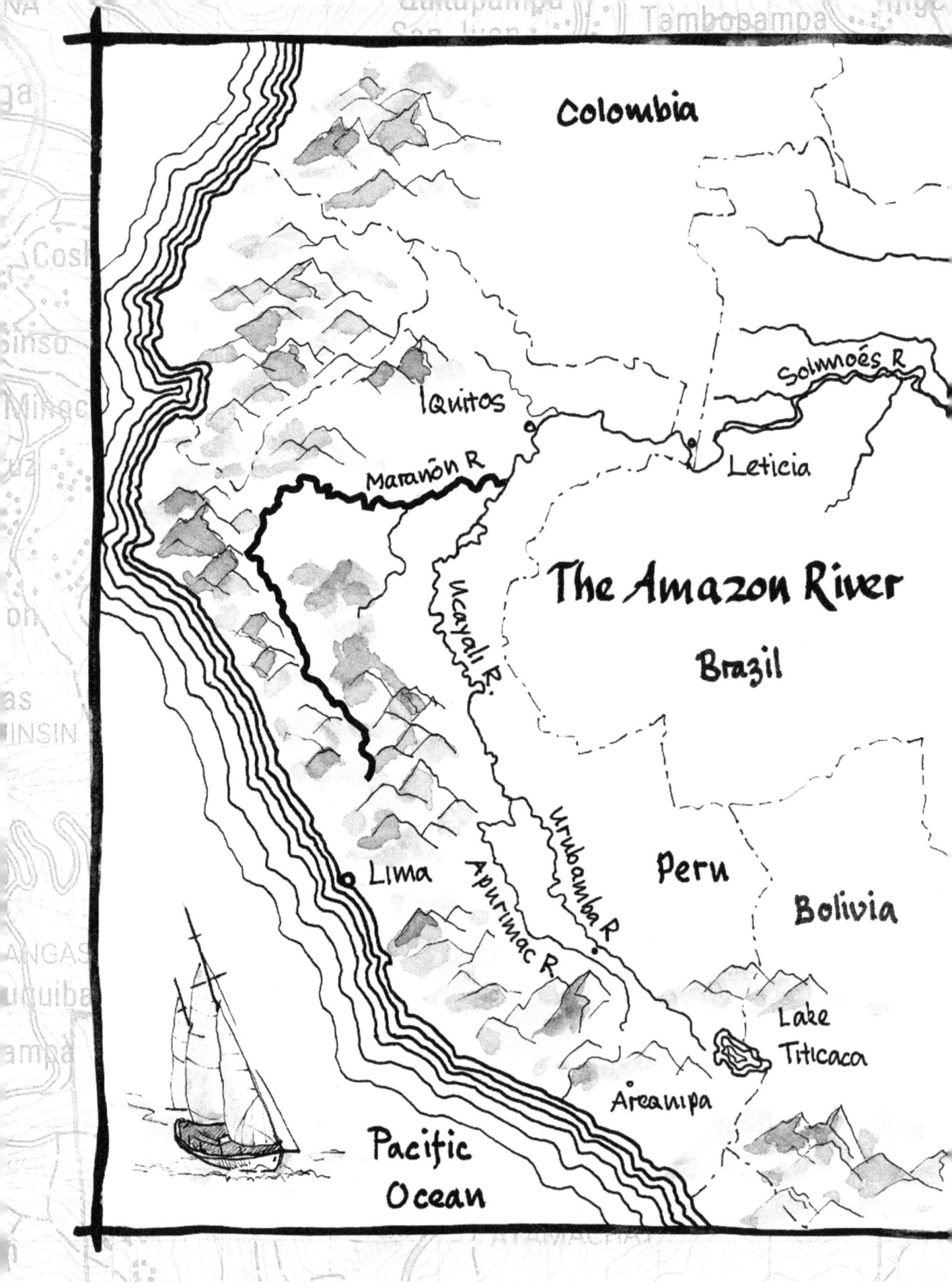

Colombia

Solimoés R.

Iquitos

Leticia

Marañón R.

The Amazon River

Brazil

Ucayali R.

Urubamba R.

Peru

Lima

Apurímac R.

Bolivia

Lake Titicaca

Arequipa

Pacific Ocean

The Marañón River
2004

Atlantic Ocean

Amazon

Manaus

Santarem

Belem

N

PART 3

Kilometers

0   200   400   600

Chapter 10

JUBILEE YEAR

A New Dream

'Consecrate the fiftieth year and proclaim liberty throughout the land to all its inhabitants. It shall be a jubilee for you' (Leviticus 25:10).

Margie put down the family Bible which we had been reading through, looked up and smiled.

'See, Sweetie, isn't this amazing! Every 50 years Israel was told to have a year of rest, to settle debts, to have a year of liberty. Well, this is your 50th year. Maybe it's your time to have a year off, settle your debts, and have a jubilee year – you deserve it!'

The idea was indeed inspiring. After 18 years farming and building up a timber business in Ixopo in KwaZulu-Natal, we had accepted an offer to sell our entire concern to a neighbouring friend and farmer, Pete Hayter. The very idea of being released from the pressures of running the timber business sounded like 'paradise' to me. The season of farming and timber had ended. Now a new, unknown season was beckoning.

I needed time to think over and absorb what had taken place. There was no better place for this than St Isadore Dam, several kilometres from Ixopo. I loaded my K1 racing kayak onto the roof of my pickup, called for Kimber, my faithful German shepherd, and set off for an hour on the water. David, my brother, would usually join me for a paddle after a day's work, but this day my dog and I were on our own. Carefully I lowered myself into the unstable sprint boat and pushed off from the shore. Soon the slender nose of the kayak was slicing through the silver-grey, glassy water. The 'swish-swish' of water against hull magically erased the stress of the past few days. A pair of fish eagles called to each other across the dam. Egyptian geese honked and prepared to roost on their favourite mud bank. My mind drifted to the events of the past few days. The reality of finally selling Flaxton Timbers struck home.

What would I do next? What new goals and dreams should I follow?

Like a bolt of lightning the thought flashed through my mind: the Marañón. 'That's it; I can do the Marañón!' It was as if that third mysterious doorway leading down to the Marañón's canyons slowly began to open. Now, with some free time on my hands, the dream could become a reality. Adrenalin shot through my system at the very thought of another river expedition. Racing thoughts whirled through my mind. Had the Marañón been run yet? Who would I take along? What would my family say? I paddled two laps of the dam, thinking, processing my new dream. My mind was in a spin. I needed some sober thought and prayer before I rushed headlong into this new adventure.

The Rio Marañón had always held a special attraction for me. Early Portuguese geographers and explorers had always recognised this river as the true source of the Amazon. On discovering the confluence of the Marañón and

The Biggs family : Me, Margie, Ben, Keetah, Jonathan, Sam

the Ucayali rivers, these explorers had decided that, with its greater volume and size, the Marañón was the true source of the Amazon.

The ancient Incas had named the Marañón the Golden Serpent, after discovering enormous gold deposits trapped in its layers of fine sand and gravel bars. According to legend, this jungle treasure house lured the Conquistadors to establish the 'seven secret cities' of El Dorado on the river in the 16th century. During the past five centuries many great explorers had pitted their strength against the river, some seeking treasure, some recognition, others barely surviving, and, indeed, others not surviving at all. So far as kayaking was concerned, it was only after

the accelerated development of kayaking as a discipline and the advances made in the construction of durable kayaks from materials such as fibreglass and, later, polyethylene, that the previously unrunnable mountain gorges had been penetrated. We could find record of only two kayak teams that had entered the inaccessible canyons of the Marañón. The first was the four-man American team led by John Wasson in 1972, and the other an American team led by Kurt Casey in 2001. Wasson's team, in fibreglass kayaks, had started below the walled Quivilla gorge, and gone as far as Bagua. Kurt Casey (whom I had kayaked with in South Africa) had made a 10-day descent of the most difficult gorge

232

section, also ending at Chugual. As far as we could establish, no one had navigated the entire river from its source in the Cordillero Huaywash to its confluence with the Apurimac and the Urubamba, 1 850 km away. The challenge beckoned, and I was more than willing to take it on. If I navigated the Marañón, I would have kayaked the three main tributaries of the Amazon River. It was an opportunity of a lifetime.

A week went by before I approached Margie and the rest of the family about my proposal. We were all enjoying a leisurely breakfast on our sunny front veranda when I raised the issue.

'Margie,' I began slowly – but, before I could utter another word, she knew that a bombshell was on its way. Nonetheless I continued. 'I've been thinking about what to do after the sale goes through. I would love to do another expedition, and the Marañón River in Peru still hasn't been run. It's something I've dreamed of for years.'

My wife patiently sat watching me, waiting for me to let it all out before speaking.

'Yes, you should do it. Go for it, you deserve it.'

Margie was not speaking in ignorance, and was certainly not naïve about what a trip like this would entail. In 1985, when we had only been married six months, she had waved goodbye to me as I left for the Apurimac. It was now 2003, and she understood exactly what it would mean. She knew the sacrifices that awaited both parties.

'When would you want to go?' she asked.

'We'd need at least six months to plan it. The best time is July or August when the rivers are still low.'

I turned to my children who were all following the conversation intently.

'What do you think, guys? Should I do it?'

I watched them wrestling to grasp what it would mean to our family – to them. We were (still are) a close family, and did everything together as a team.

Sam, my eldest son (then only 16), looked up with a clear face and big trusting eyes.

'I think you should do it, Dad,' he said. 'It would be good for you. We'll be all right here.'

My eyes turned to my other children: Keetah, Ben and Jonathan.

'Yes, you should do it, Dad,' they responded.

I was relieved. A 'no' from my family would have stopped the Marañón dead in its tracks.

'Thank you, guys. I can't tell you how much this means to me!'

The Marañón was now a certainty. The final trip in my personal trilogy had begun.

The Dream Team

On reaching the small village of Queripalca, having left Lima 26 hours earlier, the doors of our dilapidated kombi were thrown wide open. An amazing sight greeted us. The dark clouds which had hung low in the sky all day suddenly rolled away and revealed a most spectacular sight – the towering, ice-capped peaks of Yeru Paja. At 6 700 m, these are the highest peaks of the Amazon watershed, and the second highest in Peru.

The dramatic sight overwhelmed us and stunned us into silence. We remained in our seats, gaping at the view, until a polite nudge from a passenger behind snapped us from our spell. Seconds later the cloud curtain was again drawn, blotting out what we had seen. But the five of us were sure that the majestic mountains had nodded their approval of our arrival.

Our five-man team comprised four kayakers and a cameraman. Shaun Biggs, my nephew, was crammed into the backseat, half drugged by the exhaust fumes that had billowed into the vehicle for the past two hours. Of medium height, powerfully built and with a head of dark brown curly hair, Shaun (22 years old), had been my first choice as a team member. Having grown up as a farm boy in Ixopo, he had developed a love and affinity for rivers, and had risen through the ranks to become one of South Africa's top all-round kayakers, representing his country in white water sprint and marathon racing.

Sitting next to him were Graeme Anderson and Ross O'Donoghue, both 22 years old, tall and athletic, and like Shaun were all final year students at the University of Natal. Graeme and Ross had shared this love of kayaking from their school days, and it had bonded them as inseparable friends. Graeme had grown up on the Umzimkulu River near Underberg, and thus had one of the country's classic white water stretches, Thrombosis Gorge, on his doorstep. Ross, who lived in Howick, had been virtually adopted by the Anderson family, and for years the two of them

had honed their skills running the most difficult sections of local rivers. Both were regarded as the top 'extreme' kayakers in southern Africa.

Kyle O'Donoghue, Ross's older brother, had agreed at a later stage to follow us down the river to capture and document the adventure on film. I had explained to Kyle, that due to a lack of sponsors, we would be funding ourselves for the mission. Kyle was unperturbed by the shortfall, and committed himself to support us single-handedly as we made our way through the canyons. His unconditional attitude scored high in my books, and reassured me that he was the right man for the trip.

After 6 hrs in this combi we were nearly gassed by exhaust fumes.

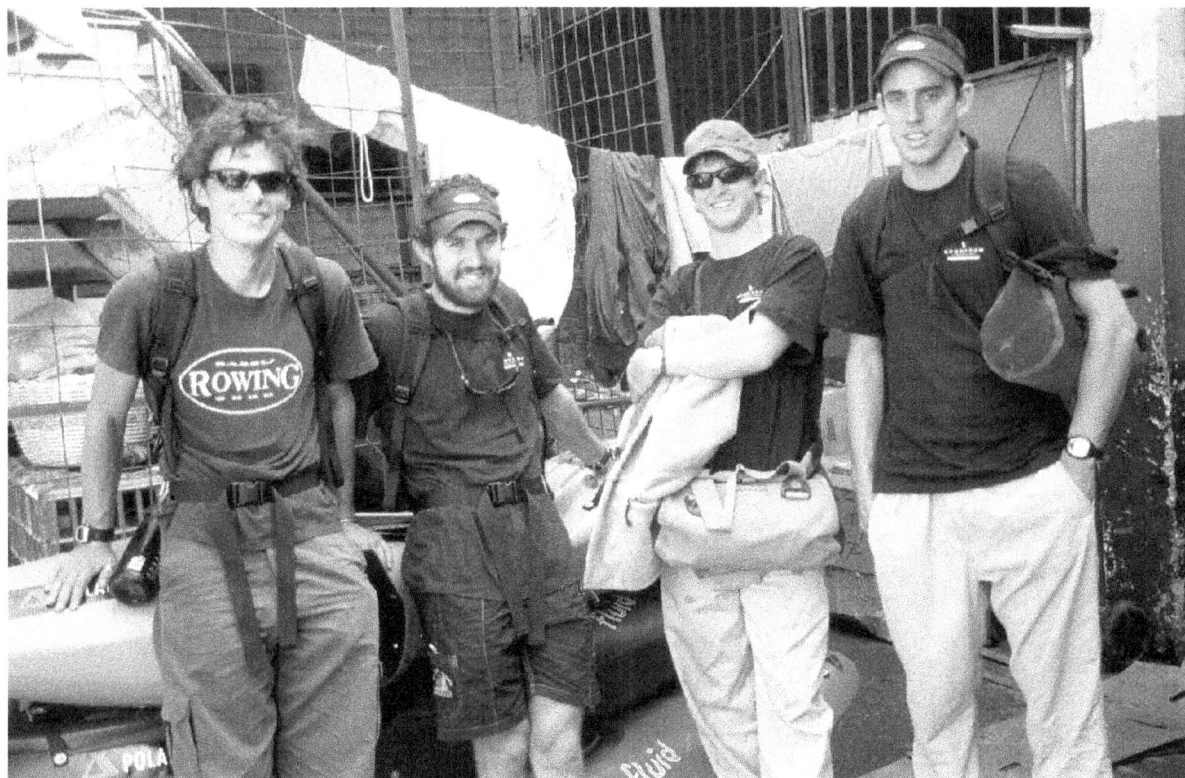

My young campañeros ~ left: Kyle, Shaun, Graeme & Ross.

François Odendaal had obviously come to mind as a member since we had travelled the first two tributaries of the Amazon together. Unfortunately he had done very little paddling since the Apurimac, and had recently undergone two operations. To expect him to manage a strenuous trip like this would be unwise. I had phoned him and invited him to produce a film of the adventure, and possibly to join us on the river itself on some of the flatter sections. François was hesitant. Understandably he was put out not to be invited onto the team, and he made no bones about it.

I stood my ground, adamant that he was not up to the task, but assured him that he was welcome to film the expedition. He cautiously accepted this proposal, but I could sense his misgiving. A month before our departure, François e-mailed to tell me that he

had been unsuccessful in raising finance for the film, and would not be able to join us.

I knew that the Marañón would now be the type of trip I enjoyed most – a lightweight, self-supporting team made up of a few handpicked kayakers.

Of Men and Donkeys

A small crowd of inquisitive villagers flocked around us, fascinated by such a strange-looking group of gringos with their unusual cargo of brightly coloured kayaks. Our belongings were ceremoniously offloaded and carried into the middle of the Plaza de Armas, where a colourful and lively carnival was in full swing. Such was the commotion and interest caused by our arrival that we soon became the focal point of atten-

Welcomed at Queripalca by the mayor himself.

Which one would you trust?
(Augustos and Shaun)

tion, and received an official welcome from the honourable mayor and his elders.

Kyle, our most fluent Spanish speaker, introduced us and explained our mission. 'We are Sud Africanos. We have come here to find the source of the Rio Marañón, and to travel down the river to its end. We need permission to pass through your village, and we also need to hire donkeys and porters to take us to Lago Coricocha. Can you help us?'

It soon became clear that our ambitious plans impressed the mayor, his elders, counsellors, and supporters. Augustos, a wiry and weather-beaten owner of many donkeys, was duly appointed to assist us with our mission. As luck would have it, we had arrived at Queripalca's original 'one-stop' shop where, in no time, Augustos supplied us with accommodation, meals, guides and vital information on the region. The slight, wiry Quechua man, with his darting eyes, Inca nose and charismatic temperament, soon made himself indispensable.

'Augustos, we need four burros to carry our kayaks up to the lake. Can you help us?' asked Shaun, whose job it was to arrange donkeys.

'Si, señor. Tomorrow morning I can have as many burros as you need,' promised Augustos. 'I have many burros,' he added, with a sweeping movement of his arms.

'Can you be here by six in the morning? We need to leave early.'

'Si, si, señor, we will be here very early.'

'How much will you charge for the donkeys and guide?' Shaun asked.

'We will talk about that at the end.'

'No, señor,' Shaun argued. 'We need to know before we leave.'

'Twenty soles for a donkey; 40 for a guide,' answered Augustos, smiling generously.

Fortunately we had found out at the plaza the going rate for a donkey was 10 soles per day, and for a guide 20.

'No, no, too expensive,' we protested. 'Ten soles for a donkey, 20 for a guide.'

Augustos paused, assessing the situation. We had obviously done our homework! But on he went, unperturbed by our objections.

'Señor, my donkeys are the best in Queripalca. They are strong and good in the mountains. Fifteen soles for a donkey, señor,' he now offered, looking hurt that we were being so difficult, 'and 25 soles for the guide.'

We discussed the price amongst ourselves, knowing that Augustos was still getting a good deal.

'Let's leave it at that,' I suggested. 'It's not much in dollars, and at least he'll feel he's making something on the deal.'

We shook hands, both parties satisfied.

At 9:30 a.m., we were still waiting for our train of donkeys to arrive. An hour later Augustos arrived with no donkeys and looked most surprised when we challenged him as to where they were.

'They'll be here now-now, no problem. My children will be here with the donkeys now, don't worry.'

At 10:30 a.m., four pitifully small burros and a small pony were herded into the courtyard. The two larger donkeys both had gaping wounds on their fetlocks, while the others were far too small for the load. We struggled to remain patient, and after some heated negotiations, we turned them down.

Augustos's reaction was dramatic. Instantly he changed into another man. His friendly, laughing eyes of the day before burned with anger. His stance seemed to say: 'How dare these ignorant gringos criticise the burros of the most respected burro owner in the village of Queripalca?'

In a flurry of frustrated fury, children, family and relatives were dispatched into the mountain slopes to find four other donkeys. Two hours later an improved batch arrived. But now there was another problem. Augustos had no suitable harness for tying kayaks on to the backs of the animals. Insisting that we tie a single kayak on the back of each burro, he

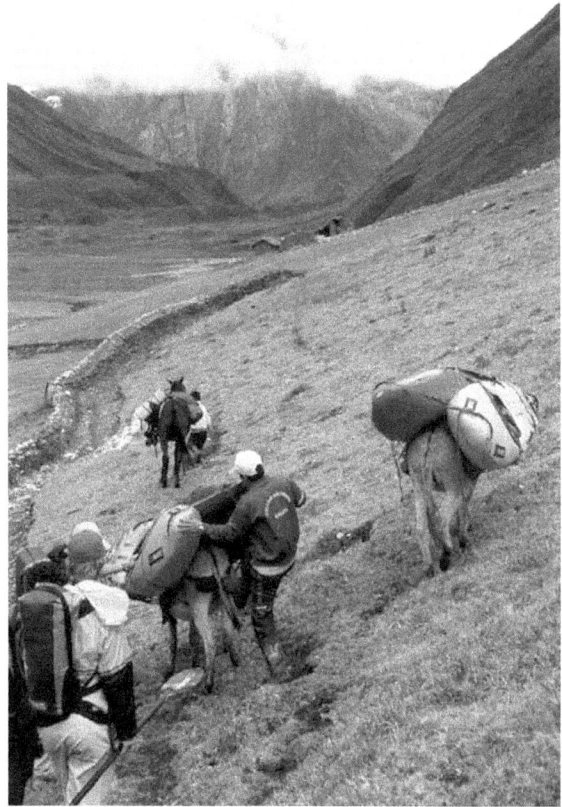

Trekking to the Cordillero Huaywash.

watched us set off in drizzle and sleet, along the stone-walled path out of the village.

After a few hundred metres the first two kayaks had already slipped off the donkeys' bony backs, and hung at a ridiculous angle. After much retying and agitation, Ross came up with a solution: have two kayaks on each donkey, one on each side, counterbalancing each other. This seemed to work well, except that we now needed only three donkeys, and that meant a price adjustment. Luis, our young guide, insisted that we return to Augustos's home to re-negotiate the deal. So back we trudged, finally agreeing on an increased price of 20 soles each for the

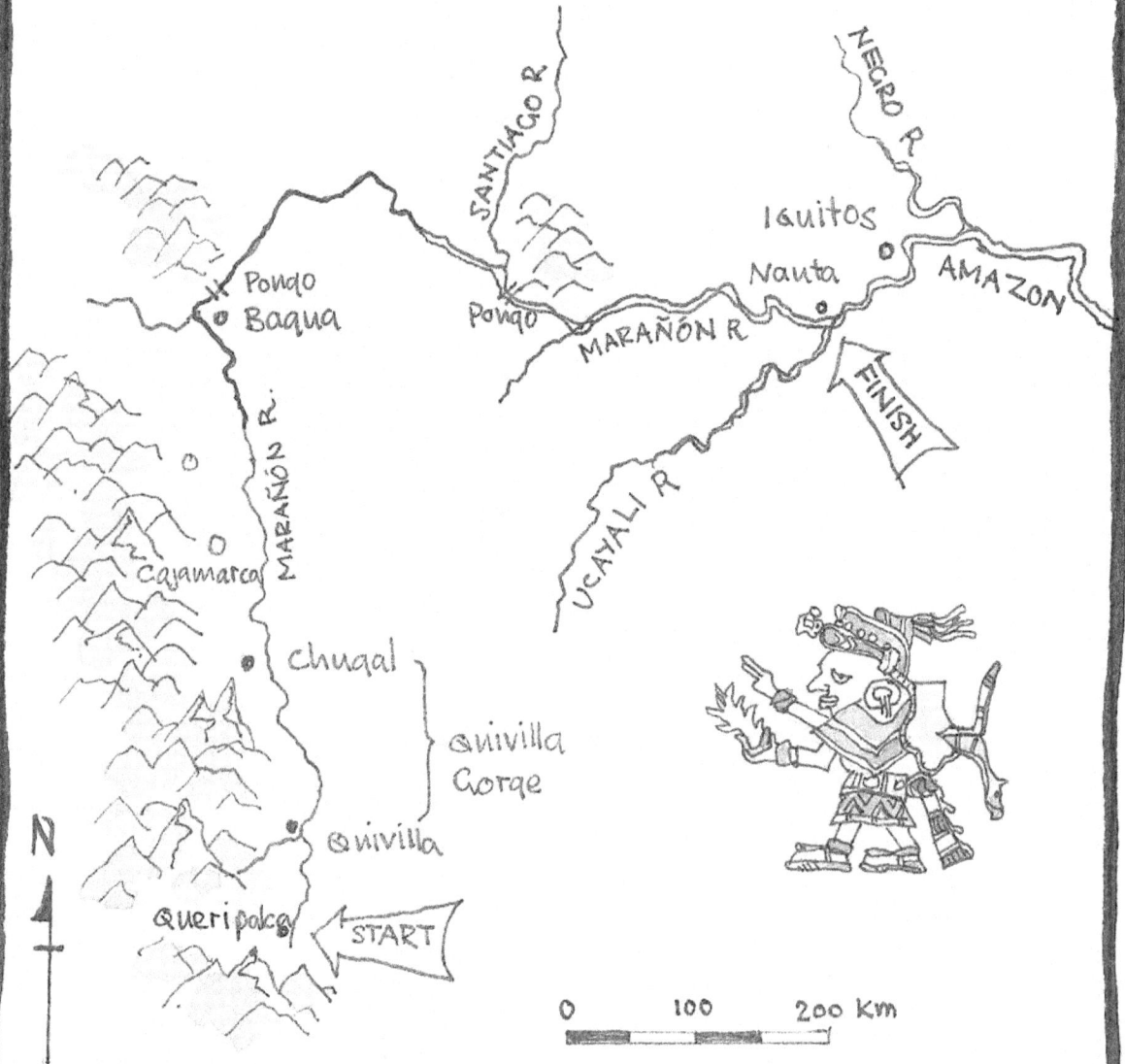

The Marañón River Expedition. 2004

NEGRO R

SANTIAGO R

Iquitos

Nauta

AMAZON

Pongo
Baqua

Pongo

MARAÑÓN R

MARAÑÓN R.

FINISH

UCAYALI R

Cajamarca

Chuqal

Quivilla Gorge

Quivilla

Queripaca

START

N

0   100   200 Km

My sketch of the source – it began to sleet so I never finished it.

three donkeys, bringing the total to the same amount as before.

With Augustos now happy with the deal, we again set off for the source.

It was late afternoon when we crested a ridge to see the greyish-blue waters of Lago Coricocha lying before us, stretched out at the base of the clouded peaks of the Cordillero Huaywash. We stood awestruck by the spectacular backdrop of sheer ice peaks, covered by cloud and mirrored in the lake's glassy waters.

'So here we are – standing at the source of the Marañón.'

Chapter 11

TREACHEROUS CANYONS

The Journey Begins

'Oh no! – look outside! Quick, look outside, guys,' came shouts from Ross in his makeshift tent. It was 6:15 a.m., and we dived for the tent opening, expecting at least an avalanche, bandits or something catastrophic.

Before us lay the most breath-taking sight. There was the lake – crystal clear, and above it tier upon tier of mountain peaks rising upwards, with the king of the peaks, Yeru Paja, standing proud and tall, beaming down on us. We stumbled out of our tents and stood dumbly, gaping in awe at our first real sight of the mountains we'd been longing to see – the mountains that had kept themselves hidden from us, and which only now shone forth in their full splendour.

Meanwhile ice and frost crunched in the grass as we tried to stomp the cold out of our feet.

'Tea, guys, where's the tea?' I called. 'We've got to celebrate with a mug of tea.'

Already Kyle had his small MSR burner hissing merrily and the old blackened pot of water was on the go.

We had been waiting for the right opportunity to photograph the team with our various sponsors' products and logos, and now was the ultimate spot and time. For the next hour, amid much laughter, we posed and sported our high-quality gear and equipment.

'Breakfast is done – come and eat,' called Ross. We swarmed around the steaming pot of oatmeal

After a few hundred metres we were
dropping over waterfalls.

porridge, our appetites back after the effects of altitude and queasiness.

We prayed before the meal: 'Lord, thank You for this most beautiful place, for your mighty creation, and for helping us arrive here safely. Today we start our journey in earnest. Please go with us and be ahead of us – protect us – be with our families back home. Thank You for this porridge. Amen.'

'Amen,' came the response from the rest of the team.

By 9:30 a.m. we had stowed our gear in our kayaks, and, to the cheers from Kyle, Luis and his Quechua compañero, we paddled into the waters of the glistening lake. By means of a small stream on the northeast corner, the Rio Nupe, we slipped through a narrow channel into a series of small cascading drops and chutes. There was just sufficient water to make the tight turns and clear the boulders. The peaty banks rose up steeply, oozing water through velvet green moss and water grass.

As we rounded the first bend, the water disappeared over a waterfall. Ross leapt out to scout and yelled: 'It's fine – we can run it.' He slipped back into his kayak and without hesitating disappeared over the 4-m vertical fall.

I chuckled at Ross's impulsiveness. 'What had I let myself into, teaming up with this bunch of daredevils?' I thought to myself. A single, piercing whistle indicated that he was fine, and that the next in line could follow. Shaun was standing by with a throw-line in case of any problem. There is always a risk running a waterfall. Five kayaks can run the same line without a hitch, and then the sixth paddler can run an identical line and slam into a submerged rock.

Graeme dropped off – then Shaun. My turn came, and I pulled a hard left sweep as I dropped over. My left rail brushed against a shallow rock and I dropped off at an angle. My boat plunged, and the next moment freezing water struck me like a steel hammer. I had overturned, and by the time my heavily laden kayak rose to the surface, it was pressed against the rock

Ross blazing a trail through our first gorge.

face. I rolled up, gasping and wide-eyed from the shock. The others were laughing.

'Cold hey, Tim! – well done.'

'Ya – you were slightly too far to the right,' Graeme added.

Graeme, Shaun and Ross had arrived in Lima a month before me and had acclimatised to the altitude and the freezing waters. This was my maiden run on the river and I knew that, as the 'old man' of the team, I was being closely scrutinised by my young friends. How did they perceive me? They had already nicknamed me Madala (meaning 'old man' in Zulu). Did they secretly view me as the one who might hold back the expedition and possibly jeopar-

dise it? I certainly had my own fears to contend with – my bad shoulder being one of them. Had the wheel of time turned a full circle? Well, I would give it a full go.

We were thrilled by the action-packed first kilometre – things were looking up. The river, however, was handing out only a taste of what was to come. We dropped over a few more drops and tight turns before reaching a shallow, rocky 'bump-and-scrape' section of gravel bars and other obstacles. Predictably, mountain weather now closed in and low drizzly clouds spattered us with sleet. The river began to steepen and we found ourselves hemmed in by a narrow gorge.

243

Lunch break - we were freezing.

Armed with his camera, Kyle suddenly appeared on the left bank. Knowing that we were in the spotlight and being captured on film, a fresh motivation and bravado took hold of us. We were now in adrenalin mode, with Ross blazing a trail through the steep and technically challenging creek. With no space to manoeuvre, we crashed our way downstream, often slamming against rocks as we negotiated the continuous drops and the steep gradient (about 70 m/km). The greatest threat was to become pinned beneath an undercut rock. If a kayak fills with water and starts to fold around your legs, you will be trapped and dependent on your mates to rescue you.

Rain and windblown sleet followed us down the river and we shivered in our kayaks. As abruptly as the small gorge had started, so it ended, and the river spewed us back into shallow gravel bars and flat water. Soon the familiar orange and brown tiled roofs of Queripalca welcomed us. We dragged our boats and ourselves back up to Augustos's house, puffing and panting from our unacclimatised condition.

Although we had only completed one day on the river, we were treated as the heroes of the day. The villagers were impressed by this first descent of their sacred river. At Augustos's house, a spirit of excitement and delight ruled; hearty backslapping replaced yesterday's wrangling over donkeys. Augustos had found his friendly eyes again; and we were lifelong friends. Graeme and Ross won the adoration of the young boys in the village by joining in their soccer games in the courtyard. One mother took me aside and told me how pleased she was that her sons could play with 'real men'. We made the most of this title over the next few days, teasing our friends about being the 'real men' around town.

Queripalca to Banos

Rays from the morning's first light beamed across the room. It was 5 July 2004 – our second day on the river – and we could have done with another two hours of sleep. The previous night's rowdy celebrations had continued through the night, degenerating into drunken chaos. The Queripalcans had shown an affinity with firecrackers, and the din of explosions had emulated a battlefield. During the early hours a thunderflash had landed in our courtyard, almost inducing a round of heart attacks!

Anyway, we quickly finished breakfast (yes, oatmeal porridge again), packed our kayaks, and bade farewell to our hosts. Augustos used sign language to show that he was still feeling dizzy and that his head was pounding. His bloodshot eyes confirmed the tale.

We dragged our loaded boats down to the shallow, fast-flowing river where a colourful crowd (those who hadn't overindulged) lined the bank. As I was about to slip into the swift current, a frantic señora – Augustos's wife – rushed to the river's edge, calling, 'havae, havae' (keys, keys). I fumbled around and, sure enough, I had walked out with the keys to our room. Soon a 'race' developed between the village's children and us, some 50 Quechua boys and girls sprinting along the riverbank, shouting and screaming until we were out of sight.

Now the first of the gorges we had spotted from the road confronted us, its dolomite walls rearing some 100 m above the river. Augustos had warned us, with animated signs, of gorges with huge waterfalls, and of places where the river disappeared underground. The latter was 'malo – muy peligroso' (bad – very dangerous). Would this be the section that now awaited us? The sides narrowed to no more than a

Anything could happen in there.

boatlength in width. Cautiously we moved forward, peering around each bend expectantly. After a kilometre of fun rapids, we broke out from the walls to find a cow peacefully grazing on the steep slope. This was obviously not the section Augustos had warned us about.

The second gorge followed shortly thereafter, its walls so narrow and sheer that no sunlight reached the river.

'No getting out of here in a hurry, even if we wanted to,' exclaimed Ross. 'It's totally walled in!'

The atmosphere inside this narrow split in the earth's surface was breathtaking. Light filtered through the gnarled and contorted trees; ferns and bracken

We found places where the sun never shone.

While I was edging up the wall with my kayak, Graeme yelled, 'Tim, my boat – catch it!' Unknowingly I had nudged Graeme's kayak which had been delicately perched on a ledge. As if in slow motion, the orange kayak slid into the current. The gravity of the situation flashed through my mind: 'lose this boat, and one of us is stranded in this gorge with no way out.' I dived into the icy water after it, only to see its stern disappear around a bulge in the rock face. Immediately beyond the bulge waited the perilous siphon. The kayak was instantly swallowed. Desperately I lunged for the rock face, found a handhold, and pulled myself out of the current. In the meantime Shaun had rushed around with a throw-line. The submerged orange hull was barely visible, wedged under rocks, the flow of the current forcing it down. Would it buckle and fold under the pressure? Helplessly we watched, glad that one of us was not trapped down there. Shaun somehow managed to attach the throw-line to the kayak's protruding handle, and Ross and Graeme pulled with all their might. Nothing budged. We tried again, using a small pulley to gain purchase. After an exhausting 30-minute struggle, the battered but intact kayak was inched out of the jam.

Sitting down on the moss-covered rocks, and relieved at having averted a crisis, we surveyed the scene around us. Tension over my careless accident was almost tangible.

'Sorry, Graeme, I didn't even realise that I bumped your boat. I'll be more careful next time.'

'No problem, Tim, at least there was no one inside. I suppose I should have made it more secure,' Graeme replied.

Graeme was gracious about the incident, but I needed no reminding that, on an expedition like this, what I had done was unacceptable. We were now trapped against the cliff on the wrong side of the river, with no option but to swim our kayaks across the stream in order to reach the right-hand side. Ross made the first plunge into the icy river. Only metres above the siphon, he shot across the stream with

draped over the small ledges, and ahead came the muffled roar of an approaching rapid. We slipped through a tricky section of tight and technical rapids, until our path became completely blocked by massive boulders and collapsed sections of cliff face. Ross, paddling up front, signalled frantically, pointing to the left bank. He barely managed to scramble onto the rocks before the river was sucked underground. With no space to exit, we clung to the side wall 'bumper to bumper', fighting the current lest we be sucked into the deadly siphon. One by one we hauled the kayaks up the sidewall and stacked them precariously on small ledges and boulders.

four powerful strokes, lunging for a protruding branch, and hauled himself out of the water. Quickly he secured a throw-line to a tree and threw it back to us. One by one, we lined our kayaks across the fast current, glancing into the jaws of the siphon as we inched past. A narrow ravine allowed us to take a near-vertical route up the sidewall, and a passage around the 150-m blockage. We struggled for a solid hour, wrestling and heaving our 45-kg kayaks up and along to a narrow, moss-covered ledge. During this exercise, I again painfully realised that I was no match for my powerful, young friends, who effortlessly shouldered their kayaks while I grunted and groaned under the weight of my own. Should I even be with these guys? I asked myself. A hard realisation was hitting home: 'I ain't what I used to be; I'm off the mark.' In all my previous expeditions I was on top of my game, up front, leading. Now the tables had turned and I was the weak link, straggling behind, making careless mistakes. Was I still up to this sort of adventure?

After a quick lunch, we pushed on downstream through the narrow canyon and the cascading rapids. Scrawny trees with papery, red bark appeared along the boulder-strewn banks, their interlocking branches straddling the river and forming a tunnel. Giant, needle-like stalactites hung from limestone walls, reaching out to something that only they could see. The river steepened and we worked our way through class 4 chutes and drops until another blockage stopped us and demanded a strenuous portage. Emerging from the dark gorge, we paddled on, only to be met by a third sheer-sided canyon. Here were more stalactites and overhanging caves. We named it Cango Canyon after the Cango Caves in South Africa.

Technical creeking ~ Ross.

Four hours later, we were literally spat out by a fast and bumpy rapid that marked the end of the day's gorges. A gushing tributary poured into the Rio Nupe from the right-hand side, almost doubling the river's volume. We realised that this had to be the alternative source of the Marañón, and the sister river to the Nupe. Although our maps showed it to be slightly longer than the Nupe, we had taken note that a section of stream was represented by dotted lines and swamps. This seemed to suggest that the stream was possibly seasonal, and flowed into a swampland. Right or wrong, we had committed ourselves to the Nupe as the source of the Marañón, and it had certainly provided us with a thrilling start to our journey. Like the Apurimac and Urubamba, the names of the Marañón's tributaries change from the Nupe to the Marañón.

We sped through some 10 km of magnificent class 3 and 4 water, and at 4:00 p.m. arrived at a beautiful, grassy riverbank with a thermal spring that drained into the river. 'Hey, guys,' I called out, 'look at this amazing spot. Let's camp here tonight – we can all have hot baths!'

'No,' said Ross, 'let's head on to Banos. Kyle is waiting for us – I'm sure we can make it before dark.'

After some hesitation, Graeme and Shaun supported Ross's call.

'But, guys,' I persisted, 'we've still got at least 15 km to go. We'll end up paddling in the dark – and we won't easily find another perfect campsite like this. Besides, Kyle won't be too put out. He's staying in a hostel at the hot baths.'

My motivation was overruled, and I decided to bow to the majority vote. It was not a serious issue, but, nonetheless, I privately wondered whether this was the pattern of things to come – being outvoted by my teammates. On the other hand, I appreciated that it would be good to join Kyle for the night. So we headed on – me in a low-grade 'sulk', my nose definitely 'out of joint' at being overruled.

Two-and-a-half hours later, at 6:00 p.m., we spotted the village of Banos in the distance. It was already dark, and after three more portages and several small gorges, we arrived at the village. A low timber bridge loomed into sight, and in shaky Spanish we called out, 'Dondes el gringos?' (Where are the gringos?). There was no response from the glowering and unwelcoming figures on the bank. 'These guys have obviously had a bad experience with gringos,' I commented. 'Normally the village folk are friendly, These guys don't like us.' We later found out that this had been a stronghold of the Maoist guerrillas, the Sendero Luminoso.

Banos was a squalid, dirty-looking town with a river frontage lined with plastic bags and refuse. We paddled on. It was now properly dark, and none of us knew where exactly Kyle would be waiting or indeed where the 'hot baths' were. After paddling three more kilometres without finding our friend, I had to restrain myself from making an untoward 'I told you so' statement. Just as I was about to call an end to the day's paddling, a small light flashed on the opposite hillside. As the light approached, we discerned Kyle's figure stumbling through the dark. It turned out that he had been tipped off by bush telegraph that four gringos were approaching in canoes, and had decided to wait for us at the river's edge. We greeted each other warmly, relieved that our night outing was over.

Banos – Cosmo Canyon (Incas' Revenge)

On the third day of the expedition, we were up and out at first light. Our host, Lenin, showed us the Inca hot baths (aqua calieintes), which we decided to try before moving on. The experience was disappointing and hardly appetising. Hand-hewn Inca stonework lined the two pools, each approximately 16 m². We were not the first there; an old man and five children were amazed to see their first ever gringos in their own hot baths. We stripped to our underpants and wallowed in the soupy, smelly water, much to the astonishment of the onlookers.

Where the Incas got their revenge.
(I had diarrhoea for the next 3 wks.)

Before we left Banos, Kyle asked Lenin to fill our drinking bottles with boiled water, since the water in the area was not very pure. Lenin took our bottles and disappeared. As we set off, he handed us our filled water bottles for which we were very grateful. Hours later, I opened mine and swigged down a large mouthful of the foulest-tasting water I have ever experienced. Within minutes, nausea and vicious diarrhoea set in, which was to plague me for the next three weeks. We did not have to be scientists to figure out what had happened. Lenin had obviously misunderstood the 'boiled water' for the warm water of the hot baths!

'That was the Incas' revenge,' Graeme laughed dryly.

We waved goodbye to Kyle who would hike on to the next bridge at the village of Quivilla, some four or five days downstream. Soon the Rio Lauricocha – a river of some 4 to 5 m³/s – flowed into the Nupe.

Entering a steep-sided section of the river, Ross paddled ahead to scout a difficult-looking rapid. Aiming for a small eddy halfway down the rapid, he failed to make it and was swept down backwards, disappearing around a bend. Graeme was quick to follow and he beckoned us to come on after him, but

there was no sign of Ross or his kayak. Searching as we sped through the rapid, we spotted the upturned red kayak floating down the river and Ross swimming for the bank. We quickly pulled him ashore and retrieved his kayak. Ross explained that as he had slipped backwards, his kayak had ploughed through a wave and collided with a submerged rock. In a flash, his boat became pinned and it capsized. Trapped under the water, the torrent forced his head down against the deck; he could feel the kayak beginning to buckle with the pressure. Using the last oxygen in his lungs, he fought his way out of the cockpit and swam to the surface.

'That's the first time I've ever seen you having to swim for it, Ross,' I called.

'Ja,' he replied. 'That could have been a bad one. It shows how quickly these things happen. It wasn't even a really difficult rapid.'

Relieved, we set off again.

'Look at the high-water mark on that tree,' observed Shaun. 'It must be 15 m above the water level.'

We marvelled at the sight, trying to figure how driftwood could be found so high in the treetops. As if eavesdropping on us, the river answered our question. We rounded a bend and discovered the most dramatic section of river. The current drove straight into a cliff face, forcing its way into an underground, boulder-strained tunnel. We scrambled on to the left bank and gazed in awe at the phenomenon. On the east side cliffs rose up hundreds of metres; on the west side, the entire sidewall had collapsed into the watercourse, blocking it completely. Scaling a section of cliff face, we were able to survey more than 600 m of river carnage. Dolomitic blocks of rock the size of houses had driven the Marañón underground. Approximately 200 m downstream, the river reappeared, angrily crashing and roaring through another 500–600 m of sieves, siphons and drops.

In relays we began the marathon task of hauling the kayaks through tunnels, under rocks, and over

Where the river went undeground ~ we went overland.

gigantic blocks of dolomite. It was five hours before we re-entered the choked river, exhausted and battered, making a 'seal launch' off a high ledge. The river swept us along for a few hundred metres before a treacherous siphon again brought us to a stop. Suddenly we realised our unforeseen predicament. We were boxed in! – we had run the rapids past the point of no return. On our left was a rapid that was impossible to run, and on our right a face of sheer rock blocked our way either upstream or down.

'Now we've done it. We're really trapped!' grumbled Graeme. 'How the hell do we get out of here?'

Climbing over the huge boulders, we found a spot where escape seemed remotely possible. A fierce 3-m channel of water plunged between two rocks. By using a kayak to bridge the chute, we could possibly drag ourselves across by lying over the kayak.

After several attempts at hurling an empty kayak across the chute, the nose miraculously wedged itself

into a crack and held fast. Securing the other end, we inched our way across, dragging ourselves over the roaring channel.

'Phew, that was close,' I chuckled nervously. 'I wouldn't like to spend too many nights on that perch.'

'Yeah,' added Shaun, 'we would have had to do some serious fishing to stay alive.'

We clambered and hauled our boats up a 50-m bank where we found a beautiful grassy terrace, perched above the river. Downstream, there was no sign of the river letting up its furious pace. The Marañón disappeared from sight in a continuous succession of surging siphons and plunging drops. Tomorrow could be another challenging day!

It was 5:30 p.m. and we were exhausted. Ross and I found time to do a quick sketch of the Cosmo canyon looking downstream, using sepia brown watercolour and then ink to finish off the detail.

The Cave

Soft rain fell during the night. We woke early and I fired up the burner for a brew of tea. Below us the roaring river reminded us of what lay ahead. Every joint and muscle in my body was tender after yesterday's five-hour portage; my left wrist was swollen and my shoulder ached. During our antics of the previous day I had sworn to myself that I would offload all my non-essential kit.

'Guys,' I said, 'this is it! I'm thinning down my gear.'

Cheers met my announcement.

'Well done, Tim, let's see it actually happen! That's what you said two days ago,' came the teasing response.

The truth was that yesterday's portage had left me exhausted and frustrated at my struggle to man-handle my kayak over the massive rocks. Ross, Graeme and Shaun had all helped, backtracking every now and then to give me a hand with my kayak. They were powerful, agile young men with a strength and endurance that I could not match.

Determined to scale down, I cleared a spot on the grassy terrace and laid out on a groundsheet each item of gear and equipment. I had an extra torch; sun cream; five small Bibles (Gideons International); my pair of Levi jeans; spare underpants; socks; a dictaphone for taking notes; harmonica; an extra jersey; a paperback book; a writing exercise book for notes and stories; toiletries; spare string and rope; a knife, etc. No doubt about it – I was a walking, talking

The Marañón disappeared under the rocks for almost 1 km.

251

convenience store! My friends howled with laughter at the display. To my embarrassment the extras weighed over two kilograms. Obviously many years had passed since I had last done a serious expedition.

'No wonder you can't lift your boat up, Tim. You've got half your wardrobe with you.'

'Well, this is the last day. There's a small cave around the corner that I spotted. I'm going to dump it all there. Maybe some young shepherd boy will find it,' I said in all earnesty. Then I went on.

'Now also remember, you guys, you already had six weeks of kayaking in Peru before I arrived. In fact, I'm amazed you're all still so disorganised yourselves,' I said, hitting back, knowing I had little chance of escaping the teasing that would follow.

'Yes, yes, Tim. Excuses, excuses. The fact is that you've got too soft in your old age; you're going to need to toughen up and be hardcore on this trip, you know!' Shaun rubbed it in, laughing.

Maybe Shaun was right. Anyway, I could not resist chuckling to myself as I watched the three of them circle like vultures around the heap of extras, unable to resist the temptation of including some of the choice items in their own gear. Ross homed in on the dictaphone, Graeme went for the spare batteries, and Shaun grabbed the spare torch. I wanted to counter-attack, but thought it would be better not to 'stir the pot' further.

Hauling our kayaks down to the river, I immediately felt the difference the lighter weight made. I

The Tantamayo confluence.

Golf course rapid.

could now at least hoist my kayak on my shoulder and leap from rock to rock without teetering and staggering like a drunkard. As we worked our way through kilometres of choked rapids, the spiritual significance of what had happened began to dawn on me. How difficult it is to throw away valued possessions! We cling to them even when they have become a threat to our lives. Throw them out! – your boat will float faster, respond to the pull of your paddle.

'This must be the Viscaro,' came Shaun's voice, jolting me out of my reflection. 'It's the tributary where Kurt started.' A strong stream of clear, greenish-grey water mingled with the Marañón. This was the stream we had travelled next to on our bus ride to Queripalca.

Kurt Casey, with a well-known and experienced American team, had pioneered the Quivilla gorge in 2001. Starting from the Rio Viscaro, the team had completed their 150-km trip at the village of Chugal. Kurt had paddled with me in South Africa, and had spent a few days resting at our farm while one of his friends recovered from a back injury. He had helped us generously in planning for this trip, advising us with logistics and notes on the river. Although we were grateful, we were naturally disappointed that we had been pipped to the post in the running of this amazing gorge.

We made our camp several kilometres upstream from the village of Quivilla – and pitched our tents on a beautiful grassy playa. Our mood was relaxed and satisfied, happy that we were doing what we loved doing most. An impressive bank of dark storm clouds marched across the sky, sending us scuttling for our tents, as huge drops of rain began to fall. The storm was short-lived and the clouds unexpectedly dispersed, exposing a sky studded with stars and a bright half-moon. We stretched out on the grassy beach, gazing at the stars as we contentedly sipped our last cups of tea for the night. Tomorrow we would be up against the Marañón's most challenging gorge. We could not wait.

Chapter 12

QUIVILLA AND OTHER GORGES

The Quivilla Gorge Epic

We paddled into the typically Peruvian riverside village of Quivilla, with its old and rusted steel bridge, its tall eucalyptus trees, and the reddish-brown tiled roofs of centuries-old buildings. Kyle was waiting for us and he was glad to see us. He had travelled alone for five days through the mountains, and was finding the experience lonely and gruelling. He wrote in his journal: 'While waiting for a bus for five hours I was harassed by a drunk guy in the plaza. Another drunk luckily came to the rescue with fists flying. Both drunks then tripped over a sleeping dog and landed in a heap on the ground.'

We exchanged stories while re-stocking provisions. We estimated that the next stage could take up to 10 days and that our kayaks must be loaded to maximum capacity. Soon the riverbank where we were packing the kayaks became a throng of excited children. The entire school had been let out to witness our departure.

According to our maps the river entered a small gorge some 2 km downstream. Kyle decided to hike along in the hope of getting some exciting film footage. We paddled around a bend and arrived at a suspended footbridge that marked the start of a 1.5-km series of rapids, siphons and blockages. Scouting the river from the left bank, we realised that the first 500 m were runnable, after which the river simply disappeared under rocks. Ross and Graeme were fired up, running alongside the continuous white water, calculating each move and each individual stroke, weighing up the risk of a mishap at each section.

I would normally have elected to portage the section, noticing the giant boulders that – halfway along – forced the water underground. In any case the rapid itself would have to be portaged, sooner or later. But then I looked at my young friends and realised that there was no way they would be seen portaging when there were those few hundred metres of exellent white water to be run.

'Yep,' I mused, 'paddle with guys 30 years younger than you are, and what did you expect would happen?

A good day for these kids
~ school closed down to witness our arrival.

movement, he peeled into the current and disappeared from sight. A shrill whistle signalled that all was well, and we followed one by one, hauling hard to reach the turbulent eddy below. The next two drops ran straight into each other. Graeme leapt out his kayak to scout, signalled that it was runnable, but showed that we should keep hard right at the second drop. Ross ran the first drop, was thrown off line and struggled over the next. A vertical paddle-blade appeared from the eddy below, signalling that the run was manageable.

Adrenalin was running high. The roar of the river was so loud that we could hardly hear each other shout. We knew that an ugly blockage lay around the

Kyle - cameraman extraordinaire.

In there is where I had my swim.

Come on, isn't this why you chose these friends to paddle with you? They've got guts and want to push their limits. I'll join them – at least we'll get some good film footage.'

There was no doubt that I was nervous. The river volume had increased to 30 m³/s, and a 'swim' here would be disastrous. In single file we entered the rapid, first Ross, then Graeme, then me, then Shaun. At the first 3-m chute our loaded kayaks plunged deep and we all scrambled for the small eddy in the quieter water. Graeme edged as close as he could to the next drop to see what lay below. His hand went up and he nodded an 'okay'. Then, in one smooth

256

next bend – no room for a mistake here! I caught a glimpse of Kyle high up in the cliffs, busy with his camera. Now it was my turn. I sprinted to get momentum, ramped over the lip, and could see immediately that my angle wasn't right. Frantically I pulled two hard-right sweep-strokes and only narrowly made the second drop. Ross and Graeme were waiting below, ready for a rescue. My kayak dived deep. I felt a strong side-current slamming against the submerged hull. I braced hard to stabilise myself when the current kicked me to the right. My kayak rose to the surface and I was whipped into a small eddy against massive black, shiny rocks.

Shaun raced into the same eddy, wide-eyed and looking unhappy. 'Phew!' he exclaimed. 'Heavy going!' Shaun had been growing quieter and quieter during the past few days, and we had noticed a distinctive bulge to his left cheek where an abscess was brewing.

Graeme had already run the next relatively mild chute, which looked okay from where we were perched. Moving into centre stream, I caught a glimpse of Graeme below pointing with his paddle towards the right. It was too late for any changes. As my boat crashed through the hydraulics, a sudden surge from the left flung me over and left me upside down. I gathered myself for a roll, struck out with my paddle, but realised to my horror that I had slipped out of my hip-braces and was dislodged from my seat.

My first roll failed, and I had a flash decision to make. I could either attempt another roll out of seat position, or try to wriggle myself back in before making another attempt. I knew that if one is not secure in one's boat, rolling is almost impossible. I reached out with my left hand, gripped the cockpit rim, and desperately tried to wriggle back into the seat. Nothing was working. I was still out of my braces, struck out with another 'loose roll' and failed again. It was now only seconds before I would be dragged, upside down, over the next drop (below which was a siphon). What should I do – stay in and keep trying to roll, or bail

Roll man, roll!

Shaun in action.

out and swim away from the siphon? Upside down, I waited for the blow from the rocks. 'No,' I realised, 'it's time to get out!'

I ripped off my spraydeck and kicked myself free. Surfacing, I glimpsed Ross's red kayak immediately above the fall. I let go of my paddles and, in a last ditch attempt, lunged, but missed. The powerful current was sweeping me over the fall. If I was right, the siphon was immediately below the drop, only metres away. 'If I miss this eddy, I'm a goner,' I thought.

Graeme - owning the Marañón.

Without the buoyancy of my kayak to help me, it seemed as if I was held forever under the thrashing water. At last I was up, gasping for air. The vertical black rocks of the siphon rose up in front of me. I swam for my life, knowing that these few strokes were my only chance. Memories of similar nightmares flashed through my mind. I cleared the siphon but was now only metres from the next fall. A jutting handle of rock caught my eye. I lunged for it, got a hold, and my body pendulumed around, swung by the current. I had to keep my grip. If I let go now I was finished. 'Concentrate. Pull your legs in.' I inched my way towards the bank, found another hold for my left hand, and wrapped myself around the submerged rock. Ten, 15 seconds passed, the current still tearing at my legs. I hunted for a foothold, found one, and lay at last, half-submerged, spread-eagle against the rock. I could hear Ross and Graeme shouting. Shaun's green kayak whipped into the eddy alongside of me.

'Hold my boat, Tim. I'm secure,' shouted Shaun.

I pulled myself out of the water, onto the rocks. What a relief, I was safe!

'You okay, Tim?' asked Shaun, with a worried expression. 'I also flipped in that last wave, and only just managed to roll before the drop.'

Ross and Graeme soon joined us.

'Hey, Madala, this isn't the place to practise your swimming!' they teased.

'Sorry, guys. I'm glad to be out of there, and not under those rocks. Where's my boat, Ross, did you see it?' I asked.

'We found it round the corner, against the bank. It's fine. It almost went into a siphon. You should just see what the river does around the corner.'

'Thanks, guys, for helping. I don't know what happened to my roll; I just couldn't get up. Crazy!' I added, dejectedly.

I had disgraced myself, not being able to roll in a tight spot. What was going on with me? 'I can't believe I failed to roll,' I said to myself. 'I can't believe it!'

During the past two months, on the Zambezi and the White Nile, I had executed hundreds of rolls in far rougher conditions.

'Well,' said Graeme, consolingly, 'remember, it's always hard rolling with a full boat.'

The river's downward gradient was now even steeper, with blockages every 20 m or so. We were running on pure adrenalin – Ross, Shaun and Graeme keen to run as much of this unrun gorge as they possibly could. I forced myself to climb back into my boat, and to follow my friends down one or two easier drops. Then I decided it was time to get out! I had had enough for one day.

'See you below the rapid. Perhaps see you at the other end of the gorge,' I said. 'I'm going to try to climb out before I have another swim. There seems to be a route over there which I think I can manage.'

'Tim, we'll keep going until we have to climb out as well. Are you sure you're all right getting your boat out on your own?' asked Graeme, thoughtfully.

'Ja, thanks. I'll be fine. You guys take it easy. Good luck.'

An hour later I hauled myself over the rim of the ravine. I was not quite sure which was more dangerous – paddling down below, or heaving a 45-kg kayak up the loose and crumbly sidewall. I took a glimpse of the ant-like figures of my friends standing on the rocks below. Ahead of them was a 100-m blockage.

Two young Quechua boys appeared from behind a rock, took one look at me, and fled behind the boulders. I dragged, and sometimes carried, my kayak along a small path before reaching a bridge across the Marañón. Kyle appeared from the opposite bank, and he was soon followed by the rest of the team who had carried out their boats after the river had

Waiting for Kyle & Shaun.

I had lots of time to sketch.

become completely blocked. We all camped at a beautiful, protected campsite 2 km downstream from the bridge. It had indeed been an action-packed day.

Toothache

Shaun with toothache.

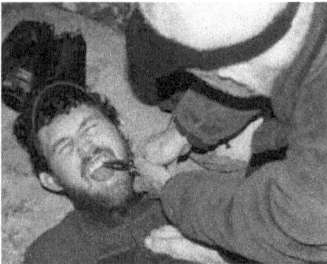

No problem
– we'll sort that out.

All's well that ends well.

Shaun's tooth had become a problem. His face was swollen and painful. We had a decision to make: either we could head on towards Chugal, which might take 10 days, or find someone in the area who could treat the abscess.

'Shaun should get treated first, before we leave,' I insisted. 'I would hate to have the thing blow up in the middle of a bad section.'

We all agreed; the only problem being how to find a dentist. Dentists did not exactly flood this region!

'How about me going with Shaun?' offered Kyle, generously. 'It'll give you guys time to rest, and I have a fair idea where these roads lead to.'

'Sounds good, Kyle, if you're up to it,' we answered.

Early the next morning Kyle and Shaun set out on their Andean hike in search of that rare commodity – a dentist.

I was glad for the break. It had been a long week, and I needed time to psyche myself up and restore my confidence. I also had to refit the kayak's seat and thigh braces, and to practise my roll, which I did in the quiet pool opposite the camp. I couldn't remember when my self-confidence was last so low. Something was wrong – or was I just too old for this sort of thing? To paddle well, one must be aggressive and bold, choosing committed lines, and being positive that you can make them. The section ahead would become bigger and more difficult if I could not build up my morale.

Taking my refitted kayak into the river, I was about to begin my rolling session when I spotted a young Quechua man sitting quietly fishing across the river. Our eyes met. I raised my hand in a wave, but he did not move. He just sat watching me, holding a fishing rod that had been cut from a tree. For the next half-hour I did one roll after another, my temples aching from the freezing water.

I turned to go, again raising my hand to my expressionless friend who, this time, raised his hand in reply. For a moment we stared at each other before he too stood up and began to move upstream. Strange as it may seem, I felt that we had shared something. Maybe he sensed my determination to overcome my mental self-doubt.

The following day I decided to explore, and found a steep footpath that led up the canyon sidewall. Tucked into the mountainside I came across a small mud dwelling with a faded red Coca-Cola sign above the rickety doorway. An elderly Quecha woman greeted me, and ushered me into her gloomy *tienda* (shop). She had been reading from a small, blue book, which I immediately recognised as the identical match to my own small Bible (Gideons International). Asking permission to see it, I opened it to

260

find a Gideons International stamp, dated 1983. I took off my daypack, and showed her my own edition. She carefully examined it in amazement.

'Englis'!' she exclaimed excitedly.

'Si, señora, English,' I replied.

An immediate bond was forged between us in the humble Andean shop that morning.

Although unable to communicate with words, we both understood that we shared a common love for our Lord and King. Having been involved with the spreading of Bibles to rural areas in South Africa, I wondered who had delivered this Bible to these remote parts.

Two days went by before Kyle and Shaun returned from their mission. Shaun looked decidedly shattered and his face was still swollen. They had travelled a whole day and night, and eventually found the house of the resident dentist in Huanuco.

They had woken him up, begged for help, and he had big-heartedly obliged, injecting Shaun with a maximum dose of powerful antibiotics. Back at camp Ross – our aspiring medico – leapt at the chance of administering the next round of injections into Shaun's buttock!

Back in Business

Keen to move on, we bade farewell to Kyle, planning to meet him again in four or five days at Arancay. After rounding the first bend we were halted by another kilometre-long ravine of rock-choked cataracts and crashing water. This time we climbed out without hesitation and began a gruelling portage along the left sidewall, sticking to animal paths and clinging to small ledges. Eventually we lowered our kayaks into the river with our throw-lines. The next few hours of

Tunnels through the rocks – our longest portage.

continuous white water were a delight, taking us deeper and deeper into the heart of the Marañón's secret wilderness.

We seemed to be completely isolated from other human beings. Yet, on our third day into the canyon from Quivilla, we rounded a corner to see figures on the riverbanks ahead of us. Approaching curiously, we found Quechua men intently panning for gold in the alluvial gravel bars. On spotting us the men gestured wildly, disbelief written on their faces that we were travelling down their sacred river. Further along we passed another group of gold seekers who had taken the game a notch further. Masked divers in wetsuits would dive into the deep pools, dropping long suction pipes into the gold-rich potholes and crevices in the riverbed while motorised pumps, mounted on pontoons, sucked up the river's treasures.

The canyon sides were now becoming more arid, with scrub and bushes clinging to the towering 1 200-m slopes. The Rio Tantamayo had cut a sheer-walled canyon through the dark granite gneisses, marking our arrival at a section that our maps showed to have a huge gradient. A thundering roar of water, forced underground, warned us that no ordinary blockage lay ahead. On the left a 200-m wall of rock overhung us, and on the right giant granite blocks of every conceivable shape were stacked.

'This has got to be the "Big Mamma" portage that Kurt wrote about,' observed Ross.

'Sure is aptly named,' muttered Shaun, as he shouldered his kayak, his jaw still swollen and painful.

We climbed under and over house-sized rocks, sometimes crawling through tunnels, sometimes through deep underground caverns. To our left the river went berserk, plunging over underground waterfalls, crashing through cataracts, booming and roaring as it hurtled through its constricted course. Hours later, in fading light, we reached the lower end, ex-

Class 5 rapids.

hausted and pitched camp on a small patch of sand between giant boulders.

'Hey, Tim, thanks for bringing us here. This is what we came to see,' confided Ross. 'It's just incredible.'

Ross was right – this is what we had come for – raw adventure.

Any conversation was almost impossible that night. A thundering underground waterfall, 20 m away, drowned our voices completely.

As we flowed along in the rhythm of the Marañón's waters, edging our way deeper into the Andes, days started to slip by almost unnoticed. Each day had become a routine of waking early, cooking breakfast, packing kayaks and beginning to negotiate our way through the endless class 3, 4 and 5 rapids.

During the traverse of a 1-km section of rock-choked river, my trip almost ended. We were carefully working our way along a steep slope when my foot slipped from under me and without warning I was down, my heavy kayak landing on top of me. In an instant the kayak started careering down the slope. I lunged at it, grabbing the bow handle, only to be dragged along behind it. Sliding down the slope toward a 30-m cliff, I had to make a quick decision! Either I could hang on to the kayak and hope to break the slide, or let it go and lose it to the river. A third option – my kayak and me both in the river, one missing, one dead – also flashed through my mind. I was now tobogganing downhill on my back, desperately trying to halt the slide. A few metres from the precipice my foot struck fast on a sturdy scrub plant, slowing me down. I frantically grasped at a tuft of grass with my free hand, and came to a halt. Peering over the drop, I looked down at the torrent of water charging head-on into a giant boulder.

'That's where I would have landed,' I thought aloud, shaking from shock. 'It wouldn't have been much fun swimming in that lot.'

'Tim, are you okay?' shouted Shaun. Carefully he climbed down to me, and together we hauled the kayak back up the cliff.

'Phew, that was close,' I chuckled nervously. 'I almost went straight over the edge, into a siphon.'

'I thought you were gone,' replied Shaun. 'Ross also slipped and landed on his paddle. The shaft has snapped . . . it's our last spare.'

At the end of the day we approached a dark canyon no more than 10 m wide – the narrowest we had seen since Queripalca. Cautiously, and on high alert, we entered the chasm with its 100-m sides. The first visible section was clear, but the resonating rumble of a big rapid warned us of heavy water action ahead. Before that, however, a footbridge came into view, constructed from two massive logs.

'This must be the bridge to Arancay,' I called.

'It might be, but there's no way to get out of here,' replied Shaun. 'There must be another place further downstream.'

'I reckon we camp right here,' I said. 'It's almost dark. If there are bad rapids in there, we'll find ourselves walled in.'

All agreed. We made camp on a small beach, tucked away at the base of a cleft in the cliff. I managed a quick sketch before Graeme cooked the meal. We sat around a glowing campfire, relaxed and at peace, loving the experience of exploring such a wild corner of the planet.

'Well, here's to this amazing river! Let's drink to the Marañón,' said Ross, raising his mug of tea as if it were iced champagne.

'Here's to Cal Giddings and his team,' I said, adding another toast. 'He was the first to explore these parts, in the days of fibreglass kayaks. Hey, Ross, come to think of it, he was here before you were even born.'

We all laughed.

'Yeah, old Kurt only just beat us to it. Why didn't you bring us here two years earlier, Madala? What happened? You were caught sleeping,' teased Graeme.

'I had my head stuck too deep in a timber yard,' I replied, laughing.

We lay on our backs, gazing up at the star-studded sky between the canyon walls.

Where Shaun ambushed the donkeys.

'Ja, this is the life,' we agreed. 'This is the life, all right.'

We rose early and paddled into the confined gorge, crashing at once through the drenching, cold waves of a class 4 rapid. Several kilometres downstream we arrived at a second suspension bridge, cutting a graceful arc between two abutments of hand-hewn stone. A well-used footpath climbed steeply from it through a cleft in the canyon walls. Ross and Graeme were to hike up this steep trail in search of Kyle at Arancay, while Shaun and I would wait on the river. These rests afforded me time to sketch and spend a few quiet hours on my own. On a long trip, where people are close to one another, time on one's own is good for more than just health. It brings back mental

balance, refreshes the senses, and motivates one for the next stage of the trip.

A Quechua man with five loaded donkeys came into sight and slowly descended the footpath. For 15 minutes he hissed and beat the terrified animals, coaxing them to cross the rickety footbridge. At last one of the smaller donkeys yielded, and, with ears pinned back, began to edge its trembling way across the swaying bridge. Once it had gained the halfway mark, the rest of the team gained courage and followed cautiously, one by one.

'I'll go and ask him where Arancay is,' Shaun volunteered.

Scrambling up the slope he intercepted the un-suspecting convoy as they rounded a sharp bend. Shaun burst out in front of them, with his bearded face and kayaking 'battledress'. The startled donkey-owner let out a yell of terror, leapt backwards, and raised his stick in self-defence. With frantic yells he and the donkeys took off at a gallop to escape the wild-looking 'antichrist' dressed in black. Shaun set off after them, shouting, 'Señor, señor, momento!' but to no avail. The convoy was in full flight, and was soon more than halfway up the slope. I rolled on the ground laughing, watching the comical scene unfold before me.

Kyle had arrived at Arancay the day before, and had bought 30 kg of vegetables, kerosene and rations. He had begun his hike back to the river and met Graeme and Ross halfway. Kyle's uncanny ability to meet us within hours of our arrival at a point was extraordinary – neither party having any idea of how long a particular section would take. His journey from Quivilla to Arancay had involved a 40-hour hitchhike through some of the most remote and iso-lated routes in the Andes. Kyle's diary read:

'. . . How do I even begin to describe today? It feels as if I awoke from reality into a dream; for the first time in ages I feel alive and excited by the world. Just spent six hours on the back of a Toyota pickup truck on the worst road imaginable – winding through the

264

mountains, calling on tiny villages with smoking roofs. A desperate chicken was pecking at my foot, its head strained through a plastic cage, as I hung on for dear life, balanced on sacks of potatoes. It seems no gringos come here. The stars came out and the temperature plummeted to minus 18 degrees as we forded streams and wound in and out of valleys . . .'

Desert Canyons and Falling Rocks

The fast-flowing Golden Serpent now swept us into an arid arena of folded pastel-coloured strata – mauves, reddish-browns, greenish-greys and ochres. The canyon had deepened to 1 500 m and for days on end we

kayaked through beautiful and challenging white water. My self-confidence had picked up since my last close shave. Although I was still weak from my bout of diarrhoea, I loved the simple routines of river life. Graeme and Ross were out hunting for the biggest and most extreme runs they could find. Shaun – off his normal top form due to persisting toothache – was paddling more conservatively, but still chose the most difficult lines. We were in a wilderness where we would sometimes travel for days without seeing a soul, and where our only company was the occasional rise of a shy otter (or circling condors, if we were lucky). Strong tributaries such as the Rio Putchca and Rio Tamajaljifa flowed into the Marañón, boost-

Me taking the chicken run.

ing her flow by 17 m³/s. After restocking provisions at the small village of Sihaus, we pushed on for the next five-day stretch to Chugal.

Rounding a bend that led us into a long class 5 rapid, we began manoeuvring our way from eddy to eddy. Ross was scouting ahead and opening our route when he was unexpectedly swallowed by a 2-m mound of turbulent water. Graeme followed closely, eddying out above the drop, from where he signalled to Shaun and me to keep well left. There was still no sign of Ross. Graeme broke out of his small eddy to look for his friend, and followed Ross's line over a massive drop. Rushing through a series of smaller drops in the left channel, Shaun and I were in time to see Graeme's upturned hull being pummelled violently by the claws of a keeper hole. Ten long seconds passed before Graeme whipped himself upright with

The lone tree.

a roll and paddled to safety. Ross appeared from behind a boulder, looking shaken, and paddled over to us.

'I've just been eaten by that same hole – it wouldn't let me go!' lamented Ross, blowing water from his sinuses. 'I ran out of air and was about to bail when I realised I had been washed out. It would have been a terrible swim.'

The rapid swept us to the beginning of another gloomy gorge with vertical cliffs. As we peered ahead an explosion of spray only metres from my kayak jerked me into alarm mode. Unbelievably, two rocks struck the water with explosive force, one narrowly missing Shaun.

'Paddle, guys, paddle! Someone's throwing rocks!' Graeme screamed from ahead.

We sprinted away as fast as we could, fearing for our lives. When we were out of range of the missiles, we looked up at the 700-m cliffs and noticed the figure of a man waving his arms threateningly at us.

'Bastard!' shouted Shaun. 'One of those rocks on the head would have killed us . . .' He was cut short by another volley, exploding all around us. Hastily we rushed on, and were soon swept into the next section of heavy white water.

'Goes with the territory, I guess,' I said, still panting.

'One of those rocks landed a few feet from me. Get hit by one of those and you're a goner for sure,' Shaun muttered, still visibly upset. 'Did you see that cultivated green patch just below him? I bet it was his plot of marijuana that he was worried about.'

The following day we reached Chugal, the point where Kurt Casey's and Cal Giddings' teams had pulled out. There were now only 250 km of canyon left before we reached Bagua and the jungle.

While studying the maps we noticed a 3-km stretch of river dropping through a frightening gradient of 150 m. To run a river of such steep gradient, and with such accumulated volume, would be mind-

Suddenly the rapids ended.

blowing – certainly the greatest challenge we had come across on the Marañón.

'Look, maybe it's where those cliffs meet the river,' said Shaun, answering my query. We rounded the next spur – only to find fast-moving flat water. Range after range passed us by, until we stopped on a sandbank for a welcome tea break. We were definitely confused. Up until now our maps had proved to be accurate. Could it be that this mighty cataract didn't even exist?

'Maybe it was Friday afternoon, and the American cartographer felt like some fun and just made it up,' chuckled Graeme.

'Well, who knows? He certainly had me worried,' I grumbled,

Two hours later, the mountain topography of the Northern Andes melted into long-inclined escarpments, covered with broad-leafed plants and high-rainfall vegetation. We realised that our desert canyons had come to an end. Ahead of us towering banks of cloud

– caused by moist jungle air colliding with the mountains – rose out of the jungle mountain ranges. We looked at each other, realising that the Marañón rapids had ended. We had made it through the canyons.

Shaking hands and laughing, we brewed a pot of tea and ate our last chocolates in celebration. Although we were relieved, we were also disappointed to be out of the land of desperate rapids and high adrenalin.

We made camp on a long sliver of sandbank under a canopy of lush branches and trees. On each side of us was the unfamiliar sight of cultivated orchards and crops. A young boy appeared from nowhere and inquisitively edged up to us.

'What's your name, my friend?' I called.

'Henry,' came the shy reply.

'Henry, we are very, very hungry. Can you find us some food?'

Our new friend responded with a blank stare and simply disappeared into the riverside foliage.

'You obviously don't look hungry enough, Tim,' joked one of my friends. 'The boy wasn't convinced.'

Twenty minutes later the comment backfired. Henry reappeared carrying our supper of four beautiful, yellow papaws in both hands.

'We'll name this place "Camp Papaya",' suggested Shaun.

Graeme and the centipede! "Whose sleeping bag is this anyway?"

For the first time on our trip, mosquitoes became a problem. Our old friends, the bloodsucking sandflies that had pestered us for 600 km, stayed behind in the mountains. After enjoying a huge campfire, I slept poorly and listened to the new, unfamiliar sounds floating across the river: a barking dog, a crowing rooster, and the occasional, haunting cries of a man. Some time later, a commotion woke me and there, next to me, a most amazing drama was in progress. Graeme had leapt out of his sleeping bag and was shining his headlight onto a giant centipede – 30 cm long! – which had reared up like a spitting cobra and was swaying back and forth. For several seconds a transfixed Graeme and the giant centipede stared each other down. After a while, there was a thump, thump, thump, and a 'squish'! as Graeme gained the upper hand and ended the challenge with the help of a sturdy length of driftwood!

At about the same time, Shaun woke from a nightmare in which a river monster was about to attack him. He shot out of his sleeping bag with a yell, closely followed by his bedfellow, another 10-cm angry centipede.

'Hey, maybe we should rename this place "Camp Centipede" in memory of our team bravely fighting off these monsters,' Ross proposed the next morning.

We set off for the last short leg to Bagua. The river glided swiftly over vast sandbanks and braided channels as it headed for the approaching jungle. Our last tea break was on a rocky island outcrop in the middle of the wide Marañón valley. We were all elated when we reached Bagua. Our dream of kayaking through the Marañón's canyons had come true, and we were all in one piece. Originally, we had planned to run this 700 km (440 miles) section in six weeks, but had completed it in only 20 days! We shared a heartfelt prayer of thanks – moments like these are sweet and unforgettable. We were doing what we loved doing and life was good.

Bagua Bridge was only 10 minutes downstream. Cheering and rejoicing, we greeted the 300-m-wide

The canyons melt away.

structure as it came into view. For the last time we heaved our heavy kayaks onto our shoulders and climbed up on to the road. An old ramshackle Kombi rattled down a track towards us.

'Bagua, señor?' we asked.

'Si, si,' he replied, climbing out to help. We loaded our kayaks, and the old Kombi roared off towards the bustling jungle town of Bagua Grande.

We soon tracked Kyle down at the Hotel Iris, where he and Shaun had left the sea kayaks four weeks previously. Two luxurious days were spent celebrating and resting in the busy town, testing delicacies from the hundreds of street stalls and markets. For the first time in the trip, we were able to telephone our friends and family back home.

Chapter 13

THE PONGOS

Kyle in a Kayak

On 25 July 2004, we loaded our 5-m sea kayaks onto a pickup and waved goodbye to our friendly hotel owner and some 65 cheering locals. Kyle was now a full member of the kayak team and he was about to attempt his first river trip on uncharted waters. Bringing him into the kayaking team had been a risky decision. What if he could not cope with the paddling? There could be no turning back once we were through the pongos (where the river narrows into a jungle gorge); there were no roads for hundreds of kilometres. To complicate matters, Kyle had a history of a weak shoulder, which was prone to dislocations. Only his reputation as a survivor and his sheer determination persuaded us. We loaded our kayaks with provisions for the 1 100-km trip to the confluence with the Ucayali, said a short prayer, and launched off from the river's edge. Ross gracefully slipped down the grassy bank only to get his kayak's nose stuck in the muddy bottom, leaving him airborne and stranded. Hooting with laughter, we watched as he struggled to free himself and maintain some form of dignity.

With the entrance to the first pongo in sight, we paddled in high spirits along the winding, flat river. Ross used this stretch to put Kyle through a crash course in river running and reading the water. We camped early on a low, sandy island, only an hour away from the pongo. Kyle had with him a custom-built, shortened guitar, which he fitted into the stern of his kayak. The quality of our campfire evenings soared as we sat entranced with Kyle's beautiful playing. Later that night, to the accompaniment of Ross and me on harmonicas, Kyle composed some hilarious lyrics for our Marañón theme song. Ah, this was living indeed.

At first light, we broke camp and set off towards the Pongo de Retema. Some residents of Bagua had warned us of the lethal consequences of running this gorge, and we were more than uneasy about what was awaiting us, especially as this was Kyle's first river trip. As we approached the 300-m cliffs of the

Five hooligans.

271

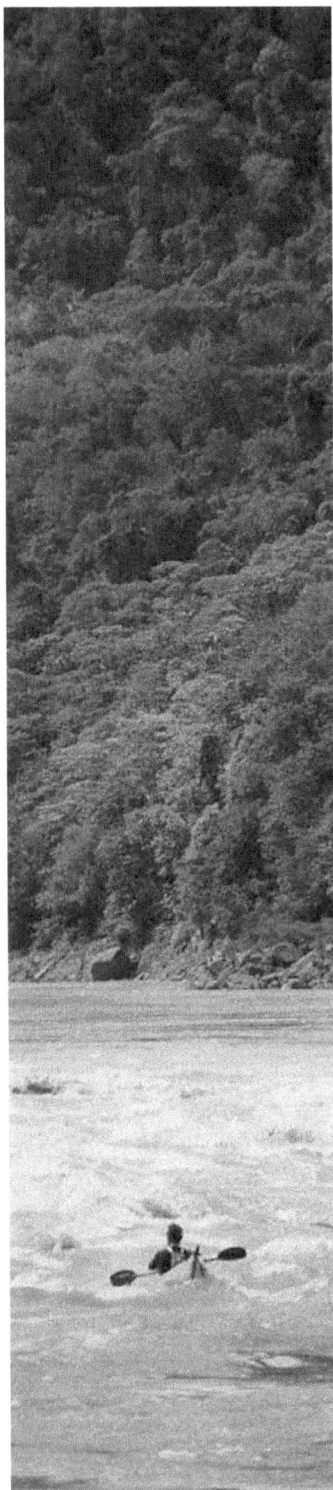

gorge, we could hear the rumble of a rapid long before we saw it. Telltale flashes of white water and spray leapt from where the disappearing river plunged into the gorge. This could be a big one!

'Hey, hey, how's that for a river in full flood!' shouted Graeme, pointing to our left where a tributary, the Rio Chichipe, added tons of chocolate-brown water to the fast-flowing Marañón.

'Keep in the mainstream and follow me,' shouted Ross to Kyle, above the roar of the rapid. The Marañón accelerated with exhilarating speed into the constricted throat of the gorge. Within seconds we were crashing through huge, exploding standing waves, struggling to control our kayaks in the surges. My spraydeck pulled off and I shipped gallons of water. I had to empty out, and I hauled myself into an eddy before the next train of waves.

Ross and Kyle were nowhere in sight. Shaun hurtled past at a good 50 km/h, yelling, 'Are you okay, Tim?' I gave him the thumbs up, finished draining my boat, and peeled out into the current. I soon saw my friends' four brightly-coloured kayaks huddled together in a turbulent eddy against the right bank. I paddled hard, broke the eddy line, and joined them to discuss tactics.

A congratulation was timely. 'Well done, Kyle, running that stuff on your first run.' I was relieved that he was all right.

'Beginner's luck,' returned Kyle, with a nervous grin.

'We still don't know what's coming next. If it's any bigger than this rapid, we could be in trouble,' warned Ross, thinking of his brother.

We certainly hadn't expected the first rapid to be so big and vicious. Maybe the villagers' warnings were right after all.

'That's the next gorge just round the corner. Looks like another big one to me,' said Shaun, peering down to where the river disappeared from sight.

'Let's go for it,' I said, 'and take it as it comes.' Heaving whirlpools made it difficult to get back into the current. Our unwieldy long kayaks were thrown around by the waves rebounding off the sides. We entered a long train of breaking waves. Kyle and Ross paddled first and soon disappeared, and I followed on. Breaking waves engulfed Kyle's kayak, submerging him under tons of water. He disappeared for a few seconds, until the yellow hull of his upturned kayak re-emerged. Kyle was out, swimming. Ross, quick to the rescue, struggled to tow him to the bank.

We broke for a brew of tea, marvelling at the way the vegetation had changed in only two kilometres, from desert scrub to emerald jungle. The river, too, had changed – in direction. It had swung dramatically east, gouging its way through the mountains and setting a new course for the Atlantic.

The rapids in the Pongos knocked us about.

Shaun and Graeme paddled ahead to film Ross, Kyle and me running the third rapid. It soon became obvious that this was the big one. Ross and Kyle disappeared in a 200-m maelstrom of waves and spray. I caught a glimpse of Kyle as his yellow upturned boat emerged from the waves, just before it disappeared into the chocolate-brown water. My next sight was of Ross towing Kyle and his half-submerged boat to the shore.

'They'll be all right,' I thought, as I made for the bank to photograph Shaun and Graeme running the rapid. The scenery was spectacular – this would be a prize photograph. Minutes passed as I waited for them to appear. At last two kayaks, dwarfed by ocean-size waves, rounded the bend, crashed through the white water, and disappeared from sight. Scrambling back into my kayak, I raced to catch up with them. The four were helping Kyle empty out his flooded kayak. I immediately sensed that the vibes were not good.

'Are you okay there, Kyle? How was your swim?' I asked, innocently.

A stony silence was the reply, and Ross's face looking like thunder.

'I just couldn't get my boat to the side,' explained Kyle. 'Every time we got near the bank, we were washed into the current again. In the end I had to swim for a good kilometre.'

I realised my mistake. Like a fool I had stopped off to film when I should have been rescuing Kyle. I was clearly in the dogbox. I kept silent for a few moments, amazed at my negligence.

'Hey, I'm sorry, guys, that was so stupid of me,' I said, apologising. 'I wrongly assumed that Ross would manage on his own!'

'No problem, Tim,' answered Kyle, but Ross remained angry and silent. Kyle's confidence was rock bottom, and he was exhausted by his two swims.

'Let's try supporting Kyle from each side whenever we get to rapids,' suggested Graeme. 'We'll make a pontoon.'

We again pushed off from the bank, Ross and Graeme each holding a side of Kyle's kayak as we

273

Riding the waves.

entered the rapids. The team effort worked like a charm, and we began to cover a good distance. That afternoon a steady rain set in. It was time to camp. After two hours of searching we found an idyllic spot. A clean, sandy beach, surrounded by towering hardwoods, beckoned us.

Mongrel to the Rescue

Enjoying our private beach, we were pitching our tents and preparing a meal when Graeme called softly: 'Watch out, we've got company.'

Silently a group of half-naked Indians, armed with shotguns and machetes, had slipped through the dense undergrowth.

'Whoa, this looks like trouble! Let's just act friendly,' I advised, quietly.

We stood to greet the intruders (or were we the intruders?). The short man leading the group raised an ancient single-barrell shotgun, pointing it towards us.

'Kyle, see if they speak Spanish,' I whispered.

'Bueños dias,' he began, but was brusquely interrupted by a string of excited, unintelligible words. We raised our hands to show we didn't understand a thing. An older man pushed forward, speaking a language that resembled Spanish.

'Where are you from and what do you want here? Why do you stay here?' this man barked at us.

'We are from Sud Africa. We are just travelling through. Tourists – we leave tomorrow,' said Kyle, trying to explain.

'Passeporte,' the short man demanded, holding out a gnarled, weather-beaten hand.

'Momento, señor,' replied Kyle, indicating that he would be straight back. He quickly fetched our dossier of documents, and returned. By this time, a hostile throng had gathered, inquisitively inspecting our equipment and kayaks.

The older man reached for our papers, scrutinising them upside down. Then, without warning, he broke out excitedly, addressing his group in an animated dialect. As the tribesmen debated our presence, the tension level spiked. Things did not sound healthy at all. Anything was possible.

It was Ross who broke in. 'Hang on, guys. I think that's their dog across the river! Maybe if I go and fetch it they'll calm down.'

Swiftly ferry-gliding the swollen river, Ross lifted up the malnourished dog, placed it in the back hatch, and returned to the campsite, where he presented the dog to one of the young men.

What Ross did took the Indians aback, confusing them. The atmosphere turned; the aggressive man's expression softened. Hesitantly he handed back our documents, declaring to his fellows that we were 'not a threat to their territory' after all. Soon the whole family appeared from the forest, realising that the warlike foreigners were not invaders. Kyle discovered that they were from the Aldinaro tribe, and eked out an existence from hunting and fishing.

'Ask if they have any food for us, Kyle,' called out Graeme.

Soon two young boys returned, each holding de-capitated (and very thin!) chickens by their bleeding necks. Our visitors helped us to revive our dying fire, coaxing up crackling flames from the wet kindling. The skewered chickens were placed over the flames while we sat, feet up, huddled around with our guests, enjoying the company – all this thanks to a rescued dog!

After Ross saved their dog, the man with the shotgun brought us a chicken.

Unfriendly Hosts

'Look guys, the Southern Cross has moved!' said Ross, pointing to the sky. 'Until now it's always appeared upstream from us. Now it's to our right. The river has turned.'

For the past month we had spent our evenings gazing up at the stars and to our favourite constel-lation. During this time, the Southern Cross had consistently arched above the canyon walls, always upstream of us. Now the Marañón had swung through 90 degrees and had thrown the Southern Cross to our right. We had at last turned from our northerly course, and were moving eastwards towards the Atlantic.

The mountain jungle opened before us, revealing a mystical scene. Soft mists hung from mountain ridges, bringing a crescendo of early morning bird and animal calls, quite different from what we had grown accustomed to in the desert canyons. Our shotgun-bearing friend passed silently by with his son, off to fish and pan for gold in the exposed sandbanks. He raised a hand to us, and without a word the two of them moved upstream through the rocks.

We launched our kayaks upstream of our camp into the tail waves of the rapid, wondering what the day would bring in this new environment. Once again our predictions of river conditions had proved unreliable. We had totally underestimated the size of yesterday's pongos. According to our maps, another five lay ahead, and after what we had been through, we had no idea what to expect. Although the river had dropped slightly, the brown flood lifted our kayaks and swept us downstream at a cracking speed of almost 20 km/h. In silence we paddled, absorbing the beauty of the early morning jungle. One or two thatched-roofed dwellings swept by, blending perfectly into the interlocking canopy.

It was tea break and we 'log jammed', holding onto one another's kayaks and drifting with the current, joking and enjoying snacks and energy bars. Kyle was having a good day and had not swum yet. His confidence and kayaking skills were improving dramatically. We were finding a rhythm to our days on the river, paddling for two-and-a-half hour sessions between rest breaks. The new sea kayaks were much faster than our stubby creek boats, and we could now easily average 75 km a day.

We had just passed a small banana-thatched village when Graeme called out, 'We've got a boat following us. They came out from that village when we passed by.'

Log jamming while we have our tea break.

Soon we heard the chugging beat of a peci-peci motor closing in on us.

'Let's spread out and keep paddling, as though we haven't seen them,' I suggested. 'I get the feeling they aren't too friendly.'

Just then, the motorised wooden canoe pulled up alongside of me.

'Passeporte, passeporte!' one of the crew shouted aggressively, leaning out of the boat, and indicating that we should return to their village for interrogation.

No, I thought, we've had enough of shotguns for a day or two. I tried to explain in my best Spanish that the current was too strong for us to paddle back upstream. They would have to tow us back if they wanted to speak to us. As one of the crew was about to tie a short towline of platted vines to my bow, I explained that Ross, who was now almost 1.5 km downstream, had all the passports. A frustrated argument broke out amongst the crew, some wanting to turn back and leave us, others punting that we be towed.

'We are South Africans. Tourists. Nelson Mandela!' I continued, playing for time. By now the other kayaks were specks in the distance, and the two who argued they should turn back won the day. Without a word or a farewell and much to our relief, they pull-started the Briggs and Stratton engine and chugged back upstream.

The sun beat down on us mercilessly all day. After our seven-hour session on the water we were all sunburned and fatigued, and badly in need of shade and food. The knowledge that we had almost 1 000 km of flat water ahead was a mental challenge, especially to Graeme and Ross, real 'adrenalin junkies', who tended to fall prey to depression the moment they were not running life-threatening rapids. Graeme tackled the flat water ordeal by not allowing himself to think further than one day ahead, less the enormity of the distance ran away with his mind. Our new motto thus became 'one bend at a time, one day at a time'.

'Passeporte señores', he shouted.

Shaun - touched by the sun.

No good campsites appeared, and we had to make do with a poor site, hot and exposed. It was one of those days when everything seemed to be against us – mosquitoes and gnats welcomed us with unprecedented vengeance, our stove wouldn't work, the firewood was wet from a recent flood, and a steady stream of locals streamed into our camp, plying us with questions.

I sensed Ross's increasing irritation. 'Amigos, I want to sleep, leave us now,' he would say, to a roar of laughter as more joined the 'fun'. One man became particularly annoyed and unpleasant because we hadn't reported to a military camp, some 20 km upstream. We patiently explained that we would be checking in at Santa Maria, 5 km downstream. But

277

We stopped at a deserted beach ~ 2 mins later ...

he was adamant, stating that the commandant had sent him to return us to the village upstream. Trying to keep the atmosphere from getting tense, we pointed out that our kayaks would take two days to reach the base, and that it was now too dark to attempt such a feat. The approaching night worked in our favour, and the group slowly lost interest and filtered off to their villages. Distant drums could be heard throbbing rhythmically, reminding me of Africa. We were left to enjoy the peace and quiet of the evening, and had begun our supper when the same young man, now intoxicated, came marching angrily with excited youngsters following him.

'Salida, salida,' he shouted, 'you must come now! The commandant says you must leave this beach immediately.' We gradually calmed the group and asked if the honourable commander could come and explain the situation himself. Only then would we gladly leave. To our surprise our friend seemed satisfied with this proposal and promised that the commander would arrive in 30 minutes. After that we must depart. An hour went by but no commander showed up. Gradually the group became tired of waiting and disappeared into the night. We slept restlessly, however, uneasy about our inhospitable hosts, and worrying about whether they would return.

Pongo Manseriche (Gold Fever)

Six days after leaving Bagua we arrived at the last of the pongos, Pongo Manseriche. This pongo is a significant landmark on the Marañón as it marks the divide between the Andean foothills and the floodplane of the jungle. Here the river explorers of the sixteenth century, coming upstream, were halted and prevented from pioneering further by the sheer sidewalls and the powerful current.

We had all been enchanted by Leonard Clarke's book, *The River Ran East*. Clarke, an American intelligence spy in World War II, undertook to seek out the famous El Dorado – the city of gold – that had lain undiscovered since the time of the conquistadors. In the 1950s he travelled with a Peruvian companion, down the Rio Perene, into the Rio Tambo, and then up the Marañón, searching for the lost cities, and surviving many a hostile skirmish with Indian tribes. Under the guise of researching medicinal plants and witchdoctors' medications, he pioneered a trail through the Gran Pajonal (one of the world's most remote wildernesses), and by canoeing up the Rio Santiago discovered the location of two of the ancient gold-mining cities. Scooping up bags of gold-rich ore, he narrowly escaped attacks by Indians and fled back to the mountains with his treasures. Clarke's adventures and bizarre stories were especially intriguing for us as they were played out on the same river we were on.

As we approached the Rio Santiago, I called out, 'Okay, guys, I'm turning left here. I guess it's time to tell you: I didn't just come for the kayaking. It's the gold I'm really after; I've got a map to one of the lost cities! See you back in South Africa,' I added playfully.

'No problem, Madala,' laughed Ross, 'but you'll need some help. You're far too old to make it on your own; you won't survive a day without us. We'll protect you – and share the bounty.'

We slipped quietly past the confluence with the Santiago. A large military camp was situated at the entrance to the river and we hoped to sneak past unidentified and unseen. The hills were shrouded in mist, and the Marañón surged into the narrows of a steep gorge. Rain began falling as we approached, and we plunged through the cresting waves of a class 3 rapid, dodging the whirlpools. Either side of the main current lay dangerous corridors of turbulent

Hunting for that gold in Pongo Manseriche.

279

Croc braai.

and confused water, caught between the hurtling main current, and the reverse current along the walls of the cliff. Small whirlpools, generated by the interface of these two water masses, sporadically pulsed and swirled, and soon became massive cycling vortexes that could easily drag a kayak below the racing surface.

Ross looked after Kyle, guiding him clear of the treacherous whirlpools and steering him safely along the main current. Shaun paddled ahead and beckoned us to join him in an eddy he had found. We had spent many nights speculating about this pongo and how we would fare; and here we were.

'Well done, Kyle,' I said appreciatively. 'You've mastered these pongos. I was almost pulled under by one of those whirlpools myself. I didn't see it coming; it caught me from behind.'

'Yeah, I can't say I'm not glad that this is our last pongo. I think it was just luck I got through.'

'Nonsense, I watched you. You handled it well,' added Graeme.

'Now where's old Leonard Clarke's goldmine?' I asked. 'I can't see any obvious sites here – the sides are too steep.'

'In his book he says it was on the right,' said Graeme.

'Well, let's keep looking. Maybe we'll see something further down.'

We shared some biscuits and raisins, then peeled out once more into the racing flow. Leaving the pongo we re-entered the endless, flat, waterlogged jungle. Soon we saw half-naked Aguaruna Indians ahead of us, laboriously panning for the fine gold flecks in the creamy white sands.

'What on earth is that?' shouted Ross, pointing at what looked like a ship moored on the left bank. We paddled up to it, speculating about what it was.

'Peru's secret missile-launcher,' joked Graeme.

'No, man,' said Shaun, 'it's an abandoned gold dredger. Look, those are huge pumps for sucking up sand.'

'It looks in reasonably good nick to me,' I chipped in. 'Hey, let's all come back and start a gold-dredging business. We'll fix it up and make our fortunes.'

'Yeah, we can build holiday bungalows on the islands and charge tourists to watch the gold pouring out,' kidded Ross.

Life in the jungle became noticeably tougher, as swarms of tormenting mosquitoes and armies of insects enjoyed our company. At each campsite we scrambled to erect mosquito nets and get a smoky fire going that would deter the welcoming committee from the Amazon's insect world from smothering us. The fire ants were our first concern – they would latch onto our feet and legs in minutes, administering a bite like the sting of a bee. The sun became hotter and more intense, forcing us to retreat into the shade through the hellish hours between 11:00 a.m. and 2:00 p.m. We gladly made use of these forced rests, but it meant setting off earlier in the mornings to make up time. I would start the fire at 4:00 a.m., and by 5:00 a.m. we would be on the river, paddling silently through the jungle.

Before the expedition began, our hope had been that we would fish for our supper. Our sponsors had generously donated a full set of fishing gear and tackle, and we had spent many evenings boasting about how we were going to live off the river. Ross had taken up the challenge enthusiastically, and hour after hour, day after day, trawled a line behind him. Alas, 450 km later he still had not recorded a single bite!

'Ross, where are the fish?' we teased. 'Did you see all the fish those Indians caught upstream? Even the little kids were hauling them in.'

'Don't worry,' Ross shouted back. 'I'll catch one tomorrow. Wait and see.'

Camp Gabriel – Pigs and Rubber Chickens

On the tenth day since Bagua, we paddled through our lunch break, completing a good 90 km by 3:30 p.m. It was another scorcher of a day and shade was badly needed. The river had risen a good 600 mm, flooding the beaches that were suitable for camping, and a strong headwind made any progress tough going. A banana-thatched roof appeared through the green canopy, standing behind a long, clean sandbank.

'Let's ask if we can camp next to that hut,' suggested Graeme. 'Maybe we can barter some food from them.' We paddled onto the beach, which would have made an excellent campsite were it not for the lack of shade. Shaun and I waded across a shallow lagoon between the sandbank and the homestead, where we were met by a wiry, tough-looking Indian man. Understanding our poor Spanish, the man – whose name turned out to be Gabriel – invited us into the two-room home, which was raised 2 m off the ground by stilts, and had a sturdy timber stairway.

'Señor, we need a place to sleep. Can we camp under those trees . . . and we also need food, chicken, meat,' we said, pointing at the fine-looking rooster that was strutting past. Gabriel's suspicious attitude softened, and he soon returned with an armful of chopped firewood and the headless rooster. Shaun and I sat back under the shade and began sketching the homestead, watching the simple, touching scenes of life in the 'Jivaro' family, and the three young children, playing an endless game of 'catch' the family pig. A huge black sow and six mottled piglets good-humouredly raised themselves from their mud holes as the stick-wielding children

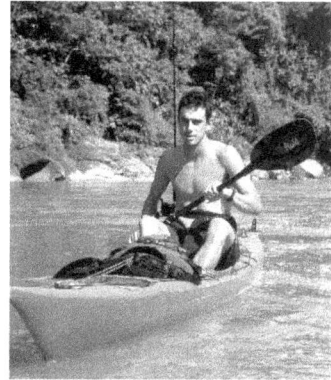

Ross trawled a line for 500 km without a bite.

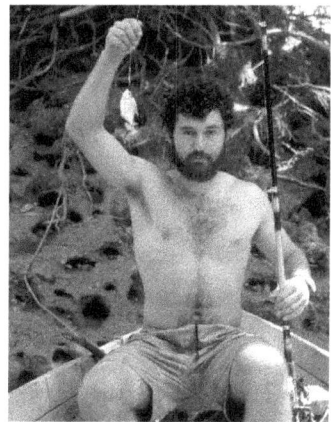

Finally Shaun catches our first fish.

Then the big one.

281

Gabriel's homestead ~ note the pig guarding the property.

scuttled them out with blows to their hindquarters. Meanwhile the mother of the home – clearly the driving force in the family – observed Shaun and I from a distance, her eyes full of suspicion.

'Hey, Shaun, you should find yourself a wife here. Check how this woman works. You'll be able to go canoeing all day and leave her to look after your bambinos.'

The good mother tirelessly carried water from the river, cooked the evening meal, chopped wood, cleaned the house, picked up and breastfed the crying youngest child (who had been knocked over by the escaping sow), and all the time kept watch over the strangers who had invaded her territory. Although very poor in possessions, the family appeared to be totally contented, living in harmony with their beautiful surroundings.

'We'd better finish our sketches, Shaun,' I said. 'It's almost quarter past six and the mossies will be

here any moment,' I called. Shaun and I had learned that at 6:20 p.m. sharp, the high-pitched whine of the 'mosquito squadron' would mark the end to a peaceful afternoon. Clouds of the pests would descend, showing no regard or respect for insect repellents, smoke from a fire, or furious swatting. We packed up our sketching tools and retreated to the camp.

It was Graeme's turn to cook supper. On a beautiful bed of glowing coals there slowly roasted Gabriel's prize rooster. But, as Ross concluded, 'This ole rooster sure got its revenge in the end. I've never tasted a bird so tough.' No matter how hard we chewed, we could not penetrate the meat.

'Sorry, guys,' said Graeme, apologetically, 'but it's not from lack of trying. If I had cooked it any longer it would have been charcoal!'

The family of pigs seemed to have foreseen what would happen. Encroaching on our private space, they came grunting and scratching around the fireside, waiting for us to concede defeat and throw them the rubbery leftovers. To overcome the disappointment of the rooster (certainly not a KFC candidate), Ross came to the rescue with his favourite fireside treat – breadsticks! Unbelievably, these delicacies had become one of the trip's highlights, always a welcome deviation from our daily rice and noodle stew menu. On this occasion Ross had traded with Gabriel for some bananas, mashed them into a mixture of flour, water, and yeast, rolled the dough into thin beadings and wound these round long skewers. We sat around the coals holding out our breadsticks, turning and watching them become brown and crispy. Meanwhile an enormous orangey moon rose from the jungle canopy, disproportionately large on the low horizon, the wide river reflecting its vivid colour on a glassy surface. Ross summed up: 'If it weren't for the damn mosquitoes and the smoke, this would be almost perfect.'

It looked as though the pigs were also stirred by the effect of the moon. They hunted down each portion of rubber rooster we tossed into the grass, squealing with delight each time a morsel was discovered, like children at a paperchase!

By 8:00 p.m. we were ready to sleep. But the sow had obviously trained a family of hard-working piglets. They kept us awake most of the night, rummaging around our mosquito nets. Some time in the early hours, I heard rustling, inches from my head. Striking out I connected the sow squarely on the nose. An ear-piercing squeal broke the night, followed by much cursing around the campsite!

'Why didn't we have that bloody pig for supper?' mumbled Graeme. 'At least we would have got some sleep.'

Each successive campsite had its own stories and laughs, and each one was duly named before we departed. After 'Camp Gabriel' we swore we would steer clear of any banana-roofed dwellings and families with herds of swine. The following night we camped on an idyllic island with long sandy beaches and abundant firewood. I slept fitfully, waking up at the sounds of scratching outside my tent, but, after the sleepless night before, I was too lazy to get up and inspect what was afoot. Just as well! The next morning our campsite was crisscrossed with the giant birdlike spoor of large caymans, some passing within inches of our tents. We aptly named the camp 'Camp Cayman'.

The highlight of the trip - Ross's breadsticks.

The next one was 'Camp Terrible'. On our scoring system, this one rated two out of ten. The sandbank was covered with mud, there was no firewood, and the adjacent lagoon spawned the Marañón's most vicious mosquitoes. They blatantly ignored the 6:20 p.m. deadline and attacked us the moment we set foot on the beach after our 90-km paddle. We decided to pack up and search for a better campsite, but rainclouds swept in and the skies opened, driving us into our tents. The driving rain doused our small fire and exhausted any chance of getting at least a mug of hot tea. Our MSR burner was still on the blink, and I vowed I would hurl it into the middle of the Marañón if it continued to bring such trouble to our camp. After a cold supper of four bananas, some crackers and half a tin of tuna, another shower finished off our evening's entertainment, and we crawled unhappily into our tents at 7:00 p.m. Throughout the night periodic crashes from the shore opposite told us that heavy upstream rains were undercutting the banks, causing giant trees to fall into the water.

A furious squall set in.

Amazon Blues

I woke with a start. It was already 5:00 a.m.; I had overslept! I stumbled out of the small tent, scratchy-eyed and determined to satisfy my tea addiction. With the campsite soaked and the firewood wet, I had no choice but to try to make peace with my enemy, the old MSR stove. Shaun must have sensed my irritation and came to the rescue. Methodically, piece by piece, we disassembled and re-assembled the small stove, pumping it, coaxing it, talking to it, but, alas, not a flame did it give, not even a splutter! By then, the mosquitoes had spotted us, had evacuated their stagnant lagoon and launched another attack. It was time to leave. Slapping and cursing the blood-sucking insects, we set off silently without tea or breakfast. No one spoke a word. It was going to be a long day! We were sore and stiff from the huge paddle of the previous day. Kyle was suffering from tendonitis in his wrist and blisters on his hands, and my old shoulder injury was playing up. If Margie had been there she would have warned me, 'Now, Tim, you're tired. Watch yourself, don't be so irritable.' And boy, I was that! Not having had my customary early morning quiet time to read and pray also had something to do with my state.

Ross, keen to reach the Ucayali in record time, wanted to reach the village of Miraflores, 75 km away. On a good day this would have been reasonable and possible, but today . . . no ways, I needed a rest!

Diplomatically I threw out a tactical suggestion. 'Hey, guys, we've had three bad nights in a row. We haven't eaten, Kyle has sore wrists, and we're all tired. Let's rest ourselves and only paddle until lunchtime. We can make 30 or 40 km and find a really good campsite.'

'No ways,' was Ross's adamant reply. 'Let's go for Miraflores. We can easily make it, and we need to restock there.'

Graeme immediately sided with Ross: 'Yes, let's just keep moving slowly and we should make it.'

Laid-back jungle life.

Shaun, by his silence, closed the vote to keep going. I fumed silently. 'The one day I badly need a rest, and old Ross starts throwing his weight around. Hang in there,' I grumbled to myself, 'don't start an argument so early in the morning.'

An hour later, I put in a last bid for an early stop, only to be convincingly outvoted yet again. Not wanting to 'pull rank', I bit my lip, and sulkily kept going, digging deep into my reserves. To aggravate circumstances, our laminated maps were playing tricks on us, punishing our morale. It appeared that, over the past two days, we had only covered half the distance we thought we had!

Afternoon thunderstorms were a common occurrence in the jungle. As we approached the Rio Tigre, one of the largest tributaries of the Marañón, a lashing squall whipped up giant waves that crashed over our decks. 'Here comes the rain,' shouted Shaun above the wind. 'It's a big one.'

The characteristic fresh smell of ozone from the approaching thunderstorm confirmed what he said. The low roar of tons of rain beating onto the forest canopy grew louder and soon we were enveloped in a white curtain of rain. Putting our heads down, we paddled against the howling wind. Visibility decreased to a few metres, and for the next 40 minutes we had little idea of where we were.

'There are some houses. Maybe that's Miraflores,' shouted Graeme above the uproar. On the left bank we could barely see a small village.

'No, it's too early. We could never have paddled 75 km,' Shaun replied.

Tim Biggs
Riverside apartments

Marañón truckers ~ floating bananas down to the market.

The usual debate ensued as to whether to pitch camp at the village or to keep going. By the time we decided to try the village we had drifted a kilometre downstream, and had to sprint back against the current. A small party stood in the rain waiting for us, welcoming us to their village.

'Is this Miraflores?' we wanted to know.

'No, this is Santa Rita.'

Miraflores was 10 km up the Rio Tigre. We dragged our kayaks across to an empty schoolroom that was offered to us for the night. Soon Ross and Graeme were taken off to a nearby lake (a cut-off of the old river's course) where there was apparently excellent fishing. I used this time to sketch, while Kyle arranged for our meal with one of the villagers.

Sitting around our host's rickety table, glowing coals in the corner beaming light across the room, we ate heartily. Kyle brought out his guitar, strumming and singing to us and within minutes guests and hosts alike were spellbound. The glowing coals, the soft shadows that danced across the reed walls, the occasional call of a jungle nightjar, all made up an unforgettable experience. This, indeed, was a night to remember. This night's enchanting mood also cast its spell on the family's eldest (and most attractive) daughter. Tears moistened her soft doe eyes, which now had room only for our romantic, good-looking campañero, Kyle. Any hopes of a midnight romance were, however, thwarted as we were escorted down the rickety stairway of the jungle home by our hosts.

'Buenos noches – mucho gracias,' we bade farewell as we walked back to our sleeping quarters. I had managed to pull out of my bad mood. I sidled up to Ross.

'Hey, Ross, sorry about being so grumpy with you today. But hey, man, you're a hard taskmaster. The one day I needed a rest you pushed us to the limit.'

'No problem, Tim. I'm sorry too,' Ross replied. We laughed, relieved to have cleared the air. My mood of wrath had not gone unnoticed.

Kyle – stole the attractive daughter's heart.

The next morning we went back and spent time fishing at the laguna. A young local boy took us out on a dugout, claiming that fishing was so good here that even unfit tourists would bring them in. Maybe this was our chance to return home with photographs of our trophies! We cast and cast, determined to break our dismal record of not having caught a single fish in the entire 800 km of Marañón River (ironically one of the world's richest fishing grounds). Ross and Graeme finally paddled in looking despondent and beaten. A favourite song (from a Terrence Hill and Bud Spencer film) with a catchy tune came to mind: 'Don't cry, little fish, don't cry, don't cry.'

'No chance of fish shedding tears with us around,' laughed Graeme. Fishermen we were not.

Does anyone have a mop for me?

A family outing.

Tim Bee

We headed on to Nauta, the last village before the confluence with the Ucayali. The Marañón wound lazily through endless meanders and islands as we paddled in V-formation, Shaun up front. A group of villagers stood waving at us from the riverbank, and I instinctively shouted back a greeting in Zulu!

'Hey, Madala,' my friends scolded me, 'you've been on this river too long now. The jungle is getting to your mind! It's time for you to go home.'

The Last Camp

Our last camp, on a wet, muddy beach, was a mixture of bitter and sweet. Our much longed-for confluence was less than 20 km downstream. As Ross stepped ashore, he sank to his thighs in thick, slimy mud.

Our old enemies the mosquitoes were waiting, and fought us fiercely. The sky turned bluish-green, and lighting strikes flashed wildly on the eastern horizon. Then the heavens opened and rain pelted down on our tents bringing red-brown torrents of water which gouged miniature canyons in the soft sand.

But nothing could dampen our spirits. The realisation that this was our last night on the Marañón overcame all grumpiness about an uncomfortable camp. We were so close to the end! The skies finally cleared and the Southern Cross rose above the silhouetted canopy. Kyle played his guitar and we celebrated with a tin of condensed milk.

'So, tomorrow, all going well, we sleep in Iquitos,' Kyle reflected. 'It'll be like another world.'

How I felt at 25.

... at 50.

... at the end of the trip.

'Yeah, I can't believe this trip is almost finished,' said Graeme, coaxing some life into the smouldering fire. 'It feels as though we've been on the river for months and months.'

'Hey, but what a trip it's been,' I came in. 'Definitely the best I've ever been on. I must really thank you, guys; you've all been stars. Especially you, Kyle, following us down the river. I think yours has been the biggest adventure of the lot. I've certainly enjoyed every minute . . . well, almost every minute.'

'How does it compare with your other trips, Tim?' asked Kyle, passing round the condensed milk.

I had to think for a while.

'Phew, they've all been so different. But for sure this has been the best by a long way. On the other trips there was tension and problems the whole way down. There were just too many people, too many logistics that could go wrong, and everyone had a different agenda. I think this trip worked well because it was so simple. Being self-supporting is the way to go, and we were a good team. We trained together and we knew each other well. About the biggest problem I had was Ross slave-driving me when I was too tired to paddle.'

We all laughed.

'You see, Ross, you've messed up our trip again,' Shaun teased.

'And which was the most difficult of the three tributaries?' asked Graeme, prying.

I pondered the question. Memories came flooding back. 'That Machu Picchu stretch on the Urubamba River was incredibly heavy going. I was lucky to make it through alive. To me at any rate, that was the most difficult section – it was just so continuous and I was so inexperienced. The Apurimac River was by far the most remote and walled-in. And there we had all the scrapping and politicking to mess things up – that was tougher than the actual river. This Marañón trip didn't have the "extreme" sections like the other rivers, yet it was on this trip that I struggled most with my paddling. My self-confidence was down and it affected my river running for sure.'

Some long moments of silence followed as we reflected on our experiences. The time to say goodbye to our river was drawing near.

I went on. 'What I've found most special and different about this trip has been that we've been able to pray about things and commit them to the Lord right from the planning stages through until now. I'm sure God has honoured us for that. I also really appreciate you guys respecting that, it meant a lot to me.'

A storm was brewing again. Strong gusts of moist air were warning us of another downpour. Our evening's entertainment was over. We said goodnight and crawled into our cramped tents.

I lay awake for hours – thinking about our journey, about my friends, about Margie and my far-off family. A deep sense of satisfaction flowed through me.

What was it about rivers that never failed to grip me? What was that golden thread which had led me on from one river to the next over the years? Wasn't it perhaps just our God-given longing and desire to live out a dream; to search for that ultimate adventure and to take life-threatening risks, throwing ourselves headlong at challenges in order to succeed? Yes – that was it. I guess there is nothing too deep about my passion for rivers. I do them just because it's what I really love doing!

The steady pattering of soft rain against the sides of my tent brought me back to reality. Sleep evaded

I just love this lifestyle.

We made it! The Marañón and Ucayali meet.

me. My mind was now in overwind. So what had I learnt these past 30 years of running rivers and adventuring? Tricky question – had I learnt anything at all? I still seemed to continually make mistakes, get really scared by big rapids, get myself into trouble. But yes, there was one thing that I had learnt from river running, and learnt it the hard way. While I tried to run my life by my own rules it just didn't work for me. I was humbled many times by big rivers. I need God in my life. He gives purpose and meaning to my life, which adds a whole new dimension to running rivers, to adventure and to one's life.

I had decided to continue by boat for the remaining 4 000 km to Bélem where the Amazon flows into the Atlantic. Although our team had completed this stretch in 1985, we South Africans had been barred from entering Brazil. I still badly wanted to experience the long jungle waterway, even by riverboat.

I woke early and set about coaxing my favourite stove to boil our customary morning coffee. We managed to squeeze out a brew before the benzene ran out, dashing any hope of porridge. Silently we packed away our tents and gear in the soft rain, sinking to our knees into the black mud as we launched our kayaks for the last stage of our journey.

'I never want to see this damn campsite again,' blurted Ross in frustration. It took us five minutes to wash the slimy mud off our legs.

Pushing out into the current, and holding our paddles tenderly with blistered hands, we drifted in silence, allowing ourselves a few minutes of reflection before the day's work began in earnest.

After only an hour's paddling, Ross shouted: 'There it is, isn't that the confluence?'

The river had split into a mass of islands and channels. Was this just another channel joining the

700-m-wide river? A fisherman appeared, pulling silently upstream in his dugout canoe, totally absorbed in the waters around him.

'Bueños dias, señor, donde el Rio Ucayali?' I called. His expression did not change nor did he reply. He simply raised his arm and pointed ahead to the confluence, 1 km ahead of us. There was the Ucayali.

'We can even see the Ucayali, and here we are asking where it is,' chuckled Kyle, critical of my terrible Spanish. 'He must think we've been touched by the sun.'

The greener, clearer waters of the Ucayali swirled and mingled with the Golden Serpent. Together the two sisters waltzed and spun along a dancing eddy line. We cheered, laughed, and yelled as our boats swung into the current of the Ucayali.

'Look, dolphins!' shouted Graeme. Metres from us, a pod of freshwater dolphins joined the celebration, leaping, snorting and carving through the water. The timing of their display was surely more than a coincidence: they had been sent to welcome us!

'Thank You, thank You, Lord, for a magnificent trip,' I prayed.

A bottle of cheap Peruvian champagne was produced and sprayed into the air. We dived into the swirling waters. It was almost 23 years since I first became acquainted with the mighty rivers of the Amazon. We were meeting again as old friends.

The journey of the three rivers had ended.

Adie Badenhorst running the Inxa Falls

pillow wave

Glossary

Big Water:	Refers to large volume rivers with massive hydraulics.
Boof:	Launching a boat over a rock or shallow ledge; derived from the sound the hull makes when it hits the water surface.
Boulder Garden:	A rapid that is densely cluttered with boulders.
Braai:	A South African term (Afrikaans) for a barbeque.
Breaking Wave:	A standing wave that collapses upstream.
Bro':	A shortened South African word for 'brother'.
Broach:	When a fast current pins a kayaker's boat sideways against a rock or other stationary object.
Cartwheel:	Flipping a boat end for end in a hydraulic.
Caymans:	Alligator-related reptile native to tropical America, especially the Amazon.
Cfs:	Cubic feet per second; measures the current's velocity at a fixed point in the river.
Class I – VI:	The international standard classifications – ranging from flat water to extreme, life endangering whitewater – used to rate the difficulty of rivers and rapids.
Clean:	Describes a route free of major rapids.
Cockpit:	Entry hole in the deck of a kayak.

interface

Eddy fence

Confluence: The point where two rivers meet.

Drop: A steep sudden change in the riverbed grade.

Eddy: Comparative calm spots found on the downstream side of rocks.

Eddy fence: A high water condition in which the eddy becomes dramatically elevated or depressed in comparison with the main current. The turbulent zone where the opposing currents collide is extremely hazardous.

Endo: When a kayak is throw end over end in a hole or hydraulic.

Eskimo Roll or Roll: The technique used to right the boat after a flip.

Falls: A major drop where the river plunges steeply over rocks or broken riverbed.

Ferry: A paddling technique used to propel a kayak back and forth laterally across the river.

First Descent: Boating a whitewater river that has never been kayaked before.

Float Bags: Air inflated bags within the interior of a whitewater boat to aid buoyancy.

Forward Stroke: A powerful speed generating stroke.

Gradient: The steepness of a river bottom. Low gradient rivers drop less than six meters per kilometre. High gradient rivers drop in excess of twenty meters per kilometre.

Haystack: A big unstable standing wave.

Hole: Also known as hydraulic or a reversal, usually forming on the downstream side of good-sized rock. Fast water passing around the obstacle and headed downstream is pulled back to fill the vacuum behind the rock. Generally the bigger the drop and faster the current, the more violent the 'infilling' action.

An Ender in a hole.

GLOSSARY

Horizon line: The waterline in front of the kayaker as the river drops away.

Ja: The Afrikaans word for yes.

Keeper: An extremely deep, violent hole that can keep and hold a boat or swimmer for a dangerously long period of time.

Line: A preselected path through a rapid.

Oroya: A cable crossing over the river with a hand-winched carriage.

Peci-peci: A motor-powered Indian canoe.

Pillow: A current rebounding off a rock or an obstacle.

Playa: A sandy beach.

Pongo: A small gorge in the jungle where the river is constricted.

Portage: To carry your kayak around a rapid.

Pourover: The current pouring over the top of a boulder and then dropping vertically, often into a treacherous hole – particularly dangerous because they appear from upstream as benign, modestly humped waves.

Quebrada: Spanish for stream.

River Left: The left side of the river as you look downstream.

River Right: The right side of the river as you look downstream.

Roll: An Eskimo roll.

Scouting: Stopping to check out possible routes through a whitewater rapid before running it.

OH NO!

Typical pourover

Sieve: A strainer created by a pile of rocks in which a boat is easily entrapped.

Sneak Route: Easiest path through a rapid.

Soroche: Altitude sickness.

Spray Skirt or Deck: A stretchy girdlike garment around the boater's waste and fastened to the cockpits rim to seal out water.

Standing Wave: A stationary river wave stopper: a powerful breaking wave or hole that kills forward momentum.

Strainer: Any obstacle on the river that allows water to pass through but not boats or people. Most common obstacles are downed trees, logjams and boulder piles.

Surf: To ride a wave on its upstream face or get stuck in a hole.

Sweep Stroke: The primary turning stroke.

Throw bag: A rescue rope coiled within an open-ended, easy to toss bag.

Tongue: A smooth V-shaped runway of water that usually offers the cleanest, deepest line through a rapid.

Undercut: An overhanging rock with water flowing underneath it; often the cause of fatal pinning accidents.

Vasbyt: An Afrikaans word meaning to persevere or to 'hang in there'.

Waterfall: A big vertical drop, usually two meters or more.

Wave train: Consecutive standing waves.

surfing standing waves